ISLAND LIVES

ISLAND LIVES

Historical Archaeologies of the Caribbean

Edited by Paul Farnsworth

The University of Alabama Press
Tuscaloosa and London

9 8 7 6 5 4 3 2 1
09 08 07 06 05 04 03 02 01

Typeface: AGarmond

∞

The paper on which this book is printed meets the minimum requirements
of American National Standard for Information Science–Permanence of
Paper for Printed Library Materials, ANSI Z39.48–1984.

Library of Congress Cataloguing-in-Publication Data

Island lives : historical archaeologies of the Caribbean / edited by Paul Farnsworth.
p. cm.
ISBN 0-8173-1093-2 (pbk. : alk. paper)
1. Archaeology and history—West Indies.   2. West Indies—Civilization.   3. Land settlement
patterns—West Indies—History.   4. West Indies—Antiquities.   I. Farnsworth, Paul, 1958–
F1609.5 .H57 2001
972.9—dc21   2001001002

British Library Cataloguing-in-Publication Data available

For the People of the Caribbean

CONTENTS

CONTENTS

CONTENTS

FIGURES AND TABLES

Figures

Tables

PREFACE

PREFACE

Historical archaeology in the Caribbean (figure 0.1) is as old as the discipline itself—not so very old by comparison with some disciplines. There have always been a handful of historical archaeologists working in the region. There have also been a few periods when the numbers have swelled, such as the years prior to 1992, when the Columbian Quincentennial sparked additional interest in, and research funding for, Caribbean projects related to Spanish colonization. As Ewen notes (in this volume), however, Spanish colonial archaeology has always taken a backseat to plantation studies in the Caribbean, at least among North American scholars.

Interest in the historical archaeology of the region is experiencing another minor boom at present as a result of the growing interest that Caribbean peoples are taking in recording, preserving, and promoting their culture and heritage; the growth of "heritage tourism" in the region; and the popularity of African-American archaeology in the United States. Certainly the Caribbean is an important region for African-American archaeology, as the contributions in this volume make clear (see the chapters by Armstrong, Farnsworth, Loftfield, Pulsipher and Goodwin, and Wilkie in this volume). It is doubtful, however, that the Caribbean will ever be viewed by most North Americans as more than peripheral to studies of the southeastern United States.

North Americans underestimate the importance of the Caribbean in the history of the United States. Long before the founding of Jamestown (A.D. 1607), Spanish towns, plantations, and trade were flourishing in the Caribbean. Although Americans today view the Caribbean as merely their backyard,

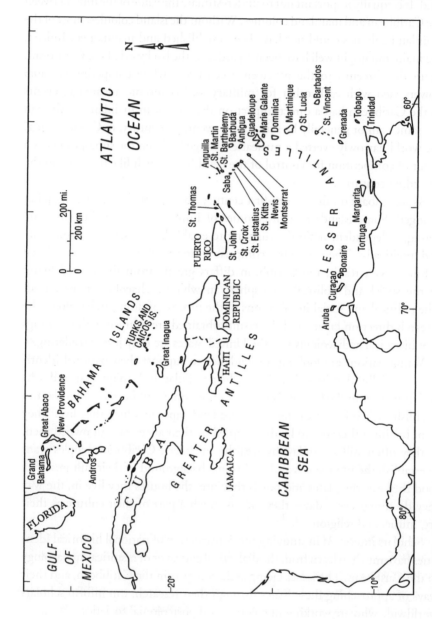

Fig. 0.1. The Caribbean.

most European nations (excluding Spain) considered their Caribbean island colonies far more important (and lucrative) than their colonies on the mainland. It is equally important not to underestimate the value of the links between the Caribbean and mainland colonies. Without the island colonies, most of the mainland colonies could not have been established and maintained. Indeed, the mainland might well have been regarded as the backyard of the Caribbean. From the fifteenth to the nineteenth centuries, while competing colonial powers vied with each other for military and economic advantage, events in the Caribbean had a direct impact on the American mainland. Although the same cannot generally be said of the twentieth century, in October 1962, the world narrowly averted a nuclear exchange between the superpowers as a result of competition for control of the Caribbean much like that seen in the preceding centuries.

As we embark on the twenty-first century, the Caribbean political map has changed. Some islands remain colonies of European nations, but most are young, independent nations struggling to establish themselves economically and politically. These nations comprise vibrant, pluralistic, transnational cultures. As a result, the Caribbean differs greatly from the United States in the social and political atmosphere in which archaeology is practiced. The political and social implications of the process of doing archaeology, the research direction taken, and the results obtained are charged with meanings that historical archaeologists in the United States are only just considering.

Young nations are looking for evidence to support their national identities, especially identities that reflect their populations' uniqueness and self-determination in the face of colonial domination. Caribbean peoples want to establish their role in creating the island landscapes in which they live. They want to affirm their ties to lands occupied by their ancestors but owned then, as they often still are today, by wealthy outsiders. Caribbean peoples want to establish the uniqueness and traditional background of their cultures. The food they eat, the plates and bowls they use, the houses they live in, the way they do things every day—these are as much a part of their culture as their art, music, and religion.

Scholars interested in studying the construction of national historical identities have much to learn from the dialectical endeavor of historical archaeology in the Caribbean. The issues facing archaeologists in the Caribbean, and their ways of approaching these issues through their research, can inform scholars worldwide who are working in colonial and postcolonial societies.

Archaeology does not and should not take place in a vacuum. A socially responsible archaeology must take into account the people involved, in both the past and the present. There can be no doubt that historical archaeology in the Caribbean has been shaped by the people of the region. This book in its organization mirrors some of their concerns and their influence on our research. I have divided the book into three sections that highlight the relationships between the chapters in each group. The alert reader will also find plenty of links between chapters in different sections.

The first section consists of four chapters (by Ewen, Delpuech, Haviser, and Watters) that introduce the reader to the literature on historical archaeology in the Spanish, French, Dutch, and British Caribbean. This scheme admittedly reflects the colonial division of the Caribbean. Although the colonial framework is still commonly used, it perpetuates the late nineteenth-century imperialist perspective. It must also be noted that, prior to the twentieth century, competing colonial powers swapped individual islands fairly regularly as military and political fortunes waxed and waned. Nonetheless, I have chosen to organize this section along these lines because, during the twentieth century, different colonial powers adopted different approaches to their Caribbean colonies that have directly affected the development of historical archaeology. The French and Dutch islands, for example, are still outposts of their European masters (Haiti is the obvious exception) albeit with varying degrees of autonomy. Historical archaeology on these islands has, in general, been dominated by government organizations. The Spanish and British islands are largely independent sovereign nations today (the Turks and Caicos Islands, Cayman Islands, Anguilla, Montserrat, and others are exceptions), and the role of government institutions in the development of historical archaeology has varied from nation to nation.

Each of the first four essays introduces the reader to significant aspects of historical archaeology in the Caribbean and raises issues for future research in the region. Ewen examines the impact of the Columbian Quincentennial, noting that it heightened scholarly interest and provided a focus for Spanish colonial research. Nevertheless, although the level of research has been maintained since that time, the focus has been lost. The result has been fragmentation of the direction of research. Ewen contends that the task now confronting Spanish colonial archaeology in the Caribbean is "to focus on the questions that count."

Delpuech indicates the problems involved in establishing historical archaeology in the French islands when it is not an established discipline in France and when previous archaeological research on historic sites on these islands has focused on the European fortifications, which symbolized European power, and on the plantation estates, which controlled the African-Caribbean population. Delpuech advocates study of the Carib Indians during the historic period, the lives and culture of the enslaved populations of the islands, and the transition to the contemporary situation, incorporating both the African-Caribbean and nineteenth-century, immigrant East Indian populations and their descendants. As in much of the Caribbean, however, a lack of resources and trained historical archaeologists has hampered progress during the past decade and will continue to do so unless the French universities and research institutions make a serious commitment to research and training in the Caribbean.

The scale of historical archaeological research on the Dutch islands since 1981, described by Haviser, contrasts with that described by Delpuech for Guadeloupe. In addition to the Archaeological-Anthropological Institute of the Netherlands Antilles, which has performed extensive research, the College of William and Mary has played a significant role on St. Eustatius and Sint Maarten, a fact that adds weight to Delpuech's point about the benefits of involving outside researchers. Haviser notes, however, that outside research teams can bring problems as well as benefits for the residents of the islands. Haviser also addresses the impact of historical archaeological research on the residents of the Dutch islands in their development of a historical and national consciousness.

Watters too comments on the important role that historical archaeology plays in establishing the national patrimony on many of the British islands. His chapter differs from its predecessors, however, in that he emphasizes the importance of nongovernmental organizations (NGOs) and resident avocational archaeologists in the past, present, and future of historical archaeology in the British Caribbean. He observes that foreign, usually North American–based, archaeologists working in the British islands have focused their attention largely on plantations during the period of slavery. As a result, studies of the contact period and of urban, military, and commercial sites have generally been no more than small-scale, locally sponsored undertakings. Much archaeology can and should be done in the Caribbean apart from the study of plantations.

The book's second section consists of chapters that focus on the development of Caribbean landscapes on three different scales. Barka deals with the settlement pattern of an entire island (St. Eustatius). Armstrong looks at one section of an island (East End, St. John). Pulsipher and Goodwin examine the landscape of one plantation (Galways). Barka's research shows how the environment and changing political and international relations, as well as global and inter-island economic factors, shaped the Statian settlement pattern. Armstrong's archaeological and historical study, which explores social relations and the changing cultural landscape of the East End, St. John, provides perspective on the emergence of a community of free persons during the period of slavery. Pulsipher and Goodwin's study of Galways Mountain, Montserrat, searches for the meaning that the place and its material culture have held for residents during the last 300 years.

Chapters in the final section examine some aspects of the development of unique island cultures and identities in the Caribbean. Loftfield's study of Barbados uses the development of a vernacular system of defense and fortification and the evolution of a local ceramics industry to examine the early stages of creolization in the seventeenth century. Both case studies illustrate components of the creolization process as manifested in this particular island. Farnsworth's study of housing in the Bahamas analyzes the complex diachronic cultural negotiation between Africans and Europeans that produced a unique Bahamian architectural heritage. Wilkie's research on the composition of the artifact assemblages from the slave houses at Clifton plantation, Bahamas, indicates that the European-made ceramics, pipes, and personal adornment artifacts recovered provide evidence of African-driven consumer choices. African cultural continuity is thus to be found not only in the craft traditions of enslaved people but also in the European manufactured materials that enslaved people appropriated as they forged their new Caribbean identities.

The themes I have chosen to emphasize here are not the only ones shared by the various chapters. Moreover, there are many connections between chapters in different sections. The ceramics recovered from the villages at Galways, Montserrat (Pulsipher and Goodwin), and Clifton, Bahamas (Wilkie), and the locally made redwares from the Codrington estate, Barbados (Loftfield), reflect some of the ways that Caribbean peoples used ceramics to express their identities during enslavement. Readers interested in the development of Caribbean architecture will find connections between the chapters on Guadeloupe (Delpuech), St. Eustatius (Barka), St. John (Armstrong), Montserrat (Pulsipher and Goodwin), Barbados (Loftfield), and the Bahamas (Farnsworth).

This volume should not be viewed as a comprehensive study of historical archaeology in the Caribbean. No one edited volume could possibly include every project and every researcher; there has been, and there continues to be, too much historical archaeology in the region. One major omission from these pages is more than brief discussion of underwater archaeology in the Caribbean. In part, this lacuna reflects the fact that the quantity of research necessitates a volume devoted to the subject. In addition, the political and methodological concerns, research agendas, and results obtained in underwater archaeology often differ so radically from those of terrestrial historical archaeologists that they do not integrate well with the contributions found here. That being said, underwater archaeology is, and will continue to be, an important contributor to the historical archaeology of the Caribbean.

Another topic that lacks a separate discussion is contact-period research on Amerindian sites throughout the region. Here again, however, separate discussions appear in the overview chapters. To date there has been relatively limited archaeological research on this period, although interest is growing and this will become a more important focus for historical archaeology in the future. Recognition of the Amerindian contributions to Caribbean cultures and populations is increasing despite their extinction at the hands of the Spanish in the Greater Antilles and Bahamas and despite European efforts to exterminate them in the Lesser Antilles. Although frequently overlooked, a small Amerindian population survives in the Caribbean, and Amerindian genetic and cultural contributions are being recognized and accepted throughout the region. As Caribbean peoples seek to recover their unique cultural heritage, the contributions of the Amerindian populations will be an important focus for future research.

The potential for Caribbean historical archaeological research in the future is vast. The resources may be limited, but the interest in the results of historical archaeological research shown by Caribbean peoples and their governments is on the rise. As this volume's contributions show, however, the research agenda will be shaped by the people of the Caribbean. They have a rich, complex cultural heritage, as well as present-day needs and problems. Historical archaeology will continue to be used to explore the former in order to address the latter. In the process, it will enrich our knowledge and understanding of the human condition, not just in the Caribbean, but globally.

Prefaces traditionally conclude with acknowledgment of the many people who have made the volume possible. I will not depart from custom, although the authors make their own acknowledgments in their respective chapters. I shall therefore be brief. First I must thank the contributors, without whom there would be no book, and acknowledge their patience with my slow-motion editorial style! I hope my efforts have helped and not hindered their presentations. The Department of Geography and Anthropology at Louisiana State University has been my permanent home during the preparation of this manuscript, although considerable work was also done during the times I spent visiting the Department of Anthropology and the Archaeological Research Facility at the University of California, Berkeley. Without the support of these institutions, the book wouldn't have been finished. Mary Lee Eggart of the Cartographic Section of the Department of Geography and Anthropology, Louisiana State University, prepared the Caribbean location maps used throughout the volume and redrafted the figures for each chapter to ensure legibility and compliance with the publisher's requirements. I also thank Judith Knight, the acquisitions editor at the University of Alabama Press, for her patience and encouragement of this project, manuscript editor Kathy Swain, and the staff of the press for all their assistance. I thank Laurie Wilkie for her encouragement, especially when it seemed easier to abandon the project, and Alexandra Wilkie Farnsworth for providing much-needed distractions at moments she thought appropriate. Finally, I thank the people of the Caribbean for allowing me, during the past two decades, the privilege of researching their past while enjoying their islands. I dedicate this volume to them.

PART 1
HISTORICAL ARCHAEOLOGY
IN THE CARIBBEAN

I

HISTORICAL ARCHAEOLOGY IN THE COLONIAL SPANISH CARIBBEAN

Charles R. Ewen

The celebration of the Columbian Quincentenary was an event that one would have thought to have been eagerly anticipated by both scholars and the general public in the New World. The consequences of the meeting of the Old World and the New became a required topic of investigation for Spanish colonial researchers in the years preceding the Quincentennial. Curiously, the islands of the Caribbean, the arena of the earliest contact, saw relatively little in the way of Spanish colonial archaeology by comparison with investigations on the U.S. mainland. This is all the more perplexing considering the fact that there are many more Spanish colonial sites in the Caribbean than in the U.S. Some of the reasons for this disparity may have been revealed during the Quincentennial commemoration itself.

A great deal of fieldwork has been and continues to be undertaken in the Caribbean. The Bullen Research Library at the Florida Museum of Natural History boasts a bibliography of over 1,200 citations (Keegan, Stokes, and Newsom 1990) and can be found online at http://www.flmnh.ufl.edu/anthro/caribarch/bullenbib.htm. Most of the citations relate to investigations of the prehistoric inhabitants of the Caribbean, with archaeological research on English plantations running a distant second. Publications of Spanish colonial research account for less than 3 percent of the references. Other bibliographies of Caribbean archaeology (e.g., Goodwin and Pantel 1978; Kelly 1988) and related topics show a similar trend.

It is difficult to find a comprehensive overview of the archaeology of the Spanish Caribbean. The primary reason is the scarcity of references and is exacerbated by the difficulty of locating sources, especially by off-island researchers. Much of the recent work in the U.S. possessions and commonwealths is contract-driven and buried in cultural resource management (CRM) site reports with an extremely limited circulation. The literature also reflects the cosmopolitan nature of the current researchers; their work appears in Spanish, English, French, and Dutch language publications. Many of these publications are virtually impossible to obtain outside the country in which they were published even if scholars knew of their existence. Still, these problems do not account for the paucity of research undertaken on Spanish colonial topics, since a comparatively large body of work is available on non-Hispanic Caribbean archaeology.

The relative lack of Spanish colonial research can perhaps best be explained as reflecting the recent development of historical archaeology in the region coupled with the incipient nationalism of the Caribbean states. Historical archaeology did not flourish in the United States until the Bicentennial celebrations. True, there were many historical archaeological projects prior to that time, but these were mainly conducted by investigators trained in prehistoric archaeology who sought to answer architectural or reconstruction-oriented questions. As recently as 1980, only a half-dozen universities offered any sort of program in historical archaeology. Even today, the list of universities offering graduate training in historical archaeology fills only a short section at the back of the Society for Historical Archaeology Newsletter. Spanish colonial archaeologists comprise a relatively small percentage of active historical archaeologists in the United States.

But what of native Caribbean researchers? The past decades have seen a rise in the number of indigenous archaeologists in developing countries around the world, and the Caribbean has been no exception. Many of these archaeologists are being trained by island universities as well. As the literature indicates, however, their efforts have principally been directed at unearthing pre-Columbian heritage. The Spanish colonial period, while not ignored, has clearly not been the focus of indigenous research. One of the reasons became clear in the Quincentennial plenary session at the 1992 Annual Meeting of the Society for American Archaeology in Pittsburgh. There a prominent Caribbean historian stated that it is "in that pre-colonial past the Caribbean people expect to encounter the confirmations of their social worth and the confidence to persevere as nations in the future" (Sued-Badillo 1992:605). Not surprisingly, much of the research undertaken by local scholars deals with the impact of the colonizing Spaniards on the indigenous peoples (e.g., Domínguez 1978; Domínguez and Rives 1995; Fernández Pequeno and Hernández 1996; Morales Patino and Acevado 1946; and Romero 1981a, 1981b).

Some knowledge of the Spanish colonial history of the Caribbean is necessary to understand the context of the Spanish colonial archaeological research completed to date and identify areas demanding additional research. The works of such social historians and anthropologists as Fernand Braudel (1979), Immanuel Wallerstein (1974), and Eric Wolf (1982) have shown that it is impossible to consider regions in a vacuum, especially in the historic period. It is, therefore, important to know something of the history of Europe at the time of the Spanish colonial effort. As this ground has been covered elsewhere (Ewen 1990a, 1991; Hoffman 1980; Parry and Sherlock 1971), only the highlights will be recapped here.

The Spanish Presence in the Caribbean

SPAIN AND THE NEW WORLD

The Spanish presence in the Caribbean has been interpreted as the logical extension of the reconquista in the Old World. Shortly before Columbus's fateful voyage to the New World, the combined armies of Aragon and Castile had finally succeeded in ousting the Moors from Granada, their last stronghold in the Iberian Peninsula. Conventional wisdom held that, having reclaimed its own country, Spain looked overseas for new lands to add to the realm. While elements of these ideas may well be true, they certainly do not tell the whole story.

Spain, on the eve of the discovery of America, did not have its own house in order. The marriage of Ferdinand to Isabella may have joined the kingdoms of Aragon and Castile, but it hardly united them. Extreme measures to force the union included the ethnic-cleansing policy of *limpieza de sangre* (purity of blood) highlighted by the expulsion of the Jews and the Moriscos (Christianized Moors). The Inquisition attempted to enforce a single faith for the nation as well. Aspects of these policies (many of those pertaining to social and racial purity) were transferred to the New World as part of the Spanish colonial policy and became a fundamental part of the Spanish colonial experience.

The political unification of Spain did not become a reality until 1517 with the ascension of the first of the Hapsburg line. Charles I, or, as he styled himself, Charles V of the Holy Roman Empire, embarked upon an ambitious campaign to extend his dominion over all of Europe. The Hapsburg zeal, and the preeminence of Spain, peaked with the reign of Phillip II (1556–1598). The succeeding seventeenth-century Hapsburg rulers (Phillip III, Phillip IV, and Charles II) were progressively weaker monarchs, with the result that the Bourbons co-opted the throne in 1700. The reforms that followed allowed Spain a brief resurgence on the world stage, but this quickly dissipated, and Spain's influence dwindled to its nadir by the close of the eighteenth century.

Close examination suggests that Spain's initial interest in the New World was driven more by the desire for capital to use in its Old World campaigns than by a desire for new territory, although territorial acquisition was not ignored. The mineral riches of the New World were meant to finance Spain's ambitious program to revive the Holy Roman Empire and unite Europe under a Catholic monarch. These aspirations proved ruinous and meant that Spain was perpetually at war with at least one of its neighboring countries. It also meant that the New World never commanded the Crown's full attention. The fortunes of the colonies, however, waxed and waned in accordance with those of the mother country.

THE CARIBBEAN BOUNDARIES

The Caribbean can be defined as a collection of islands including the Greater Antilles (Cuba, Hispaniola, Jamaica, and Puerto Rico); the Lesser Antilles (the Leeward and Windward Islands stretching east to south from Puerto Rico to the South American mainland); and the Bahama Islands to the southeast of the Florida peninsula (figure 1.1). The coasts of northern South America (the old Spanish Main) and Central America, and the Gulf coast of the United States, are often included in what is called the Circum-Caribbean area. However, for the purposes of this essay, the focus will be restricted to Spanish colonial activity on the islands of the Caribbean.

COLONIAL PERIOD

The Spanish colonial period in the Caribbean began with Christopher Columbus's first voyage of discovery to the New World in 1492. The wreck of the *Santa Maria* on Christmas Eve of that year obliged the Admiral to leave thirty-nine members of his crew on the northern coast of what is now Haiti. The ill-conceived settlement of La Navidad had been destroyed by the local Arawaks by the time Columbus returned to plant his second colony in 1493. The new venture, La Isabela, was situated farther to the east in an area that commanded a good route to the gold fields of the interior but possessed a

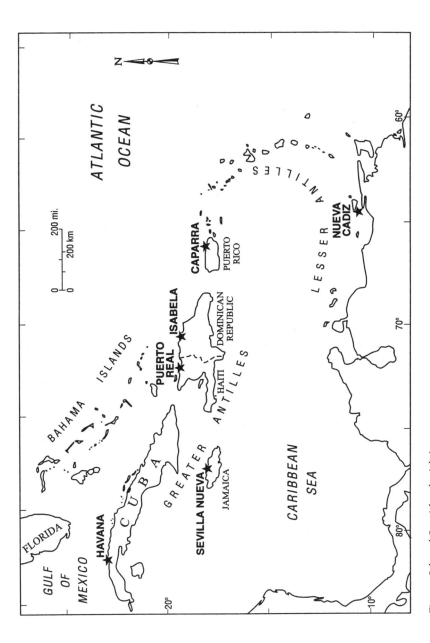

Fig. 1.1. Selected Spanish colonial sites.

poor harbor. This colony lasted only five years before the colonists moved to Santo Domingo on the southeastern coast of the island.

Spain surveyed and subdued most of the Caribbean during the first half of the sixteenth century. During this period, the coastline of the Caribbean basin was mapped and the Greater Antilles conquered and colonized (Hispaniola in 1505, Jamaica in 1509, Cuba in 1511, and Puerto Rico in 1512). The Lesser Antilles were charted, but according to McAlister, "no incentive . . . existed for conquering the smaller islands. They held no gold, most had dense forest cover that made them unsuitable for grazing, and, while northeast trades made them easily approachable from the Atlantic, contrary winds hampered access from settlements in the Greater Antilles" (1984:138). Moreover, the native inhabitants of the Lesser Antilles proved more bellicose than the Arawaks of the Greater Antilles, which further discouraged any colonial plans of the Spaniards.

This flurry of activity was not sustained in the islands of the Caribbean. The vast mineral wealth of the New World was to be found in mainland South America and Mexico. Within a decade of their subjugation, the Caribbean islands had become merely a staging point for mainland expeditions and the location of backwater farms maintained by less ambitious colonists to supply the more important colonial ventures. "By the 1560's the insular Caribbean was only sparsely settled. Santo Domingo was its only major city, and it had seen better days. Havana was only beginning to stir as a rendezvous and revictualing station for fleets bound homeward to Spain" (McAlister 1984:138). Still, although Spain did not place great value on its island possessions, it jealously guarded them and denied other nations access to them.

IMPERIAL PERIOD

The enslavement of the native inhabitants of the Caribbean through the *encomienda* system, effectively destroying the indigenous population, did little to enrich the Spanish colonists. The Spanish policy of mercantilism ensured that the Caribbean-born Spaniards were exploited economically as well as socially. Colonists were permitted to trade only with Spain (even intra-colonial trade was greatly restricted) and Spanish-born *peninsulares* had higher status and more privileges than island-born *criollos*. The policy of placing peninsulares in the governing political offices, while snubbing the more qualified criollos, became a source of growing social unrest in the islands.

The mercantilist policies of Spain also precluded any non-Spanish ship from legally plying the waters of the Caribbean. The wealth of the mainland colonies and their shipping, however, attracted hordes of smugglers and worse. With the decline of Spanish power at home and abroad, the seventeenth century came to be known as the Golden Age of Piracy in the Caribbean. Although Spain fortified its ports and had employed a convoy system to protect its treasure fleets since 1542, French, English, and Dutch buccaneers continued to prey upon the colonies with varying success (see Hoffman 1980). The western third of Hispaniola was abandoned to the French in 1605, and the English captured Jamaica in 1655.

The Bourbon reforms of the early eighteenth century briefly reversed the fortunes of the Caribbean colonies. Trade was opened to other Spanish ports besides Seville, and an intra-colonial trade was finally permitted. The Crown even granted some foreign companies licenses to trade with the colonies. This measure produced at least some revenue for the Crown, as commerce with foreign smugglers had been rampant among the ill-supplied colonial towns. Unfortunately for Spain, the newfound prosperity did not persist beyond the second half of the century.

DECLINE

Although Spain kept most of her New World colonies into the nineteenth century, she ceased to be a major colonial power long before that time. In 1763, Spain was forced to cede Florida to England in order to regain Havana, which had been lost during the Seven Years War. Spain did gain substantial territories in North America (Louisiana in 1764 and Florida once again in 1783), but a close inspection reveals that these gains were orchestrated by other nations merely to keep territory out of the hands of more powerful rivals. Impotent Spain was regarded as a safe custodian for lands of uncertain worth. After the American Revolution, Spain's own colonies followed suit and either won their own independence or were captured by more powerful nations.

A Short History of Caribbean Historical Archaeology

PRE-QUINCENTENNIAL

Spanish colonial archaeology before the Quincentennial era loosely followed the general developmental trend apparent in historical archaeology. The earliest work tended to focus on standing structures (e.g., Goodwin 1946; Palm 1945, 1952) and artifact studies (e.g., Goggin 1960; Mendoza 1957). Interestingly, one of the earliest Spanish colonial studies in the Caribbean (Morales Patino and Acevado 1946) addressed the Contact period, preceding the Quincentennial emphasis by nearly half a century. It is also noteworthy that Hispanic archaeologists have been part of the Caribbean scene from the beginning.

A pre-Quincentennial literature guide (Ewen 1990b) assessed Spanish colonial archaeology and, by taking a topical approach, was able to identify certain "core interests." The major concerns of Spanish colonial researchers fell into the following areas: (1) Contact period, (2) missions, (3) settlements and architecture, (4) material culture studies, and (5) shipwrecks. However, by the eve of the Quincentennial, investigation had advanced to the point where the compilation of synthetic works on Spanish colonial archaeology was possible (Milanich and Milbrath 1989; Thomas 1990).

QUINCENTENNIAL

Despite the anticipation, the Columbian Quincentennial was a bust. The North American public never really responded to the Quincentennial as it had to the U.S. Bicentennial. A couple of disappointing movies, a mildly successful series on public television, an unsuccessful Jubilee, the pathetic exhibit that the United States placed in Expo '92 in Madrid, and a rash of books on "Columbus the Man" made little real impression. The more successful celebrations focused not on Spain's efforts in America but rather on the consequences of contact (i.e., the Smithsonian Institution's "Seeds of Change").

In an effort to explain the reasons for the Jubilee's failure, some archaeologists tried to blame the public's lack of interest on reports that the Quincentennial was politically incorrect. Many of the Columbian texts vilified the role of Spain in America. Kirkpatrick Sale's *Conquest of Paradise* (1990), not content with bashing Columbus, indicted all European males as well. The University of California, Berkeley ignored the Spanish discovery and declared 1992 the year of the Native American. Its example was followed by the United Nations declaring 1993 the year of indigenous peoples. The Episcopal Church went along with this idea and produced literature comparing Columbus to a pirate and worse. In retrospect, though, one wonders how much these efforts really hurt the Quincentennial celebration; any publicity, negative or otherwise, should have heightened awareness of the event.

It was predictable that the Quincentennial would receive little attention in the United States. The United States is still largely an Anglo-centric nation, which explains why the American Bicentennial got all the good press. Spanish colonial archaeology *did* benefit, however, from the Quincentennial. Scholarly interest was raised. These efforts have been chronicled in the Organization of American States' newsletter, *Quincentennial of the Discovery of America: Encounter of Two Worlds*. Several synthetic works were published on recent Spanish colonial archaeological research. Most notable were the three-volume

Columbian Consequences (Thomas 1990) and the popular *First Encounters* (Milanich and Milbrath 1989).

Fieldwork that started during the Quincentennial was generally successful. A multiyear project initiated at Isabela, Columbus's first planned colony, and involving archaeologists from Florida, Venezuela, and the Dominican Republic, focused on the excavation of the public and private sectors of that settlement. It is already telling us much about Spanish colonial adaptations. The community-oriented archaeological work has continued at St. Augustine, Barrio Ballaja, Puerto Rico, Habana Viejo, Cuba, and other Spanish settlements in the Caribbean and Florida. The underwater archaeologists, far from idle during this period, included both contract- and academic-based research groups scouring the Caribbean (e.g., Keith 1989; Salas 1989; Smith, Myers, Lakey, Keith, Thompson, Smith 1985). The excavation of the Emmanuel Point wreck (possibly one of Tristan de Luna's ships) combined investigations on both land and sea (Smith 1991).

POST-QUINCENTENNIAL

What impact did the Quincentennial have on Spanish colonial research as it headed into the twenty-first century? Even with the availability of synthetic articles (e.g., Deagan 1988; Deagan and Cruxent 1993), it is difficult to assess the state of recent research, but the direction of scholarship appears not to have altered greatly. A decline in activity might have been anticipated following the end of the anniversary. No such decline seems to have occurred, however; as much or slightly more research is now under way as when the Quincentennial began.

If nothing else, the Quincentennial provided a focus for Spanish colonial research. Grant-hungry scholars eager to tap into the Quincentennial "El Dorado," symposium organizers, book editors, professors on the lecture circuit, and others all tried to link their research to the Columbian Voyage of Discovery or its consequences. With the disappearance of this theme, researchers are returning to previous research questions that are often of a site-specific or regional nature.

The current fragmentation of effort is, perhaps, the most unfortunate aspect of research in the wake of the Quincentennial. Many of the research connections with the Quincentennial were admittedly tenuous and reflected mercenary considerations, yet the occasion provided a focus for the scholarly efforts. Other, general research topics, such as community studies or a reexamination of reified demographic changes, have been proposed. It remains to be seen what integrating themes, if any, emerge.

What has Spanish colonial archaeology contributed to Caribbean research in general? When compared to the body of Caribbean archaeology, investigations at Spanish colonial sites account for a relatively small proportion of the total. Given the difficulties in retrieving citations, especially those appearing in local journals of limited circulation, the bibliography appended to this volume has probably omitted many accounts of investigations in the Caribbean. As the same limitations apply to the production of bibliographies on prehistoric projects, however, one must assume that the proportional difference is fairly accurate. The imbalance did not shift appreciably during or after the Quincentennial as Contact-period research continued to concern itself with the impact of the Europeans on the native peoples (e.g., Fernández Pequeno and Hernández 1996; García Arévelo 1990). Still, the work that has been conducted on Spanish colonial sites has made some important contributions to the discipline.

The Topical Approach

Previous assessments of historical archaeology in the Spanish Caribbean have been organized according to a variety of criteria. The chronological perspective indicates trends in the research, whereas a regional approach illustrates the priorities and background of various researchers. Both approaches are important for the understanding of Caribbean scholarship but lack an integrating theme. Similarly, when research is divided according to the geographic origin of the archaeologist—North American versus Island—the result is polarization of an area that has, for the most part, been characterized by cooperation.

A topical approach permits projects to be grouped according to various "core interests" in Spanish colonial archaeology. Topics identified in the literature include: underwater sites; settlements and architectural studies; material culture studies; specialized analyses; and processual studies, especially those focusing on the Contact period. Such an organizational scheme, which quickly reveals areas where research has been scant or even nonexistent, should help identify neglected topics meriting attention in the future.

Underwater

Underwater archaeology in the Caribbean, unlike its terrestrial counterpart, has tended to focus on the Spanish colonial period (Lakey 1990; Smith, Keith, and Lakey 1985). This essay will only scratch the surface of a vast corpus of work. Spanish shipwrecks naturally attract archaeologists, treasure hunters, and the public in general. In many cases, the activities of amateur archaeologists have prompted professional archaeologists to become involved either directly or indirectly. The depredations of unscrupulous treasure salvors have spurred some governments to attempt to regulate underwater salvage operations. Government regulations are often administered or assisted by an archaeological representative of the government in question. The data recovered often amount to little more than an inventory of wreck sites and recovered artifacts and are very hard for scholars to access (e.g., Keith 1980; Parrent 1990).

In some cases, treasure hunters and archaeologists have formed an uneasy alliance, or at least the archaeologist has been granted access to the treasure hunter's collections (e.g., Marken 1994). The ethical implications of such collaborations have been hotly debated in the archaeological community (Elia 1992). One side claims that the data will be lost to science if the archaeologist does not seize opportunities to study the material recovered by treasure hunters. The other side is equally adamant in opposing professional archaeologists' interaction with treasure hunters, claiming that it may lend legitimacy to the undertakings of the salvor in the public's eyes and thus encourage further depredations on the dwindling database. While discussion of these issues falls beyond the scope of this essay, they have a very real effect on research in the area.

Much of the effort involved with Spanish shipwreck archaeology involves the location and identification of specific wrecks (J. L. Hall 1992, 1993; Irion 1990; Lopez Perez and Sanson 1993; Morris 1990). Historical research in repositories such as the Archivo General de las Indias in Seville provides crucial background for these investigations. The documentary data will often include a description of the general area where a ship was lost and an inventory of its cargo. Yet the documents only indicate where to look and what to look for. It is the archaeologist who finds the wreck and recovers evidence that confirms its identity.

Shipwreck archaeology by its nature has obliged its practitioners to concentrate on the study of artifacts and ship architecture. The contributions of the nautical archaeologist in the latter endeavor have been significant, since relatively few blueprints exist of early Spanish sailing vessels. In fact, it was not until Eugene Lyon's (1989) discovery of a document in Spanish archives that any description of Columbus's vessels existed beyond what type of ship they were, although research had previously been conducted to investigate this matter (e.g., Keith et al. 1989). Nautical archaeology has demonstrated its ability to put real data planking on the historical frame of ship architecture.

The artifacts found at shipwreck sites have an even broader application to Spanish colonial archaeology. One of the greatest strengths of a shipwreck site is the chronological control that it affords the archaeologist once the wreck has been identified. The shipwreck is, to use a term that is hackneyed but accurate, a time capsule. In many cases the archaeologist knows the exact day (and sometimes the hour!) that the ship sank and, hence, when the artifacts came to be deposited. Such control is invaluable for refining the ceramic chronological sequence for the New World. Indeed, many see this as the greatest contribution of the nautical archaeologist, since the data can be used to date other sites underwater as well as on land.

Unfortunately, the nautical archaeology of the Spanish Caribbean has not, in general, progressed much beyond this point. Some tentative attempts have been made to study shipboard life and to trace the origin, type, and distribution of artifacts (e.g., Bass 1972; Keith 1987), but these topics remain largely unexplored. It is to be hoped, as more extensive projects are undertaken, possibly with the cooperation of treasure salvors, that archaeologists will undertake processual studies examining such themes as "life at sea in the colonial period" or "trade patterns in the Caribbean" (cf. Borrell 1983a).

TERRESTRIAL

Spanish colonial archaeology that concerns itself with terrestrial sites also exhibits unrealized potential—unsurprisingly, given the relative paucity of work in the area— and presents a wide field for future research. A few of the core interests of terrestrial researchers will serve to illustrate the present state of knowledge in Spanish colonial archaeology and the potential for future avenues of inquiry.

Artifacts. The concern with artifacts as chronological markers as well as status indicators and evidence of site function is typical of archaeology and is well reflected in this particular interest within historical archaeology. The concern with the description and classification of the material culture of Spanish colonial sites forms the bulk of the published literature. Most prevalent among the material culture categories is, not surprisingly, ceramics.

The groundwork for ceramic studies was laid by John Goggin's pioneering *The Spanish Olive Jar: An Introductory Study* (1960) and *Spanish Majolica in the New World* (1968). These works mostly built on sites that Goggin had studied in the Caribbean but on which he had published little. Subsequent work by Deagan (1987a), Lister and Lister (1974, 1976, 1984, 1987), James (1988), and Marken (1994) built upon the basic framework constructed by Goggin. An interesting study by Vaz and Cruxent (1975) attempted to use thermoluminescence to source the clays used in majolicas recovered in the Caribbean. Other technical analyses include Myers et al. (1992) and Myers and Olin (1992). A number of ceramic studies have investigated culture contact and acculturation in the Caribbean. Domínguez (1978, 1980, 1984), Ortega and Fondeur (1978a, 1978b), and Smith (1986) have studied evidence for transculturation as the syncretic ceramic traditions are conceived in the Spanish-speaking Caribbean.

Unfortunately, other categories of artifact in the Spanish Caribbean have not received the same extensive study as Spanish ceramics. The only synthetic studies of nonceramic artifacts deal with shipwreck artifacts recovered off the coast of Texas (Arnold and Weddle 1978; Olds 1976) and Deagan's (1987a) examination of glassware as well as ceramics. This is not to say that there are no descriptions of nonceramic artifacts from the Caribbean (e.g., Brill et al. 1986, 1992; Stahl 1992). Most site reports, both nautical and terrestrial, describe all classes of artifacts recovered from a particular site. However, little comparative work on these data has appeared in print.

Subsistence. Subsistence analyses are an important facet of interdisciplinary research that has come to characterize archaeology in the Caribbean during the last decade. Faunal and floral analyses have provided insights into the diet of the Caribbean colonists (Reitz and Scarry 1985; Wing 1989). In addition, they have shed light on trade patterns at the sites of Puerto Real (Ewen 1991; Reitz 1982, 1990) and La Navidad in Haiti (Deagan 1989b; Ericson n.d.); Old San Juan in Puerto Rico (Crane 1990); Sevilla Nueva in Jamaica (McEwan 1984); and Nueva Cadiz off the coast of Venezuela (Wing 1961) (figure 1.1). Such specialized analyses are even beginning to appear in shipwreck studies such as the current work on the Spanish wreck in Pensacola Bay (Derrow 1995).

Settlements and architecture. Virtually every major Spanish colonial settlement in the Greater Antilles has seen some amount of archaeological investigation (figure 1.1). Unfortunately, the reporting of this work has been uneven. The work in Cuba (Leal 1993) is difficult to access; the current political situation has limited communication between Cuban archaeologists and the rest of the archaeological community.

In Cuba, most of the reported investigations have taken place in Havana (Davis 1996; Domínguez 1981, 1984; Fernández Pequeno and Hernández 1996; Romero 1981a). Although Santo Domingo was the official capital of the Caribbean, Havana soon outstripped it in wealth because of its strategic location near the mainland and on the main shipping lanes. As the Cold War winds down and interchange between scholars becomes freer, Cuba may

and presumed historical weather patterns (Judge 1986). This debate is not likely to be resolved anytime soon and will, no doubt, heat up in 2092.

Another, more accessible prize also continues to elude the Columbus hunters, namely the wreck of the *Santa Maria*. This Holy Grail of Spanish shipwrecks remains undiscovered despite repeated attempts to find it. The ship is thought to lie in relatively shallow water somewhere near modern Cap Haitien, where it ran aground. A couple of anchors purporting to be from the ship have been recovered (one is in Chicago, the other in Santo Domingo), but their provenance is suspect. Since the vessel was stripped to build the fort at La Navidad, it may be that little remains. Perhaps this explains the modesty of recent efforts to locate the wreck (Keith 1989).

Three long-term projects on the island of Hispaniola have focused on the earliest Spanish colonial efforts in the Caribbean. The presumed site of La Navidad has been located (Hodges 1983, 1984, 1986) and then mapped using an extensive magnetometer survey (Deagan 1987c). Situated within the fifteenth-century Arawak village site of En Bas Saline, the evidence for the ephemeral Spanish presence (the small site lasted for less than a year) required painstaking survey and excavation to gather evidence for the identification of the site. The recovery of European metal fragments and the bones of European mammals (notably ship rat) in an otherwise prehistoric context are compelling clues to the ill-fated settlement (Deagan 1989b).

Investigations at the nearby town of Puerto Real (c. 1503–1578) (figure 1.1) examined Spanish colonial adaptations to the New World, specifically in the areas of domestic life, Spanish-Indian and Spanish-African interaction, town planning, and international commerce. The site became a laboratory of the Early Contact period for students from the University of Florida and resulted in two master's theses (McEwan 1983; Smith 1986); two doctoral dissertations (Ewen 1987; Willis 1984); and two books (Deagan 1995; Ewen 1991). Other publications concerning this site include Hodges (1980), Fairbanks et al. (1981), Marrinan (1982), Shapiro (1983), Reitz (1986), and Williams (1986).

Farther east, another project by the University of Florida in cooperation with the Dominican Republic has Kathy Deagan and Jose Cruxent uncovering the site of La Isabela (figure 1.1). The site is surprisingly well preserved, given the techniques employed by some of the early investigators. Work by Cruxent (1989) has focused on the walled city proper of Isabela, where the Admiral's house, church, and other public buildings were located. Deagan has concentrated her efforts in the residential section of the town and in an area across the bay, where a kiln and evidence of other work-related activities took place. The ongoing work has already shown that the colonial pattern at this site differed from that seen at other sites occupied less than ten years later (Cruxent 1990; Cruxent and Deagan 1992; Cruxent, Deagan, and Arevalo 1993; Deagan 1989a; Deagan and Cruxent 1992).

Future Trends

Spanish colonial research in the Caribbean is likely to exhibit continuity in the future. That the themes of the Quincentennial are still valid can be seen from the program of the Twelfth Annual Center for Archaeological Investigations Visiting Scholar's Conference, held in 1995 at Southern Illinois University. The conference focused on building a new framework for the study of culture contact in archaeology. Claiming that the Quincentennial had both aided and hindered culture contact studies, this conference presented the merits and limitations of approaching culture contact through world systems theory, models of evolution, and theories of acculturation and ethnicity. Certainly, these discussions provide guidance for future research.

A broad, anthropological research topic that would complement the current research of Spanish colonial archaeologists would be to define and test a Spanish colonial pattern. Deagan (1983a) derived such a pattern from her work in St. Augustine, which was tested at Puerto Real (Ewen 1991). Basically, the pattern is defined by conservatism in those socially visible areas associated with male activities, coupled with Spanish-Indian acculturation in the less-visible female-dominated areas. Williams (1993:118–119) had trouble accepting this pattern, citing the works of Foster (1960) and Fuentes (1992) pertaining to Spanish colonial adaptations in Mexico and Peru. Van Buren's (1999) work near Potosí does not appear to support the full hypothesis either. Do the questions raised by these writers invalidate the hypothesis, or do they merely suggest the need for its modification? Perhaps the Spanish colonial pattern changes through time (i.e., as the site passes from the Contact period to initial settlement and eventually to imperial state) or varies somewhat from place to place (i.e., from North America to the Caribbean to South America). Perhaps a pattern can be established by comparing Spanish colonial sites with contemporary sites of other colonial powers. How are the Spanish sites different, how are they alike, and how do we account for this? Is there a universal colonial pattern? Why or why not? This is fertile ground for inquiry.

Spanish colonial scholars in the post-Quincentennial era have more data at their command than their predecessors. The advent and development of computerized databases will continue to make references and actual data more accessible. New documents are being discovered in old archives, and as the end of the Cold War brings greater access to archival sources in Cuba, this trend is likely to continue. The expanding synthesis of the material culture improves our ability to interpret new excavations and to reinterpret old data. Spanish colonial archaeology in the Caribbean must continue to focus on the questions that count, whether the task is to reconstruct past lifeways, discover patterns in the colonial process, or explore the cognitive processes of the colonists themselves. Such issues transcend the immediate question "Did Columbus sleep here?" and keep Spanish colonial archaeology integrated within the larger frameworks of history and anthropology.

2

HISTORICAL ARCHAEOLOGY IN THE FRENCH WEST INDIES
Recent Research in Guadeloupe

André Delpuech

Historical archaeology is a discipline still struggling for recognition in the French West Indies. The limited development of archaeological research on the colonial period in the islands of Guadeloupe and Martinique (figure 2.1), as we will see, is due to several reasons. First, we must change the state of affairs in French territories overseas, where archaeology in general has remained isolated and nearly nonexistent until very recently.

The islands of the French West Indies, more than 7000 kilometers distant from metropolitan universities and research centers, have rarely attracted the attention of professional archaeologists, who are more interested in Paleolithic, Gaelic, and Roman France; in the classical civilizations of Greece or Egypt; or even, in the Americas, in the "great" Maya and Inca civilizations. As a result, the French Ministry of Culture did not create an official Regional Department of Archaeology in Guadeloupe until 1992 (Delpuech 1996a).

I was assigned the responsibility of designing and implementing an archeological policy for the administrative region of Guadeloupe, which includes the islands of Basse-Terre, Grande-Terre, Marie-Galante, Les Saintes, La Désirade, Saint-Barthélemy, and the French part of Saint-Martin (figures 2.1 and 2.2). In Martinique, a French territory administered separately, a similar service had been created in 1986. At this writing, not one university, either in the French West Indies or in France, deals with the archaeology of the Caribbean.

This chapter was translated from French into English by Laurel Suter, Miriam Touchton, and Paul Farnsworth.

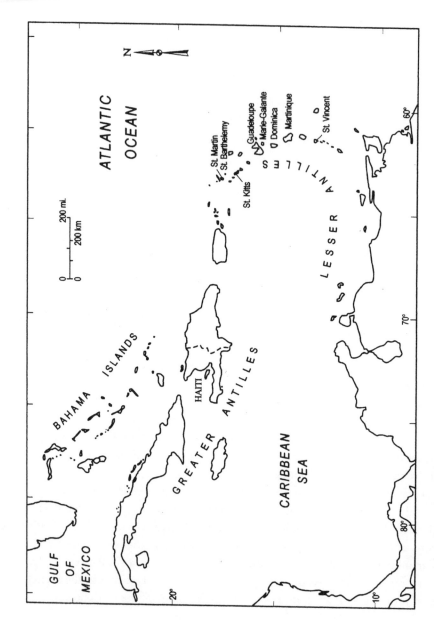

Fig. 2.1. Selected Caribbean islands.

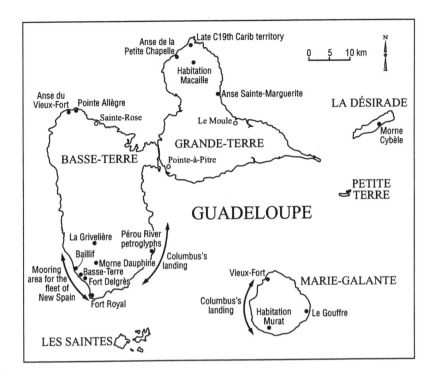

Fig. 2.2. Selected sites in Guadeloupe.

It must be remembered that historical archeology begins in the Caribbean in 1492 with the arrival of Christopher Columbus and also that for the French West Indies it really only begins in the seventeenth century. In France, however, there is no archaeological tradition for the modern and contemporary periods. The Middle Ages themselves have been a focus for French archaeologists for only two or three decades. Real archaeological research concerning periods after the Renaissance is the exception and has appeared only very recently in some large urban salvage excavations. Under these circumstances, the complete absence of historical archaeology in distant overseas territories is not surprising.

Until now, the discipline of archaeology for the people of Guadeloupe and Martinique was in every way synonymous with pre-Columbian studies. The rare research that has been carried out on the islands for over fifty years has been devoted to the prehistory of the Amerindian groups, the Arawaks or Caribs. It wasn't generally thought that archaeology could even make a simple contribution to historical knowledge. Accordingly, archaeology was considered as contributing solely to heritage, without having any research objective:

people were satisfied with clearing the walls of an impressive colonial building, the only purpose being to emphasize them. The methods were expeditious. The archaeological context mattered little as far as anyone believed, given that the history was already known. Particularly for the early periods of French colonization, the second half of the seventeenth and the beginning of the eighteenth centuries, the very detailed accounts of several well-known chroniclers (Fathers Du Tertre, Breton, Labat, etc.) gave some researchers the impression of total knowledge of the situation.

Sometimes archaeological involvement could be considered but only to corroborate certain facts described in the texts. The archaeology was regarded simply as proof of a historical event: archaeological reconnaissance could be used to find the landing place of Columbus in 1493; the excavations at the D'Anglemont estate, on the heights of Saint-Claude, were going to reveal the details of the epic of Louis Delgrès and the rebels of 1802 who sacrificed themselves there at the time of the reestablishment of slavery by Napoleon Bonaparte. Elsewhere, certain layers from fires were considered to correspond to specific attacks by the English. Obviously, these examples fail to take into account the limitations of archaeology, but above all, they accord little importance to archaeology's abilities and its range of applications as a historical discipline in its own right.

Last, we must not lose sight of the social and political context in the French territories in the Americas. In these territories, which had been colonies since 1635, French departments from 1946 onward, and places where slavery had been abolished in 1848, historical science is not neutral. The people of Guadeloupe and Martinique today are mainly of African or even East Indian descent. The Amerindians have disappeared; individuals of European extraction are made up of recent arrivals (*métros*) absent from the historical debate, and *blancs-pays,* descendants of colonists and slave owners. Until now, and by no accident, archaeology has been presented as a science exclusively concerned with pre-Columbian Amerindians, who have no descendants and belong to a remote, somewhat unreal, past. Archaeology has intervened only infrequently in the field of more recent history and only to excavate a certain fort or sugar estate, the symbols par excellence of colonial domination and slavery. It should therefore come as no surprise that most of the population has not been interested in archaeological heritage.

Once I had been appointed to Guadeloupe in this pioneering context, having been a prehistorian by training and a specialist in Amerindian research, I tried to initiate and develop a certain number of research projects in different areas of historical archaeology. Here I present some of the projects accomplished during my seven years in charge of the Service Régional de l'Archéologie de Guadeloupe, from 1992 to 1999, where, with the assistance of a number of French researchers, the first deliberate policy was initiated to develop historical archaeology. I have also summarized some study directions and research themes that in my view need to be developed.

From Christopher Columbus to Richelieu

THE SECOND VOYAGE OF CHRISTOPHER COLUMBUS

On November 3, 1493, after a twenty-one-day voyage, Christopher Columbus, leading seventeen ships and 1500 men, arrives at the island called *ouaïtou-coubouli* by its inhabitants, which he will name Dominica because he discovered it on a Sunday. Unable to find an accessible port on the Atlantic coast, Columbus moves toward the neighboring island of Aïchi, or Aulinagan, which he will call Marie-Galante, after the flagship of his fleet (figure 2.2). Landing here in the afternoon, Columbus plants the Christian cross and, royal banner in hand, solemnly takes possession of all of the surrounding archipelago in the name of the crowns of Castile and Léon. The Lesser Antilles enter into European history (Yacou 1992).

On the following day, November 4, the Admiral of the Ocean Sea directs his fleet toward a large island where he can see mountains from afar. Steering for the waterfalls of Carbet, Columbus sends a light vessel on reconnaissance toward a small Amerindian village. He baptizes the island of Caroucaera in the name of Sainte-Marie of Guadeloupe, virgin protector of soldiers and sailors.

Although the exact location of Columbus's landing remains a controversial subject, it was probably somewhere on the Côte-au-Vent, the "Capesterre," of Guadeloupe. According to an established tradition, the first arrival would have taken place near the Grand Carbet River. From there, in search of a place to anchor, the fleet would have traveled back to the Bay of Saint-Marie, farther to the north. A monument to Christopher Columbus was erected in this small town at the beginning of the twentieth century. In fact, it remains difficult to specify the locations of these landings: the descriptions of this part of the second voyage remain vague, and it is futile to search for archaeological traces of this event. In contrast, a letter by Diego Alvarez Chanca, who accompanied Columbus, notes the presence of numerous Carib villages along the coast followed by the fleet: "All along the shore, one saw many small villages whose inhabitants fled at the sight of the ships." These Amerindian settlements have yet to be located.

A letter from the Admiral dated January 1494 and reporting the stopover in Guadeloupe states, "I found in their houses baskets and large boxes filled with human bones and heads suspended in each house; I also found a large piece of stern post from a Spanish ship, I believe that it came from the one which I left here last year near Fort Navidad" (Yacou and Adelaide-Merlande 1993:89). Las Casas makes the same observation in his *Historia de las Indias:* "They found in one of the houses a piece of wood from a ship, which the sailors call the stern post, and which greatly astonished them. They imagined that this part had washed up here after being pushed by the winds and the currents from the Canary Islands or that it came from the ship which the Admiral had lost in the island of Hispaniola during the first voyage" (Yacou and Adelaide-Merlande 1993:100).

Fernando Colon's *Historia del Almirante de las Indias* in chapter 46 ("How the Admiral discovered the island of Guadeloupe and what he saw there") includes the passage:

> The ships having anchored, they went ashore to explore a village which they had noticed near the coast. . . . The presence in one of these houses of an iron baking dish was a cause of astonishment. . . . Although this baking dish was made of iron, there was nothing astonishing in how these Indians of the island of Guadeloupe who were Caribs used to travelling as far as the island of Hispaniola in order to rob had been very well able to steal it from the Christians or other Indians of Hispaniola. It could equally be that they had carried away into their houses part of the hull or any other parts of the ship which the Admiral had lost in order to obtain the iron parts that comprised it, unless it was another wrecked ship which the winds and the currents had, from our coasts, pushed to this place. (Yacou and Adelaide-Merlande 1993:95)

These observations of possible European objects in the hands of the Carib Indians of Guadeloupe in November 1493 are interesting. One should note that the quoted passage documents the first historical archaeology observation in the Americas. In any case, if the facts are confirmed, they are also, as noted by witnesses of the time, proof either of exchanges of Spanish objects during Columbus's first voyage between the Tainos of Hispaniola and the Caribs of Guadeloupe or of the possibility that there was another transatlantic voyage to the Lesser Antilles before 1493. The first hypothesis would not be surprising, in view of the trade contacts and warfare between the Amerindians of the Greater and Lesser Antilles. The second hypothesis would obviously be quite revolutionary.

On November 10, 1493, Columbus leaves Guadeloupe for Haiti and travels north along the arc of the Antilles. From April 9 to April 20, 1496, on his return voyage, Columbus will call again at Guadeloupe to gather supplies before sailing for Spain.

THE SIXTEENTH CENTURY IN GUADELOUPE: THE SPANISH AGAINST THE CARIBS

Columbus approached the islands with a preconceived idea: he wanted to meet the ferocious man-eaters whom the Taino Indians had described to him the year before. From the first village at which they landed, the Spaniards took four or five human bones. Columbus interprets the remains as proof that the inhabitants of Guadeloupe are truly the ferocious Caribs or Canibas eaters of humans described by the Tainos. The term "Cannibals" was appropriated by the Spanish to designate not only the Kalinagos of the Lesser Antilles but also all the people who resisted evangelization and colonization, whom the Spaniards saw as monstrous creatures.

Because of the trade winds, the natural ports of the Lesser Antilles received, throughout the sixteenth century, the majority of the ships making for the New World. From 1593, as the Terre Ferme fleet continued to favor Dominica and in addition Martinique, the single and almost obligatory port of call for the fleets of New Spain became Guadeloupe (figure 2.2), which retained its importance even for a few years after French colonization in 1635 (Moreau 1992). Father Breton, a French chronicler from the middle of the seventeenth century, reports furthermore that "the Island of Guadeloupe was the meeting point for the fleet to take water from our Basseterre River, which was consequently called la Rivière de la Pointe des Galions" (Breton 1978).

The Caribs violently opposed the Spanish, resisting the attempts at colonization of their islands, particularly that by Ponce de Leon in 1515. After 1525, the Caribs of Guadeloupe, weakened numerically by numerous slave raids, were relieved by the warriors of Dominica. These warriors, with the assistance of their "brothers" from the continent, continued to attack Spanish settlements until the seventeenth century. At the same time, more peaceful and commercial contacts were established with the French, the English, and the Dutch who had come to the Antilles to seize Spanish riches. Perceived as allies with the same objective, these pirates and buccaneers were received as honored guests by the Caribs. They exchanged manufactured goods, particularly of metal, for tropical products and fresh food. These exchanges, which continued for nearly a century, allowed the Europeans to familiarize themselves with the natural environment of the Antilles, including its food resources, and with Amerindian technology.

To date, no archaeological trace of this "Spanish" period of the sixteenth century has been discovered in Guadeloupe. In the absence of permanent installations in the archipelago, moreover, the chances of discovering traces of this period remain very slim.

Given the important visits made by Spanish vessels, archaeologists might conceivably find the remains of certain shipwrecks. In the vicinity of Baillif, Côte-sous-le-Vent (figure 2.2), Jean-Pierre Moreau has conducted research in vain for the traces of sunken ships from the fleet of New Spain in 1603 (Moreau 1988). According to the archival sources and notably the account of Juan de Salazar, the shipwreck occurred on August 2, 1603, as the ships were anchoring following a storm and an attack by the Carib Indians. Before abandoning the ships, the Spanish set fire to the three shipwrecked vessels, which were then plundered by the Indians. A Spanish rescue expedition came in 1614 to save what remained. The Spanish left a chart representing the location of one of the shipwrecked vessels commanded by the marquis of Montesclaros. According to this chart, the anchorage was located in a wide open bay protected to the north by plateaus and to the east by a strip of land. Near the anchorage three rivers descended from the mountains. The anchorage was very deep, and the vessels could have come close enough to the coast to moor among the trees. This document is not very precise, and the zone to be surveyed is therefore very wide. Overall, the topographic conditions and heavy sedimentation along the length of the Côte-sous-le-Vent make it unlikely that the wreck would have been preserved and still less likely that remains from this period will be detected.

THE PÉROU RIVER PETROGLYPHS

In his *Relation de l'île de la Guadeloupe*, written in 1647, Father Breton notes in a rather unexpected way the Spanish presence in the islands preceding French colonization:

> Many believe, and not without reason, that the Spaniards, as they were the first Europeans to discover our Guadeloupe, were also the first inhabitants.
>
> (1) because there have been found horseshoes and some plowshares which are not used by our savages.
>
> (2) because there has been found, and we have seen it, a stone weighing about three tons in the large Cabseterre River seven hundred paces from

the sea, on which are engraved various representations of men, women and children. Among others, in the middle there is the face of a large man with a long beard and wearing a cap on his head drawn a little like theirs. There is also the head of a little boy wearing a garland that is shown on this stone a little like a count's crown. The heads of the women are all unadorned. At the end of the stone there is a death's head with large crossbones underneath it, and at the bottom a form of coat of arms of their kind. It appears that it had more figures than are apparent now, but water has erroded them and even made one side of this stone fall down, which has not maintained its original form. The stone appears rather old, and made by other hands than those of the savages. (Breton 1978)

Further, Father Breton introduces the hypothesis that this rock had been engraved by three Spanish monks who were staying in Guadeloupe around 1600.

In fact, this is a case of pre-Columbian petroglyphs, of which a large number are known in the south of the island of Basse-Terre. They can be dated to the first centuries A.D. (figures 2.2 and 2.3). They were rediscovered in 1888 and then again in 1990. For the history of archaeology in the Antilles, this mention of petroglyphs in 1647 by Father Breton is remarkable.

Archaeology and the Historic Carib Indians

The Caribs at the Time of European Colonization

With the effective seizure of the islands of the Lesser Antilles by Europeans, the process of evicting the Carib Indians entered a decisive phase. Within a few decades, the Amerindians had been eliminated from the new colonies and simultaneously a trade in enslaved Africans had been established. In 1625, the indigenous population of Saint Christopher (St. Kitts) was massacred and the island divided between England and France. The year 1635 proved to be crucial, with the seizure by the French crown of Martinique and Guadeloupe by d'Esnambuc, de l'Olive, and Duplessis. The islands of Les Saintes and Marie-Galante as well as the northern region of Saint-Martin were annexed after 1648. Very quickly and inescapably, colonial logic imposed itself. One enters then into a classic process, repeated everywhere on the American continent, of attacks, reprisals, and peace treaties. Inexorably forced back toward the most undesirable lands, the too trustful Indians, less well armed and weakened by diseases imported from the Old World, suffer terrible demographic losses. The last Caribs see their territory reduced finally to the islands of Dominica and Saint Vincent by the treaty of 1660, signed at Fort Saint-Charles (today Fort Delgrès) in Basse-Terre.

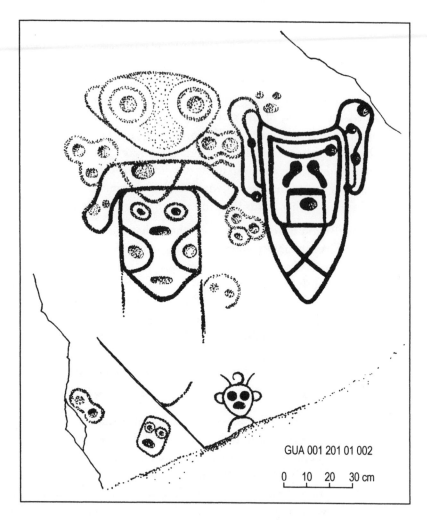

GUA 001 201 01 002

0   10   20   30 cm

Fig. 2.3. Amerindian petroglyphs from the Pérou River, Capesterre-Belle-Eau, described by Father Breton in 1647. Recorded by A. Gilbert.

Although Guadeloupe, along with Dominica, is regarded as one of the principal islands of the Island Caribs—and many historical chronicles describe the presence, life, and customs of these Amerindians at the time of European colonization (Breton 1978; Du Tertre 1978; Labat 1979)—there have not been found, to date, any confirmed Amerindian remains from this period. No historic Carib site has been identified, and on an archaeological level, the material culture of the last Amerindians of Guadeloupe remains unknown. For now, in the archipelago of Guadeloupe, as in the rest of the Lesser Antilles, the most recent Amerindian site is a prehistoric one at Morne Cybèle on the small island of La Désirade, in the vicinity of Grande-Terre, Guadeloupe (figure 2.2). This archaeological site is on a steep promontory 200 meters above sea level. Excavated in 1984 by Pierre Bodu, then in 1994 by Corinne Hofman and Menno Hoogland (Hofman 1995), the site has produced distinctive ceramics characterized by a decoration of punctations adorning the edges of the pottery and some idols but exhibiting some resemblance to the Suazoid style. A *guaiza,* or human head in *Strombus gigas,* indicates a connection to the Taino culture of the Greater Antilles. A radiocarbon date puts the occupation of Morne Cybèle in the years 1440 to 1460. It is therefore the most recent site currently known in the southern Antilles. Preceding Columbus's arrival by only thirty to fifty years, this site might conceivably be associated with the Caribs described by the chroniclers.

For the sixteenth century, when the Carib presence was still significant, one major goal for current archaeological research is therefore to reveal sites occupied when the Spanish and other Europeans arrived in the region. One could ultimately characterize the material culture of the Island Caribs and compare it to that of the groups in preceding centuries. As in the Greater Antilles and the rest of the Americas, it would be very interesting to study the impact of the arrival of the Europeans on the Amerindian way of life—the exchanges, the borrowings, and the processes of the Amerindians' eviction and destruction.

THE LAST CARIBS OF GUADELOUPE

In 1660, Governor Houël gave the Caribs of Guadeloupe the lands considered least fertile and farthest away from Basse-Terre. Located between Pointe de la Grande Vigie and Pointe des Châteaux, to the northeast of Grande-Terre, these territories were eaten away little by little, during the eighteenth and nineteenth centuries, by fields of sugarcane. Documents that trace the history of these last Caribs are sparse (Lafleur 1992). In 1730, seventy-six "savages, savagesses and their children" were counted. Among those recorded in the registers of legal status, one notes in Baie-Mahault on June 14, 1749, the baptism of Magdeleine, Carib, the daughter of Caribs living on the Ilet à Christophe, in the Grand Cul-de-Sac. It is interesting to note that some Amerindian artifacts have very recently been discovered on this tiny islet, hardly emerging from the Grand Cul-de-Sac: could these be remains dating from the historical period? Archaeological excavations are scheduled there.

In 1825, the existence of seven or eight Carib families is indicated at Anse du Petit Portland, on the east coast of Grande-Terre. An article in a newspaper from 1855 discusses the "last savages" taking refuge in the furthest Carib part of Anse-Bertrand, at Pointe des Châteaux and near the port of Moule. In the registers of legal status, the names of some individuals are preserved. For example, at Le Moule, on June 20, 1819, the birth of Néphise, daughter of Elisabeth, Carib and free.

In 1882, in the extreme north of Grande-Terre, a group of fifteen people and their relatives, descendants of the Carib of Anse-Bertrand, claim 200 hectares to the west of Pointe de la Grande Vigie, to the north of the Pistolet estate. Their petition to the authorities will be the last claim document by the Amerindians. Thereafter they melt into the population of Guadeloupe. There remains a cadastral map from 1884 delimiting the layout of a Carib Territory (figure 2.2). The location and archaeological excavation of the estate remains to be carried out.

The First French Forts of the Seventeenth Century

As in many places in the Americas, early archaeological research focused on "historic" places from the beginnings of colonization—the founding places in some ways for French legitimacy on these American islands. In this context, the primary date is 1635, which saw the official seizure of Guadeloupe by the French, the same year that Martinique was taken and ten years after the division of Saint-Christopher (St. Kitts) between France and England. It is, however, important to note that, until there is some Guadeloupean historiography addressing the blackout on all of the "Spanish" sixteenth century, one moves directly from 1493 and the discovery by Christopher Columbus to 1635 and the arrival of the French. It is as if 142 years of history had been erased.

THE FRENCH COLONIZATION OF 1635

Guadeloupe was occupied by Charles Liénard, sieur de l'Olive, and Jean Duplessis, sieur d'Ossonville, with the permission of the Compagnie des Isles d'Amérique. They left Dieppe on May 25, 1635, with 500 men, and after a short stay in Martinique, they landed on Guadeloupe and took official possession of it on June 29, 1635. I will not go into the details here of the historical events that followed, which have been described by various chroniclers and commented on by numerous historians. For present archaeological purposes, I will raise only the question of the original establishments of that first French colonization and their locations.

Initially, the French settled at Pointe Allègre, at the northern end of Basse-Terre (figure 2.2). Their stay was brief, lasting only six months, and disastrous.

Badly prepared, the small French colony experienced famine and rivalry between factions. The two leaders of the expedition built two forts near each other, with chapels and housing. Many colonists died quickly and were buried in the vicinity. On this last point, during the 1970s, the discovery of skeletons by Maurice Barbotin in this area at Anse de Nogent led him to suggest, among others, the hypothesis of some remains belonging to this historical episode (Barbotin 1978). No archaeological evidence attests to this hypothesis.

Charles de l'Olive, remaining the only person in charge after the death of Duplessis, decided to abandon the northern point for the southern end of the island of Basse-Terre. According to Father Du Tertre, an important Carib village surrounded by provision gardens was located in this southern zone. The gardens were coveted by the French colonists, who drove out the Caribs and, at the beginning of 1636, built in this area Fort Royal, which became Vieux-Fort l'Olive and then Vieux-Fort (figure 2.2). In about 1643, the new governor, Houël, preferred the current site of Basse-Terre, finding it more favorable for anchoring ships. Vieux-Fort became nothing more than an advanced defense position for the capital.

In addition to the narratives of the chroniclers, we have some maps from the seventeenth century that mention these various forts. However, the scale and the precision of these documents remain insufficient to easily locate any remains that might have been preserved. In the north of the island, in the area of Pointe Allègre, current toponymy has preserved the memory of these first establishments: Pointe du Vieux-Fort; Rivière, Anse, and Etang du Vieux-Fort; Pointe and Anse du Petit-Fort; and the hamlet of Plessis-Nogent. The area remains little urbanized; however the erosion of the eastern coast is severe and could have resulted in the disappearance of many sites. To the south, at the current Vieux-Fort, some people see the site of the fort of 1636 as coinciding with the coastal batteries between the contemporary lighthouse and Anse Dupuy. These batteries date from the eighteenth and nineteenth centuries; no archaeological evidence currently exists to place the original fort there. The sparse surveys carried out on the sites of Vieux-Fort and Pointe Allègre were too limited and superficial to provide results. It would be appropriate to carry out much more thorough investigations to find any trace of these ephemeral buildings.

The same question arises concerning the location of the first French installation on Marie-Galante in 1648. There also, the texts, the old maps, and the current toponymy direct researchers to the northwest of the island, toward the current hamlet of Vieux-Fort (figure 2.2) and the surrounding, evocatively named places: Anse du Vieux-Fort, Pointe Fleur d'Epée, Anse de l'Eglise, and so forth. By chance, this area has been very isolated and very little urbanized: the remains of the middle of the seventeenth century have quite likely been preserved here. It would therefore be appropriate to find the means and a qualified team of researchers who will devote themselves to the task. This is one of the important goals for archaeology in Guadeloupe for the years to come.

Fort Delgrès (formerly Fort Saint-Charles) of Basse-Terre

In about 1650, Charles Houël, governor of Guadeloupe, had built on the edge of the Galion River a fortified house intended to protect the roadstead and the developing borough of Basse-Terre (figure 2.2). The sources, relatively abundant for the eighteenth century, are much rarer and, above all, less precise about the early phases of the fort's arrangement: even the date of construction of this first building cannot be determined precisely.

According to the chroniclers, the structure began as a simple square building constructed on a terrace that was soon reinforced by four projecting corners, then surrounded by a wall to defend against external attacks. In 1667, the engineer François Blondel, charged with producing an evaluation of the fortifications of Guadeloupe, made a harsh assessment of the fort, which he considered badly conceived, badly built, in danger of collapse, and, in a word, useless. He recommended that work be undertaken to strengthen the fort's defenses.

Another project, presented by the engineer Payen in 1682, was partially carried out a few years later in anticipation of English attacks. Houël's old fort was surrounded by a parapet protected by a ditch. Both were extended eastward in order to include a hill dominating the fort and to form a battery for cannons (figure 2.4). At the end of the seventeenth century, when a new conflict with England appeared inevitable, Governor Auger entrusted to Father Labat the responsibility of reinforcing the fort's defenses:

> It was thus I had made . . . the internal and external parapet walls of the fort, to maintain the earth, and the defective fascines of which they were composed. I had made a demilune to protect the door with a drawbridge; a large open cistern, serving as a ditch for a flanking entrenchement, which cut the length of the fort in two, in order to protect the keep and to be possible to withdraw there and hold fast, if the enemies were able to seize the artillery battery. (Labat 1979)

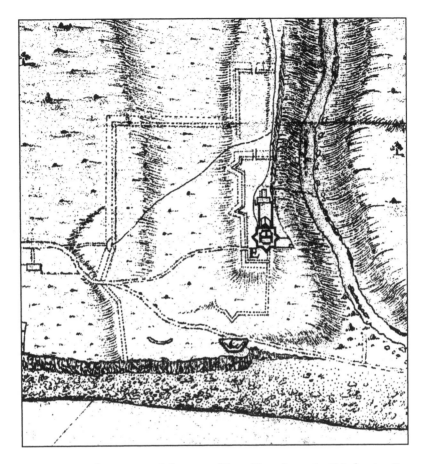

Fig. 2.4. Extract from a map of the town of Basse-Terre, June 26, 1686, showing Fort Saint-Charles (now Fort Delgrès). Centre des Archives d'Outre-Mer, DFC Guadeloupe no. 17A.

The improvements were not sufficient to stop the English, who seized the fort in April of 1703. On retreating, the French blew up the keep and finally destroyed it.

In the second half of the eighteenth century, the old fort was restored. Covered parapets were built for protection from direct shots by enemy ships, the bastions on the sides facing the sea and Basse-Terre were reinforced, the barracks and warehouses located inside the fort were repaired, and new warehouses and workshops were installed on the esplanade outside the fort. These buildings were, a few years later, included in new fortifications that extended in the direction of the town and the sea with the construction of bastions and demilunes inspired by Vauban's principles. These fortifications, carried out on the eve of the French Revolution, gave the fort its final appearance.

In 1995, in the plan for the restoration of the old eighteenth-century prison of Fort Delgrès by the Monuments Historiques, an archaeological assessment was carried out, under the direction of Dominique Bonnissent, at the site of the original fortified house of Governor Houël (Rousseau 1996) (figure 2.5).

Trench 1, located at the northeast corner of the prison, exposed various structures corresponding to several stages of construction. The oldest remains are those of a wall (M1) made of coarsely squared blocks of volcanic rock, which served as foundation for one of the walls of the prison. On them lies a pink coating and, still surviving in it, the impressions of flagstones or squares corresponding to the flooring, which may have belonged to the house of Governor Houël. The walls M2, M3, and M4, belonging to the same structure, mark a second phase of construction. This structure remains, for the moment, difficult to interpret. Perhaps it dates from the first enclosure of the fort visible on the 1667 plan? Two walls (M5 and M6), of a different style from the former, seem to correspond to the barracks erected in 1766.

Trench 2, carried out along the front of the prison, permitted the discovery of the continuation of wall M1 reused for the construction of the building. The presence of considerable fill against this wall indicates extensive alterations, perhaps related to the demolition of one of the salients of the fortified house.

Trench 3 revealed a wall (M7) that, by its execution and its orientation, could correspond to a section of one of the salients of Houël's keep. Because of a still unexplained alteration, the partial destruction of the walls had been filled up by several layers of fill, which produced an abundance of artifacts consisting of fragments of marquetry, faience, ceramics, glass, and metal objects.

Trench 4, located at the angle formed by the prison and the parapet of the seaward bastion, revealed a wall (M9) built on the original ground surface and made of stone rubble framed by two stone facings of small, very regular dimensions. This wall seems to belong to the star-shaped structure, although its method of construction differs appreciably from those walls attributed to the keep.

The artifacts recovered are characteristic of a military occupation: musket balls, uniform buttons, pipes, and glass bottles. Other remains provide us with information about everyday life in a fort in the Lesser Antilles during the seventeenth century (fragments of marquetry, combs, scissors, faunal remains) and about trade (imported plates and bowls, manufactured goods).

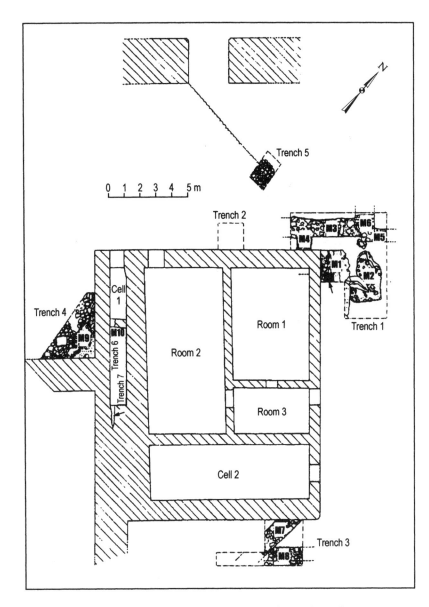

Fig. 2.5. Archaeological excavations in 1995 at the site of the eighteenth-century prison (hatched), Fort Delgrès, Basse-Terre. Recorded by D. Bonnissent.

This limited exacavation made it possible to demonstrate the area's indisputable potential in recovering some remains of the fortified house of Charles Houël and in defining the original topography of the site. Other, later buildings and structures were also discovered, showing the complex evolution of this area, the oldest part of the current fort. An excavation campaign of greater extent is still necessary, however, in order to better understand the complex evolution of this oldest area of the fort. The detailed study of artifacts remains to be carried out.

Urban Archaeology: The Development of the Towns and Boroughs of Guadeloupe

The French Antilles are far from the founding of urban growth that marked the earliest beginnings of the Spanish conquest of Hispaniola. Even in the large French colony of Saint-Domingue (present-day Haiti), there are not, strictly speaking, foundation acts for towns but rather a long and slow process of developing urban phenomena in response to a series of circumstances or needs (Bégot 1992).

The town was initially just a port, the first accessible roadstead, like that of Basse-Terre, in Côte-sous-le-Vent. Here the custom of anchoring began with the sixteenth-century Spanish fleets and would be the origin of the future capital of Guadeloupe. Saint-Pierre in Martinique occupies a similar geographical and topographic position. Although Pointe-à-Pitre truly emerged only under the English occupation of 1753–1759, in 1667 Blondel and then Payen, the King's engineers, drew the attention of the metropolitan authority to the superiority of the offshore area at Petit Cul-de-Sac, which has quiet waters, compared to the roadstead of Basse-Terre, which is open to all hurricanes. Having an accessible roadstead applies to all the settlements whose location is still linked to the shore.

Urban archaeology in Guadeloupe is still in its infancy. The investigations have, until now, been devoted to urban architecture and principally that of the nineteenth and twentieth centuries. Real archaeological research has scarcely begun and allowed to address the two earlier centuries, for which few buildings remain standing.

BASSE-TERRE

In Guadeloupe, Basse-Terre was organized under the protection of the fortified house of Governor Houël beginning in 1660, simultaneously the military quarter, or to be strictly accurate, the "parish of the town of Basse-Terre," and, farther north, in the flatter part, the commercial sector, or the "borough of Saint-François" (figure 2.2).

The development of Basse-Terre thus takes place without preestablished order. Topographic logic guides the functional distribution of the quarters, which are set up with support points (fort and military annexes, churches, and convents). But the results are modest all the same, as one can judge from R. P. Plumier's picture of Basse-Terre in 1688 (figure 2.6). Behind its parapet of dry stones and fascines, the town is just one unplanned cluster stretching along a large street parallel to the shore, with the semblance of cross-streets and certain focal points like the fort, the Jesuit church, the Carmelite convent, and the charity hospital. The early town is completely immersed in the countryside with its woods, its savannas, and its fields. However, there are the symbols of the town that count, the symbols of military and religious power: the fort, the home of the governor, and the churches and convents.

Because of its commercial, administrative, and religious functions, Basse-Terre became the capital of the island. Although it was destroyed many times by wars, fires, earthquakes, and hurricanes, the town of Basse-Terre, which had many gardens and vast properties belonging to the religious orders or the administration, and which developed slowly because of the economic dominance of Pointe-à-Pitre beginning in the eighteenth century, has a strong probability of having preserved traces of its birth.

At this writing, the first archaeological endeavors primarily relate to the town's origins in the seventeenth century. The initial investigations carried out by the Service Régional de l'Archéologie have consisted of documentary research: detailed examination of records, old maps and land surveys, descriptions left by the chroniclers, and so forth. This work, complemented by a careful inspection of the evolution of small portions, has made it possible to identify and locate, more or less precisely, the principal buildings of the old town and reconstruct the urban framework of the time, which has not fundamentally changed.

So far, however, there has been no true archaeological excavation of any significant extent. Some pinpoint excavations or certain observations during construction and repair work have affirmed the potential of this urban zone. A rescue excavation must be carried out before the current Palais de Justice is enlarged over the site of the cemetery of the old Hôpital de la Charité. A real urban archaeology policy is ineffectual, unfortunately, in the absence of a research team on the spot or in France. As at the neighboring borough of Baillif, the only studies remain too specific to Basse-Terre.

Fig. 2.6. View of the borough of Basse-Terre in 1688 by Father Plumier. Bibliothèque Nationale, Cabinet des estampes, JD 18 fol.

BAILLIF

In September 1995 Hurricane Marilyn caused the rivers of Côte-sous-le-Vent in Basse-Terre to flood at many points. On the banks of the Baillif River, close to its mouth, pre-Columbian and colonial remains were thus fortuitously uncovered. A very limited, urgent salvage excavation took place on the right bank of the river (Delpuech 1996b). At the bottom of the stratigraphy, an Amerindian occupation level of the recent Saladoid style, from the third to the fourth centuries A.D., was discovered. Elements dating from the colonial time were found in the three excavated areas.

In area 1, close to the sea, were exposed the remains of a drain that allowed used water to run off toward the river. This drain, made up of river pebbles embedded in lime mortar, was covered with ceramic tiles. In area 2, the floor level of a house was sealed by a layer of ash and charcoal. The destruction of this structure by fire could correspond to one of the fires reported in the documents. To the east and the west of this area, visible in the cut of the bank, walls attest to the presence of many other structures. One could see how the river had come to cut these areas, which extended toward the south. Area 3, the innermost area, corresponded to a pit from colonial times that contained a great quantity of ceramics. These artifacts remain poorly dated for lack of detailed study.

The structures exposed probably correspond to those of the first village of Baillif established on the right bank of the river between 1640 and 1703, the date of its abandonment. In 1637, the Dominican fathers built a monastery on a hill dominating the Baillif River, around which the borough of Saint-Louis developed, while another borough formed on the right bank of the Baillif River, at the foot of Morne de la Magdeleine, where the fort built by the Boisseret family around 1650 dominated (figure 2.7). At the end of seventeenth century, this second borough was twice flooded before being set on fire by the English in 1703. The site was moved. At an unknown time, the Baillif River was diverted from its course to pass more to the north, where it destroyed part of the remains of the first village. The remains uncovered in the current bank of the river relate, without any doubt, to that first establishment of the second half of the seventeenth century, preserved between the current bed of the watercourse and the cliffs of Morne de la Magdeleine, as indicated by discoveries made during terrace work for contemporary houses. These dwellings and a road have prevented the necessary extension of the excavations.

Religious Archaeology: Churches, Chapels, and Convents

Religion is one of the foundations of colonization. From the very start, religious orders were present to evangelize and maintain the "true" Catholic faith in the French Antilles. Chapels, churches, and convents were built immediately upon French settlement in order to establish the divine presence in this new world. These institutions were to give structure to the country. At this writing, however, no program of archaeological research has yet been undertaken in Guadeloupe to investigate the establishment of the first religious buildings of the seventeenth century and their evolution. The only relevant studies come from a salvage excavation at Anse-Bertrand, in a marginal area of the Guadeloupean archipelago.

ANSE DE LA PETITE CHAPELLE (ANSE-BERTRAND)

The fortuitous discovery of human bones on a stretch of beach in the north of Grande-Terre, following the passing of Hurricane Luis in September 1995, led the Service Régional de l'Archéologie to undertake an archaeological assessment on the beach evocatively named "Petite Chapelle" (Delpuech 1998) (figure 2.2). The excavations carried out by Michel Pichon and Xavier

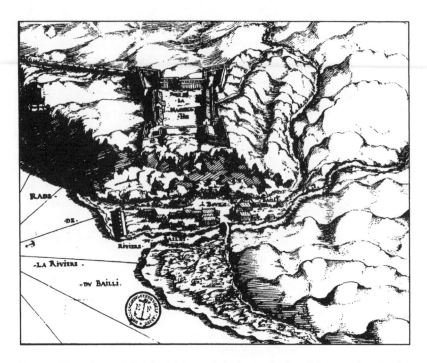

Fig. 2.7. View of Fort de la Magdelaine and the borough of Baillif in 1667 by Blondel. Archives départementales de la Guadeloupe.

Rousseau have shown that a very eroded cemetery was located there; two skulls were found in the southern trench. Above all, the work revealed the substructure of an old chapel. The modest building, of which only the foundations and one or two courses remain, exhibits two phases of construction (figure 2.8).

Phase 1 shows a building of rectangular plan with one nave finished with a semicircular apse. The walls were made of mortar rubble set on a shallow foundation consisting of pebbles that was covered on both sides with a white coating. Wooden posts, of square or rectangular section, were embedded in the internal face of the walls. The building, 6.50 meters wide, is preserved to a length of 8.30 meters. The remainder of the building has been destroyed. Some terra cotta tiles seem to correspond to the floor level of phase 1.

In the second phase, the chapel is entirely rebuilt according to the same rectangular plan with a single nave, but this time it is finished with a plain apse. The walls consist of heterogeneous materials: small rubble, pebbles, and coral covered on both sides with a white coating. The choir is lengthened by

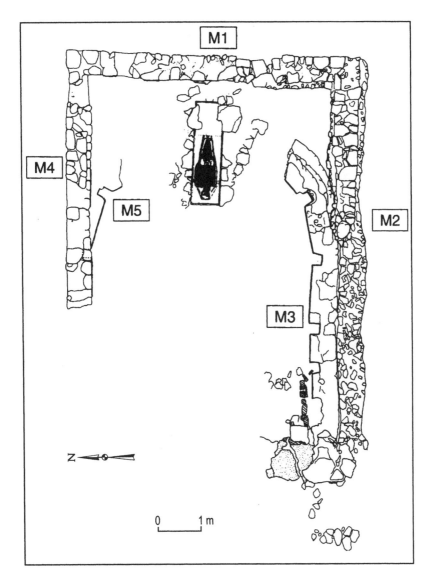

Fig. 2.8. Excavations in 1996, Anse de la Petite Chapelle, Anse-Bertrand. Recorded by M. Pichon.

approximately 1 meter. The level of floor had to be raised approximately 0.30 meter to cover the structural remains of the first phase. We found remains of neither the pavement of flagstones nor tombstones. All had been salvaged, apparently, after the final abandonment of the cemetery, which encircled the chapel, at the beginning of the twentieth century.

During this second phase, a masonry burial vault, covered with an interior coating, had been inserted in the choir. The burial in the vault is that of an adult male whose coffin was decorated with brass nails to form a large cross. Brass buckles, probably belonging to his clothing, were found on the chest of the individual. The placement of the burial and the richness of the coffin testify to the social importance of the deceased. The skeleton could have been buried at the beginning of the nineteenth century, but it is a reuse, some bones having been found at the bottom of the burial vault.

The site is on the territory of the township of Anse-Bertrand, located to the north of Grande-Terre. This area was colonized only starting from the beginning of the eighteenth century, when the rise of the sugar industry pushed the colonists to clear new land. The archives made it possible to identify the chapel mentioned as dedicated to Sainte-Rose. It was used by the inhabitants of the area before the creation of the parish of Anse-Bertrand in 1737 and the dedication in the borough of the parish church in 1739. The chapel was probably built in about 1700–1720. The two phases of construction seem both to belong to the eighteenth century. It is not possible to be more precise at this time.

The families buried in the chapel appeared on a list of inhabitants drawn up in 1737. The surrounding cemetery, according to a local informer, was used until the First World War. The chapel had disappeared from memory, although traces were still visible at that time. The site kept the name of "l'anse de la Petite Chapelle." Called the "cemetery of nobility" by the locals, the abandoned cemetery, surrounded by a wall, survived until the 1960s. Located on the edge of sea, on a small terrace exposed to the swells, it was eroded little by little. The bones uncovered by the passage of the hurricanes of 1995 appear to be the last remains of this burial place.

Archaeology of Plantations and Slavery

In Guadeloupe, archaeological research on rural life has remained largely limited to the sugar estates and has particularly consisted, until now, of architectural and technical study of the remains related to the manufacture of sugar: animal, water or windmills, sugar-houses, purifiers, drying ovens, works, and so forth. Other types of activities, such as the exploitation of tobacco, indigo, or even coffee, are definitely less known, at least in the early phases of colonization. Architectural analyses of the "master's houses," the large residences of which a certain number remain standing and still inhabited, are another well-documented area. For the remainder, and in particular for all that relates to the conditions and the lives of the enslaved populations, one must note that no investigation worthy of the name has been carried out on the ground until the present time.

Sugar Estates

As in all the Antilles, the history of a large part of the Guadeloupean archipelago is inseparable from that of the sugar industry. To quote some figures, at the end of the nineteenth century, 464 sugar mills were operating. Most often, there only remains today the ruins of the mills, the majority from the eighteenth century (270 on the entire archipelago in 1750). Some rare animal mills survive. Water mills (143 in 1829) had been very widespread on Basse-Terre with their essential installations, notably the aqueducts. Large numbers of windmills on Grande-Terre and Marie-Galante (252 in 1829) best symbolize this sugar past.

A large number of studies have been carried out on the history, the economy, and the sugar estates, especially during the last few years under the impetus of Danièle Bégot, of the University of the Antilles and Guyana (Bégot 1991). In particular, an inventory of the estates has been undertaken. It consists of the systematic survey of all the architectural elements and furnishings (above all the machinery) preserved on the ground. The recent campaign of reconnaissance and survey, for example, made it possible to inventory nearly seventy sugar estates in the townships of Port-Louis and Anse-Bertrand, to the north of Grande-Terre (e.g., the Habitation Macaille, shown in figure 2.9). An archival study completes the description of the industrial remains.

The work of surface recording, however, takes into account only one small part of the actual estate. In the majority of cases, the permanently constructed buildings alone are apparent, that is to say, those related to the manufacturing process of sugar: mills, sugar-houses, and so forth. All the rest—the wooden infrastructure, slave huts, stables, embanked works, etc.—remain unexplored. Simple topographic observation of these places is often sufficient to restore part of the organization of these agricultural and industrial undertakings.

Some research conducted in the last few years sets in motion the first beginnings of plantation archaeology. They remain, however, too limited.

Habitation Murat (Grand Bourg of Marie-Galante). The archaeological research carried out on the Habitation Murat (Grand-Bourg of Marie-Galante), on the island of Marie-Galante (figure 2.2), came in the development project for the Habitation to be the location of an ecomuseum by the Conseil Général of Guadeloupe. It has, thus, a primary heritage goal, the objective being to locate and identify the various buildings that made up the operation so that they can be integrated into the restoration program.

The first excavations carried out in 1997 by the Service Régional de

Fig. 2.9. Windmill, Habitation Macaille, Anse-Bertrand. Photograph by E. Mare.

l'Archéologie related to the animal mill (figure 2.10) (Delpuech 1999a). The Murat estate possessed, in effect, one of the rare examples of a structure of this type still preserved in Guadeloupe. The animal-traction mill at the Habitation Murat appears as a circular platform seventeen meters in diameter delimited by a wall with sixteen sides made of limestone blocks. Two openings in front of the access ramps allowed for the supply of cane and the removal of bagasse.

Several excavations were carried out in different areas of the mill. A layer of gravel resting on a floor of mortar was discovered over the whole of the surface. At the center of the mill, excavation exposed the base on which the machinery of the mill rested. This base, made up of an elaborate collection of materials that arrived unassembled, included several grooves intended to receive the beams of the wooden frame that supported the rollers. Ten iron brackets, undoubtedly used for securing the rollers, were found. The vat for receiving the cane juice and the outlet channel had disappeared as well as the level where the animals circled. The location of the pipe for the removal of the sugarcane juice in the wall makes possible the precise reconstruction of the level of the floor to thirty centimeters above the gravel.

The small amount of material recovered by the excavation is attributable on

Fig. 2.10. View of the 1997 excavations of the animal mill, Habitation Murat, Grand-Bourg de Marie-Galante. Photograph by X. Rousseau.

the whole to the nineteenth century, although some elements of the twentieth century are mixed in. The material consists essentially of metal artifacts: brackets, nails, and various fragments including a hoe blade. Shards of glass (jars, bottles) and some sherds of pottery were also recovered. This research remains very limited. Apart from its importance in the context of heritage, this investigation hardly contributes new information on the operation and dating of the mill.

Indigo Works

Indigo, or rather the indigo plant, is a shrub that generally grows in hot and dry areas. The preparation of indigo, which is purplish blue in color, begins with the fermentation and decanting of the leaves, which are steeped for a long time in stone tanks or basins arranged in steps. The resulting substance is used to dye fabrics. The manufacture of dye was particularly developed on the islands of Marie-Galante and Grande-Terre, with their favorable climatic conditions, which yielded three-quarters of the total production of Guadeloupe between 1686 and 1719. On Marie-Galante, production was maintained until 1735, as is evident from the remains still visible, particularly in the area of Galet à Capesterre, at the east of the island, before it disappeared completely with the establishment of sugarcane monoculture.

An inventory of the indigo works in the east of Marie-Galante, in the area of Galets (Capesterre) has been carried out recently by Yolande Vragar and Xavier Rousseau. About fifteen indigo works have been discovered (Delpuech 1999b). The manufacture of indigo required an installation comprising three to five vessels or tanks, organized in steps. The indigo works discovered all had this same basic organization: a steeping tank, a beating tank, and a settling tank. Water was always drawn from a well located in the immediate vicinity.

Surveys and excavations were carried out in 1998 on a well-preserved indigo facility at the place called Le Gouffre, on the coast (figure 2.2). The site is distinguished by the quality of its construction but also by its particular arrangement, which differs from that of other indigo facilities in having two sets of tanks aligned in parallel (figures 2.11 and 2.12). The tanks, 3.50 meters per side on average, are built with blocks of coral bound with lime mortar. The interior of the basins is covered with a mortar of broken tile carefully smoothed with lime. A drain hollowed out level with the bottom of the basin permits the liquid to be shifted from one tank to another. The walls, with an average thickness of 0.65 meter, are preserved to a height ranging between 0.60 meter and 1.70 meters, which seems to correspond in at least some cases with the original elevation.

Each steeping tank has, on the upper faces of the two side walls, four cavities that face each other two by two. They are probably the holes that held the assembly of posts and cross-pieces supporting the lid that covered the tank. This mechanism, described in the documents, was intended to keep the bundles of indigo under water and to contain the fermentation. Other notches and grooves hollowed out in the lateral face of the wall that separated the steeping tank from the beating tank (on the beating tank side) mark the location of a mechanism supporting the beaters, which agitate the water in order to oxygenate the liquid and turn it blue. The two settling tanks, still buried and covered with broken stones, could be only partly revealed. Their state of preservation is quite poor. The well, located about ten meters behind, is partly destroyed and filled. It consists, as is generally the case in this area, of a simple hole made to reach a passage of the karst network. The upper part had been furnished summarily with a facing of coral blocks.

Fig. 2.11. View of the indigo facility at Le Gouffre, Capesterre de Marie-Galante. Photograph by X. Rousseau.

Fig. 2.12. View of archaeological excavations at the indigo facility at Le Gouffre, Capesterre de Marie-Galante. Photograph by X. Rousseau.

From among the many agricultural practices, Guadeloupe experienced a strong development of coffee cultivation, mainly in the eighteenth and nineteenth centuries on the Côte-sous-le-Vent of Basse-Terre, which was unsuitable for cane cultivation. Many coffee plantations survive in a state of ruin on the steep slopes of the volcanoes of Basse-Terre. Many of the wooden structures have been subjected to very significant degradation with the passage of time, accelerated by the repeated passage of hurricanes. Tourist development of the area has involved making the most of some of these sites and the resumption of coffee production on a modest scale.

One of the major sites, La Grivelière, in the valley of the Grande Rivière of Vieux-Habitants (figure 2.2), is one of the most remarkable examples of such activity. The estate preserves the assemblage of professional and domestic buildings that were typically found on such plantations: master's house, manager's house, workers' huts, undershot wheel, pulping machinery, drying sheds, and so on.

Restoration work at La Grivelière has been in progress since 1995. A complete topographic survey of all the existing buildings and structures, visible or exposed by excavation, has been made (figure 2.13). The buildings currently in place are essentially wooden, with construction dating, for the oldest, to the beginning of the nineteenth century, but the archaeological excavations carried out by Gérard Richard at the time of the restoration work on the master's house have provided evidence of structures that may go back as far as the eighteenth century. On the other hand, the domestic garbage dumps have provided some datable items (porcelains, bottles, pipes) from the end of the eighteenth century, the second half of the nineteenth century, and the beginning of the twentieth century. A survey of the hydraulic system shows a logical use of water, with distribution to the group of buildings starting from a catchment on a stream for the undershot wheel, the master's house, the fountains, coffee or cacao washing, and the pigsty. Some excavations near the workers' huts have revealed old structures (channels, old walls).

CONDITIONS AND MATERIAL CULTURE OF SLAVE POPULATIONS

Until now, the archaeology of Guadeloupean estates has been almost synony-mous with industrial archaeology, with study only of the buildings related to production. Equally studied are the masters' residences where they have survived. The rest, and in particular all of that which concerns the material culture of the slaves and indeed everyday life, apart from the work of the

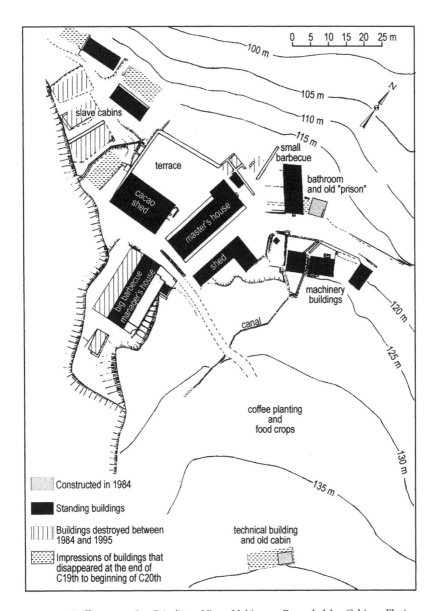

Within the figure the following labels appear:

0 5 10 15 20 25 m

100 m
105 m
110 m
115 m

N

slave cabins

small barbecue

bathroom and old "prison"

terrace

cacao shed

master's house

shed

big barbecue
manager's house

machinery buildings

120 m

canal

125 m

coffee planting and food crops

130 m

135 m

Constructed in 1984

Standing buildings

Buildings destroyed between 1984 and 1995

Impressions of buildings that disappeared at the end of C19th to beginning of C20th

technical building and old cabin

Fig. 2.13. Coffee estate, La Grivelière, Vieux-Habitants. Recorded by Cabinet Florian Simon, Conseil Régional de la Guadeloupe.

plantation, remains unknown on an archaeological level. No slave cabins have ever been excavated.

The questions remaining to be answered by such research, however, are numerous and important. In particular, research should focus on the identification of African traditions: how these African characteristics can survive, disappear, or change in a new environment and under unnatural living conditions. Archaeology can make it possible to approach certain fundamental aspects of life on the plantations about which the texts say little. Examples would include: the dimensions and spatial arrangement of the housing, domestic furnishings and utensils, foodways, and the identification of artifacts related to religious practices or even funerary customs. This is a completely virgin field of investigation for future research in the French Antilles and beyond.

Cemeteries of the Colonial Period

The potential of colonial funerary archaeology on Guadeloupe, with its parish cemeteries and its estate cemeteries where owners' families were buried, has been known for a long time. In addition, the very numerous finds of human bones that have been recorded and collected sometimes included undisturbed skeletons, out of all context, most often on sand beaches. Very often, these places have been considered, without any historical or archaeological proof, to be slave cemeteries.

The discovery by Maurice Barbotin (1978) of the burial places of skeletons on the beach at Nogent, to the north of Basse-Terre, has already been mentioned. Other sites are known: at the Raisins Clairs beach (Sainte-Anne), at the Autre-Bord beach (Le Moule), and in a place with the evocative name of Anse des Corps (Petit Canal). An iron ring, identified as a slave collar, was discovered at Raisins Clairs beach around the neck of a skeleton (now in the collection of the Schoelcher Museum). Recently Gérard Richard has also uncovered, at Pointe des Pies in Saint-François, several historical burials.

These past projects have been very specific, without research questions and, above all, without a true team of specialist physical anthropologists. The various authors have often reached their conclusions too fast and with too little argument. The term "slave cemetery" is used without justification. The sites in question are in fact colonial cemeteries whose status is unknown to us at present. We know nothing, either about the structures with which they are associated or about the populations buried there. It is all the more necessary to develop research on this topic, as we have available, in fact, little written information on the funerary rites of the slave populations apart from the anthropological, demographic, or pathological aspects.

Several salvage projects on funerary sites in 1995 and 1996, following the passage of hurricanes, inaugurated the research on colonial period cemeteries (Courtaud, Delpuech, and Romon 1999). Their inventory began, at the same time as archival research, with the collection of information on the available sites. A planned project was implemented on the site of Anse Sainte-Marguerite (Le Moule) under the direction of a team of anthropologists from the University of Bordeaux.

ANSE DU VIEUX-FORT (SAINTE-ROSE)

Following the hurricanes of 1995, the strong swells damaged the beach of Cluny, also called Anse du Vieux-Fort, to the north of Basse-Terre (figure 2.2), exposing scattered bones and an undisturbed burial. The beach has been a subject of marine erosion for a long time. The presence of burials at this place proves all the more interesting because we are in the supposed area of the founding of the first fort built by the French upon their arrival in Guadeloupe in 1635 (see above), as the name Anse du Vieux-Fort indicates.

Four burials have been excavated in an urgent salvage operation (Pichon and Vragar 1997; Delpuech 1998). They were simple primary burials in coffins oriented east-west. The individuals, all adults, one female and three others of undetermined sex, were lying extended supine, their heads to the west. The disturbed remains of two children were collected on the surface, one above burial 1, the other in the immediate vicinity of burial 3. The four burials are very close to each other and seem to be the last at this site. The sea and the mining of sand destroyed the rest of the cemetery.

Burial 3 revealed five bone buttons. Burial 4 revealed four bone buttons as well as two rectangular iron buckles. All the buttons have five holes and exhibit a distinct peripheral rim. These indicators, which tend to date the burials to the eighteenth century, lead us to discount any connection with the original French establishment. The small group of burials, with its diverse membership distant from any known religious building, suggests no hypothesis other than that this was a slave cemetery associated with an estate, even if no decisive indicator exists to support this conclusion and the exhumed population sample is much too small.

MORNE DAUPHINE (SAINT-CLAUDE)

The funerary site of Morne Dauphine was discovered fortuitously following a landslide caused by Hurricane Marilyn. Several undisturbed skeletons were observed in the cut in the ground on a steep slope. The cemetery is located on the interior of the lands of Matouba, in the township of Saint-Claude (figure 2.2). Matouba is a plateau located between 450 and 650 meters high, around 10 kilometers to the north-east of Basse-Terre. The cemetery is on a steep slope on the right bank of the Cacador ravine, 100 precipitous meters above the streambed.

Nine burials were excavated in an urgent salvage operation (Delpuech 1998; Rousseau, Pichon, and Vragar 1997). They are simple, primary burials in coffins, situated northeast-southwest perpendicular to the slope. The individuals, all adults, two males, one female, and six others of undetermined sex, were lying extended supine. The disturbed remains of an immature individual were found on the surface. Three other very eroded burials were cut through by an excavation trench. No observations could be made.

Burial 7 revealed three bone buttons with one single central hole, all located in the sacro-lumbar region. A glass bottle was found between the edge of the pit and the coffin, level with the head of the individual, in burial 8. Additional bone buttons and another glass bottle were collected by hikers. The anthropologically recovered sample is small and badly preserved. We do not know the extent of the cemetery beyond the zone uncovered by the landslide. We have no precise marker that would enable us to date its use. The cemetery seems not to be directly associated with any building.

The lands located in this section of the heights of Matouba have belonged since 1719 to the Guischard family. They were divided little by little into several estates because of marriage alliances and successive sales. This cemetery is found on the Habitation Grand Val, in an area of steep slopes at the margins of the property. The diversity of membership (men, women, and children) lends weight to the hypothesis that this is an estate cemetery. Its remoteness and its topographic position encourage us to form the probable hypothesis that it was a slave cemetery.

ANSE SAINTE-MARGUERITE (LE MOULE)

The cemetery of l'Anse Sainte-Marguerite is located on the eastern littoral of Grande-Terre, on the Atlantic coast (figure 2.2), in the dune field of the Anse Sainte-Marguerite beach in the township of Le Moule to the south of the village of Gros Cap. It was formerly known for important pre-Columbian remains and for many historical burials that have since been destroyed during sand mining and by marine erosion. No true scientific study had been carried out on this funerary site, which local tradition regarded as a slave cemetery. After some preliminary excavations in 1994, a large-scale planned excavation has been in progress since 1997 under the direction of Patrice Courtaud.

Reported here are some first results of the 1997 and 1998 seasons of study (Courtaud 1997, 1998; Delpuech 1999a, 1999b). Stripping of 300 square meters was carried out, representing only a small part of the entire burial ground, which is very extensive. The distribution of the tombs is very variable. Certain areas are less dense, with broad spaces between, while others show a high density with many intersections. Seventy-one burials have been uncovered.

All of the individuals except one were buried in coffins, extended supine. The coffins were well built with many nails. A study of their architecture is currently in progress. It seems that there is homogeneity: the coffins were built with six vertical boards, the smallest at the head and the feet, and two horizontal boards.

The tombs are mainly simple burials, with the multiples, primary and secondary, accounting for only 6 percent. All the funerary structures have an east-west orientation. In 86 percent of the cases, the skull is directed toward the west. The reversed positions correspond to children's burials and the burial of one adult. This last burial is notable for the fact that this is the only one that did not entail a coffin. The immature individuals less than five years old are all shallowly buried in direct proximity, even above, an adult burial. The burial intersections do not seem random but show the deliberate intention of bringing certain individuals closer in space and in "the beyond." This positioning implies an awareness in space, and also in memory, of the placement of the burials and the identity of the deceased.

Burial S56 stands out for the filling of the upper part of the grave with limestone and coral blocks. This burial also stands out because of the unusual nature of the coffin (figure 2.14). This coffin was upholstered; upholstery tacks associated with fabric were recovered at various places. The tacks were arranged on the periphery of the lid and outlined a cross on the lid that was found, after the lid had collapsed, on the chest of the deceased. The nails on the periphery of the baseboard indicate that it too was upholstered. A total of 157 bronze tacks were found, including 30 for the lid design. Even though the nature of the coffin appears very different, the tomb is nonetheless clearly integrated in the funerary assemblage, as shown by its orientation, form, and position in comparison with the other burials. Moreover, in 1999, two burials were found that had a surface architecture made of limestone and coral pieces assembled using mortar. The first was associated with a child and a man, and the second revealed the remains of a young woman.

The total population exhumed after two seasons had risen to 68 individuals. It consisted of 30 children, 4 adolescents, and 34 adults. Of the total population, 81 percent were less than thirty years old. None of the adults had

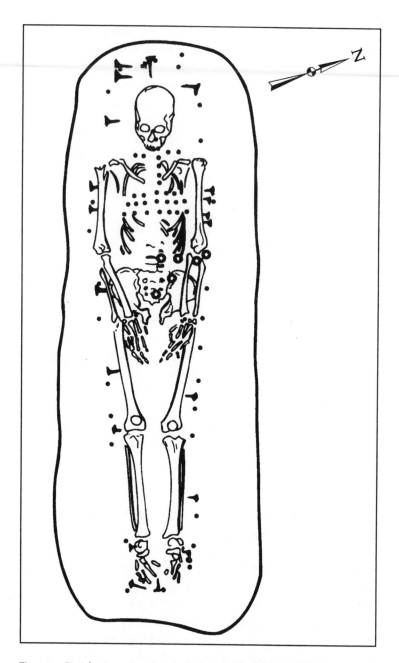

Fig. 2.14. Burial 56, 1998 archaeological excavations at the colonial cemetery of Anse Sainte-Marguerite, Le Moule, showing the nails of the coffin and the upholstery tacks in the form of a cross. Recorded by P. Courtaud.

the characteristics of very old individuals. There is a considerable proportion of immature individuals, primarily young children (76 percent of these are less than five years of age). The sex ratio is 1:1.35 (37 percent males, 50 percent females, and 13 percent of undetermined sex). The state of health is rather poor, in particular as regards the teeth and the ankles.

The preserved elements of clothing consist of buttons, in bone and mother-of-pearl, found on the area of the pelvis and the lumbar region. The bone buttons were either simple and with a single hole or well engraved on one face and with five holes (figure 2.15). The mother-of-pearl buttons, less numerous and of much smaller dimensions, had four holes. Bronze pins located at the feet and skull were also recovered in five graves.

With certain exceptions, this sepulchral assemblage conforms completely with Christian rites. The primary question at the moment is the function of the burial place. Is it a cemetery of slaves associated with a colonial estate, or is it the parish cemetery of an old borough of Sainte-Marguerite that has since disappeared?

No archaeological evidence permits us to differentiate slave burials from those of colonists. Although we might estimate that, in the second half of the eighteenth century, nine-tenths of the North Grande-Terre was servile and thus that a cemetery of this extent could only be a slave cemetery, we cannot prove this conclusion in any way. The presence of "rich" burials with upholstered coffins or even with a masonry structure seems rather to indicate a parish cemetery. Note that a map from the second half of the eighteenth century shows, on the beach where the cemetery was established, an old borough of Sainte-Marguerite that seems to have disappeared rapidly.

We should obviously not exclude the possibility of a "mixed" cemetery, in which slaves and free men were buried on the same site at the same time, or even the possibility that one type of cemetery succeeded the other. The continuation of these studies should make it possible to resolve this crucial point. On the one hand, the extension of the excavations will provide a sufficiently large sample of the population for biological studies, and genetic analyses may permit us to differentiate the African and European populations. On the other hand, archival studies should permit us to place this cemetery in its eighteenth-and/or early nineteenth-century context.

Conclusion: An Archaeology to Be Built, a History to Be Rediscovered

Through the few examples of the first research undertaken recently, one can see that the areas of investigation for historical archaeology are vast and the

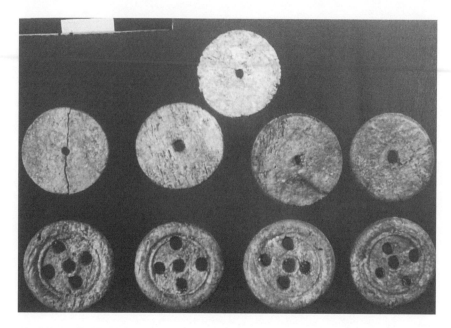

Fig. 2.15. Bone buttons from the 1997 archaeological excavations at the colonial cemetery of Anse Sainte-Marguerite, Le Moule. Photograph by P. Courtaud.

significant part that this discipline can contribute to our understanding of the history of Guadeloupe and the French West Indies, which is based too exclusively on written sources. Whole chronological periods or particular areas thus remain largely misunderstood because very few documents provide evidence, and no archaeological trace has yet been found in the French Antilles. The "Spanish" sixteenth century and the historic Carib Indians are topics that demand further investigation.

Another archaeological area that remains far too neglected deals with the everyday life of slaves on the plantations. Aside from some texts issued by the dominant power, there remains very little documentation on the habitats, foodways, material culture, and even funerary rites of the enslaved groups, although in the last-named area, we have seen the beginning of research with the first excavations of cemeteries. Research on African cultural heritage focuses on study of the places where the slaves lived, whereas industrial archaeology, which has produced many results, is interested above all in the architecture, techniques, and economy of the owners of European origin. Guadeloupe is the largest island of the Lesser Antilles and has in the mountains and the forests of Basse-Terre a relatively vast backcountry that harbored some camps of escaped slaves, the black maroons. Even if, by definition, these living places have remained uncertain, it is nonetheless true that if located precisely the traces would be extremely interesting for studying their arrangement and operation.

Urban archaeology must develop. An understanding of the birth and development of colonial towns in the seventeenth and eighteenth centuries requires thorough archaeological investigations. The results may then be compared with the historical traditions that originated in often incomplete documents far from the realities of colonies remote from the central European power. It is sometimes difficult to distinguish in the drawn plans of towns the real parts from those remaining from urban projects that never came to fruition. Similarly, by comparing manufactured goods resulting from official trade with goods smuggled in, we can clarify the real networks of economic relations. The history and the life of the urban slaves are another area to be explored.

Finally, archaeological inquiry should not be confined to the early centuries of colonization. Archaeology can be involved up to the twentieth century. The nineteenth century is a decisive period that witnessed society's passage from the old regime to contemporary Guadeloupe. The transition from the system of sugar estates to central factories constituted a determinant phase in the economic and social history of the islands. The abolition of slavery in 1848 remains the major event. Its consequences can lend themselves to analysis from an archaeological perspective: what became of the plantations after emancipation and after the former slaves became sharecroppers? How did the exploitation of new geographical areas and the transformation of the environment take place? How were the new Indian immigrants integrated in the second half of the nineteenth century?

The areas for research are vast. This archaeology remains to be built. It will require much long, sometimes tiresome work in the field and in the laboratory: detailed surveys, large-scale archaeological excavations, and thorough studies of archaeological artifacts. The archival historian and the archaeologist must work in tandem to confront the data, to place the remains and materials back in their context, and to derive the best documented syntheses.

This work will require years of labor. Above all, it will not transform the economy, a real political stubbornness, the financial resources, and especially the human resources. The French universities (beginning with that of the Antilles and Guyana), and the scientific organizations such as the Centre National de la Recherche Scientifique, are the only institutions that can inaugurate and continue such research at a high level, by employing professors and research archaeologists working in the field of colonial history of the Antilles and providing a quality education to the students.

3

HISTORICAL ARCHAEOLOGY IN THE NETHERLANDS ANTILLES AND ARUBA

Jay B. Haviser

Five Caribbean islands constitute the present Netherlands Antilles: Curaçao, Bonaire, Sint Maarten, St. Eustatius, and Saba. The island of Aruba was a part of the Netherlands Antilles until 1986, but it now has direct ties to the Netherlands. The Netherlands Antilles and Aruba are currently partners within the realm of the Kingdom of the Netherlands. They are autonomous with respect to internal policy, local government, and legal currency. Just as each of these individual islands has had a varied history, so too has each had a varied array of material culture studies and historical archaeology investigations, ranging from amateur antiquities collectors in the nineteenth century to extensive professional research during the last fifteen years.

In this chapter, the issue of cultural transformation will be discussed but with less focus on the historical contexts of the early colonists and with more attention to the results of interaction between the Netherlands Antillean peoples and a myriad of material culture researchers. The chapter is intended as a reference source summarizing the material culture research done in the Netherlands Antilles and Aruba. I have written, however, not from a particularistic archaeological approach to the available data but rather with the intention of providing an overview of the types of research that have been undertaken on these islands and the impact of this research on the islands' modern populations. Interested readers will find here both sources for more information about specific historical archaeology investigations and insight into how the act of conducting historical archaeology affects the lives of Antillean peoples.

This chapter will first review the geography and cultural development of the islands before turning to each one's specific historical archaeology or material culture research. Finally, indications will be given as to the impact that historical archaeology research has had on the residents of these islands in their development of a historical and national consciousness.

Geographic Background

The Netherlands Antilles and Aruba are physically separated into two groups of three islands that are often called the Dutch Windward and Dutch Leeward groups (figure 3.1). The Dutch Leeward group consists of the islands Curaçao, Bonaire, and Aruba. These islands are in a linear pattern about 40 to 70 kilometers distant from and roughly parallel to the northwestern coast of Venezuela. Aruba is situated about 78 kilometers west of Curaçao, which is located in the center, and Bonaire about 60 kilometers to the east of Curaçao. Curaçao is the largest of these islands, with an area of 444 square kilometers, whereas Bonaire has 288 square kilometers and Aruba 190 square kilometers. Curaçao and Bonaire each have an associated smaller island, which have both been inhabited: Klein Curaçao and Klein Bonaire. All of these islands are semidesert, with an average of about 520 millimeters of rainfall per year and a coverage of predominantly xerophytic vegetation. The climatic conditions on these islands means that they have minimal potential for productive large-scale agricultural activities.

Geologically, Aruba is a part of the continental shelf extending from the Paraguana peninsula in Venezuela and is thus primarily composed of limestones, quartz-diorite, and basaltic diabase, which is evident as a generally flat topography less than 190 meters in elevation. Gold deposits found in Aruba resulted in the commercial exploitation of this resource for a short period.

In contrast to Aruba, Curaçao and Bonaire are geologically true oceanic islands of undersea volcanic origin, with primarily basaltic diabase present and various coastal limestone terraces, evident as generally hilly terrain with some small mountains reaching up to 375 meters on Curaçao and 240 meters on Bonaire. The islands' natural resources that have been exploited commercially include dyewood, phosphate, copper, magnesium, and salt.

Within the Dutch Windward group are the two islands of St. Eustatius and Saba and the southwestern half of the island Sint Maarten–St. Martin. The St. Martin half of the island is French territory. These islands form a rough triangle pattern. Sint Maarten lies to the north, within 10 kilometers' distance between the adjacent islands of Anguilla and St. Barts; St. Eustatius

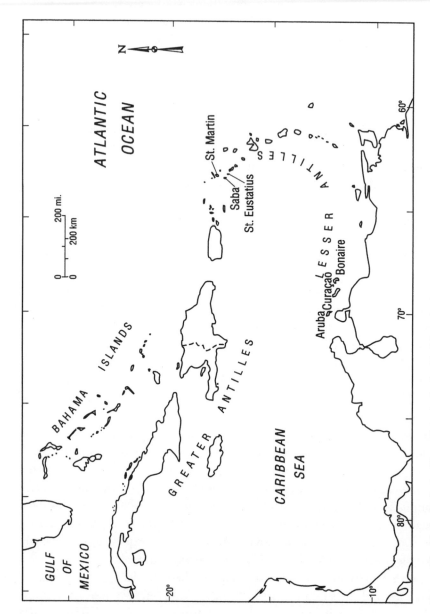

Fig. 3.1. The Netherlands Antilles and Aruba in the Caribbean basin.

is to the south, about 5 kilometers northwest of St. Kitts, and Saba is about 25 kilometers northwest of St. Eustatius. The Sint Maarten half of that island has an area of 34 square kilometers, St. Eustatius has an area of 21 square kilometers, and Saba has an area of only 13 square kilometers. Although some xerophytic vegetation is present on the islands, there is an average rainfall of about 1100 millimeters per year, considerably more than has been noted for the Dutch Leeward group.

Geologically, these islands are of open-air volcanic origin, with primarily andesitic, basaltic, and dioritic bedrock, evident as very steep hilly terrain, with some sloping plains. Sint Maarten has a maximum elevation of 391 meters, St. Eustatius has the peak of a volcano at 600 meters in elevation, and Saba at 870 meters has the highest elevation in the entire Kingdom of the Netherlands. The sloping, smooth topography of Sint Maarten and St. Eustatius, combined with good rainfall, offered excellent potential for large-scale agricultural plantations, whereas Saba had less possibility for large-scale agriculture due to its small size and proportion of suitable topography. Other commercially exploited natural resources on these islands included salt on Sint Maarten, sisal and pumice on St. Eustatius, and sulfur deposits on Saba.

Cultural Background

All of the islands of the Netherlands Antilles and Aruba were inhabited at some period during prehistoric times by Amerindian peoples who had migrated from the South American mainland. The indigenous people who inhabited these islands at the time of contact with Europeans were from various branches of the Arawakan linguistic family. The Amerindians of the Dutch Leeward Islands have been identified as of the Caquetio ethnic group. The Dutch Windward Island Amerindians probably had an affinity with the Taino ethnic group.

The earliest European encounters with the islands of the Netherlands Antilles began with the reported sighting of Sint Maarten, St. Eustatius, and Saba by the 1493 Columbus expedition, but no landings were made on the islands. In 1499, Amerigo Vespucci landed on the island of Bonaire and spent two days and one night on the island, after which he landed at Curaçao for one day. Later on, the Spanish established a small colony at Curaçao and a post at Bonaire from about 1520 until 1634. Aruba had a small Spanish post from 1527 to 1636. In the Dutch Windward group, the Spanish presence was less significant. No Spanish settlement was made on St. Eustatius or Saba, and the Spaniards occupied Sint Maarten only briefly from 1633 to 1648.

The Dutch presence on the islands began with visits to Bonaire in 1623 and to Sint Maarten in 1624, both landings being primarily for the collection of salt. In the case of Bonaire, some Spanish and Portuguese prisoners were left on the island. In 1634, the Dutch invaded and took the islands of Curaçao and Bonaire from the Spanish. Two years later Aruba entered the sphere of the Dutch Leeward colonization. The French established small colonies on St. Eustatius and St. Martin starting in 1629. In 1635, Saba was claimed by the king of France. In 1631, the Dutch and the French simultaneously occupied Sint Maarten. On St. Eustatius the Dutch in 1636 replaced the French who had been there. In 1640 Dutch settlers from St. Eustatius established a colony on Saba, where the French had never actually settled.

In the mid-seventeenth century there began a long period of changing flags for many of the Netherlands Antillean islands. In 1633 the above-mentioned Spanish occupation of Sint Maarten ran out both the Dutch and the French, who recouped the island in 1648 and split it into Dutch and French halves later that same year. Thereafter Dutch Sint Maarten was occupied by French and English forces during various periods up to 1816, when the Dutch regained control of the island that has lasted until the present day. On Saba, French attacks in 1689 were successfully repulsed, but the English occupied the island several times for periods of a few months to as much as seven years, until 1816, when the Dutch took permanent control of the island. The cultural influence exerted by the English may be gauged by the fact that by about 1780 the Dutch language had all but disappeared on Saba.

Thanks in part to the large Jewish population allowed to relocate in the Netherlands Antilles, St. Eustatius had become a commercial hub for the entire region by the early eighteenth century. Its importance is apparent from the frequency with which the island was invaded and conquered. From 1636, when the Dutch first took St. Eustatius, to 1816, when the Dutch regained permanent control of the island, there were twenty-two flag changes on the island, by the French, the English, and the Dutch. It should be mentioned that in 1690–1691, numerous Dutch planters fled St. Eustatius and took refuge in the Danish islands of St. Thomas and St. Croix to avoid French seizure of their property. As a result the Dutch became the largest national group on St. Thomas at the time. In addition, St. Eustatius played a key role in the shipment of armament supplies to the North American colonies during the American Revolution. One result of the numerous military encounters on the Dutch islands was the recurrent building of fortifications and the rebuilding of the towns after attacks that are apparent from the abundant reuse and reconstruction noted in historical archaeology research.

In the Dutch Leeward group, the islands were far more stable in regard to Dutch control. There was only one French capture of Curaçao in 1713, lasting for some days, and two captures of all the islands by the English, in 1801–1803 and 1807–1816, after which permanent Dutch control was established. This relative stability permitted Curaçao to emerge as a major trading center for the region and, together with the climatic conditions, focused the island's economy in the direction of commerce rather than plantations.

The first Africans were brought through the Netherlands Antilles, as part of the Dutch transatlantic slave trade to the Caribbean, as early as the 1640s. Thousands of Africans were used as slaves on the predominantly large-scale plantation islands of Sint Maarten and St. Eustatius. Even larger numbers of Africans passed through the islands of St. Eustatius and Curaçao, as a part of the Dutch slave trade to the Spanish territories and other lands. On Bonaire, imported Africans accounted for a small proportion of the population. On Aruba the African presence was extremely small, and on Saba no African presence was evident during the slave period.

As well as being of significance to the economic development of the Netherlands Antilles through their commercial sale and their labor on the plantations, the Africans also had an important impact on the subsequent cultural formulation of the islands. In places where the Africans were a small proportion of the population, the influence of African genetic and cultural traits is, logically, smaller, whereas on the islands with majority African populations, the genetic and cultural influence of Africans generally predominates. Several important events, such as the 1750 and 1795 slave revolts on Curaçao, partly contributed to the eventual emancipation of the slaves in the Netherlands Antilles in 1863. After the emancipation period various economic, settlement, and social systems began to alter dramatically on islands that had large African populations. Less of a shift occurred on the islands with little African influence. Particularly in the postemancipation period, other non-European ethnic groups, such as Lebanese, Chinese, and Madeiran Portuguese, also migrated to parts of the Netherlands Antilles. These groups formed the multiethnic base of the peoples who are now more evident on some of the islands, such as Curaçao, and less evident on others, such as Saba and St. Eustatius.

Of particular importance to historical archaeology are those internal systems that produce, directly or indirectly, large quantities of material evidence, such as economic systems. For the Netherlands Antilles, there were a variety of economic systems for the different islands. The island of Curaçao had primarily a commercial exchange economy throughout its history, including an early emphasis on the African slave trade, with agriculture, mining, and salt production as only minor supplements to the overall system. Curaçao's sister island of Klein Curaçao was heavily exploited for phosphate in the late nineteenth century. St. Eustatius, like Curaçao, also developed and maintained a large commercial economy, again reinforced by slave trade, until the beginning of that island's economic decline in 1781. St. Eustatius, however, relied to a large extent on a plantation economy of various crops, with sugar the greatest in importance.

The island of Sint Maarten had a predominantly agricultural plantation economy, with surplus for export, accompanied by salt production. Saba had a small-scale economy of agricultural production for local consumption, some minor export of woven handcrafts, and nineteenth-century sulfur mining, and Saban people themselves were in demand for their navigation skills and seamanship. On Bonaire, agriculture, livestock, and salt production were the primary basis of the economy. On Aruba, livestock production and minor agriculture were the economic mainstays, with gold mining a very short-term economic resource in the late nineteenth century. In the early twentieth century, the economies of Aruba and Curaçao shifted heavily toward the petroleum industry, with the construction of two large oil refineries on those islands. Furthermore, by the mid-twentieth century, all of the islands had directed all, or part of, their economic systems more toward the tourism industry, particularly Sint Maarten and Aruba.

Historical Archaeology Research in the Netherlands Antilles

As one begins to integrate the historical background of the islands with the material culture research conducted, it becomes evident that research topics on the islands vary with each island's historical contexts and geography. The types of research undertaken on the islands have generally reflected their relative mix of plantation, commercial, and military activity. Nonetheless, each island has abundant sites representative of other areas of study that have yet to be fully investigated. As elsewhere in the Caribbean, the complex interaction of international, financial, and local interests determines which sites are to be investigated and by whom.

In regard to fields of research related to historical archaeology, there are various history, anthropology/sociology, architecture and ethnographic studies that cover some, or all, of the islands, and a few examples will be mentioned here.

Some of the more important early collections of maps and documents pertaining to the Dutch colonization are located at the Dutch National Archives in The Hague, Holland, including the Dutch West India Company documents. The Netherlands Antilles Government Archives in Curaçao also has documents that date mostly to the period after 1830. For the Spanish period of colonization in the Dutch Leewards, some references can be found in Hernéandez (1868–1882) as reproductions from the Royal Archives in Seville, Spain. For secondary historical sources covering all of the islands, see the publications by Teenstra (1836), Hamelberg (1901–1909), Knappert (1932), Wright (1934), Hartog (1953–1964), and Goslinga (1971, 1979). In addition, researchers should consult the 1917, 1969, and 1985 editions of the *Encyclopedia of the Netherlands Antilles* (Ayubi, Boerstra, and Versteeg 1985; Cruxent and Rouse 1969; Ten Kate 1917). These sources are supplemented by island-specific publications by numerous authors including Attema (1976), Hamelberg (1899), and Hartog (1965, 1976a, 1976b) for St. Eustatius; Maduro (1961), Renkema (1981), Congregation (1982), Hartog (1968), Felice Cardot (1973), and Hartog (1996) for Curaçao; Mansur (1989) and Hartog (1988) for Aruba; Johnson (1979), Hartog (1965, 1975), and Hofman (1987) for Saba; van Nooyen (1985), Hartog (1978), and Euwens (1907) for Bonaire; and Johnson (1987), Glasscock (1985), and Hartog (1965, 1981, 1994) for Sint Maarten.

Closely related to the historical studies, and directly related to historical archaeology, are publications about the historical architecture of the islands. These architectural investigations include Ozinga (1959), Newton (1986), Prunetti (1987), Buddingh' (1994), and a series of posthumous publications by Hartog (1997a, 1997b, 1997c) for Curaçao; Temminck-Groll (1982, 1989) for St. Eustatius and Sint Maarten; Newton (1988) and Klomp (1980) for Bonaire; Denters (1979) and Peterson (1985) for Aruba; and Brugman (1994) for Saba. A Dutch-language publication by Floore, Gawronski, and Ortiz-Troncoso (1995) contained a limited outline of historical archaeology research of the Netherlands expansion in the Caribbean, but this was primarily a list of historical sites.

In addition to history-oriented studies of the islands, various anthropological and sociological studies are relevant to a thorough historical archaeological investigation. Some of these studies include publications by Keur and Keur (1960) for the Windward islands; Crane (1971) on Saba; Klomp (1983) on Bonaire; and Hoetink (1966), Brito (1991), Allen (1991), Römer (1991), Gansemans (1989) and de Paula (1967), and Ayubi (1996) on Curaçao.

Various popular or semiprofessional sources of information on the islands are also useful for their contribution to historical reconstructions. They include local journals and magazines, such as *Lantèrnu* and *Kristòf* on Curaçao; *Discover* on St. Martin-Sint Maarten; and newsletters from historical foundations and museums on the different islands. There are also numerous ethnographic artifact collections associated with most of the museums in the Netherlands Antilles and Aruba, some of which have corresponding publications; see, for example, Brenneker (1969–1975) and Juliana (1976–1978, 1988) for Curaçao.

What follows is a basic discussion of the historical archaeology and material culture research that has been conducted thus far on each of the individual islands of the Netherlands Antilles and Aruba.

St. Eustatius

The island of St. Eustatius has been the primary focal point for both the earliest and the majority of historical archaeology research in the Netherlands Antilles undertaken thus far. The earliest intentional historical sites documentation was conducted by J. P. B. de Josselin de Jong as part of an archaeological/ethnological expedition to the Netherlands Antilles sponsored by the Leiden Ethnological Museum in 1923 (Effert 1992).

Although some less well documented investigations were conducted in the waters around the island by R. Marx in 1961, the first systematic professional historical archaeology investigation on this island, and the first for the Netherlands Antilles as a whole, began in 1981. The 1981 St. Eustatius project was a joint land/underwater survey and land excavation investigation undertaken by the College of William and Mary, the University of South Florida, and Edwin Dethlefsen with the approval of the Archaeological-Anthropological Institute of the Netherlands Antilles (AAINA) (Dethlefsen et al. 1979). The College of William and Mary participated as a summer field school headed by N. Barka; the University of South Florida conducted an underwater survey by S. Gluckman and K. Hardin and a land survey made by J. Haviser. One result of this early work was that N. Brito, a native-born Curaçaoan working at the AAINA, later studied historical archaeology at the College of William and Mary.

After the first summer of work, over 100 archaeological sites, primarily plantation ruins, had been located and mapped on the island; the underwater wharf structures of Oranje Bay had been mapped; and limited excavations had been conducted at the Dutch Reformed Church, Fort de Windt, and the Lower Town warehouse district. Some of the results of this work were presented in a symposium at the 1982 annual conference of the Society for

Historical Archaeology held in Philadelphia (Barka 1982; Dethlefsen 1982; Garland 1982; Hardin and Gluckman 1982; Haviser 1982).

A second William and Mary field school on St. Eustatius was conducted by Barka in 1982. Gluckman returned on behalf of the University of South Florida, Dethlefsen left the project, and Haviser now represented the AAINA. The field survey and mapping continued, as did excavations in the Lower and Upper Town warehouse districts (Barka 1983). From 1981 until 1994, the College of William and Mary continued either general historical archaeology field schools or specific historical archaeology excavation programs on St. Eustatius (Barka 1985, 1987a, 1987b, 1988, 1991b, 1996a, 1996b). The University of South Florida discontinued its participation after the 1982 field season. The AAINA participated from 1982 to 1985 with Haviser conducting land survey and mapping and with W. Nagelkerken conducting underwater survey and artifact recovery in Oranje Bay intermittently from 1983 to 1991 (Nagelkerken 1985, 1986, 1987, 1988a, 1988b, 1993a).

On St. Eustatius, historical archaeology research has focused on various plantation complexes, some forts, underwater work in Oranje Bay, and, most extensively, urban/commercial sites. An important aspect of these urban studies has been the investigation of different ethnic populations on the island such as the Jews, with the excavation of a synagogue and the comparative study at the Protestant Dutch Reformed Church. Furthermore, the field school context of the research on St. Eustatius has produced several synthetic reports of the historical archaeology results, such as works on acculturation by Kandle (1985) and Colono ware ceramics by Heath (1988, 1991, 1999). The field school aspect of the historical archaeology research on St. Eustatius has also generated more student reports of the data recovered from the excavations than exists for the other islands. The relevant publications and manuscripts include Hinote (1981), Kochan (1982), France (1984), de Passalacqua (1987), Bequette (1991), and Delle (1994). Many historical sites on the island with potential for historical archaeology research remain to be investigated.

Sint Maarten

As with St. Eustatius, de Josselin de Jong made a survey of the island of Sint Maarten in 1923. Apart from noting some historical sites, however, he made no historical contribution. In the 1950s and 1960s, several individual families, including the Buncampers, the Beaujons, and the Wilsons, amassed extensive ethnographic artifact collections that were placed in a small museum on the island in 1960. This museum was later closed, and most of the artifacts were lost, although a few specimens survive in the current museum and at private residences.

With all the attention paid to St. Eustatius by professional historical archaeologists beginning in 1981, it is ironic that Sint Maarten received so little attention considering that one must travel through Sint Maarten to reach St. Eustatius. Barka, Gluckman, and Haviser visited such historical sites as Belvedere at the time but made only surface observations without doing an actual survey, mapping, collecting, or excavations. Eventually, various historical archaeology sites were recorded for Sint Maarten by M. Sypkens-Smit (1982) in 1981 and by Haviser (1988) in 1987, although both of these site listings were incidental to surveys of prehistoric sites.

The first extensive historical archaeology excavations were conducted at the Fort Amsterdam site in 1987 by J. Baart (the city archaeologist for Amsterdam, working in cooperation with the AAINA). Baart conducted excavations at the Fort Amsterdam site again in 1989, with an additional minor test excavation at the Frontstreet 118 site, and made surface collections from the Bishop Hill site (Baart 1990, 1992; Baart, Knook, and Lagerwey 1988). While the mapping and excavations were under way at Fort Amsterdam, Nagelkerken, representing the AAINA, performed underwater survey and mapping around the peninsula on which the fort rests.

In 1989, the College of William and Mary, under the direction of Barka, conducted a survey and mapping at the Welgelegen estate on Sint Maarten (Barka and Sanders 1990). This was followed from 1990 to 1992 by a survey and mapping of various historical sites on the Dutch side of the island, these being primarily plantation estates of the eighteenth and nineteenth centuries (Barka 1991a, 1993). Barka then organized a symposium at the twenty-fifth meeting of the Society for Historical Archaeology, where he stressed the need for emergency action to preserve sites on the island (Barka 1992; Baart 1992; van der Hoeven 1992; Kraai 1992; and Richardson 1992). The result was that the AAINA submitted draft contracts for the control of archaeological research on the island (Haviser 1993c), and the island government of Sint Maarten drew up an official historic sites protection list for the island (VROM 1994).

Underwater survey and mapping directed by K. Bequette was conducted in 1994 and 1995 at the *Proselyte* shipwreck site of 1801, off the coast of Sint Maarten (Bequette 1995). During the 1994 field season, Bequette and S. Sanders were also called upon to make an emergency soil profile drawing of historic burials eroding from a road cut at the Bishop Hill cemetery site (Bequette and Sanders 1995).

More recently, Haviser conducted a systematic survey with test excavations at the Belvedere plantation as a mitigation project for the urban planning office of Sint Maarten in 1996, which sought to delineate areas requiring protection from development (Haviser 1996a).

On agriculturally productive Sint Maarten, historical archaeology has focused on individual plantation complexes or on the dominance of the Fort Amsterdam fortification as an integral part of the battles fought for the island. Again, private residences, African descendants' sites, other immigrants' sites, salt factories, anchorages, and other forts have yet to be thoroughly investigated.

In the context of Sint Maarten–St. Martin, it can be mentioned that, on the French side of the island, archaeological research has almost completely focused on the prehistoric period. Some mention has been made of historic sites in the prehistoric site surveys of Sypkens-Smit and Haviser and in various popular articles about the architectural monuments by R. Richardson as editor of *Discover* magazine.

SABA

Historical archaeology research on Saba has been rather limited, beginning with de Josselin de Jong's observations in 1923 and his few actual site identifications. In 1983, Haviser conducted an islandwide archaeological survey for the AAINA that identified both prehistoric and historic sites outside the developed residential areas (Haviser 1983). This survey of Saba includes the location and mapping of numerous historical sites and abandoned historic village complexes dating from the eighteenth century through the twentieth. Of these, most had never been mapped before, including Mary's Point, Cow Pasture, and Middle Island.

During a prehistoric archaeological investigation on Saba in 1987, C. Hofman and M. Hoogland of Leiden University also noted historic components at the Kelbeys Ridge site, for which they acquired radiocarbon dates (Hofman 1993; Hoogland 1996). Also noteworthy is a doctoral dissertation on historical architecture by F. Brugman, which presents an extensive analysis of the historical structures on the island and has considerable importance for historical archaeologists (Brugman 1994).

On Saba, the smallest island in the constellation, the limited historical archaeology research has concentrated on entire village complexes as subjects of investigation, in lieu of large plantations, which did not exist. Other potential historical archaeology sites, such as residences, a sugar factory, anchorages, and the sulfur mines, have been recorded only with site location mapping and limited surface collections.

In the Dutch Leeward islands, a Dutch pastor named A. J. van Koolwijk carried out amateur investigations in an effort to locate various historical archaeological sites on the islands in the 1870s and 1880s and wrote letters to the Ethnological Museum in Leiden (1879). The museum's director later published some of the results of van Koolwijk's finds (Leemans 1904). For Curaçao, van Koolwijk tried unsuccessfully to find the Spanish village of Ascension but was able to identify several prehistoric sites during his search. This attempt was followed by the previously mentioned archaeological/ethnological field research of de Josselin de Jong, who was also on Curaçao in 1923. Few historic sites were actually identified at that time, however.

During the 1950s and 1960s, P. Brenneker, E. Juliana, and C. Engels conducted extensive amateur collections of ethnographic materials on Curaçao. The Engels collection forms the basis of the Curaçao Museum exhibits. Most of the Brenneker and Juliana collections were in the possession of the AAINA and now form the basis for the National Archaeological Anthropological Museum (NAAM), which has replaced the AAINA since 1998. These three sources represent some of the largest ethnographic artifact collections for the island to date and an important reference base for material culture research on the island. Juliana has published information relating to the artifacts in the form of art, poetry, stories, and other literature. Brenneker's series, called *Sambubu* and published from 1969 to 1975, describes artifacts and activities of potential importance to historical archaeology research.

During a short visit in 1965, the Venezuelan archaeologist J. Cruxent visited Curaçao and identified some historical archaeology sites. Cruxent processed the first radiocarbon dates for historical archaeology sites on the island, with a date of A.D. 1610 from the Spanish-period Gaito site (Cruxent 1965).

From the 1950s to the 1990s, several historical architecture studies were written with a particular bearing on historical archaeology studies and should be mentioned here. These studies include Newton (1986), Prunetti (1987), Monsanto and Monsanto (1991), and Buddingh' (1994). In 1990, Coomans, Eustatia, and Newton published an edited volume discussing historical architecture in the islands. Brito (1989) completed her master's thesis with an archival study of eighteenth-century merchants on Curaçao. De Haseth (1984) wrote a thesis on African-Curaçaoan kitchens, and Rosalia (1996) wrote a dissertation on African-Curaçaoan music, both for Leiden University.

The actual historical archaeology conducted thus far on Curaçao has investigated a wide variety of sites. Professional historical archaeology research on Curaçao has primarily been conducted by the AAINA, beginning in 1982 with an islandwide land survey for prehistoric and historic sites. The historic sites first reported in this survey were mostly of the protohistoric period (Haviser 1987, 1989a, 1989c). The AAINA also conducted excavations at the San Hironimo site on Curaçao, a Spanish-Amerindian settlement of the sixteenth century called Ascension, which van Koolwijk had sought (Haviser and Maduro 1990). Later, Haviser and Brito conducted archaeological tests over much of the urban Punda district on Curaçao in 1990 (Haviser and Simmons-Brito 1991, 1993). This effort was followed in 1991 by excavations at the Zuurzak site, believed to be a Dutch slave camp from the late seventeenth century (Haviser 1992; Haviser and DeCorse 1991; Haviser and Simmons-Brito 1995). In 1994, the AAINA conducted excavations and mapping at two Seinpost sites, Dutch optical telegraph stations of the early nineteenth century (Haviser 1995b, 1996b). In 1995, a historical archaeology field survey and excavations were conducted by the AAINA at a slave-period and postemancipation African settlement in the Kenepa area of Curaçao (Haviser 1995a). One result of these excavations has been a comparative study of Curaçaoan slave houses and West African house structures that identifies sociological repercussions of the slavery system (Haviser 1995a, 1997a, 1997b, 1999, 2000, 2001a, 2001b). Furthermore, in preparation for the tourist development of Daai Booi Bay, Haviser conducted an archaeological survey with test excavations in 1997 that identified Spanish-period artifacts, a nineteenth-century Dutch fort, early twentieth-century salt warehouses, and a World War II observation post (Haviser 1997b). More recently, sixteen human burials from a late seventeenth-century Protestant cemetery were excavated from beneath the floor of a Jewish synagogue in the urban center of Willemstad. This study is being conducted by Haviser (archaeology), van Langenfeld (history), and Khudabux (physical anthropology); a preliminary report was presented in 1999 (Haviser, Khudabux, and van Langerfeld 2001).

Beginning in 1988, W. Nagelkerken conducted various underwater historical archaeology investigations on Curaçao for the AAINA. These studies include some general underwater surveys of the bays on the south coast; underwater mapping and excavations from 1988 to 1995 at the 1778 shipwreck *Alphen* in Sta. Ana Bay; and underwater survey and excavations along the wharf area of Handelskade in the commercial Punda district (Nagelkerken 1990, 1991, 1993b, 1994, 1997, 1998a, 1998b). More recent underwater research has been conducted by Nagelkerken at the *Mediator* shipwreck. The *Mediator* was a nineteenth-century Dutch coal transport vessel (Haviser 1997d).

The large size of Curaçao, in comparison to the other islands, and its multiethnic character, are certainly indications that much more historical archaeology research is possible for the island. Numerous sites are present on the island from various ethnic groups and social classes. These offer potential for future research. They include urban and rural post-emancipation African, Asian, and non-Dutch European sites; sites related to Caribbean and South American immigrants; industrial sites; anchorages; and Dutch plantations, urban/commercial centers, and forts, which are now simply recorded with site locations.

Bonaire

Actual historical archaeology research has been minimal on Bonaire, with early historical sites mentioned by G. Bosch in 1836 and A. van Koolwijk during his amateur surveys in the late nineteenth century; again, no specific sites were located. Later amateur surveys conducted by R. van Nooyen, F. Booi, and P. Brenneker focused primarily on prehistoric sites on Bonaire. Some of the van Nooyen and Booi artifact collections noted in the Bonaire Museum, however, are historical materials. In addition, amateur scuba divers have located various underwater sites, particularly shipwrecks, off the coast of Bonaire, none of which has been professionally documented or investigated.

Some historical archaeology was conducted on Bonaire by Haviser for the AAINA in 1990 as part of a larger study concerning the Amerindian culture history on the island from prehistory to the present (Haviser 1991). The first actual historical archaeology excavations, however, were conducted at Fort Oranje, an eighteenth- to nineteenth-century fortification site, in 1997 by the AAINA (Haviser 1997c; Haviser and Sealy 2000). Plans have been made for further historical archaeological investigation by Haviser, with excavations scheduled at World War II military sites on Bonaire and Curaçao.

Aruba

Like Bonaire, Aruba has seen little actual historical archaeology research. The general focus of archaeology has been more on the prehistoric sites, some of which do have historic components, including, for example, an interesting reference by van Koolwijk to a historic-period Amerindian urn burial ceremony (van Koolwijk 1879). Various ethnographic artifact collections can also be noted in the Aruba Archaeological Museum.

The only investigations to date that relate closely to historical archaeology, on Aruba, are architectural and historical studies by Peterson (1985), van Alphen (1990), and Stienstra (1988) of Aruban gold-mining activities from

1824 to 1915, which include site plans, photographs, and detailed historical accounts.

It is interesting to note that the two islands of Bonaire and Aruba with rather large areas yet limitations for large-scale agriculture and minor commercial ports have been severely neglected by historical archaeologists, who have mainly focused on plantation complexes, forts, and commercial centers for research. Indeed, except for the limited industrial archaeology conducted on Aruba, and investigations of the fort on Bonaire, historical archaeology has been only incidental to the prehistoric research done. A wide variety of historical sites remain that have potential for future historical archaeology research on these islands.

The Cultural Impact of Historical Archaeology Research in the Netherlands Antilles

Official recognition of archaeology as a direct responsibility of the Netherlands Antilles government began with the formation of the Archaeological-Anthropological Institute of the Netherlands Antilles in 1967 under the direction of E. Ayubi. The initial focus of the institute was on cultural anthropology and prehistoric archaeology investigations until the introduction of historical archaeology to the research curriculum in 1981. Thus we can say that historical archaeology is still in the early stages of development for the Netherlands Antilles and Aruba. Apart from St. Eustatius and Curaçao, the islands have seen very little professional historical archaeology research thus far. The cultural impact of the small amount of historical archaeology that has been done, however, overshadows the actual quantity of research. Indeed, it was noted from the beginning by Dethlefsen (1982) that the very act of conducting historical archaeology on these islands goes well beyond any scientific contribution to become a social, political, and economic focal point. In the following discussion, I mean not to place blame on, or otherwise demean, any historical archaeology conducted in the Netherlands Antilles but rather to identify positive and negative aspects of cultural transformation that relate to the introduction of historical archaeology research onto the islands.

The topic of cultural transformations in this context calls to mind Trigger's view that contact and change due to the manipulation of the archaeological past may be regarded as having three organizational frameworks: the nationalist, the colonialist, and the imperialist (1984). To these aspects we might add issues bearing on the definition of ethnicity, such as the importance of self-perception by a group (de Vos 1975), and the incorporation of differing views of the complexities of sociocultural continuity (Smith 1982).

The entry of North American and European archaeological teams into these small island societies for long periods of time has dramatic social implications. Consider the delicate nature of the information sought, the actual historical background of an island's ethnic community. Many anthropologists regard historical perspective as an essential part of an ethnic identification, yet it is also vulnerable to romanticism and generalization (de Vos 1975; Ferbel 1995; Haviser 1995c, 1998a, 1999; Mintz 1974; Smith 1982). The way a community perceives and accepts historical archaeology and the historical data produced reflects the culmination of each island society's cultural transformation in response to the organizational framework of the archaeology conducted. The social impact differs, depending on whether the AAINA directs archaeological projects using local workers (i.e., a nationalist approach) or whether large groups of outsiders come in to conduct research (i.e., an imperialist approach) and then leave the island.

One social aspect of these different relations is that the involvement of local workers in AAINA projects generally results in additional indirect involvement of those workers' family members and friends, all participating within the same social codes of behavior. When a project's directors and workers are brought in from another culture (such as a summer field school), the general result is insulation and relative isolation from local social contexts. Sometimes there is also the negative aspect of introducing moral and/or dress codes not accustomed to the local population. There is also an aspect of introducing new female role models for local women when foreign researchers enter the society. From an outsider's perspective this would seem to be a positive aspect for local women; however, in practice, as was noted by Brito during her fieldwork, the local population is more often shocked at the concept of female manual laborers (Brito, personal communication).

A local community's eventual perception of a project, and thus the project's value to that community, are clearly affected by its relationships with the researchers. In the AAINA case, the local investigators are perceived by the general community as conducting research for the local good albeit on a small scale. On the other hand, foreign researchers are generally perceived as "inquisitive tourists" with little to offer the local community. Even though the researchers make some economic contribution to the community through local expenditures, sometimes supplemented by other assistance such as support for museums, a sense of personal connection with the population is often lacking. This reaffirms the importance of involving local personnel in an archaeological investigation, a point that has also been noted in the context of other countries by Graham and Mills (1990).

On the islands of St. Eustatius and Sint Maarten, most of the research has been conducted by North American and European archaeological teams. The local working population has been minimally involved in the actual excavations, with the exception of some few cases in the early years of the St. Eustatius project. Yet, ironically, the island government officials have played a large role in the negotiations for the work. As Nash (1981) has noted, sometimes access to foreign specialists reflects social status within a community. Thus, in the case of St. Eustatius and Sint Maarten, much of the general population regards the historical information generated by the archaeologists as being meant for the elite of their community and therefore as being of less relevance to themselves. Meanwhile, any financial contributions to the community, whether made through direct compensation or by other means, often fail to change this public perception.

The strategic historical relation of St. Eustatius with the North American colonies during the American Revolution suggests that it is more than a coincidence that North American archaeologists have focused on that island. This has also been perceived by some of the local population as a North American investigation of North American history, not theirs. Further in this regard, the focus of excavations at predominantly European descendants' sites clearly emphasizes an imperialist orientation to the research interests of the investigators, rather than relating to the interests of the local African descendent population. In contrast, the nationalist historical archaeology by the AAINA on Curaçao focuses on African descendants' sites and reflects strong local demand and local involvement in research plans for the island.

Other cultural transformations resulting from the advent of historical archaeology on the islands clearly includes a general increase in the local appreciation of the intrinsic value of historical sites and objects. By association, the increase in local awareness of the value of the material culture has also developed into a greater sense of self-value and self-esteem among most of the island communities. Therefore, knowing that the grounds for self-esteem are an important part of identity within an ethnic group (Stein 1980), the very practice of historical archaeology reinforces ethnic identities on the islands. In addition, the historical data generated by archaeological research, when accepted by the local communities, build a stronger sense of historical perspective and association with ethnic and national groups beyond the confines of each individual island. This greater transnational identification has been implicated as a defining aspect of national development in the Caribbean (Olwig 1993).

An increased appreciation of the value of old material things has had some negative consequences. Local individuals have occasionally plundered and destroyed important land and underwater sites to recover newly realized "valuables." Sometimes, too, the sense of personal identification with people in history gives way to a more symbolic representation of things in history, as Haviser (1995c) noted on Bonaire. On the other hand, the new awareness that historical material things are valuable has led to the establishment of numerous museums on the islands with the historical period as a focus. When possible, properly excavated historical artifacts are used in these museum exhibits rather than random collections, most of which were made by amateurs such as van Koolwijk, whose orientation was colonial. A concern for artifacts' proper contexts is much more important in exhibits now than it was before rigorous education in historical archaeology came to the islands. Nonetheless, museum exhibits remain dominated by modern ideological orientation, partly molded by the historical archaeologists, a phenomenon that Shanks and Tilley (1987) noted elsewhere.

There is currently a museum on each island in the Dutch Windwards, with a museum of professional quality on St. Eustatius, thanks to the cooperative efforts of the St. Eustatius Historical Foundation and the College of William and Mary. On Bonaire, where less historical archaeology has been conducted, there is a single folk museum and a new artifact exhibition room at the restored Fort Oranje. On Aruba there are several small museums, the largest being focused on the prehistoric period. In contrast, Curaçao currently has nine historical museums, with more planned. Whereas the other islands with their smaller populations can afford only a single museum, Curaçao has a larger, more affluent, multiethnic population. In addition, archaeological research on prehistoric sites began to influence the Curaçao community many years earlier than it did most of the other islands. With the development of historical archaeology, Curaçao has shown a particular maturity in national pride and local appreciation for historical research, thereby stimulating a greater enthusiasm for museums. Clearly, then, the museums have felt the impact of the archaeological orientation on the islands, whether more imperialist, as on St. Eustatius, or more nationalist, as on Curaçao.

In connection with museums, local public education about historical archaeology has been growing in popularity and acceptance on the islands. New school textbooks about archaeology are being used in both the Dutch Windwards (Haviser 1990) and the Dutch Leewards (Haviser, Sillé, and Garcia

1995). On an international note, the Venezuelan government invited the Netherlands Antilles to present a professional course on Dutch diagnostic artifacts (Haviser 1998b). This event stimulated local interest on Curaçao in historical archaeological research. This interest reflects not only the growing local population's awareness of their historical past but also an awareness of the link between that past and the methods by which it is researched through historical archaeology.

Education about historical archaeology has begun to reach the government legislatures as well (Haviser 1989b). As a result, national laws regarding historical monuments are being borrowed from Dutch laws of the 1940s, revised on various occasions up to 1989. The islands of Curaçao and Sint Maarten have official "monuments lists" of historical sites that are designated for protection (DROV 1989; VROM 1994), and the other islands are currently considering passing similar laws. The stimulus for these laws is increased historical awareness on the islands, for which the development of historical archaeology is partly responsible. The national and local governments alike have come to see that historical archaeology can be valuable as it ensures that historical sites on the islands are properly recorded and in some cases restored to their original appearances. Evidence for this appreciation includes the appointment of an archaeologist to the official Monuments Advisory Council (Monumentenraad) established on Curaçao and subsequent outline of selection criteria for archaeological sites (Haviser and Ansano 1993). In addition, AAINA has submitted draft contracts to control the quality of archaeological research on the islands of Curaçao and Sint Maarten (Haviser 1993a, 1993b).

There are still cases where developers have produced pseudohistorical constructions for tourists, but the increase in education and awareness of historical archaeology on the part of local developers and governments (Haviser 1993a, 1993d) has helped curb these pseudohistorical tourism projects. There has been greater focus on more correct restorations, for example, at the government guesthouse on St. Eustatius (Temminck-Grol 1989), the courthouse on Sint Maarten (Kraai 1992), and downtown Willemstad on Curaçao, which has now been placed on the UNESCO World Heritage List (DROV 1990). Indeed, national leaders are becoming more aware of the vast wealth of historical sites in the Netherlands Antilles and Aruba and view these sites as opportunities for economic development through tourism that can be realized with the assistance of historical archaeology.

The growth of museums and increased education about history are also intimately tied to the rapid development of the tourism industry over the last fifteen years. In response to the need for the islands to distinguish themselves from the rest of the Caribbean, the unique historical structures and character of the Netherlands Antilles and Aruba have been the subject of economic development for tourism for some years now (Brito 1991; Haviser, Brugman, and Newton 1989; Henriquez 1990; Römer 1990; and others). Some social and economic effects relating to the tourism industry partially attributed to the introduction of historical archaeology include the above-mentioned development of museums, publicity information about the unique historical aspects of the islands, and historic restorations of numerous monuments and districts for tourists to visit. As Nash (1977) has warned, however, small-scale societies must be particularly careful of the potentially overwhelming impact that tourism can have by creating a service economy in which the community's traditional aspects are engulfed by transitional aspects. Thus, using historical archaeology as a tourism development tool requires an extra sensitivity to the interests of the local population regarding which historical sites are presented and how they are presented.

The imperialist, and occasionally colonialist, bias of North American and European historical archaeological research toward selecting sites of European descendants, mentioned above, is difficult in this respect because it has stimulated a general impression that European properties are more important than the properties of other ethnic groups on the islands (Haviser 1985). Indeed, the presentation of plantation life demonstrated to tourists can be from the perspective of the adaptability and achievements of the African slaves and freemen/women. This is the current program of research for Curaçao (Haviser 1995a; Haviser, ed. 1999), and not only to focus on servitude and the landowner's properties. Granted that the work of archaeologists is itself a part of the cultural process that perpetuates national histories and identities, and what the local population presents to tourists expresses that contemporary social production. Historical archaeology has clearly benefited the tourism industry on these islands, but the Netherlands Antilles and Aruba as the host country must still prepare for adaptation to a new sociocultural reality within and among the ethnic groups and classes in the islands.

Without a doubt, the debut of historical archaeology has contributed to a growing awareness in the Netherlands Antilles and Aruba that these islands have a unique historical significance, not only for the local inhabitants, but also for the Caribbean region and the world. This increased historical consciousness is having a direct impact on the development of a national pride and a confident identity. At the same time, however, the contact with foreign researchers is introducing the islands' people to new social codes and new forms of social relations, thereby contributing to cultural transformation within Antillean society. Just as historical archaeology is beginning to expand in the Netherlands Antilles and Aruba, so too are these islands developing as nations with the reinforcement of some traditional perspectives and the absorption of some influences from abroad. A deeper historical consciousness is helping in the formation of a more mature national identity, and, subsequently, that historical self-perception is contributing to social and economic growth.

4

HISTORICAL ARCHAEOLOGY IN THE BRITISH CARIBBEAN

David R. Watters

Great Britain possessed more island colonies in the Caribbean during the colonial era than any other European power. Most of these islands are now independent nations that remain linked with the United Kingdom as members of the British Commonwealth. Their past connections are manifested today in numerous ways, ranging from use of the English language and the parliamentary system of government to an unbounded enthusiasm for cricket and to customarily driving on the left side of the road. The historical sites of these islands testify to the close ties existing in the past.

This chapter provides an overview of historical archaeology and related subjects in the British Caribbean, or, as it is more commonly known, the British West Indies. It focuses on selected smaller islands in the eastern Caribbean Sea, mainly those in the Lesser Antilles island chain. Islands individually receiving coverage in the subsequent chapters of this volume—Barbados, Montserrat,

I am grateful to Desmond Nicholson of the Museum of Antigua and Barbuda, Alissandra Cummins of the Barbados Museum and Historical Society, and David Robinson of the Nevis Historical and Conservation Society for providing pertinent information and publications and for reviewing and commenting on earlier versions of this chapter. I also thank Henri Petitjean Roget of Musée Schoelcher, Guadeloupe, for discussing historical archaeology in the French Caribbean and Paul Farnsworth for his willingness to allow the inclusion in the bibliography, at the last minute, of newly found references. I also acknowledge the help of Stanley W. Lantz with production of the photographs and Jennifer Brown with manuscript revisions.

and the Bahamas—are dealt with minimally in this chapter, as are some other islands (Bermuda, the Cayman Islands, Jamaica, Trinidad, the British Virgin Islands) and the former colonies of British Honduras (Belize) and British Guiana (Guyana) on the continental mainland.

Spain made no sustained effort to settle the Lesser Antilles islands, preferring instead to focus its colonizing efforts on the larger islands of Hispaniola, Puerto Rico, Cuba, and Jamaica in the Greater Antilles. Consequently, the vacuum in the eastern Caribbean attracted other European powers, first as bases for their privateers (who often switched to outright piracy) and second as locations for their colonizing attempts beginning in the 1620s. The English, French, and Dutch ultimately dominated the Lesser Antilles islands; in doing so, they created a colonial-era pattern in this archipelago that persists to the present day. Great Britain eventually obtained the greatest number of islands as colonies, but the two largest islands (Guadeloupe and Martinique) have been French possessions from the beginning, and France also controlled the larger Windward Islands (e.g., St. Lucia, Grenada) for much of the colonial era. Dutch colonists emphasized trade and commercial enterprises, unlike the British and French settlers, for whom the acquisition of suitable plantation land was foremost. Although the Dutch presence in the Lesser Antilles was geographically restricted, comprising the small islands of St. Eustatius, Saba, and St. Maarten (the latter shared with French St. Martin), it was nonetheless economically formidable (see the chapters by Haviser and Barka in this volume).

Caribbean Perspectives

In the British Caribbean, a conceptual distinction exists between the ways historical archaeology is perceived by visiting foreign archaeologists, who generally have professional training, and by resident local researchers, who usually are avocational archaeologists. Historical archaeology in the guise known to most North American practitioners, as an anthropologically based discipline and a distinct component of the field of archaeology, does not have an equivalent counterpart in most of the British Caribbean. For local researchers, the field of archaeology serves as the common denominator; whether the time period studied is the prehistoric or historic era is of secondary importance. Very few resident researchers in the British Caribbean (Jamaica excepted) regard themselves as exclusively, or even primarily, historical archaeologists.

The differing perspectives exist for a number of reasons. First is the concern for "national heritage" in recently independent nations, each of which is in the process of defining and characterizing the individuality of its particular cultural patrimony (Cummins 1994a). This process establishes the nation's unique national character and simultaneously distinguishes it from other island nations. Residents relate first and foremost to their islands, identifying themselves as Dominicans, Antiguans, Vincentians, or Kittians and only secondarily as West Indians, a situation that stands in sharp contrast to the tendency of outsiders to lump the citizens of these islands as West Indians. Archaeology therefore plays an important role in establishing the national patrimony, and it does so irrespective of whether the research focuses on prehistoric or historic occupants of the island. Residents of Caribbean islands today regard the prehistory of the indigenous people as part of their own national patrimony, although Native Americans continue to exist as distinct ethnic groups on very few islands (e.g., Dominica, St. Vincent). This involvement with national patrimony is clearly illustrated in Nicholson's publications on the archaeology and history of the country of Antigua and Barbuda (Nicholson 1983a, 1983b, 1991, 1992, 1993a, 1994a, 1994b).

Second, the more broadly based ideas of cultural heritage and historic preservation have attracted greater interest than historical archaeology. Stabilization of standing structures garners attention and resources, from both local governments and international agencies, more readily than buried archaeological remains, whether historic or prehistoric. This bias exists partly because structures are readily visible. Such structures, however, also have much greater potential to characterize national patrimony, to educate the citizens about their heritage, and to enhance tourism, which are prospects appealing to local governments with limited economic resources. Efforts by the Society for the Restoration of Brimstone Hill (now the Brimstone Hill Fortress National Park Society) on St. Kitts (Matheson 1982, 1987) and Friends of English Harbour (1972) on Antigua exemplify these endeavors.

Third, neither archaeology nor anthropology is taught as a distinct discipline in the educational system of the British West Indies, and there are no departments of anthropology at the three main campuses of University of the West Indies (UWI) on Jamaica, Trinidad, and Barbados. To some degree this situation reflects the distinction between archaeology and anthropology (primarily social anthropology) in Great Britain. Archaeology, in the few recent cases when it was incorporated into the UWI curriculum, was placed in the history department. Kofi Agorsah, an anthropologically trained archaeologist, was until recently a UWI faculty member at the Mona campus in Jamaica, where he instituted an academic program based on his primary research interest, the maroons of Jamaica. His project incorporates archaeological, ethnographic, and historical data (Agorsah 1994), and within the British Caribbean it comes closest to matching the North American perspective on historical archaeology.

Non-governmental Organizations

In the British Caribbean, the principal entities involved in research on historical and prehistoric archaeology, and concerned with historic preservation in general, are the non-governmental organizations (NGOs). Archaeological research is generally not conducted by government agencies, although governments may retain control of the formal process to authorize such research, especially where foreigners are involved.

The NGO normally most directly involved with archaeological research is the local archaeological and/or historical society. These almost always comprise persons having an avocational interest in archaeology rather than professional training, and their members usually include both citizens of the island and foreigners who reside there. Members are united by their interest in the history and archaeology of their island. On many British islands in the Lesser Antilles, the local society began as an informally structured group that was bound together by the common interests of its members, but they have tended to become more formalized NGOs, with elected officers, newsletters, dues, and publications. In almost every case, one or two persons took the lead in creating and sustaining the archaeological and historical society (e.g., Father Jesse and Robert Devaux on St. Lucia, founded 1954; Fred Olsen and Desmond Nicholson, Antigua, 1956; and Earle Kirby, St. Vincent, 1963). The formation in 1981 of the Anguilla Archaeological and Historical Society exemplifies the continued creation of such societies by interested persons.

Museums form a second set of NGOs involved with historic preservation. The history of museums in the English-speaking Caribbean has been well researched and documented by Alissandra Cummins (1989), director of the Barbados Museum and Historical Society. Sections of this chapter draw heavily on her study. Many museums in the British Caribbean interpret both the natural environment and cultural patrimony (Cummins 1993). These institutions often include artifacts from prehistoric and historic sites in their exhibits to establish a chronological framework for the history of the island. Other museums that focus upon or emphasize history, archaeology, or anthropology include Guyana's Walter Roth Museum of Anthropology, Nelson's Dockyard Museum at English Harbour on Antigua, the Museum of Nevis History (formerly Hamilton House Museum, the birthplace of Alexander

Hamilton), St. Vincent's Archaeological Museum in that island's famous Botanical Gardens, and some of the museums of the Institute of Jamaica. The creation of museums on newly self-governing islands reflects a concern with national identity and patrimony, although some time usually elapsed before such museums were in operation (e.g., Grenada National Museum in 1976, Museum of Antigua and Barbuda in 1985). Other islands that chose to maintain close ties with Great Britain and remain Crown colonies, however, likewise developed museums (Montserrat in 1976, Cayman Islands in 1990, and Anguilla, under construction at this writing), thus indicating that the growing interest in cultural patrimony does not correlate exclusively with independence.

The final set of NGOs are the national trusts, following the British model, established in the 1960s and 1970s. A national trust is created by an act of government and thus technically differs from archaeological and historical societies and museums, which are for the most part nonprofit associations in the private sector. National trusts are "quasi-NGOs." Some are closely affiliated with their governments, whereas others operate largely independent of government (see Cummins 1989:82–98). National trusts, because they are concerned with the natural environment and cultural heritage, may oversee national parks, biological preserves, historical monuments, and museums and interpretive centers as well as research activities associated with these entities. Efforts to identify, preserve, and restore historic structures have been a major commitment of the national trusts, as exemplified by the Montserrat National Trust's work on forts at Bransby Point and St. George's Hill and the St. Lucia National Trust's efforts at the military sites on Pigeon Island and Morne Fortuné.

Persons interested in preservationist issues are frequently associated with the various NGOs (and in some cases government agencies) that exist on an island and are driving forces behind them. Desmond Nicholson, for example, was important in creating the Antigua Archaeological Society (later the Historical and Archaeological Society) and subsequently in developing the Museum of Antigua and Barbuda; Robert Devaux served as director of the St. Lucia National Trust and as secretary of the island's Archaeological and Historical Society; and Lennox Honychurch has played key roles with the Dominica Institute and the Dominica National Park Service. The NGOs and preservationists are in the forefront of efforts promoting local legislation to protect the cultural heritage, although passage of such laws has unfortunately been spotty.

The case of the Nevis Historical and Conservation Society (NHCS), founded in 1980, illustrates the growth of an NGO and the breadth of work that it undertakes. It began with a volunteer staff that wisely sought guidance from others in the region (e.g., Matheson on St. Kitts, Nicholson on Antigua) who were already knowledgeable about the practical aspects of forming and operating such an organization. In 1984, the NHCS commissioned a feasibility study conducted by David and Joan Robinson, two volunteers in the U.S. Peace Corps, who were serving on Barbados. In 1985, the first full-time attendant was hired, and the Robinsons were appointed curators. The NHCS also enlisted the assistance of Samuel Wilson, a professionally trained American archaeologist investigating Nevis's prehistoric archaeology. The NHCS established a storage system for collections, obtained yearly reports and interpretive data from researchers, and began producing its first exhibits. In 1987, the NHCS began a long-range program to evaluate a historic district for Nevis's main town, Charlestown, including a study of its buildings by a Nevisian architect as a historic preservation master's practicum (Hobson 1989) that became the basis for classifying buildings for inclusion in the historic district. The NHCS started a project to investigate the historic Jewish community of Nevis, which is being carried on through excavations by historical archaeologists from North American universities, with a long-term goal of restoring the buildings (Terrell 1994a, 1994b; Wilson 1993a). The NHCS also supports a study of the economics of plantation life at Coconut Walk, which will become the first large-scale research project at a Nevisian plantation. The NHCS research mandate extends to the island's biodiversity and natural environment (e.g., a study of its orchids).

The success of these architectural, archaeological, and ecological programs inspired the NHCS to establish the Nevis Field Research Center to facilitate studies by qualified researchers and to enhance the educational opportunities afforded to Nevisians. The Nevis Historical and Conservation Society, with more than 500 members, is the largest NGO on Nevis. It has dramatically expanded its educational and research programs, yet the society's strength continues to reside in its membership, individuals with an abiding interest in advancing an understanding of the national patrimony and heritage of Nevis.

This section emphasizes island-specific NGOs concerned with historic preservation. However, historic preservation issues in the West Indies also involve regional organizations, such as the Caribbean Conservation Association (CCA), Museums Association of the Caribbean (MAC), and Island Resources Foundation (IRF), which often collaborate on projects with international organizations such as UNESCO (Delatour 1984) and the Organization of American States (OAS). A collaborative venture between MAC and OAS resulted in the first directory of Caribbean museums (Cummins 1994b), which contains information on museums and their collections for the Spanish, French, Dutch, and British Caribbean. A cooperative project by the CCA and the IRF produced eight country environmental profiles, each of which has a separate section on historic sites in the nation (Innis 1991–1993). A model cultural heritage act was prepared and is being circulated under UNESCO's Caribbean Regional Museum Development Project.

The International Association for Caribbean Archaeology, founded in Martinique in 1963 by avocational and professional archaeologists interested primarily in prehistoric archaeology, has held fifteen biennial congresses at venues in the Spanish, French, Dutch, and British Caribbean. Archaeological and historical societies or museums hosted congresses on the British islands of Barbados (twice), Grenada (twice), St. Lucia, Antigua, St. Kitts–Nevis, and the Bahamas. A definite trend at the recent meetings is the inclusion of an increasingly greater number of papers on historical archaeology, ethnohistory, the Contact period in the Caribbean, and underwater archaeology, to the point where these topics command a separate session. The same trend is evident as well in the proceedings of the congresses (cf. Alegría 1993; Crespo and Guisti 1995; Kelly and Armstrong 1991; Loftfield 1991; Nicholson 1990).

Research in Historical Archaeology

Historical archaeology conducted by foreign archaeologists in the British West Indies is dominated by work at plantations and especially at sugar estates. This research is temporally restricted to the later seventeenth, eighteenth, and early nineteenth centuries, from the commencement through the decline of sugar production. Work in the earlier period, the early and mid-seventeenth-century settlement of the Lesser Antilles, and the later period, after emancipation (in the 1830s in the British islands), is uncommon (Kelly and Armstrong 1991). Caribbean plantation archaeology projects are usually interdisciplinary, involving some combination of archaeological, historical, anthropological, geographical, or ethnohistorical perspectives. They have been applied to individual plantations (Armstrong 1990; Delle 1998; Goodwin 1987; Handler and Lange 1978; Higman 1998; Pulsipher 1991; and see other chapters in this volume) and to islandwide surveys of plantations (Boomert, Ortiz-Troncoso, and van Regteren Altena 1987; Clement 1997; Eubanks 1992).

Local researchers have contributed through documentation of plantation buildings, such as inventories of cane-crushing mills on St. Vincent (Kirby 1973) and Marie-Galante (Barbotin 1975), a French island. The Museum of Antigua and Barbuda has produced a computerized list of 111 standing

Fig. 4.1. The famous double windmills of Betty's Hope estate, Antigua.

mills on Antigua alone (Desmond Nicholson, personal communication 1994), one of which, at the Betty's Hope estate (Carstensen 1993; Goodwin 1994), is being restored (figure 4.1). The St. Lucia National Trust (Devaux 1975) and the Museum of Antigua and Barbuda (Nicholson 1994a) have produced comprehensive surveys of their historic sites. The Institute of Jamaica produced an excellent compilation (Higman 1988) of plantation plans and maps culled from the island's archival sources.

Surveys of historic structures on the low-lying limestone islands of the Lesser Antilles, which did not produce sugar or other commercially important crops in the colonial period, are rare. Barbuda's sites are documented (Nicholson 1994a; Watters 1980a, 1997; Watters and Miller 2000; Watters and Nicholson 1982); some information is available for Anguilla (Douglas 1986). Farnsworth (1996, 1999, this volume) and Wilkie (1999, this volume) are investigating sites in the limestone islands of the Bahamas.

Research on British Caribbean military fortifications has been conducted almost exclusively by local researchers through surveys and inventories of structures and armaments (Crandall and Dyde 1989; Nicholson 1994b). Excavations at forts are very rare. Documentary research, however, has provided plans and historical data (e.g., military units serving) for some renowned fortresses:

Brimstone Hill, St. Kitts (Smith 1992); Shirley Heights, Antigua (Jane 1982); Cabrits, Dominica (Honychurch 1983); and the Garrison, Barbados (Alleyne and Sheppard 1990).

Research in urban settings has been limited to surveys of standing structures for proposed historic districts (Cloyd 1984; Hobson 1989; Thomas 1990) and historical treatises of individual towns (Innis 1985). The archaeology of urban commercial enterprises is unknown in the British Caribbean (apart from research at submerged Port Royal, Jamaica), but it has been a hallmark of research on St. Eustatius in the Dutch Caribbean (Barka, this volume).

Studies of material culture are a high point of Caribbean historical archaeology. They range from primarily descriptive (Hannon and Hannon 1976; Hanrahan 1990, 1993) to analytical (Nicholson 1979, 1980, 1993b) to interpretive articles (Handler 1963a; Mathewson 1973). Imported and locally made ceramics have been a focus of material culture studies. Virtually identical imported ceramics are found at British sites in North America and the Caribbean, a situation that has led to the successful application of Stanley South's mean ceramic date formula to European ceramics in the British West Indies (Nicholson 1979; Watters 1997; Watters and Nicholson 1982).

Ceramic research has emphasized Afro-Caribbean pottery in a variety of cultural contexts, including the British islands of Barbados, Jamaica, Antigua, Nevis, Barbuda, Anguilla, and Montserrat (Handler 1963a, 1963b, 1964; Mathewson 1972b, 1973; Nicholson 1990; Olwig 1990; Petersen and Watters 1988; Petersen, Watters, and Nicholson 1999), Dutch St. Eustatius (Heath 1988, 1999), Danish St. Croix (Gartley 1979), and French Martinique (England 1994). Interesting differences in manufacturing techniques in the British islands have been noted. Barbados is characterized by wheel-thrown, kiln-fired ceramics produced by men, whereas on Antigua and Nevis pottery was hand-built (coiled), fired on an open hearth, and made by women (Watters 1997). Only beginning to be investigated are centers of ceramic production (England 1994; Loftfield 1991, 1992, this volume) that supplied the local sugar industry and also probably provided commodities for trade elsewhere within the Caribbean.

Research on the historical archaeology of enslaved Africans brought to the British West Indies, and their offspring born in the islands, has focused on slavery in the plantation context, including detection of the slave village and identification of material culture remains (Armstrong 1990, 1991; Handler and Lange 1978; Watters 1987). Osteological analysis has provided data on the harsh lifestyles, diseases, and traumas experienced by slaves in British islands (Armstrong and Fleischman 1993; Corruccini et al. 1982; Handler and

Corruccini 1983; Mann et al. 1987; Watters 1994) and in the broader Caribbean region (Courtaud, Delpuech, and Romon 1999; Crespo and Guisti 1992, 1995; Khudabux 1991, 1999; Rivero de la Calle 1973; Ubelaker and Angel 1976). Oral histories of Africans, enslaved or emancipated, are scarce but important (Mathurin Mair 1986; Smith and Smith 1989).

The maroons, another segment of the African population of the Caribbean, have been a focal point of study by anthropologists and historians because of their successful escape from slavery, establishment of viable communities, and resistance to efforts by the planters to subdue and reenslave them. The maroons of Jamaica and Guyana are most renowned within the British Caribbean, but maroon societies existed in other areas of the Americas as well (Price 1973). Maroons in Jamaica are active participants in collaborative efforts with scholars to document their past (and present) heritage through oral history studies and archaeological and ethnographic research (Agorsah 1994). Historic records attest to the presence of maroon settlements on some small islands of the eastern Caribbean, such as Dominica (Honychurch 1984:69–75). On Antigua (Gaspar 1985:171–214), a maroon camp existed by 1684 in the still forested mountains of the southwest section of the island. Marronage ceased on Antigua once the forests had been cleared for cultivation, when the requisite isolated terrain no longer existed. N. A. T. Hall (1992:124–138) indicates that a similar situation precluded maroon settlements in the Danish West Indies. Marronage was most successful and sustained in larger islands such as Jamaica (Agorsah 1992), Hispaniola (Arrom and García Arevalo 1986; Peguero Guzmán 1989; Vega 1979), and Cuba (La Rosa Corzo 1989, 1991).

Historical archaeology has neglected other segments of the colonial society of the British West Indies, a circumstance that arose largely because the plantation has been the focus of study. Data available for whites are derived almost exclusively from research at great houses and thus are heavily biased toward the planters. Field research at a great house is rarely undertaken in isolation; it is normally just one component in a broader plantation archaeology project (e.g., Armstrong 1990). Research related to overseers, indentured servants, merchants, soldiers, and other white components of the society is essentially nonexistent. The research on the Jewish population of Nevis is an exception. Archaeological research has also neglected the "freedmen" segment of the colonial population, which encompasses persons of mixed racial ancestry ("free colored") as well as free blacks, whether manumitted or freeborn (Handler 1974:1–6). Lack of archaeology at urban, commercial, and military sites is the principal reason for the research status of these components of colonial society.

Knowledge of the Contact period in the Lesser Antilles is unsatisfactory

(Wilson 1993b). The Native American populations resident in the region, the sporadic contact between Amerindians and Europeans in the sixteenth century, and the seventeenth-century settlement by the French, English, and Dutch are all poorly researched topics. Research on the archaeology of indigenous peoples of the Contact period is primarily conducted by persons versed in prehistoric archaeology, who have been mainly interested in locating sites and identifying artifacts unquestionably associated with Native Americans during the Contact period. A second concern has been to correlate archaeology with oral histories and historical accounts of the "Carib" inhabitants of the Windward Islands (and possibly the entire Lesser Antilles). Taino Indians in the Greater Antilles told Columbus about the Caribs during his first voyage, but the first direct contact between Caribs and Europeans took place in 1493 during his second voyage. Caribs retained control of their islands in the sixteenth century and vigorously resisted European colonization throughout the seventeenth century but were no longer a significant threat on most islands by the close of the eighteenth century.

Archaeologists have attempted to validate Carib material culture, to address the timing of migration, and to define the spatial aspects of Contact-period occupation (Allaire 1980, 1994, 1997; Boomert 1986; Davis and Goodwin 1990; Honychurch 1997). Anthropologists, historians, and linguists have reassessed ethnic affiliation by reexamining colonial documents (Boucher 1992; Hulme 1992; Hulme and Whitehead 1992; Moreau 1991; Petitjean Roget 1990; Sued-Badillo 1978). Even with previously unknown documents becoming available (Howard and Howard 1983), the "Carib problem" is still not satisfactorily resolved. The ethnic diversity of the indigenous populations throughout the Lesser Antilles during the Contact period is still not adequately understood.

A distinctive Contact-period society, the "Black Caribs" of St. Vincent, resulted from the admixture of Native Americans and Africans. They have received little attention from archaeologists, but their 1797 deportation by the British and subsequent settlement of the Caribbean coast of Central America have been well studied by Gonzalez (1988).

Historical archaeology in the British Caribbean can draw upon regional histories (Hamshere 1972), histories of individual islands, such as Grenada (Devas 1974), Dominica (Honychurch 1984), Barbados (Beckles 1990), and Montserrat (Fergus 1994; Wheeler 1988), a considerable literature about slavery in the West Indies (e.g., Bush 1990; Gaspar 1985; Goveia 1965; N. A. T. Hall 1992; Higman 1984), and conference and symposium volumes (Alegría 1993). A wide range of useful articles are found in a number of Caribbean serials, including but not limited to the *Journal of the Barbados Museum and Historical*

Society (Handler 1963a, 1972; Handler and Jacoby 1993; Loftfield 1992); *Journal of the Virgin Islands Archaeological Society* (Brown 1979; Dick 1977; Gartley 1979; Gjessing 1974; Hannon and Hannon 1976; Nicholson 1979; Ubelaker and Angel 1976; Vescelius 1977); *Jamaica Journal* (Aarons 1984; Agorsah 1992; Armstrong 1991; Mathewson 1972a, 1972b, 1973; Mathurin 1975); *Caribbean Geographer* (Hudson 1989; Satchell 1989); and *Journal of Archaeology and Anthropology of the Walter Roth Museum of Anthropology* (Hanrahan 1990, 1993; Watters 1980a). Very often the most current research reports are found in society newsletters (e.g., Hubbard 1990, 1994; Murphy 1989, 1993; Nicholson 1994c; Terrell 1994a, 1994b).

Future Directions

The potential for historical archaeology in the Caribbean has barely been tapped. This statement applies to the British West Indies and equally (and probably more so in some cases) to the French, Danish, Dutch, Spanish, and Swedish Caribbean (St. Barthélemy was a Swedish possession for a century). Today an island in the Lesser Antilles is regarded as being of British, French, or Dutch heritage, but its past associations are likely to be more nebulous, since the European power that ultimately possessed the island may not be the same nation that initially settled and controlled it. Events in the European colonies in the Caribbean often resulted from decisions made by governments in the distant European homelands. The Caribbean colonies were active (although sometimes unwilling) participants in the historical events that swept the region.

Administrative control of certain islands switched back and forth between European powers as a result of military actions and treaty provisions, and these changes occurred with such frequency as to seem almost routine. Thus, between 1626 and 1802, Tobago changed hands twenty-two times among Dutch, Spanish, British, Courlander, and French settlers before it was finally ceded to Great Britain in 1815 (Eubanks 1992:3, 64–76). Grenada was possessed first by France (1654–1762) and then by Britain (1763–1779), was captured by the French (1779), was returned to Britain by treaty (1783), and subsequently faced an internal rebellion (Devas 1974). St. Lucia routinely shifted between Britain and France, changing hands at least fourteen times in little more than a century (Jesse 1970:16–28). Thus, although it may be technically correct to classify Tobago, Grenada, and St. Lucia as British-heritage islands, such classifications are static and ignore the dynamic historical reality of these islands. They tend to obscure the influences of other European nations as well as the influences of the African and later the Asian (East Indian) segments of the population. The efforts of newly independent countries to define their individual national patrimonies and identities reflect their concern with the dynamic aspects of their cultural heritages (Cummins 1994a).

To date, historical archaeology in the British Caribbean has been limited, for the most part, to the recovery of data at individual sites or to site surveys of individual islands. Archaeologists working in the Caribbean region, whether they are residents or foreigners, tend to focus on a single island. Intra-island and inter-island comparisons are inhibited by this tendency toward single-site- and single-island-oriented research. As a result, comparative studies are essentially nonexistent in the British Caribbean, even for plantations, which constitute the best-studied and best-documented category of historic sites. Intrasite comparison will benefit from future investigation of such currently unstudied components of plantation staff as overseers (Hall 1989).

Yet it is at the comparative level of analysis, not the particularistic level, that the Caribbean holds great promise for historical archaeology. Comparative studies of sugar plantations among British islands, and ultimately among the British, Dutch, French, Spanish, and Danish islands, would be fruitful lines of research. Individual components of the plantation infrastructure (industrial buildings, slave villages, great houses) (figure 4.2) or entire plantations could be compared. Comparisons of older and younger plantations could illuminate the conversion in crops from the earlier tobacco and indigo to sugar as well as provide information on technological innovations in sugar processing. Comparisons could be extended to plantations dating to the French and British occupations on a single island, a circumstance pertinent to the Windward Islands in particular; in the case of Jamaica, it could be the Spanish (Aarons 1984; Lopez y Sebastian 1982) and British periods. Plantations are used as examples because they are better studied, but similarly structured comparisons could be applied, once the requisite field research was accomplished, to urban, military, and commercial historic sites in the British Caribbean. At the level of material culture studies, a broad-scale comparison of Afro-Caribbean ceramics, incorporating technological and social aspects, would be a logical outgrowth of the largely island-specific studies that have been concluded to date.

The opportunities for urban archaeology and especially for studies of commercial enterprises will most likely remain limited in the future. The seaport cities and towns established in the colonial era remain as urban areas in British Caribbean islands today, and most historic district structures are privately owned. Sizable excavations in such circumstances are highly

Fig. 4.2. Restoration of "moulin Bézard," one of the windmills on Marie-Galante, French Antilles. Comparison with British mills (Fig. 4.1) clearly shows certain structural elements of French mills differ.

improbable, but small-scale testing programs are more reasonable. A greater opportunity exists for research at deserted colonial towns, some of which, although they are few in number, are significant sites because they have been neglected, overgrown, and concealed since soon after being abandoned.

The British Caribbean affords an excellent opportunity for archaeological research at historic military complexes, including naval facilities and army fortifications. These very impressive bastions of colonialism, because they remain generally intact or at least in good states of repair, have been a focus of historic preservation. Preservation efforts focus on structure stabilization and, in certain instances, some level of interpretive signage. Few military sites

Fig. 4.3. River Fort's martello tower and attached gun platform guarded the principal roadstead of Barbuda.

Fig. 4.4. The well-preserved officers' quarters at Blockhouse Hill built to protect naval dockyard facilities at English Harbour, Antigua.

have undergone systematic surveys or excavations, apart from work done by local archaeological societies. Military complexes on Antigua and Barbuda (Nicholson 1994b) exemplify the variety of sites available for research, which range from naval dockyard facilities to extensive fortifications to small stand-alone defensive structures such as martello towers (figures 4.3 and 4.4). Most military sites are in the public domain and are administered by national trusts or government national park authorities, in contrast to many plantations and most urban sites, which are privately owned. Historical archaeologists working at military sites could investigate rarely studied segments of colonial society—European soldiers and sailors stationed there, local militiamen, and slaves who soldiered in the famous British West India regiments (Buckley 1979). Beyond military personnel, there were the slaves furnished (usually grudgingly) by planters to construct the fortifications, the families of the soldiers, and the numerous civilians who serviced the military.

Contact-period research will continue to employ the direct historical approach in an effort to locate Native American sites known (through historic documents and maps) to be occupied during European settlement of the region. Cody Holdren's (1998) recent presentation of the results of her direct historical approach, as applied to Grenada, is a case in point.

One research direction deserving future investigation by historical archaeologists is evidence of relationships between British colonies in the Caribbean and North America (Carrington 1988). Canada and the United States (before and after the American Revolution) had economic and social ties with British Caribbean possessions to a degree that is usually not appreciated. Movement of people from North America to the Caribbean and vice versa, whether as visitors, immigrants, or traders, was by no means uncommon. George Washington visited relatives in Barbados on the only trip he ever took outside the United States. The life of Isaac Royall reveals the connections even better. Born and raised in Massachusetts, where he became a merchant mariner, Royall at the age of twenty-three moved to Antigua in 1700, where he acquired a sugar estate, amassed considerable wealth, and married and raised a family. In 1737 he moved back to Massachusetts, settling with his family and twenty-seven slaves in Medford, where he died in 1739 (Hoover 1974). Links between colonial Barbados and Charles Towne, a settlement made by Barbadian colonists near Wilmington, North Carolina, is being investigated by Loftfield. Farnsworth (1996; cf. Gerace 1982) is researching plantations established by Loyalists who emigrated to the Bahamas following the American Revolution (Saunders 1983). The British North American colonies became a primary destination for freeholders (often former indentured servants) departing the West Indies, especially after their small parcels of land began to be acquired by the expanding estates of the sugar planters.

Material culture studies of evidence for trade between the North American and Caribbean colonies would be a worthwhile line of investigation. Steen (1990:table 1) provides information on the variety of materials being exported from the North American colonies; durable goods such as pottery would be preserved in West Indian sites. Steen (1990:table 2) tabulates the number of ships entering and clearing Charleston, South Carolina, during four periods. The quantity of ships arriving from, and departing for, the West Indies dramatically exceeds the numbers of ships traveling from/to the four other sources/destinations (Great Britain, northern colonies, southern colonies, and other ports). The West Indies is second (behind Great Britain) in terms of percentages of total tonnage entering and clearing Charleston's port. Steen (1990:table 3) lists sixteen individual West Indian islands (and two multiple island entries), including British, French, Dutch, Danish (but no Spanish) islands, as sources/destinations for ships entering/clearing Edenton, North Carolina; Antigua alone accounts for almost 25 percent (twenty-five of ninety-eight) of these West Indian records. To date, there has been no attempt to document North American pottery or other durable goods within archaeological contexts in the historic sites of the British West Indies.

Museums in the British Caribbean will become more directly involved with archaeology, not only from a research perspective, but also as the primary repositories for artifacts. Cummins (1993:37–42) determined that 86 percent of surveyed Caribbean museums held archaeology collections (prehistoric, historic, marine). The expansion of collections is largely attributable to archaeology, almost all archaeological materials are stored inadequately, and a high level of archaeological activity is having a major impact on regional museum development. The Museums Association of the Caribbean is ensuring a level of professional training for West Indian museum personnel through regional workshops, networking, and annual general meetings. In the future, museums could be logical bases of operation for West Indian archaeologists, where they would serve as curators, especially on smaller islands where there are no universities affording teaching affiliations. Local NGOs will endure as strong advocates (e.g., Nicholson 1994c) of the need to protect the cultural heritage physically and legally. The success of the cooperative ventures undertaken by regional NGOs in the recent past will make possible more collaborative projects in the future and will promote the sharing of resources and expertise throughout the Caribbean.

Archaeology in the British Caribbean will continue to benefit from collaboration by resident and foreign researchers. The avocational status of past resident researchers, however, will be augmented gradually by West Indians who receive professional training as archaeologists. Persons from Jamaica, St. Lucia, Antigua, and Trinidad have completed or are finishing graduate-level training programs at universities in the United Kingdom, Canada, and the United States. Involvement with local archaeological and historical societies, museums, or national trusts initially sparked their interest in archaeology. The growing interest in national patrimony will support the demand for undergraduate archaeology courses at the University of the West Indies campuses. For the foreseeable future on many Caribbean islands, the resident avocational archaeologists will remain most directly and substantively involved with historical (and prehistoric) archaeology and historic preservation. In this sense, professionally trained archaeologists, whether they are foreigners or West Indians, will supplement but not supplant the avocational archaeologists in the British Caribbean.

PART 2
CARIBBEAN LANDSCAPES

5

TIME LINES
Changing Settlement Patterns on St. Eustatius

Norman F. Barka

St. Eustatius (commonly called Statia) is best known as a major Caribbean entrepôt that supplied arms and supplies to North America during the American Revolution (Jameson 1903). In addition to being a bustling port, however, the island was also a community of diverse people from many lands—merchants, craftsmen, plantation owners, and slaves—a place where people lived, worked, and died. As such, it forms a valuable laboratory for many kinds of archaeological and historical research. This chapter will consider the island community using the settlement pattern approach.

Willey's (1953:1) pioneering book on the Viru Valley defined settlement patterns as "the way in which man disposed himself over the landscape." This societal and holistic approach merges archaeology and ecology and offers an effective way to study past human behavior at various levels (e.g., Ashmore 1981; Wilson 1989). Researchers have delineated three basic levels for study: the individual structure, the arrangement of buildings within a community, and regional studies of interrelated communities linked by economic, religious, and/or political systems (Chang 1968; Trigger 1967). Attempts have also been made to define determinants of settlement patterns—subsistence, ecology, wealth and rank, social and religious organization, and so forth (Trigger 1968).

The author wishes to acknowledge the help of Patti Kandle, who made many valuable comments about the archaeology and history of Statia. Sondra Jarvis prepared the fine artwork in this chapter.

Settlement patterns were the built environment of a sociocultural system as well as a means of communication in the society (Paynter 1982).

The historical past of St. Eustatius is especially suitable for settlement pattern analysis. The island's finite spatial dimensions and the widespread use of masonry construction facilitate the study of site distribution. This chapter will define settlement patterns on St. Eustatius as they were during the 360 years after initial European colonization and will examine the ecological, historical, and/or cultural factors that have influenced their development. The chapter will consider the types of sites that can be found on Statia, how these sites were distributed over the landscape at different times in the Statian past, and why certain settlement patterns exist.

The Statian Database

Small islands such as Statia are, in effect, communities with precise horizontal boundaries. As such, they are manageable units that can be studied in both particular and holistic dimensions. The study of past individuals, groups, buildings, material culture, and so forth relies upon the partnership of historical archaeology and documentary history. The Caribbean islands are especially suited to studies of cultural variation and adaptation through time and space. The study of the European colonization of St. Eustatius and other West Indian islands can offer significant comparisons with North America, as many of the same nationalities inhabited both regions.

Despite its small size, nearly 300 archaeological sites have been located on Statia through survey and excavation (Barka 1985). The presence of so many sites on a small island reflects both Statia's vibrant past and the relative paucity of modern development and construction by comparison with some other islands. The amount of surface artifacts and masonry ruins is sometimes staggering; English, Dutch, and French material culture occur in large amounts. Ceramics and glass have come from Statia in greater variety than from most North American localities. Since 1981, archaeological survey and excavation have uncovered new and more detailed information about the development of Statian culture and society.

Unfortunately, the historical database is scarce, mainly because historical records have not been preserved over time. The majority of known historical documentation is available through the works of Hartog (1964, 1976a, 1976b), Attema (1976), Keur and Keur (1960), and Goslinga (1971, 1985). New historical documents are being discovered as well (Barka 1996a). Approximately twenty-seven historical maps/drawings of eighteenth- or nineteenth-century Statia are available for study, although they vary in completeness and usefulness.

Island Geography, Ecology, and History

The physical environment of Statia, including landscape, climate, fauna, and flora, influenced settlement patterns on Statia (Attema 1976; Keur and Keur 1960; Stoffers 1956; Versteeg and Schinkel 1992; Westermann and Kiel 1961). St. Eustatius is the most southerly island of the three Dutch Windward Islands group (Saba, St. Maarten, St. Eustatius). Statia is a very small island, measuring a maximum of about 5 miles (northwest-southeast) by circa 2.5 miles, with a land area of circa 8.2 square miles. The island, formed by volcanism, has three main topographic zones or landscapes: volcanic hills in the northwest, a large volcano (the Quill) in the south, and an agricultural plain in the center. Each zone occupies roughly one-third of the island (figure 5.1).

The volcanic hills can be characterized as the eroded remnants of an older volcano, with rugged terrain and numerous high hills, such as Boven (964 feet), Gilboa Hill (586 feet), and Signal Hill (769 feet). Two well-developed valley systems reach the sea; both are dry except during heavy rainfall. Additional smaller guts run into the agricultural plain. The Quill, a relatively young volcano reaching a maximum elevation of 1973 feet above sea level, forms 75 percent of the land surface (together with the agricultural plain) of Statia. The crater of the volcano has an elevation of 895 feet and a bottom 1200 feet in diameter. The crater supports a tropical rain forest. The flat glacis of the Quill, chiefly on its northwest side, is known as the *cultuur vlakte*, or agricultural plain. This plain, with an area of circa 1400 acres, varies in elevation from 100 feet to 250 feet; it abuts the volcanic hills and is bordered on the sea by steep cliffs some 60–150 feet high.

Culturally, the Statian landscape can be divided into three areas: the Lower Town, the Upper Town, and the "country." The Lower Town is a narrow strip of beach two miles long, bounded by the Caribbean Sea on the west and high cliffs to the east. The west, or leeward, side of Statia is the major anchorage area for ships, as the Atlantic or windward side is quite rough. The Upper Town, also known as Oranjestad, is the urban area of Statia. It was built above the Lower Town on a portion of the agricultural plain. It is divided from the Lower Town by high cliffs and is connected to it by several steep paths. The "country" is a modern Statian designation for all other areas of the island outside the Lower and Upper Towns.

Statia has a maritime savannah climate, characterized by drought and rainy

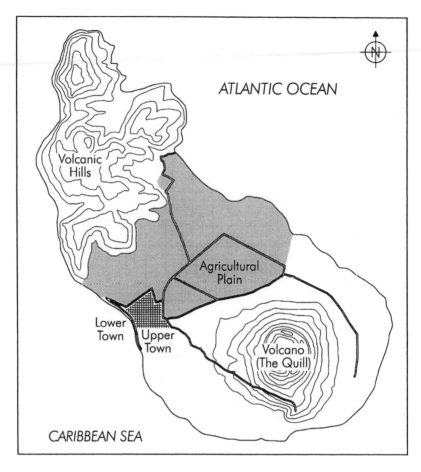

Fig. 5.1. Topographic zones of St. Eustatius.

periods. Precipitation is erratic, and crops are likely to fail every three to four years due to lack of moisture. Rainfall varies between 37 and 48 inches per year, most of which falls in the latter half of the year. The mean monthly rainfall in dry periods can be as low as 1.2 inches. Due to extensive deforestation, heavy rainfall is channeled through natural guts to the sea except where collection points have been built. Although some wells and localized underground freshwater lenses are present, the main source of potable water is rainfall collected in cisterns.

In general, soils are poor because of the dry climate, extensive erosion, and excellent runoff drainage. Soils in the volcanic hills are shallow except in some guts where loamy soil has accumulated; in most cases, land in this northern area of the island is steep, stony, and inaccessible. Similar poor conditions exist on the upper slopes of the Quill, which are quite steep. The remainder of the island has better moisture-retaining soil, which has built up over pumice to form a loose, dusty black surface soil. The agricultural plain has the best soil on Statia, although it may suffer severely from drought, causing frequent crop failures. Northeast to east trade winds cause excessive drying out of the volcanic soils.

According to Stoffers (1956), over the last three centuries of human occupation, unproductive bush replaced the original forest vegetation. European colonization caused clearing of the majority of the primary forest and erosion of the landscape. The present-day landscape is far different from the green, forest-clad islands seen by Columbus in 1493 (van der Valk 1992:18). In pre-Columbian times, much of Statia was probably covered by a deciduous seasonal/dry evergreen forest (van der Valk 1992:23). The primary natural vegetation has been preserved to some extent on the higher slopes and in the crater of the Quill, where it varies between montane thicket, elfin woodland, dry evergreen forest, evergreen bushland, and different kinds of seasonal forest. The most common type of vegetation on the island today is thorny woodland, including acacia shrubs mixed with cherry and mimosa as well as cactus plants, so that many areas of Statia are difficult to travel in. Along the coastal areas, there are low flattened trees and bushes, as well as sea grapes, plants with fleshy leaves, and manchineel woodlands.

Native fauna is not very extensive or varied. There are no mammals except those introduced by Europeans, namely cattle, sheep, goats, pigs, donkeys, horses, dogs and cats, rats, and mice. Lizards are common, iguanas are present, and a few snakes live in the Quill. Other animals include large edible land crabs, fish, other sea animals, and birds.

The Golden Rock site on St. Eustatius was inhabited in the seventh, eighth, and ninth centuries A.D. (Versteeg and Schinkel 1992:229). The native descendants of these or other peoples were long gone at the time of the first Spanish sightings of the island, perhaps as early as 1493. Although first settled by the French in 1629, Statia was permanently settled by the Dutch in 1636. The Dutch chose the island because it was uninhabited, protected from trade winds (on the leeward side), and favorably situated for trade with other nearby Dutch and non-Dutch islands (Hartog 1976a:20). Statia was settled at a time of Dutch commercial expansion.

From its beginning in 1636, the history of Statia alternated between prosperity and depression. Since that date the island changed hands at least twenty-two times, passing back and forth between the Dutch, French, and English, with the Dutch becoming the eventual permanent owners (Hartog 1976a:23). The three European powers had major economic and political interests in the north Caribbean area that prompted alternating forceful occupation of Statia and other islands. Many nationalities influenced Statia's history and development, but Statia spent most of the time under Dutch rule and control. Thus, Statia has a long history of settlement that reflects an often turbulent era.

Although agriculture was important to Statia for most of the island's history, the island achieved real prosperity in the eighteenth century as a free port and entrepôt. Enormous quantities and varieties of goods could be bought and sold on Statia, either legally or illegally. Trade with French and English islands was very profitable for an international group of merchants who resided on Statia (Barka 1996b). The North American trade became especially important for both sides during the American Revolution. American rebels purchased arms and ammunition from Statia, often from British merchants. As the nineteenth century approached, Statia's role as a trading depot lessened with shifts in world trade patterns and the rise of the United States as a major economic force. Statia entered a long period of decline, which in some respects still continues today.

Site Types

For purposes of this study, the numerous archaeological sites and standing buildings on Statia will be broadly classified into six functional categories: domestic buildings, both rural and urban; plantations and farms; public buildings; commercial buildings; religious buildings and cemeteries; and military forts/batteries. Each category exhibits different characteristics in terms of structural features, spatial arrangement of those features, artifact/ecofact content, and possible location on the landscape. In addition, all categories of sites probably show variation through time.

Domestic Buildings

This category can be defined as everyday living sites characterized by the presence of a dwelling, often accompanied by outbuildings, cisterns, and/or baking ovens. Domestic trash deposits, containing or consisting of pottery, glass, faunal remains, and so forth, are usually present at such sites, both above ground and below. Constructed of local volcanic stone or imported lumber or Dutch yellow or red brick, dwellings vary considerably by date and owner's social status.

The wood and masonry structures on Statia can be classified into two broad styles, traditional and modern. Modern wood houses have a simplified

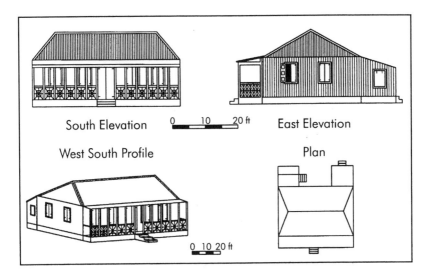

Fig. 5.2. Bungalow-style dwelling with verandah (after Sanders 1988a).

framing pattern covered with plywood or zinc sheets fastened with wire nails. Foundations may be of concrete blocks. Modern masonry dwellings are constructed of materials such as concrete blocks with a mortar of Portland cement; the ground floor and foundations may be poured concrete. Floor plans differ from those of traditional buildings.

Traditional wood houses have a wood frame with major joints hewn and pegged, a rectangular floor plan, the use of wooden sheathing and cladding, and foundations of stone, brick, and/or wood (figure 5.2). Of nearly 400 buildings studied in Oranjestad, 214 (56 percent) were of the traditional wood type; they were sometimes built on earlier foundations (Sanders 1988a, 1988b). Several nineteenth-century buildings of the traditional wood style exist today; these are usually single-story structures built on a masonry foundation. More buildings of this date may exist in the town, but the perpetuation of materials and construction techniques means that nineteenth-century houses are often indistinguishable from twentieth-century wood-framed houses (Sanders 1988a:44).

Traditional masonry houses have walls built of imported red or yellow brick or local volcanic or imported stone, using a local lime mortar. The traditional interior wall finish is a stucco layer (Plan D'2 1989). Traditional masonry buildings include structures considered to be representative of historically documented houses that were once present on the island, especially in the eighteenth century. Very few of these structures survive today. Numerous archaeological foundations/ruins, however, date to the eighteenth and/or nineteenth centuries, especially to the c. 1780–1820 period, a time of high population on Statia. No seventeenth-century dwellings can be positively identified either above ground or below.

All known historic traditional masonry dwellings are substantial, both in size and in construction. They share three characteristics. (1) All are solidly built of volcanic stone and/or Dutch brick. In addition, some use imported Bermuda limestone blocks for basement walls or other features. Captain William Peniston of Bermuda remarked in 1853: "Any one from Bermuda could not help being forcibly struck with the style of the old buildings in the upper town, most of them being built of the Lime and Soft Sandstone brought from Bermuda in the 17th century" (Peniston 1966:62). Peniston probably observed surviving eighteenth-century buildings, and the importation of Bermuda stone probably dates to the eighteenth century rather than the seventeenth. (2) The historic traditional masonry buildings are relatively large in size, have one or two stories, and in some cases have basements. (3) Specialized features may be associated with the buildings. The country house of Johannes de Graaff, commander of Statia from 1776 to 1781, for example, has a brick duck pond that measures 33.6 feet by 9.7 feet (Barka 1996a). This particular feature at Concordia has been identified both archaeologically and from documents (figure 5.3).

All known eighteenth- and nineteenth-century historic traditional masonry dwellings belonged to Statia's merchant or government elite. These include the Simon Doncker House, de Graaff's country estate, the Lampe House, the estate of Welgelegen, and several other structures. In a description published in the *St. Eustatius Gazette* on October 17, 1794, Johannes Heyliger offered for rent his "lot of land at White Hook, in the Town, called Mount Pleasant, with the buildings thereon, consisting of a sizeable dwelling house, containing a large hall, two chambers, and a cellar, an outhouse of two rooms, a spacious kitchen with an oven therein, a horse stable and other necessary buildings" (Triplett 1995:40).

Little is known about the dwellings of average people or the poor in the eighteenth or nineteenth centuries, but they undoubtedly fit somewhere within the traditional wood category as outlined above. Housing for enslaved Africans was associated with sugar plantations. Possible slave sites, in the form of low elevated areas, have been found in association with the English Quarter plantation (France 1984), and rude-looking slave structures, made of wood or brush, were sketched by Zimmerman the elder in 1792 (Zimmerman in Attema 1976:plate 12).

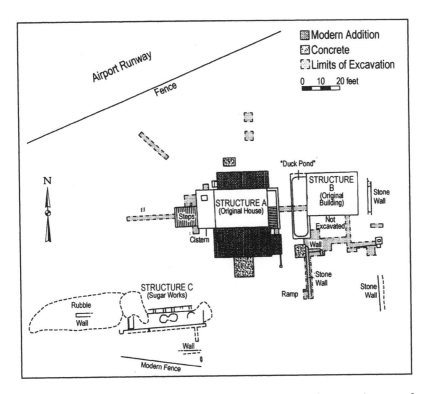

Fig. 5.3. Plan of structures at Concordia plantation, with duck pond to immediate east of main house (after Barka 1996a).

Cisterns are usually associated with dwellings, as rainwater runoff from roofs into cisterns provided the main source of water. In recently built homes, cisterns are constructed beneath the dwelling. In all earlier homes, cisterns were built as a separate structure adjacent to the dwelling; many times, older cisterns were reused. Cistern size was generally limited by structural design: too wide a roof would compromise the strength of a brick arch. Traditional cisterns were large stone and brick structures, consisting of a below-grade water storage chamber, with a brick barrel vault frequently exposed above the ground surface. The cave-in of the covering brick arch appears to be the most common cistern damage, especially in larger cisterns; cistern size could be increased lengthwise, however (Harper 1990:51–52).

Bake ovens, also constructed of brick and stone, can still be seen in use today by a minority of the population. Bake ovens were separate structures located in the yard downwind from the dwelling, usually on the west side (Monteiro 1990:105–106). Bread was made by building a fire in the main baking chamber in order to heat up the stones/brick; the ashes were removed and bread was baked by the heat absorbed within the stones/brick.

Plantations/Farms

Plantations were basically larger economic units, as opposed to smaller farms or plots of land, which managed various types of resources for profit, using enforced or paid labor. Sugar plantations on Statia usually have a number of masonry industrial or factory buildings and features, such as a boiling house, curing house, animal mill or windmill, storage rooms/buildings, and animal pens in a concentrated area (figure 5.4). A dwelling for the owner/overseer is generally located nearby, as is slave housing. An 1816 painting by Samuel Fahlberg of Retreat plantation on the neighboring island of St. Maarten, illustrates this situation. The painting depicts the substantial houses of two overseers or owners, a circular animal mill next to a smoking/boiling house, and neatly arranged groups of slave dwellings situated between the industrial buildings and fields of sugarcane.

Recent surveys of ruins on Statia indicate that the plantation site can be identified by the presence of various industrial and building features (table 5.1). Although about eighty-eight sugar plantations existed at any one time on Statia, most ruins of these complexes are not well preserved. About forty-five plantation sites have been located through survey; nine plantation sites have been mapped/studied, and all show variation in layout and architectural design, which may reflect differences in date of construction, nature of the crop being grown, wealth/social status of the owners, and/or other characteristics.

Public Buildings

Public or government buildings are present on Statia today, and such structures existed in the past: buildings to house the governor and council, a courthouse, a jail, etc. On Statia, these buildings were located within Fort Oranje and in a central location within the Upper Town.

Commercial Buildings

The commercial structures built for eighteenth-century trade were masonry and/or wooden warehouses. Although many merchants may have lived in a warehouse, the shape, size, and location of most warehouses distinguish them from ordinary domestic dwellings. Packed closely together along the shore of the Caribbean Sea on the western side of the island in the Lower Town, warehouses were mostly large and rectangular (figure 5.5). Measurements of

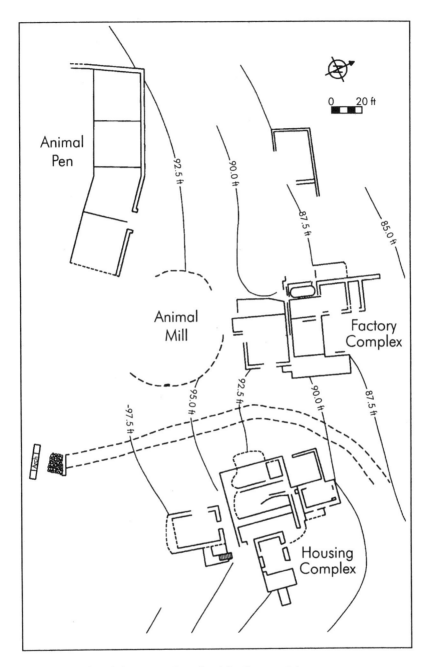

Animal Pen

Animal Mill

Factory Complex

Housing Complex

0   20 ft

92.5 ft

90.0 ft

87.5 ft

85.0 ft

97.5 ft

95.0 ft

92.5 ft

90.0 ft

87.5 ft

Fig. 5.4. Plan of English Quarter plantation (after France 1984).

Table 5.1. Sugar Plantation Features, St. Eustatius (from Barka 1996b; Delle 1989; France 1984). X denotes observed presence of the named feature.

Plantations	1	2	3	4	5	6	7	8	9
Windmill	X								
Animal Mill	X		X	X	X		X	?	X
Boiling House	X	X	X	X	X	X	X	X	X
Dwelling	X			X			X		X
Animal Pen	X			X			X		
Warehouse?	X								X
Curing House		X	X				X	X	
Outbuilding	X	X		X		X	X		X
Cistern			X	X	X	X	X		X
Well			X						X
Gateway				X			X		
Cemetery			X	X					

Key to plantations: 1 Fair Play; 2 Golden Rock; 3 Benners; 4 Schotsenhoek; 5 Roots; 6 Site P8810; 7 English Quarter; 8 Princess Estate; 9 Concordia.

warehouse ruins indicate certain common dimensions (in feet): 40 × 20; 40 × 15; 60 × 29; 44 × 24; 52 × 32.

Several warehouses have been archaeologically tested. Site SE1 is located under cliff erosion just to the north of the Bay Path (which leads to the Upper Town). At a depth of about seven feet below grade, a variety of well preserved late eighteenth-century warehouse walls and features were found, situated in good stratigraphic contexts. This site indicates that warehouses situated against the cliffs may be better preserved than those across Bay Road, on the ocean side. Site SE19, located in the central area of the Lower Town, was mainly a trash deposit situated in a narrow alley between two warehouses. The deposit contained a rich assemblage of late eighteenth-century ceramics, fancy glassware, faunal materials, and so forth. Site SE391, located on the beach side of Bay Road, was a warehouse ruin visible at grade. It measured 21 × 20 feet, with walls 1.6 feet thick. An excavation trench placed through it yielded a good stratigraphic context and a well-preserved floor made of yellow bricks set on edge.

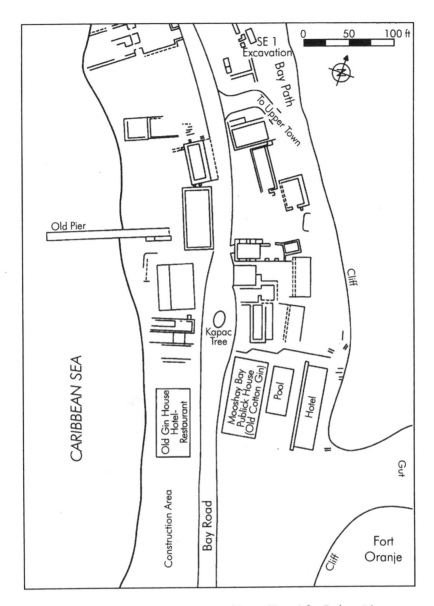

Fig. 5.5. Plan of visible warehouse ruins, central Lower Town (after Barka 1985).

Additional information about warehouses is available from contemporary drawings and eyewitness accounts. Two drawings show individual buildings close-up. A 1774 drawing details the central Lower Town, which is very congested, with large buildings often three or four deep. In addition, a central road (Bay Road) is visible, with warehouses that are generally situated at right angles to the road and beach, although some are parallel to the road. Roofs vary from hipped to vertical Dutch gables. At least one building with a fireplace may be a kitchen. Several possible jetties are depicted, as are Fort Oranje, the Dutch Reformed church, and the de Windt House in the Upper Town.

A later drawing of the central part of the Lower Town by Samuel Fahlberg in 1829 shows buildings that were constructed of wood, stone, and/or brick, probably with wooden shingles as roof covering. Many of the buildings have overhanging upper floors. One building with curved Dutch gables and dormers may have been the West India Company (WIC) warehouse (Kandle 1985:171). Another building shows a half-hipped roof, although the majority have hipped roofs. Two buildings with chimneys may have been kitchens.

Religious Buildings and Cemeteries

Religious buildings are usually distinguished from nonreligious structures by their size and architecture. Churches usually have cemeteries, although cemeteries sometimes occur alone (figure 5.6). Of the fourteen known cemeteries on Statia today, five are directly associated with church buildings (standing or in ruins); the cemetery of the Jewish congregation was located about one mile from the synagogue. Eight cemeteries were private, family, or government graveyards located in the Upper Town or in the country (Paonessa 1990). Various churches and one Jewish synagogue were present in Statia in the eighteenth century, and ruins of these structures are visible today. The nineteenth and twentieth centuries saw the development of other congregations and church structures.

Military Forts/Batteries

Forts and batteries are defensive military works constructed of masonry and/or earthen walls, with or without flanking ditches; artillery is usually present (figure 5.7). Larger forts have buildings located within them; smaller batteries may have a barracks separate from the artillery position. The largest military outpost on the island is Fort Oranje, situated since the seventeenth century on the cliffs of the Upper Town overlooking the main anchorage. Smaller military works ringed the island in the eighteenth century (Barka 1991c; Howard 1991).

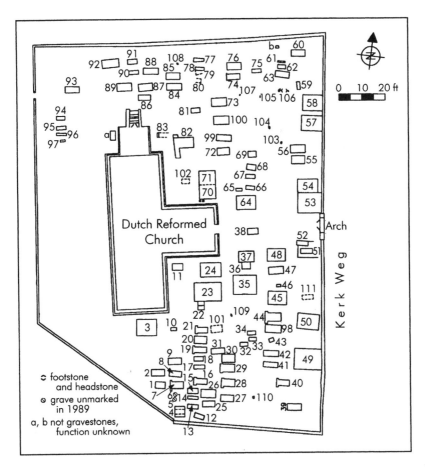

Fig. 5.6. Plan of Dutch Reformed Church cemetery (after Paonessa 1990).

Site Distribution

Five time lines, or horizons, have been chosen to document site distribution and shifts in settlement patterns: the seventeenth century, 1742, 1781, circa 1840, and 1996. The seventeenth century is a largely undocumented period. For the eighteenth and nineteenth centuries, some documentation does exist, as historical maps dated to 1742, 1781, and circa 1840 each depict the island in detail. These maps will serve as essential frameworks and guides for a study that uses archaeological, architectural, and historical evidence to discern settlement patterns. A few additional dated maps exist for Statia. Twentieth-century and

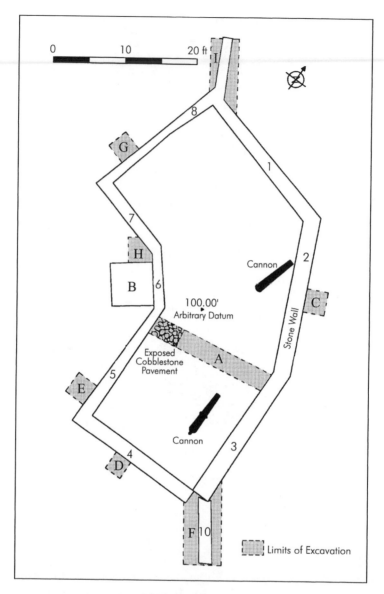

Fig. 5.7. Plan of excavations, Battery Concordia (after Barka 1991c).

modern Statia will be examined using a variety of ethnographic and historical sources as well as present-day observations. The particular time lines chosen are thought to be representative of major shifts in the history of Statian lifeways and settlement patterns.

In 1629, the French became the first Europeans to live on Statia, although their stay was temporary. In 1636, the Dutch West India Company authorized the establishment of a colony on the island for the purpose of growing crops for the European market. Pieter van Corselles led fifty colonists. They erected a fort on the ruins of an older French fort (Goslinga 1971:262). Tobacco was planted, followed by sugarcane (after mid-century) and cotton (Attema 1976:17). Within a short period, tobacco was being exported to Flushing (Goslinga 1971:263). By 1650, the colony was thriving. Tobacco plantations extended onto the slopes of the hills, and cotton production was very successful as well (Hartog 1976a:33). After tobacco and cotton, coffee was a high-ranking agricultural product, as was indigo.

At least one warehouse was built in about 1630, probably in the Lower Town (Attema 1976:18). In Statia and Saba, the earliest enslaved labor consisted of Indians, but after 1650, enslaved Africans replaced the Indians almost entirely (Goslinga 1971:336). Little is known about seventeenth-century life on Statia. Documentation is almost nonexistent, and maps are unknown. One exception is the account of De Rochefort, who wrote in 1666 that the inhabitants of Statia live in "neat houses, and those well furnish'd" (Kandle 1985:29). He also mentions one church, as well as "storehouses so well furnish'd with all things requisite to life." The church was probably the first Dutch Reformed Church, presumably destroyed by the French in 1689 (Hartog 1976a:142). Located east of the present Upper Town, the ruins are visible today with the island's oldest tombstone, dated 1686 (Paonessa 1990:25). The rural location of this church may indicate that it served as a central focal point for a scattered population.

No standing buildings dating to the seventeenth century remain today; some eighteenth-century buildings may contain elements of earlier buildings, but seventeenth-century features have not been identified. The numerous stone ruins on Statia are difficult to date, but the majority probably date to the eighteenth and/or nineteenth centuries. No seventeenth-century archaeological sites have been found, although scattered artifactual evidence turns up now and then. Such sites are difficult to recognize, given the paucity of datable seventeenth-century artifacts.

At least three forts are known to have been built in the seventeenth century on the Caribbean side of the island, in or to the north of the present Upper Town: Fort Oranje (1636); a fort on Gilboa overlooking Tumble Down Dick Bay, dating to circa 1686–1689; and possibly Fort Amsterdam in the Lower Town. In 1701, Fort Orange consisted of an entrance gate, four bastions with deteriorated guns, a run-down powder house, guards' quarters, a house used for church services, three water tanks, and the commander's house (Attema 1976:22). A dispersed settlement pattern of plantations or farms likely existed, mostly or solely in the agricultural plain, increasing in number toward the end of the seventeenth century as more land was cleared.

The Upper Town may have been started sometime in the late seventeenth century, but for most of that century, Statia's dispersed population and agrarian economy made a concentrated town area unnecessary, even though the population in 1662 had reached 1174 individuals (71 percent enslaved). De Rochefort reveals a population of about 1600 men in 1666 (Kandle 1985:26). If these figures are accurate, Statia had grown very rapidly in population in the three decades since initial settlement by the Dutch. In the main this growth undoubtedly reflected success in the tobacco and sugar markets. At least six sugar works were present on Statia in 1666 (Deerr [1950] as quoted in Delle 1989:178). In 1688, Statia had five sugar mills in operation (Goslinga 1985:128).

By the 1670s, large amounts of merchandise were available for sale at low prices (Kandle 1985:39). Trade with the English and French increased, and much of it was illegal. Many islands were able to sell tobacco to the Dutch at Statia, even though sugarcane had taken its place as the major crop (Kandle 1985:40). In 1689 during King William's War, Statia was captured by the French because Statia was a "valuable trading post, well stocked with slaves, sugar, and European merchandise to be sold to all comers" (Crouse [1943] as quoted in Kandle 1985:43). Statia throughout the seventeenth century was a major supplier of European goods as well as enslaved Africans; slaves were increasingly in demand in the islands as sugar became the dominant crop (Kandle 1985:44).

Time Line: 1742 Plantations

The 1742 Dutch map is the earliest surviving plan of the entire island of St. Eustatius. Basically, it presents a settlement pattern dominated by plantations, which are located not only in the agricultural plain but also in the volcanic hills and on the slopes of the Quill. Both the Upper and Lower Towns are inhabited but not to the extent shown on the 1781 map. Only a few military sites are present (figure 5.8).

DOMESTIC BUILDINGS

All information about domestic sites relates to the Upper Town, which on the 1742 map appears as one line of buildings on the eastern side of the main road. The most densely constructed area appears to have been across the road from

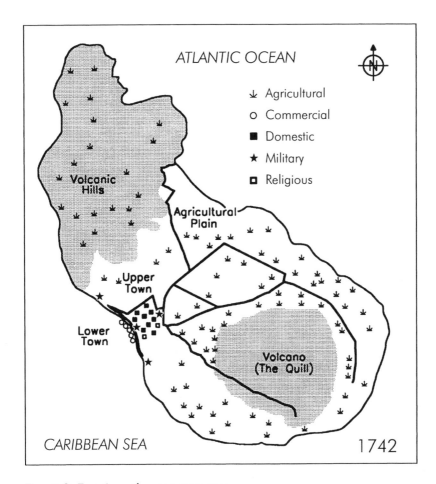

Fig. 5.8. St. Eustatius settlement pattern, 1742.

Fort Oranje and toward the south. One of the earliest references to the Upper Town is a request in 1715 by the island governor to authorities in Holland for permission to expand the town's limits onto West India Company land, as space within the town had become too cramped (Attema 1976:33, 34). By 1722, the population of the island was 1204, only a slight increase since 1662. The population grew steadily, however, so that in 1741 a total of 1778 people (539 whites, 1239 enslaved Africans) lived on Statia. Housing was scarce, it seems, and rental of a house was very expensive (Attema 1976:35).

By the early 1740s, the street grid was well developed; the 1742 map shows a network of roadways (Triplett 1995:31). Three parallel roads begin in the Upper Town and radiate out into the country. Roads continue around the

Quill. One road runs parallel to the west coastline of the island at the level of the Upper Town. At least two roads proceed into the rugged volcanic hills to the north. The depicted road network connected all parts of the island to the Upper Town.

Both masonry and wooden buildings were probably constructed in the town. The house of Simon Doncker, a successful merchant, is identified on the 1742 map. The house, which still stands, is constructed of Dutch yellow bricks; it has two stories, with hipped roof and basement. Archaeological excavations revealed another eighteenth-century foundation on the south side of the present structure (Barka 1985).

PLANTATIONS/FARMS

In 1715, eleven sugar estates were in operation, and another twelve would soon follow (Goslinga 1985:131). In 1731, a planter boasted that he exported 700 hogsheads of sugar annually. By the 1740s all arable land was under cultivation, and it was no longer possible to expand agriculture (Goslinga 1985:138).

The 1742 map lists seventy-six plantation owners and shows the location of eighty-eight plantations and/or landholdings. Each plantation is identified by one to four houses, sometimes in association with a smaller outbuilding; landholdings are identified only by number, with no houses indicated. Eleven plantations are located in the rugged volcanic hills. The majority are situated in the agricultural plain, and a surprising number on the lower slopes of the Quill. Sugar and other commodities were grown on the plantations, as indicated by the cargo of the ship *Johanna en Agatha,* which left Oranjestad for Amsterdam on July 14, 1750, with 494 hogsheads of sugar, 23 bales of cotton, 59 barrels of indigo, 2 barrels of ginger, 3122 hides, 1 parcel of pock wood (weighing 178,245 pounds), and 614 rolls of tobacco (Goslinga 1985:208). There is some uncertainty as to how much sugarcane was actually grown on Statia, however, as foreign muscovado imported from other islands was refined on Statia. There is also notice in some records of neglected sugar plantations and insufficient supplies of labor (Goslinga 1985:28, 29).

Nothing is known about housing for enslaved Africans, which must have existed at all plantations. Enslaved Africans brought into Statia to be sold stayed in temporary quarters in the Lower Town. In 1726, and on into the eighteenth century, enslaved Africans were held in a house built in the Waterfort, situated inside old and defunct Fort Amsterdam. This two-story structure was built to accommodate 4–500 slaves and measured 54 feet × 21 feet (Attema 1976:29,30).

PUBLIC BUILDINGS

There is no specific information about public buildings as a category of sites. Structures like the Government Guest House, however, were probably in use by this time.

COMMERCIAL BUILDINGS

The eighteenth century brought increasing prosperity for Statia, and the island became known as "the golden rock." Economic growth was based upon trade with French and British islands and the British North American colonies. Many different commodities were traded, one of which continued to be sugar, for which demand soared in the 1740s (Mintz 1985:67–68). The Lower Town began to become a trade locus during the first half of the eighteenth century. In 1739, the island commander noted that foreigners were setting up shops and trade in Statia (Attema 1976:38). The 1742 map shows at least nineteen buildings in "Het Dorp beneden" (the Lower Town). The buildings are probably symbolic, and the exact placement and number of buildings is unknown. No road is shown in the Lower Town; the buildings depicted extend farther to the south and north than the buildings of the Upper Town. The Bay Path connecting the Upper and Lower Towns is clearly depicted, although it is not labeled (Kandle 1985:159–160). By 1743, a *waag*, or weighing house, stood on the bay, as did some dilapidated warehouses (Goslinga 1985:35).

RELIGIOUS BUILDINGS AND CEMETERIES

Several religious structures are known to have been standing in 1742. A Jewish synagogue had been built in the Upper Town in 1739 (Barka 1988; Hartog 1976b). A Jewish cemetery was first mentioned in 1730 (Hartog 1976b:17); the earliest gravestone in it dates to 1742. In 1752, or earlier, an Anglican church formed in the Upper Town (Hartog 1976a:70, 116; Kandle 1985:84). In 1755, the second Dutch Reformed Church was built overlooking the Lower Town; the earliest tombstone in it dates to 1762 (Paonessa 1990:29).

Many plantations probably had associated cemeteries, as the following examples indicate. The Benners Family Graveyard was located northwest of town on Benners plantation. Tombstones date between circa 1728 and 1802, with five or six of the nine marked stones dating to the 1730s (Delle 1989:96; Paonessa 1990:41–42). The Groebe family graveyard is located at Schotsenhoek plantation, also northwest of the Upper Town; three gravestones date to 1750, 1770, and 1795, respectively (Delle 1989:111, Paonessa 1990:46–47). At English

Quarter, ten marked graves have stones dating from 1735 to 1759 (Paonessa 1990:47–48).

MILITARY FORTS/BATTERIES

Several military sites are shown on the 1742 map. A battery at Tumble Down Dick Bay and a "Nieuwe fort" both appear to the north of the Lower Town. Another battery, Dolien, is shown to the south of Lower Town. Several earlier military sites continue in use: Fort Oranje in the Upper Town and Fort Amsterdam, which by now has been converted to the Waterfort, a slave containment area.

Time Line: 1781 Trade

The 1781 map was made during the French occupation of Statia. When it is compared with the 1742 map, one is struck by the decrease in the number of plantations, the increase in the number of military sites, and the growth of both the Lower Town and the Upper Town (figure 5.9). In this period, Statia reached its peak in terms of trade and population. As a consequence, the majority of archaeological sites and assemblages date to the late eighteenth century. Evidence for this conclusion comes from creamwares and pearlwares, which dominate the ceramic material culture of Statia; china glaze, or pearlware with blue painted Chinese motifs, is especially common.

DOMESTIC BUILDINGS

Compared with the 1742 map, the 1781 map shows the Upper Town as a larger and clearly defined unit of settlement. Between 1742 and 1781 the Upper Town increased greatly in size and number of inhabitants. Four streets run northeast-southwest, and an equal number of streets lie at right angles to them; the town has not yet achieved the three-grid layout plan characteristic of the mid-nineteenth century. A total of circa seventy-five buildings are depicted along these streets, located northeast and southeast of Fort Orange; the buildings shown are symbolic of actual frequency. At least 400 buildings were already present in 1772, as a hurricane reportedly destroyed or damaged this many houses in the Upper Town (Triplett 1995:34–35).

A variety of buildings must have existed in 1781, ranging from a minority of substantial masonry buildings to more numerous wooden structures. A document from 1783 mentions that a majority of the houses in the Upper Town were wooden and stood very close together in some streets (Attema 1976:35). In 1792, Zimmerman wrote that most houses in the Upper Town

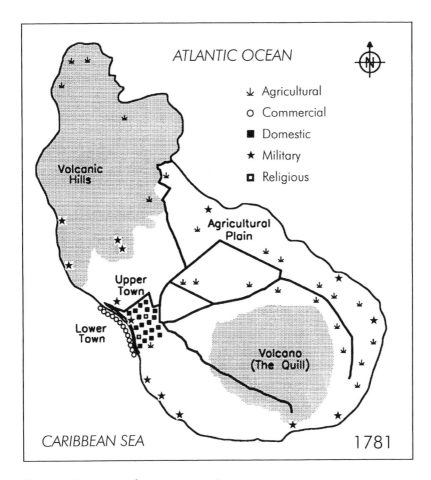

Fig. 5.9. St. Eustatius settlement pattern, 1781.

were "of a single story with a roof of eight or nine feet" and had a veranda on the ground floor (Kandle 1985:183). He also has a drawing of a two-storied wooden house built on a stone foundation, with a central gallery and a hipped roof.

PLANTATIONS/FARMS

The 1781 map divides the agricultural plain and slopes of the Quill into contiguous fields or plots of different dimensions and shapes. Each field is delimited on the map by roughly dotted lines and sometimes roads. Of some sixty fields represented on the map, about nineteen are filled with dots, lines, or brushlike symbols; about forty-one fields have no such filling. The open fields lacking dots may represent fields in use. In addition, about thirty-one small black rectangles probably represent buildings. Twenty such buildings are shown within small dotted boxes within some fields, and eleven structures are depicted in the open (not within a dotted box). Many fields have no buildings. Only a few fields and buildings are located in the volcanic hills. The number of plantations had apparently diminished from eighty-eight in 1742 to about twenty in 1781; a census of 1790 states that there were twenty individually owned plantations (Attema 1976:46). A 1775 map shows about seventy-six plantations on Statia, but it is an exact copy of the 1742 map, and therefore its accuracy is held in question. Zimmerman's letter of 1792 says that there are many sugar plantations on Statia; an exact number is not indicated.

Public Buildings

Several large buildings situated in the center of the Upper Town, immediately east of Fort Oranje, date to the eighteenth century. They were probably in use by 1742 and definitely in use in 1781. One standing structure is the Government Guest House, named and used as such in the twentieth century. It presently functions as a government office building. Although its eighteenth-century function is unknown, this building and two adjacent structures, now merely foundations, were probably government or public buildings (Barka 1986, 1989, 1990), given their characteristics and central location (figure 5.10). Commander Jan de Windt's mention in 1772 of the "Secretariat" and the adjacent "Secretary's House" may refer to two of these buildings (Attema 1976:34).

All three structures share attributes of form and size that lend credence to nondomestic functional interpretations. The Guest House is much larger in size than domestic buildings. The eighteenth-century portion of this rectangular building has exterior dimensions of up to 75 feet in length by 21 feet in width (Barka 1990). Constructed of yellow brick, it has two stories with a full basement; an indoor oven is present in the basement, as are Dutch-type air vents. The two adjacent foundations, although smaller in size (interior dimensions of 21.2 feet × 13.75 feet and 29.2 feet × 12.6 feet), share a number of features with the Guest House: they were solidly built of brick and had two stories, with basements and air vents. One structure had a large, complete domed oven at one end of the basement; the other lacked an oven but had a complete below-grade storage room with a vaulted ceiling that was connected at one time with the structure's basement. This area of Oranjestad had many more large buildings in the eighteenth century than it does at present.

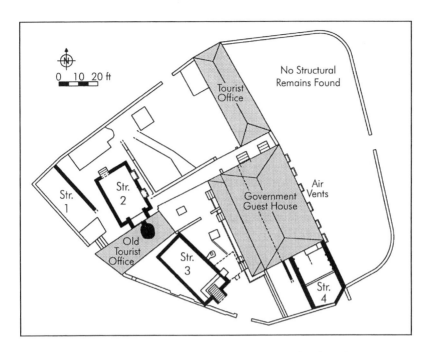

Fig. 5.10. Plan of Government Guest House complex with archaeological structures 1–4 (after Barka 1990).

Commercial Buildings

It was in the 1781 period that the Lower Town reached its ascendancy and maximum size, a pattern confirmed by both documentary and archaeological evidence. The 1781 map shows a seemingly symbolic representation of fifty structures in the Lower Town, stretching nearly the entire length of the habitable area along the beach. In places, warehouses stand in three parallel rows, and one roadway goes between the main rows of buildings.

There is additional evidence regarding the placement and characteristics of warehouses. A 1774 drawing depicts the central Lower Town as a congested area with buildings three to four deep at right angles or parallel to a central road and the beach. Janet Schaw, a traveler from Scotland, visited the Lower Town in 1775. She gives a colorful description, mentioning that the town consists of one narrow street a mile long, where a wide variety of goods were sold, including rich embroideries, painted silks, flowered muslins, shoes, hats, shovels, gloves and stockings, Portuguese wines, and other items (Schaw 1971:135–138). A 1780 drawing, made by an artist on a ship, shows numerous warehouses on the beach as well as several paths leading from the Lower Town to the Upper Town. In addition, Cornelis de Jong, a Dutch naval officer, in 1780 reported a shortage of storage space in the Lower Town for commodities brought from Europe (Goslinga 1985:146). He also observed that there were a large number of warehouses along the seafront. Some of them served as living quarters; others had two stories and were joined to houses across the street by a bridge (Attema 1976:38). In 1786, the Lower Town had 280–300 warehouses (Goslinga 1985:153). By 1790, there were perhaps as many as 600 warehouses (Zimmerman [1792] in Kandle 1985:184).

The majority of the warehouse ruins, if not all, in the Lower Town today date to the late eighteenth century. Visible stone ruins number at least 121, and ruins completely buried probably number in the hundreds. In addition, modern construction has destroyed many ruins. Archaeological research has resulted in the testing of 5 ruins and the mapping/photographic survey of all exposed warehouse ruins. Warehouse buildings were built close together, as if space was at a premium. This crowding of buildings can be observed not only in visible ruins but also in the archaeological excavations.

Religious Buildings and Cemeteries

A description of the 1780 hurricane mentions that a cathedral and four churches were left standing (Triplett 1995:36). By 1781, a large and diverse community had developed on Statia. Religion played an important role in this development, as witnessed by the increased presence of churches of different denominations, mainly in the Upper Town. An enslaved Statian named Black Harry is credited with having introduced Methodism to the island in the eighteenth century (Hartog 1976a:115; Kandle 1985:87). A Methodist church was not built until the nineteenth century, however. An Anglican church was established in 1752 in the Upper Town to the west of the present-day Methodist church and its graveyard. Only ruins remain today (Hartog 1976a:126). The earliest dated gravestone in an associated graveyard is 1755. A second Dutch Reformed Church was built in 1755 south of Fort Oranje on Kerkweg (Church Road). Measuring eighty-nine feet in length, the church had a tower sixty-three feet high at the north end (Attema 1976:65; Hartog 1976a:62–63). Lutherans held services in a large rented house circa 1780 and later built a church (Hartog 1976a:93, 126). A Roman Catholic Church for "foreigners" was located in the Lower Town. It appears on an Italian print dated around 1772 and is marked "private" (Hartog 1976a:70). Schotsenhoek Cemetery is a plantation graveyard that dates from this period with eleven graves, five marked 1750, 1770, 1795, 1965 (Delle 1989:110–111).

MILITARY FORTS/BATTERIES

Military sites ring the island on the 1781 map and reflect the increased militarism brought about by the French/British conflict associated with the American Revolutionary War. The ruins of these sites are, for the most part, visible today (Barka 1991c; Howard 1991). Some of these sites may originally have been constructed by Commanders Johannes Heyliger (1743–1752) and/or Jan de Windt (1753–1775): Fort Hollandia (1748) on the Caribbean side of the island; Fort de Windt on the south end of the island; and batteries on the east and northern coasts, such as Correcorrie, Lucie, Turtle Bay, and Concordia (Hartog 1976a:26). Apparently, all entrenchments and forts built by the Dutch were in severe disrepair in 1781 (Attema 1976:40–41). By November of 1781, however, the French had occupied Statia, and they restored the neglected forts and fieldworks. By the end of 1782, Johannes De Graaff mentions that the island had been brought "in a formidable state of defence" (Hartog 1976a:97). Forts Panga and Bouille, the latter named after the French commander, were built. Soon a ring of forts and fortifications connected by roads surrounded the whole island. The 1781 map locates and names fourteen military sites, including Fort Oranje, Fort Panga, and twelve batteries.

Time Line: 1840 Decline

A spurt of trade activity sent the population soaring to an all-time high of nearly 8,000 people in 1790. By 1818, however, the population had dropped to under 2,668 people, reflecting a sharp economic downfall after 1795–1800 (Hartog 1976a:102). From 1781 to 1816, the island was under the control of the English or French. It returned to the Dutch in 1816. In the early nineteenth century, the inability of merchants to recover earlier trade networks, especially with the United States, marked Statia's collapse as an international port (Kandle 1985:71). The nineteenth century saw severe economic decline and population loss, which is reflected in the 1840 settlement pattern (figure 5.11).

The map made by A. H. Bisschop Grevelink, government secretary from 1839 to 1846, shows the island anchorage, roads and paths, a few batteries, two cemeteries in the Upper Town, government land inside and outside town, a marketplace in the town square, and other features.

DOMESTIC BUILDINGS

An earlier map of the island, dated circa 1820, made by a naval lieutenant named W. Blanken, shows the Upper Town as two grids of streets. The map for the circa 1840 time line shows the same grids and adds a third to the north.

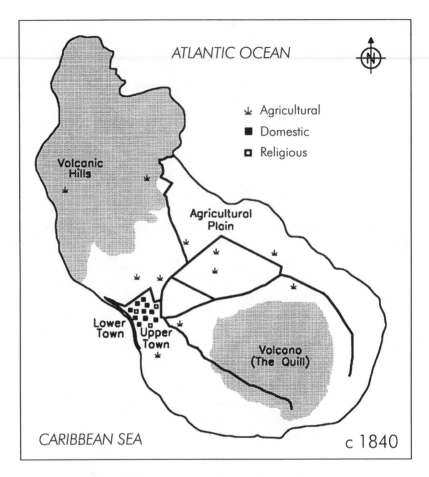

Fig. 5.11. St. Eustatius settlement pattern, c. 1840.

The three-grid pattern essentially matches the modern configuration of the older part of the Upper Town and suggests that expansion to the north took place between the 1820s and the 1840s. The Upper Town is larger by one-third in circa 1840.

Little is known about the houses of the period in the Upper Town from documents or from present-day research. Only a few traditional wooden or masonry buildings survive that can be dated to the nineteenth century. One is a physician's house on Prinsesweg, which in the twentieth century housed the first museum of the Historical Foundation. In 1816, a visitor named van Lennep Coster wrote that the Upper Town had two or three straight streets and that most houses were wooden and were well looked after (Attema 1976:47). In 1853

Captain William Peniston from Bermuda visited the governor, who "was living in his fine Mansion with its beautiful Marble Halls" (Penniston 1966:62–63). He was probably referring to Johannes de Veer, who was lieutenant governor from 1837 to 1854. De Veer lived on the east side of the Upper Town in a large brick house known as Welgelegen, the ruins of which are called "the Mansion" (Hartog 1976a:18).

PLANTATIONS/FARMS

In 1829, only fourteen plantations remained on Statia; after 1835 "people began to demolish the plantations and sugar mills constructed during the golden period, in order to sell the red and blue bricks" (van den Bor 1981:55). A map dating to 1830 depicts about thirty-eight plantations (Hartog 1976a:124), but it may be inaccurate. Only ten plantations appear on the map made in about 1840. They are located in the volcanic hills (two plantations) and in the agricultural plain (eight plantations). Each one has two to nine buildings together with a representation of an animal mill (a circle with a dot in the center). Only Fair Play plantation has a windmill as well. In addition, eight locations were apparently used as cattle or livestock farms. An 1847 copy of the circa 1840 map shows the same number of plantations but adds certain information, namely that the plantations produced sugar, molasses, rum, and bay rum and that cattle farms and government land produced yams, cattle, cows, horses, mules, and sheep.

In 1853, Captain William Peniston mentioned that "just under the eastern side of Tumble-Down-Dick [bay] towards the west lies Sentching Hook, a large sugar estate owned by the Martiney family with its ancient walls, its large sugar mills worked by Mules. To the southwest are extensive yam and Sweet-potato fields their only substitute for bread. There are also a few Cochineal fields" (Peniston 1966:60). Peanuts were also being exported in 1855 (Hartog 1976a:128).

PUBLIC BUILDINGS

Captain Peniston mentions a prison and the government house, "a fine building with marble floors," both in the Upper Town (Peniston 1966:60). The government house may be the Government Guest House building. Another type of venture that may have been government-sponsored was the establishment of a leper colony in an isolated area north of the Lower Town, along the beach near Billys Gut. This small colony was established in the 1860s and operated into the 1920s. Several buildings and a small cemetery remain today.

Because of a severe decline in trade, the Lower Town essentially went out of business after the first decades of the nineteenth century. Both natural and human events hastened its demise. A hurricane in 1819 began the destruction of the warehouses. In order to provide some income, warehouse bricks were salvaged to sell off the island; 80,000 bricks were sold in 1855 (Hartog 1976a:126). Other moneymaking efforts were also attempted, such as the manufacture of trass. Trass, a volcanic earth, makes a good mortar when mixed with water and was used extensively on eighteenth-century Statia. In 1816 trass was exported to St. Barths and later to Curaçao. In 1845, 10,000 barrels were shipped to Puerto Rico (Hartog 1976a:131).

RELIGIOUS STRUCTURES/CEMETERIES

The 1847 map shows the location of the Dutch Reformed church, the Methodist church, and the Roman Catholic church, all in the Upper Town. The latter church dates to 1843; a Catholic priest was stationed in Statia in 1841 (Hartog 1976a:117). The Methodist church was built of wood in 1825 and later (1843) of stone. A plantation graveyard at Concordia, located outside the Upper Town southeast of the airport, has one stone dating to the year 1845.

MILITARY FORTS/BATTERIES

After St. Eustatius finally returned to the Dutch in 1816, military defenses became unimportant. The circa 1840 map shows the military forts and batteries depicted on the 1781 French map but notes that they are in ruins. Only Fort Oranje continued to function as a governmental entity.

Time Line: 1996 Suburbia

The patterns of nineteenth-century settlement continued well into the twentieth century (figure 5.12). Except for the Upper Town, Statia must have looked fairly uninhabited in the early twentieth century. Economic difficulties continued, as did population decline. Beginning in 1925, many Statians emigrated to Aruba and Curaçao in order to work in the oil refineries or in other jobs, since there was hardly any work on Statia. By 1948, only 921 people lived on Statia. Those people remaining tried to develop income-producing work with a variety of products, such as sisal growing, a revival of cotton growing, trass or mortar production, cattle and hog production, and the cultivation of yams and other crops (Hartog 1976a:128–134). In the 1950s, people began to return to Statia, so that the population gradually increased to 1421 in 1974 and

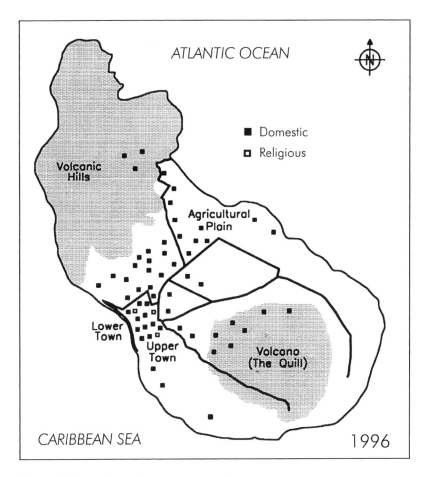

Fig. 5.12. St. Eustatius settlement pattern, 1996.

around 2000 today. With the gradual development of better transportation and roads, together with electricity (introduced in 1966), suburbanization began, resulting in a redistribution of people and settlement.

DOMESTIC BUILDINGS

A recent architectural survey of the Upper Town revealed a total of 397 buildings, the majority of which were of the traditional wooden type. A surprising number of modern buildings, most of which had been built in the period 1920–1960, were also present (Sanders 1988b:5). Today many buildings in the Upper Town are empty, and many parcels of land in the town are vacant. In the past few decades, most Statians have moved out of the Upper

Town into nearby housing developments, that is, suburbs of the Upper Town. Jeems, Concordia, Golden Rock, and the recent Princess developments are examples of modern suburbs, with fairly dense housing built upon good farming lands on the agricultural plain. An influx of American and Dutch retirees has accelerated real estate development on the north and west lower slopes of the Quill, and hundreds of modern houses are now present outside the main urban center. Building codes now exist requiring that cisterns of a certain size be constructed beneath all modern buildings.

Although vacant lots are plentiful in the Upper Town today, they may not have been so in the nineteenth century (and possibly in the earlier twentieth century), when more people lived in the town. Archaeological survey and excavation on a few lots have always yielded artifacts and sometimes buried walls. Modern Upper Town inhabitants also use old cisterns and bake ovens when available.

Plantations/Farms

In modern Statia, agriculture/cattle production is a small-scale venture because of the dry climate and the hard work involved. The majority of foodstuffs are imported. In the earlier twentieth century, various attempts were made by the government to encourage agricultural production and stockbreeding. Except for some successes in sweet potato and yam production, however, farming and stockbreeding never caught on in this century (Hartog 1976a:132). Some potential moneymaking crops were grown for a limited amount of time. The growing of cotton was revived in 1903, when a ginnery was located in the Lower Town. The peak year of production was 1919, when 250 people were employed. Sisal for rope manufacture began in 1905. In 1921, its peak year of production, 494 acres were planted, but production ceased in 1928 (Hartog 1976a:130). About fifty acres of sugarcane for making rum were still grown in the first quarter of this century at Fair Play plantation. After 1925, however, when migration to Aruba and Curaçao began, this also came to a stop (Hartog 1976a:125). In the twentieth century, therefore, there were very few farms and plantations.

Public Buildings

For most of the twentieth century, government officials had offices primarily in buildings located in Fort Oranje. With the recent renovation of the Government Guest House, most official offices have moved into this structure and a few adjoining buildings, although some occupy other buildings in the

Upper Town. Other public buildings in the Upper Town include schools, day care facilities, a library, a museum, and a hospital.

COMMERCIAL BUILDINGS

As in most of the nineteenth century, nearly all of the warehouses in the Lower Town are ruins and are therefore not used. Much of the Lower Town is uninhabited except for the presence of various businesses, which include several restaurants, two hotels, a dive shop, a power station, and the island's only gas station. The main shipping pier is also located in the Lower Town. Some commercial establishments occupy former warehouse buildings; others occupy space created by the bulldozing/leveling of old warehouse structures. In addition, there are now many commercial establishments in the Upper Town, namely banks, shops, restaurants, bars, and a few hotels.

RELIGIOUS BUILDINGS AND CEMETERIES

There are three religious congregations in the Upper Town today, the Roman Catholic, the Methodist, and the more recent (1921) Seventh-Day Adventist. The current Roman Catholic church was built in 1910 with stones taken from the ruins of the Lower Town (Hartog 1976a:116). The present stone church of the Methodists dates to 1825.

Several cemeteries were started in the twentieth century. The Berkel Family Cemetery in the Upper Town has been in use since circa 1929, based on the earliest dated stone. It contains 11 marked graves (Paonessa 1990:42–43). The Kongo Cemetery, also known as Duinkerk Cemetery, is located immediately outside the Upper Town on Mansion Road. The exact date of its establishment is unknown, and no gravestones with legible names are present. The latest burial reported in the cemetery was in 1968. The cemetery was presumably reserved for Kongo people, persons whose ancestors had come from the Congo region of West Africa (Paonessa 1990:44). Salem, or Government, Cemetery, northwest of the Catholic cemetery, is the largest cemetery on Statia, with 168 marked graves. The oldest dated gravestone is 1912 (Paonessa 1990:38).

MILITARY FORTS/BATTERIES

Fort Oranje has the only fort buildings in use today, for nonmilitary purposes. Some of the eighteenth-century batteries, such as Fort de Windt and Concordia, have been restored by the government and have become tourist attractions.

Summary and Discussion

SEVENTEENTH CENTURY

Although information on the seventeenth century is scarce, agrarianism was clearly dominant. Farms and plantations were scattered in the agricultural plain, with both owners and slaves or workers living at their place of work. There was little settlement in what was to become the Upper Town except perhaps toward the end of the seventeenth century, when a few military sites were clustered near Fort Oranje. At least one church site from this period is known to have been located near the center of the island. Commercial activities were beginning, and several warehouses may have been built in the area later known as the Lower Town.

The initial settlement of Statia and its continuous development must have been difficult, given the island's extensive tree/brush cover, relative dryness, and lack of water. During its first thirty years the colony appears to have been exclusively engaged in a rural, agricultural existence. This was a conservative, closed community focused on farming, family, and relationship with the WIC (Kandle 1985:102). Demanding circumstances were gradually overcome, as is apparent from the success of tobacco and other exports to Holland. Sugarcane gradually became the main crop, as European consumption of sugar increased fourfold between 1660 and 1700 (Mintz 1985:67–68). Rural plantations developed with an increasing supply of enslaved labor. Statia was mainly a plantation island, but its importance as a storage place and transit harbor for enslaved Africans increased gradually (Attema 1976:21).

1742

The evidence for the 1742 pattern comes almost entirely from documents. Although many ruins on Statia may belong to this period, they have not yet been positively dated or identified. No archaeological assemblages have been excavated that predate 1750. The dominant settlement scenario had emerged by 1742. Plantation settlements were dominant. Every available plot of land was used to grow sugar and other crops. What stands out is the large number of plantations in every possible part of the island, from the volcanic hills to the higher slopes of the Quill. Many of these areas were difficult to reach, and many had much poorer soils than the agricultural plain. The Upper Town had been formed and continued to grow in size. The Lower Town had many warehouses, reflecting increasing trade connections and interests. Several churches and one synagogue were located in the Upper Town. Military sites were clustered on the western side of the island, overlooking the main ship anchorage.

The initial growing of sugarcane in the seventeenth century gradually led to the maximization in the number of sugar plantations in the period around 1742, when all marginal lands of the countryside were planted in sugarcane or other crops. In the 1700–1740 period, the market for sugar was excellent; consumption tripled over previous levels (Mintz 1985:67–68). Enormous profits were reaped, and many of the island's developing elite invested in land and sugar plantations. At the same time, inter-island trade had become an important source of profit as well. At some point in the early eighteenth century, the growing presence of merchants changed Statia's main role in the Caribbean community from agrarian to commercial. Traders differed from farmers in their geographical orientation and outlook (Kandle 1985:103–104).

1781

By 1781, Statia was in its golden age, an economic state achieved through extensive inter-island trade networks. Commercial warehouses filled all available space in the Lower Town. In contrast, plantations had drastically declined in number. Trade relationships had soared, as indicated by the many warehouses in the Lower Town, increased numbers of merchants, and a high population. More people lived in an enlarged Upper Town, which had many wooden and masonry dwellings. Military batteries and forts ringed the island.

Statian commerce increased dramatically in the period circa 1750–1790, when the island assumed an economic importance beyond the production of sugar and other commodities. It developed into the Caribbean's largest entrepôt and free port. Vast quantities and varieties of goods were sold to all comers, including the French, the English, and the Americans. Statia saw voluminous international trade. After 1760 as many as 2700 ships sailed into the island's harbor yearly, reaching a peak of 3551 ships in 1779 (Hartog 1976a:40). Merchants from many different countries set up shop in Statia to profit from a lucrative trade that was often illegal (Barka 1996a). Goods of all kinds were available for purchase, including weapons, gunpowder, pottery, hardware, shoes, canvas, linen, soap, and horses, to name but a very few. Many food-related items were exported from Statia in 1779 as well (table 5.2). These goods were probably grown on other islands for sale and export on Statia.

1840

In the period from 1840 to the twentieth century, a general economic and population decline set in. There was no need for military sites, and there was a lack of commerce in the Lower Town. There were no functioning warehouses.

Table 5.2. Food and Other Exports from St. Eustatius in 1779 (Hartog 1976a:39-40).

Commodity	Exports in Pounds	Exports in Gallons
Sugar	24,000,000	
Coffee	9,000,000	
Tobacco	13,000,000	
Cocoa	457,000	
Cotton	187,000	
Indigo	416,000	
Hides	756,000	
Rum		622,000
Syrup		14,500

Plantations and farms were scattered and fewer in number, and the Upper Town expanded as the population left the rural countryside.

Changing patterns of world trade, especially with the rise of the developing United States, meant that the entrepôt on Statia was no longer relevant in the nineteenth century. Merchants left the island, and the Lower Town became inactive. At the same time, sugar prices collapsed in 1840–1870, making it impossible to sustain sugar production at a profitable level on marginal lands (Delle 1994:53; Mintz 1985:144). Although some sugar plantations were operating past the mid-nineteenth century, there were relatively few such industrial concerns on Statia. Another factor that led to the demise of this industry and others on Statia was the abolition of slavery in 1863 and the resulting social change on the island. Plantations were abandoned and the owners reduced to poverty. Enslaved Africans became free laborers, but there were no employers. Gradually government became the only employer (Hartog 1976a:128). Formerly enslaved Africans abandoned the countryside and moved into the Upper Town, resulting in more urban housing and a severe decline in the number of people living in the agricultural plain.

People continued to leave the island. In 1875, whalers on their way to Cape Hatteras began to call on Statia in order to take in supplies. Young Statians enlisted to work on such ships. In 1917, 57 young men left the island, and 20 others did so in 1918 (Hartog 1976a:128). By 1884, only 1600 people (only 50 of whom were white) lived on the island, only one-fifth of the number residing there in 1790 (Hartog 1976a:127).

There are virtually no farms and very little agriculture. The Upper Town has lost population and buildings, and suburban living has greatly increased. Domestic dwellings outnumber other types of buildings on Statia today. They are found in the Upper Town but are primarily located in new suburbs in the country on both the agricultural plain and the lower slopes of the Quill. A few houses and one restaurant are situated in the volcanic hills. The Lower Town is a collection of ruined warehouses, with a few modern businesses such as hotels/restaurants geared to tourists, a gasoline station, an electricity-generating plant, and a pier. Numerous oil tanks, part of a commercial oil-mixing facility, occupy the volcanic hills, and a large oil pier extends outward on the northwest side of the island. The east and south sides of the island remain relatively uninhabited because these areas lack electrical lines.

Conclusion

The distribution of archaeological sites on Statia testifies to an abundance of activities past and present. Stone ruins and artifacts vary with time and space. This evidence, together with available historical data, provides a framework of settlement information about the Statian past. Statian settlement patterns have obviously changed during the past three centuries. The distribution of buildings and cultural features on the landscape has been influenced by societal, social, political, and economic developments as well as by the ecology of the island.

The shape of the landscape, volcanic soils, lack of rainfall, and other ecological factors greatly affected farming and settlement. The Atlantic Ocean side of the island (the east) has remained comparatively free of population because of higher winds and rough seas. A harbor was safer and easier to approach on the leeward or west side of Statia, which is much calmer, with fewer coral reefs. Access from ships to land via small boats was relatively easy onto a long, fairly wide, and flat stretch of beach, which eventually developed into the main warehouse district or Lower Town. The beach had various disadvantages: it was open to attack from pirates and privateers, goods stored there could be captured even though the rest of the island might escape, and it was open to ocean damage during storms. Convenience weighed heavily, however, in its selection as the warehouse district (Kandle 1985:101–102). Archaeological research has established that the main ship anchorage was 500–800 meters offshore (Nagelkerken 1986). The high cliffs above the Lower

Town provided a good place for town development because they afforded both protection against attack and a good view of the anchorage area.

The dry climate of Statia and its marginal soils made agriculture difficult, but in the first half of the eighteenth century, plantations were established in all areas of the island, including some that even today are rugged and inhospitable, such as the northern volcanic hills. The less than favorable conditions apparently did not deter Statians from growing crops when prices were high.

Politics and international relations often influenced trade and the resulting settlement development. In the seventeenth and eighteenth centuries, numerous wars were waged in Europe and the Caribbean area between the European powers. The Seven Years War (1756–1763), for example, firmly established Statia as a smuggling center to British and French islands and to North American colonies (Jameson 1903; Kandle 1985:51). These adversarial relationships often prohibited legal trade between warring nations. This situation benefited the Dutch and their open port policy on Statia, as the island became a major entrepôt where enemies clandestinely traded with one another. In 1780, Britain declared war on the Dutch due to their role in the American Revolution. Trade between the English and the Dutch continued, however, and British merchants on Statia even sold goods to the American rebels (Jameson 1903).

Favorable global and inter-island economic conditions fostered opportunism, especially on the part of the Dutch and the West India Company. Economic success on Statia necessitated an ever-increasing labor supply, which in turn meant more housing on the landscape. In 1790, the population reached a peak of circa 8,000 people, the majority of whom were enslaved. The majority of enslaved peoples were probably rural and agricultural, although many worked in the warehouses and in the Upper Town. Members of white society were mostly urban dwellers—shopkeepers, hotel keepers, ship chandlers, carpenters, fishermen, soldiers, and government officials, many of whom walked to the Lower Town to work (Kandle 1985:95).

As population increased, Statian society became more heterogeneous (Kandle 1985:6). This diversity undoubtedly had an effect on housing styles and settlement. Jews, well established on Statia in the eighteenth century, had a synagogue and a cemetery in the Upper Town (Barka 1987a,1988; Hartog 1976b). The locations of their houses are unknown. A document dating to 1781 names about 800 citizens, probably merchants, as having come to Statia from a variety of countries, including England, Scotland, France, Italy, Germany, Bermuda, the West Indies, and North America (Barka 1996a:230). Gradual adoption of the English language and the growing dominance of English material culture perhaps increased uniformity during the latter half of the eighteenth century (Kandle 1985:4).

Fluctuating sugar prices in the European market were undoubtedly mirrored in the number of functioning plantations on Statia. Sugar consumption increased fourfold between 1660 and 1700 and increased dramatically again in the period up to 1775 [Mintz 1979 in Delle 1989:177–178]. Trade was to become dominant in the second half of the eighteenth century, as was warehouse construction in the Lower Town, with a resulting decline in sugar production. Toward the mid-nineteenth century, sugar prices dropped; at this time there were fewer than a dozen operating sugar plantations on Statia. Sugar was no longer a luxury that could offset expensive transportation and the productive inefficiency of small plantations on marginal land (Delle 1989:179). More efficient plantations, such as English Quarter, did survive for a time.

As economic conditions deteriorated in the nineteenth century, Statian trade collapsed. There was a migration of the vast majority of the population, from 8000 people in 1790 to fewer than 2000 in 1847 (Kandle 1985:139). Furthermore, agriculture was affected by the abolition of slavery in the mid-nineteenth century. The weakened economic system encouraged emigration, further reducing the size and composition of the population. In 1884, in a population of 1600, only 50 individuals were white (Hartog 1976a:127). The population decline greatly reduced the quantity of housing and other structures on the island. Today, concerned citizens are trying to promote a renovation of the historic core of the Upper Town in order to preserve the past and also to encourage people to live in the urban area. As population of the island steadily increases, more residential development will probably occur on lands where sugarcane and other crops once grew.

6

A VENUE FOR AUTONOMY

Archaeology of a Changing Cultural Landscape, the East End Community, St. John, Virgin Islands

Douglas Armstrong

In the late eighteenth century a small Creole community comprised primarily of people of color emerged within the East End quarter of St. John, Danish Virgin Islands (figures 6.1, 6.2). This chapter presents data recovered from an intensive archaeological survey using Global Positioning System (GPS) instrumentation to locate house sites in the steep and rugged terrain once occupied by the East End community. The survey is part of a broader archaeological and ethnohistorical examination that explores social relations and the changing cultural landscape of the East End community. The field

This project was funded by a grant from the Wenner-Gren Foundation. Fieldwork was carried out with the support of Syracuse University's Summer Sessions. Special thanks are due to Elizabeth Righter (USVI-SHPO) for her encouragement and consultation and to Kenneth Wild (National Park Service) for his continued interest in support of the project. Fieldwork was completed with the able assistance of Edward Carr, Dorrick Gray, Mark Hauser, Benjamin Kanpeyeng, Elizabeth Kellar, Melody Mitchell, Douglas Pippin, Bonnie Ryan, Margaret Wood, and dozens of volunteers from the Virgin Islands and Syracuse University. Thanks are due to the many owners of lands in the East End Quarter who allowed us to survey their property. In particular I thank the Baptiste, George, and Sewer families. This project was initiated in 1995 with the encouragement of Dr. Bernard Kemp (St. John resident and economist) and Mr. Guy H. Benjamin (East End resident, author, and past superintendent of schools for the U.S. Virgin Islands). The Global Positioning System survey benefited from technical support provided by the staff of Syracuse Blue Print. Particular thanks are due to David Knight and Lolli Prime for their continuous encouragement, support, and generosity.

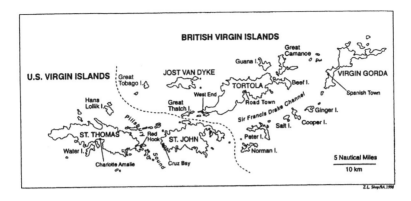

Fig. 6.1. Regional map showing St. John.

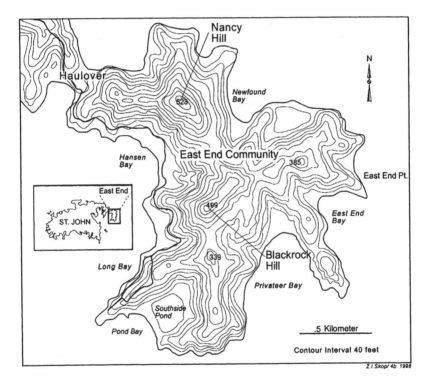

Fig. 6.2. Map of the East End (St. John insert).

The East End Community, St. John / 143

study, combined with historical research, allows us to document the emergence and maintenance of a distinct community through the immense historical changes of the eighteenth century through the early twentieth (see Hall 1992; Kemp 1990; Olwig 1978, 1985, 1990, 1995; Tyson 1984; Tyson and Highfield 1994).

The survey and historical research on the community show that the location and configuration of East End living areas changed over time. Settlement associated with initial plantations, or *plantages* (the Danish term for plantation), gave way to dozens of small freeholding house sites. An initial provisioning plantation was replaced by a group of widely dispersed planter houses located on and near ridgetops and the north side of the island. Over time, with the shift from plantation to freeholding, house sites began to cluster on the upper flanks of the hills above Hansen Bay. Finally, house sites shifted down the hill, so that there was an early twentieth-century cluster near the shoreline of Hansen Bay. These shifts are associated with increasing numbers of individual house sites through the nineteenth century as small one- to five-acre parcels were carved out of extended family holdings. This chapter will place the archaeological survey data in historical context and explore the social organization of the community as it shifted in cadence with external trade and internal social dynamics.

The archaeological study of the changing cultural landscape of East End, St. John, illustrates the dynamic, nonstatic nature of cultural transformation in the Caribbean (Wilson and Rogers 1993:6). It illuminates the active and creative roles of African-Caribbean communities, households, and individuals. Recent studies of African-Caribbean cultural transformation involving slavery in Jamaica have shown that the social and cultural systems that emerged under the harsh restrictions of slavery represent modifications from traditional African or European cultural systems (Armstrong 1990, 1992, 1998). This study explores similar systems of change within a society that negotiated a metamorphosis to freedom while creating its own distinctive cultural domain (see Armstrong 1990, 1998; Higman 1998; Mintz 1974; Mintz and Price 1976; Yentsch 1994). In so doing, the study builds upon a growing body of archaeological research examining African-Caribbean living contexts on plantations (Armstrong 1985, 1990, 1992; Farnsworth 1992, 1996; Gartley 1979; Handler and Lange 1978; Howson 1990; Pulsipher and Goodwin 1982; Watters 1987, 1994) and in maroon settings (Agorsah 1994, Arrom and Garcia-Arrévalo 1986).

The Creole community on St. John's East End emerged in the late eighteenth century and the early nineteenth century during a period in which plantation slavery and international mercantilism dominated social and economic interaction in the Danish Virgin Islands and the Caribbean region as a whole. The existence of this mostly free community sheds light on unique and variable situations in which African Americans could, and did, work within and around the dominant power structures to create and maintain their own social and economic system. This community thus represents a setting of diversity within the African Diaspora. The East End community used its "marginality" and petite, or small-scale, social and economic interactions to facilitate the maintenance of freedom on the margins of the dominant economy, which continued until the mid-nineteenth century to be based upon enslaved labor. This community represents an important locus of variation within the overall social and economic pattern of the region.

Background of the East End Community

In order to establish a land-based foothold in the Caribbean, the Danish crown (King Christian V) claimed the islands of St. Thomas and St. John in 1671. These islands had previously been occupied by native Caribbean populations and had been the site of small-scale and generally impermanent occupations by the Spanish, Dutch, French, and English. The first quarter of the eighteenth century was a period in which the demand for sugar and cotton was booming and there was ready access to enslaved laborers from Africa. Moreover, with the expansion of sugar plantations and urban populations on St. Thomas, there was an ever-expanding need for provisions to feed all sectors of society. Permanent Danish settlement of St. John was not established until 1718, after most of the arable lands of St. Thomas had been developed (Bro-Jorgensen 1966:218; Caron and Highfield 1981:8; Low and Vals 1991:6; Olwig 1985:13).

In 1718, the Danish West India and Guinea Company established a settlement at Coral Bay, St. John, in an effort to "transform that wilderness [St. John] into fruitful and populated land" (Oldendorp 1987:26; see also Westergaard 1917:127–130). The initial settlement, including a Company sugar plantation and a garrison, were soon followed by an array of sugar, cotton, and provisioning estates. St. John, as a whole, is a small mountainous island with little level ground, an irregular coastline, and many small bays with anchorages (figure 6.2). Only Carolina plantation, the Company plantation at Coral Bay, and a few small plantations on plateaus and valleys on the interior and north coast have contiguous level lands exceeding 100 acres. Hence, although sugar production was an important economic feature of this island from its earliest settlement, many of the island's estates engaged in a mix of sugar, cotton, and provision production. Although 109 plantations had been established on St. John before 1733, only 21 (one-fifth) were engaged primarily in the production of sugar (Olwig 1985:14).

The lands that were to become the setting for the East End community were not patented until 1725. Johan Jacob Creutzer (or Croitzer), the patentee, and his descendants are listed as the owner on the 1728–1739 land lists (Rigsarkivet 1728–1739). The land list indicates that Creutzer owned an estate measuring 3000 × 1500 Danish feet (112.5 Danish acres, or 110 U.S. acres) (Magana, Tyson, and Driskell 1989:23; Rigsarkivet 1728–1739). He probably controlled the entire parcel east of Haulover estate, however, or the area now known as East End. Creutzer, who was an employee of the Danish West India and Guinea Company, is listed as a "ship chandler." This occupation is defined as either a person who makes candles or, as applied in this case, a retailer of supplies and groceries and provisions (Webster 1993:190). Hence, in all probability the East End was used for provisioning directly by the Company. The 1728 land list indicates that Creutzer had thirteen enslaved laborers working his land and that it was officially defined as a cotton plantation. Neither Creutzer nor any other free person is listed as being present on the land (Rigsarkivet 1728–1739). Over the next decade between nine and twenty slaves are listed as residing on the estate, but at no time is the owner or any white manager listed. Hence, although the estate may have been overseen by Creutzer, or even by the manager of another estate in the area, the daily activities of the enslaved laborers were, at most, loosely supervised.

The expansion of both sugar and provisioning estates through the 1720s and early 1730s was marked by a significant increase in the number and proportion of enslaved laborers to a total of 1087, as compared with 208 whites (a 5:1 ratio; Westergaard 1917). Several of the estates produced small quantities of cotton, but the majority were primarily engaged in the production of a wide range of provisions (Bro-Jorgensen 1966: 218–222; Olwig 1985:14; Westergaard 1917:129–131). These provisions included land-based food crops needed by sugar estates, urban populations, and garrisons. Provisions such as cassava, corn, yams, beans, pepper, and squash were probably grown in garden plots and terraces throughout the East End. In addition, fruit trees were planted near houses and in protected guts and shorelines. Commodities such as charcoal were made by burning native hardwoods. Areas such as the East End produced an array of coastal and maritime provisions, including a wide variety of shellfish and fish. Laborers also built small craft for local trade and participated in the exchange of local produce and the redistribution of imported mercantile goods ranging from ceramics to wine and spirits.

Many of the laborers on both sugar and provisioning estates were *bussels,* or new arrivals from Africa, rather than *Creoles,* who were born in the islands. Westergaard's study of the Danish islands (1917:160) reports not only that the whites were vastly outnumbered by individuals recently uprooted and transported from Africa but that many of the estates were managed in absentia, either by planters living on St. Thomas or by overseers called *mesterknecht* (Caron and Highfield 1981:8). It was an illegal but common practice on St. John to use mesterknecht overseers as the primary supervision of plantations (Caron and Highfield 1981). The rapidly growing enslaved population of St. John was confronted by drought and a destructive hurricane in 1733. Moreover, the conditions faced by the laborers, who included a large number of recent arrivals from areas near Danish forts on the Gold Coast of Guinea, were compounded by the posting of a harsh new slave code in September 1733 (Knox 1852:69–91; Westergaard 1917:166). In November 1733 the enslaved population, led by a core group of bussels from Amina (Akan speakers from the area of Elmina in Ghana), staged a revolt (Pannet 1994:19–23).

Oldendorp (1987), Westergaard (1917), and Caron and Highfield (1981) all appear to assume that the bussels of St. John were Amina rather than individuals taken into slavery by the Amina at Elmina castle. As part of their argument, Caron and Highfield (1981:9–10) maintain that the newly arrived Amina were accustomed to dealing with Europeans as equals through their centuries of contact and interaction at Elmina and on Ghana's Gold Coast. These new arrivals on St. John had had long and intimate contact with firearms and with a range of socioeconomic classes of Europeans. This background contrasted sharply with their treatment on St. John as chattel slaves. This backdrop, combined with the intensification of food and water shortages of 1733 and the general practice of management from a distance by the planter elite, set the stage for and fueled the rebellion of 1733–1734.

The resistance to enslavement began at the fort at Coral Bay and spread across the island. The leaders of the rebellion gained control of much of the island for nearly a year before the French assisted the Danes in regaining control of both the island and its laborers (Caron and Highfield 1981:17; Westergaard 1917:199–212).

There is no direct evidence that the slaves residing upon the East End provisioning estate were involved in the revolt nor how they were affected by it. With the restoration of control, however, the island continued to produce sugar and provisions. During this period, the East End became even more closely associated with Company management as Creutzer's lands at East End St. John passed to Jens Hansen (between 1735 and 1737), who later became governor of St. Croix from 1747 to 1755. Peter L. Oxholm surveyed the area in preparing a map of the island that was first published in 1780. He wrote notes indicating not only that Governor Hansen had been a previous owner at East End but that Hansen had used the land for the production of provisioning crops including an array of fruit trees (Oxholm 1780 in Low and Valls 1991:14–150). Neither Creutzer nor Hansen actually lived on the lands that would become the East End community, but each sent managers and slaves to produce provisions that found a ready market on the island through their connection as chandler and governor. Hence, from the area's initial settlement, the plantations of the East End were primarily engaged not in cash crops for external markets such as sugar and cotton but in the production of food and supplies for local consumption. Recognition of the importance of local provisioning is indicated by ownership of lands by key company and government officials. Even under this early management, however, the small numbers of enslaved persons working the lands had some autonomy because of the small scale of the operations and the emergence of fishing and maritime transport as part of the provisioning system.

The St. John *matricals* (Danish land tax lists) for 1756 and 1757 record the transfer of lands from the estate of Governor Jens Hansen to a group of planters including women and men from the George and Sewer families. These families came over from Spanish Town, Virgin Gorda, in the British Virgin Islands (Rigsarkivet 1755–1915). This group was related to planters who were already established in St. John. The families also retained ties, both familial and economic, with their close neighbors in the British Virgins. Over the next forty years, the lands continued to be used for the production of provisions by this group of white and mulatto landowners and their enslaved laborers. The matricals for 1759 indicate that the East End was co-owned by Charles Joris (George), Johannes Sewer, and William Jores (George). Immediately preceding this group on the matricals is a listing for Peter Soor (Sewer) along with a woman and four children. They are listed as a white family without land. The following year (1760) the same Peter Soor (Sewer), along with Michael Ladler, joins the initial trio of East End landowners. Peter Soor (Sewer) and Johannes Sour (Sewer) had been listed as living on their grandmother's land in 1758.

Over the next decade, between four and six primary individuals appear as the owners of this 2000 × 1500 parcel, with Martha George named in place of her deceased husband William Joris (George) in 1769. Interpretation of East End land ownership is assisted in the 1770s by the division of an East End quarter out of the more heavily populated Coral Bay quarter. In 1772, the five principal landowners are followed on the matrical list by Phillip George and Nancy, the widow of Charles George, Jr. In that year, St. John was struck by a major hurricane that has been called the "worst in the history of man" (Varlack and Harrigan 1992:25). The following year's matrical suggests that the storm, or related events of that year, had a devastating impact on the East End planters; four of the five planters listed on the 1772 matricals were replaced by relatives in 1773. Only Charles George, Sr., survived. It appears that Martha George, Peter Sewer, Johannes Sewer, and Michael Ladler all died, or at least passed their land on to Martha George's daughter-in-law Nancy, Michael Ladler's widow, and Phillip Sewer. At the same time the large East End land tract is divided, with Charles George, Sr., and Nancy, the wife of Charles George, Jr., amassing 2000 × 500 parcels and Michael Ladler's widow and Philip Sewer holding 2000 × 250 parcels. In the following years Charles George's widow, Nancy George, remarries, taking Antoni Kembeck as her husband in 1777, and the widow of Charles George, Sr., and their son Abraham are listed as splitting a 2000 × 500 parcel into equal shares in inheritance. Gemie George is listed as holding what had previously been Michael Ladler's land.

A landowning group consisting of Martha George (the widow of Charles George, Sr.; 250), Abraham George (250), Antoni Kembeck (500), Gemie Sewer (250), and Phillip Sewer (250) controls the lands until 1785, when Antoni, Gemie, and Phillip are replaced by Benjamin Lind. Lind obtains a significant 2000 × 1000 holding (or two-thirds of the collective lands). Lind, who did not live on the land, also held lands in Cruz Bay and Coral Bay. In addition he held the post of master of provisions for the St. John garrison and may very well have used his land and connections at East End to supply a variety of provisions from his East End cotton/provisioning plantation.

Through the eighteenth century, as demand for sugar remained strong, St. John joined its Caribbean neighbors in a dramatic, if temporary, expansion of sugar production. Sugarcane became the dominant crop on the island. The number of slaves increased on St. John from approximately 1000 in 1733 to 2500 by the end of the century. In 1800, sugar plantations averaged about 400 acres and 100 residents (Tyson 1987). By 1805 more than 90 percent of the island's enslaved population worked on sugar plantations (Olwig 1985:14). Much of the island thus saw a shift from provisioning to agro-industrial sugar production, with the average sugar estate cultivating 85 acres of cane on an average of 110 acres of cultivated land using an average of 103 slaves (Green Pedersen 1979:21; Olwig 1985:14 after Bro-Jorgensen 1966:220–22). Although the scale of production on St. John pales in comparison with that of the plantations of the Greater Antilles (Jamaica being British; Hispaniola being French and Spanish), this era saw the peak in the island's sugar production.

Despite the shift toward sugar production elsewhere on the island, the East End continued to engage in the production of both land- and sea-based provisions, specializing in commodities needed to sustain the growing plantation and urban populations of St. John, St. Thomas, and the neighboring British Virgin Islands. During the eighteenth century the East End became firmly established as a source of provisions for its neighbors. At this time the area was occupied by Anglo descendants, many from the British Virgins, along with small numbers of enslaved Africans. From the standpoint of legal ownership, the matricals indicate a gradual consolidation of lands under the names of key individuals through the turn of the century. At this point, there had been considerable intermarriage and union between all sectors of the community. The nineteenth century featured the gradual dividing out of small parcels to family members while the larger, encompassing tracts were held by the principal elders of the George and Sewer family.

Peter L. Oxholm provides a description of the area and its settlement and provisioning patterns during the late eighteenth century (Oxholm 1780 in Low and Valls 1991:14–150) (figure 6.3). Oxholm noted that the area was practically uninhabited except for "a few fishermen who live in some old huts on the beach" (Oxholm 1780 in Low and Valls 1991:14). Oxholm, whose mission included military assessment, was impressed neither with the organization of defensive structures on St. John nor with the conditions faced by these shoreline inhabitants. He describes small, overcrowded houses and notes that "despair and misery are seen here in the extreme and one cannot observe it without compassion. In some places whole families are found living in huts built for only half as many" (Oxholm 1780 in Low and Valls 1991:14). Oxholm's notes describe details ranging from clothing to housing and furnishings. With regard to clothing he states, "The most important have shirts and one pair of long trousers or a skirt, which constitutes their entire wardrobe." In their houses he observed that the only piece of furniture for some households of four of five people was "a bench, covered with banana leaves," which served as both bed and bench. Their diet is described as being limited to "yams and fish along with a drink of water" (Oxholm 1780 in Low and Valls 1991:14). Oxholm spent five days walking about the area, which he found to be extremely steep, difficult terrain.

In notes published with the original map, Oxholm described the deterioration of provisioning plantings at the East End estate previously owned by Governor Hansen. Prior to the rebellion of 1733, "on the East coast previously owned by Governor Hansen, there were many animals, fruits and other products, enough to supply neighboring islands" (Oxholm 1780 in Low and Valls 1991:15). The association of such trees and provisions associated with an earlier era at the East End suggests the importance of provisioning. Oxholm's picture of diminished provision production may have resulted from

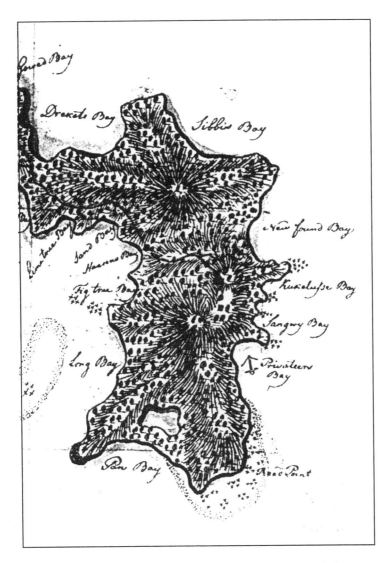

Fig. 6.3. East End of St. John. Section of a map by Peter Oxholm, 1780 (Rigsarkivet, Copenhagen).

his having observed a short-term change following a storm in the 1770s (see Varlack and Harrigan 1992:25). He was possibly also seeing a shift in the organization and focus of provisioning from plantation-based fruit crops to a broad-based system of individual and collective production of goods on land and sea organized by the emerging and increasingly free population of East End. In any case, the cultivation of fruit trees appears to have given way to a combination of fishing (which Oxholm observed), charcoal production, and a range of crops grown in provisioning gardens. Oxholm does not mention cotton production in the area, and matricals indicate only minor plots of land engaged in cotton production.

By the beginning of the nineteenth century, the East End community had begun the gradual transformation from small-scale cotton/provision plantations operated by planters using the labor of a few slaves to a community of many small landholdings (one-five acres) located within larger communal/family owned lands. This shift is illustrated in the recorded transfer of lands after 1800 but had probably been in effect since the 1780s or 1790s. In 1801 East End estates began to be listed in the matricals under the names Hansen Bay, Newfound Bay, and Haulover (versus the earlier practice of simply listing the landowner). Over the next forty years the estates shifted to property held in common under the name of elders representing the primary families. More than thirty-five separate households and land parcels were gradually divided out of the main Hansen/Newfound lands, however. This shift in the cultural landscape coincides with, and illustrates, the emergence of the East End community. The shift may well have been facilitated by the fact that provision farming, although an important element in sustaining the plantation and mercantile system of the islands, was not in itself a means of producing significant capital for planters, even as absentee investors. A diverse system of provision, procurement, and trade, however, could sustain the emerging and locally based East End community. This multifaceted system was flexible enough to sustain the community through recurrent drought, storm, and earthquake. Moreover, it could play off multinational colonial conflicts, which regularly interrupted formal mercantile trade on a larger scale in the region (see Nissen 1792–1837). The East Enders used their ties throughout the region for petite-scale capitalization and probably suffered no interference because they exerted a stabilizing effect on localized economies throughout the region.

For the island as a whole, the economy continued to be dominated by sugar production through the 1840s; even before emancipation in 1848; however, the number of sugar estates and the scale of sugar production had decreased dramatically (Tyson 1984). During this period the economy as a whole shifted more toward the broad-based provisioning system already in place on the island's East End. Island populations decreased as sugar plantations closed. Laborers escaped an oppressive Labor Act of 1849 and made their way to neighboring islands (Magana, Tyson and Driskell 1989; Tyson 1984). By 1915 only one plantation still cultivated and processed cane (Tyson 1984). The population of the East End, however, remained fairly constant through the late nineteenth century and the early twentieth. During this time small settlements were found throughout the island and included clusters of house sites along the shore of Coral Bay, Majo Bay, Cruz Bay, and Hansen Bay/East End (Olwig 1985, Tyson 1984). Karen Olwig reports that by 1915 75 percent of the rural population lived on provision-based sites, and a distinctive peasant culture had emerged on the island (Olwig 1985). After an examination of the island matricals, Magana, Tyson, and Driskell (1989:17) point out that a significant proportion (approximately 20 percent) of the small plots were located in the East End (Rigsarkivet 1755–1915). Hence, in the latter decades of the nineteenth century, the broad-based provisioning economy, found earlier in the East End, became a fixture of the island as a whole. The archaeological survey of the East End, in combination with historical documentation, allows us to examine the shift from plantation to freeholding and the emergence of the community from the late eighteenth century through the early 1900s.

Archaeological Survey

Historically the East End of St. John was remote, and its lands were considered of little economic value. The area was therefore not well mapped. This lack of accurate mapping was fostered by a rather inhospitable survey environment. The area features steep slopes and irregular ridgelines. The arid East End supports a mixed vegetation of subtropical plants along with cacti and agavi, which, although not covering sites with a tropical canopy, severely impede line-of-sight surveying. These factors have significantly contributed to the irregularity of professional survey results in the area. They also effectively prohibited us from relying on previous survey data in locating sites. Given these conditions, we opted to use GPS instrumentation to plot sites located through an intensive walking survey of the East End. The GPS survey was conducted using Leica instruments and Wild software. Field recording was assisted by the Survey Department of Syracuse Blue Print, Inc.

Our archaeological objectives also contributed significantly to the choice of GPS as a methodology for site location. With more than fifty uncharted sites in the area, it was important to reduce error in plotting location. The Danish were meticulous keepers of tax and census records. Their information, however, is useful only if individual house sites can be accurately distinguished and plotted. Precise location of house sites using the GPS survey, combined with archaeological sampling, has permitted us to plot trends in the use of the landscape. The survey has allowed us to obtain a fine-grained analysis of a community over time, a task that would have been difficult to achieve using traditional surveying methods. The archaeological survey of the East End identified the estates defined in the tax records and shown on the 1780 Oxholm map (figure 6.3). As the archaeological aspect of this project progresses, the pinpoint location of house sites and features will be useful in projecting trends in the use of the landscape. GIS layering will allow us to plot out a whole series of information, including not only location and topography but also material use, diet, and even trends in distribution of members of a household across the landscape over time. In short, we have an opportunity for a fine-grained analysis of a community over time, which can be significantly enhanced by detailed information on location.

The location of the East End in relative isolation on St. John not only fostered the emergence of this free community but also served to protect its residual archaeological sites from destruction by development and from casual vandalism by collectors of bottles and curios. Unfortunately, this isolation has also acted to limit recognition of the important cultural and social traditions expressed by the existence of persistence of this free community. Furthermore, factors that have protected these sites for centuries are no longer working to protect them. The recent past (since the 1960s) has brought paved roads, unplanned development, natural devastation (e.g., a series of recent hurricanes), and increased foot traffic to even the most remote section of the East End. Moreover, the last generation of East End residents to predate the establishment of the St. John National Park is aging.

The physiography (topography, soils, and rainfall) of East End, St. John, was not conducive to agro-industrial production associated with Caribbean sugar plantations. The area was therefore settled relatively late, as secondary cotton and provisioning estates. The five East End estates depicted on Oxholm's 1800 map of St. John were small-scale operations that used between one and thirteen enslaved laborers. As was typical for the Danish Islands, by the late eighteenth century the proprietors were not Danes but rather descendants of the settlers on the neighboring British Virgin Islands (Tortola and Virgin Gorda). The five men and women listed as owners of the property that become the estates Hansen and Newfound Bay were grouped together on the annual tax list.

The initial plantations were patented as strips of land of varying widths that transected the island on a north-south axis, a system that is grossly incompatible with the undulating landscape and did not conform to land use or to traditions defining land ownership (figure 6.4). These early plantations are clearly represented in the archaeological record and are distinct in design, construction, scale, and layout from later freeholdings (figure 6.5). Moreover,

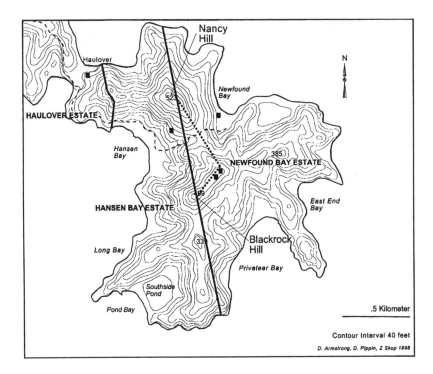

Fig. 6.4. Map of St. John indicating early estate boundaries (approximate).

nearly all of these sites were reused and modified by free blacks in the postplantation era.

In the early 1800s, sons and daughters of the initial group of settlers began to be listed separately on the land lists. Although the principal owners of the encompassing estates are initially listed as being of white or mulatto ancestry, blacks, including those of direct African ancestry, ultimately become significant owners of community land. Given the mixed ethnic heritage of the community, typical divisions into categories of European and African or black and white really do not adequately account for the integrated amalgam that was present. Hence, though the phrase "people of color" is useful in defining the people of the East End community, it is perhaps better to simply refer to them as part of a Creole community. Until 1820, actual acreage associated with land tax lists continues to show formal land ownership in the names of as many as five family heads (including both men and women). This situation changes dramatically after 1820, with the formal listing of nine small landholdings of less than 5 acres by free blacks, a number that increased to seventeen over the next decade.

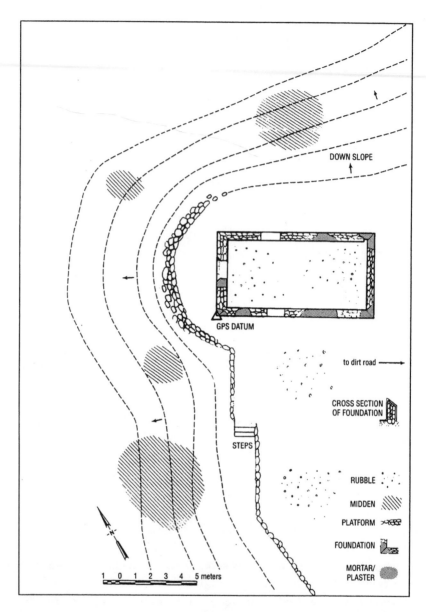

Fig. 6.5. Early cotton/provisioning estate, Haulover, St. John.

The increase in settled residences is illustrated in the location of sites dating to this period (figure 6.6). Geographically, houses were located throughout the East End study area, with house sites on the northern coast (Newfound Bay), along the ridgelines, and on the southern coastline of Hansen Bay. The community was sustained and augmented through births (as indicated in the Moravian church records) and by the arrival of new slaves and free persons from the British Virgins (documented in census data and in Moravian church records). North coast settlements provided quick and direct access by small craft to Tortola, less than a mile to the north. The ridgetop houses provided access to the expanding acreage of terraced fields and were within easy walking distance of north and south coast bays. This distribution of settlements is confirmed through the location of house sites before 1848 (figure 6.6).

Probate records for Catherine Ann Ashton, who died in 1831, describe the personal holdings of an East Ender from this period (St. Jan Probate Records 1831). Of note is the fact that her house is located on the flank of Newfound Bay (northern coastline), and her boat, the sloop *Kitty*, was anchored at Hansen Bay (southern coastline). Historical records, including baptismal and church registers from Emmaus Mission and the annual land lists, indicate that well before 1800 the free community of the East End interacted regularly at Coral Bay. Hence the community was rooted in both the Danish and the British Virgin Islands.

Unlike their enslaved counterparts from St. John, the East End group moved freely between islands, visiting the British Virgins regularly and trading local and imported commodities at Charlotte Amalie on St. Thomas, from boats constructed in the small East End bays. Nissen, a maritime merchant based in St. Thomas, repeatedly logged descriptions of small trading vessels used to transport goods between islands and to unload larger vessels in the bays of the Danish and British Virgin Islands (Nissen 1872–1937). Interaction with British Virgin Islanders and East Enders was facilitated in the early 1800s by international power struggles that brought British administration of the Danish Islands during the periods 1801–1802 and 1807–1815. Interestingly, the beginning of the 1807–1815 British governance coincides with the British abolition of the slave trade. Hence, not only did British control facilitate interaction and commerce between the East End and its immediate neighbors on Tortola, but it fostered an environment open to the autonomy of the East End population.

Interaction between the British Virgins and St. John was based on proximity and descent, as a large portion of the East End population arrived in St. John from the British Virgins. Even after the Danish took the islands

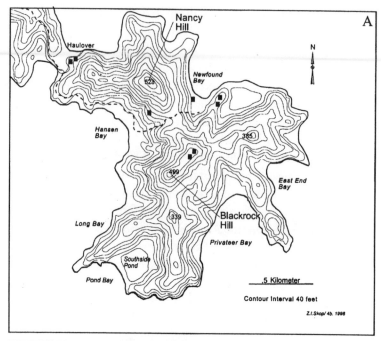

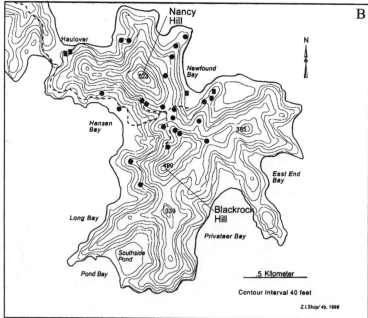

Fig. 6.6. Maps depicting East End, St. John site locations: (A) 1800; (B) 1810–1848.

back, interaction with, and support for, the free black community from the British Islands was facilitated by policies leading to emancipation. Whereas the Danish administrators resisted reform, the British established policies that included banning the trade of slaves and, ultimately, emancipation. Slaves from St. John began to abandon the estates and fled to the British Virgins on small vessels from the many isolated bays on St. John's north coast (Hall 1992).

In the 1830s, in an attempt to arrest the flight of slaves, the Danish government attempted to regulate trade by small craft on the island and to monitor the bays of the northern coastline. Small vessels, including those built and used by East Enders, were registered and formal cargoes documented. Then as now, however, the undulating coastlines, the multiplicity of small bays and coves, the proximity to neighboring islands that fell under an array of colonial jurisdictions, and the petite nature of both craft and cargo all worked together to prohibit effective monitoring of the small craft. Still, the closer scrutiny of administrating officials seems to have had some effect.

These external changes seem to have coincided with the village's shift in its focus to the south coast. Newly registered boats like the *Harmony*, which was built in the East End, were registered to owners in Hansen Bay on the south coast. Meanwhile, the growing community subdivided its holdings as new generations of East Enders established their residences up and down the canyon sides adjacent to Hansen Bay. By mid-century, settlements had decidedly shifted toward the southern coastline and Hansen Bay (figure 6.7).

With emancipation in 1848, the community, augmented by additional arrivals from St. John and the British Virgins, was able to expand its trade and interaction as it already had a web of trading partners spanning many islands. By 1850, some thirty landholders are listed in the tax lists, many on smallholdings whose names—"Rebecca's Fancy" and "Eva's," for example—identified the primary landowners. Most were 1- or 2-acre parcels. A few, such as Signal Hill, had as many as 5–8 acres. All were rather informally carved out of the larger family holdings. Although the community may have developed understandings concerning the specific boundaries between many of these parcels, very few property lines were recorded in deeds, and none were formally surveyed.

Gradually through the later decades of the nineteenth century, the houses on the north shore were abandoned, yet trade and interaction, including intermarriage, continued to tie this community to both British and Danish spheres of influence. The distribution of sites dating to the turn of the century shows the community concentrated on the southern hillside and shoreline of Hansen Bay (figure 6.7). By the time of the American takeover of the Danish

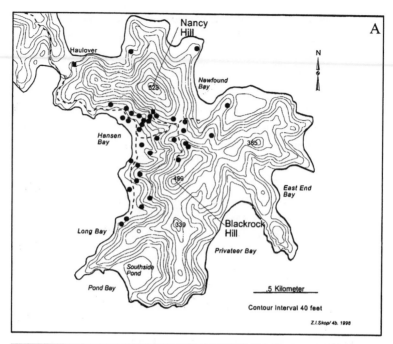

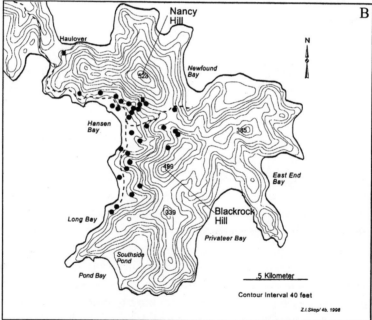

Fig. 6.7. Maps depicting East End, St. John site locations: (A) 1848–1900; (B) 1900–1917.

Virgins in 1917, the center of activities was clearly on the south side. Over the first two decades of the twentieth century, the population became more concentrated in the southern coastal area, with trade and education (East End school) organized from the shoreline.

The communitywide shifts described here are reflected in changes in the configuration of specific house sites encountered through intensive survey, mapping, and preliminary excavations. Two house sites will be used to illuminate internal, site-specific changes within East End residences: (1) estate Hansen Bay, a plantation turned freeholding; and (2) Rebecca's Fancy, a small half-acre residence and plot carved out of estate Hansen Bay.

The early cotton/provision plantations of Hansen Bay included lands spanning north and south shorelines, with an initial house site on the hilly flanks above the bay that was known by the same name. The plantation house is clearly discernible in the formal layout of three platforms. A pair of platforms supported the primary residence, which, like other early East End cotton plantations, was oriented with the long axis of the primary residence perpendicular to the slope of the hill. A small cook shed and a brick and stone oven completed the planter's residence area. A lower platform served as a pathway to and around the residence. A separate platform contained an additional three structures, at least two of which show evidence of early occupation, presumably by enslaved laborers. These structures may have served the dual purpose of storage warehouse and residence for laborers.

By 1840 the cotton and provisioning plantation had given way to residences occupied by free blacks. No longer operating as part of a cotton plantation, the two later houses were now listed as separate one-acre holdings, called Windy Hill (Timothy George was head of household in 1850) and Nancy Hill (Christian Hughes was head of household in 1850). These house sites served as residences for persons involved in a broad-spectrum economy based on provision, fishing, and trade. The old planter's residence was reused and reorganized, with new doorways and a window designed to catch the breeze.

A second example illuminates elements consistent with small landholdings of the mid-nineteenth century. During this era, the community was in the process of shifting its focus to the south side and shore area of Hansen Bay. This site, known as Rebecca's Fancy (owned by John J. Henry and Salome Rebecca Henry, c. 1860), is a 1.5-acre parcel (figure 6.8). It was occupied from the mid-nineteenth century through 1917. In contrast to the Hansen Bay/Windy Hill complex, Rebecca's Fancy consists of a single platform on which is located a single house structure, an associated cook area, and an oven. Like many other houses from this era, it was built parallel to the slope of the hill, with two

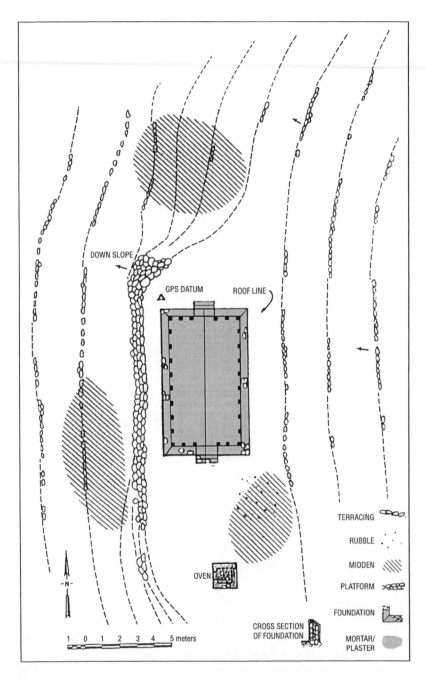

Fig. 6.8. Rebecca's Fancy, late nineteenth-century house and yard compound.

rooms and multiple doorways and windows. Much of the daily activity of the household took place outside the house on the terraced platform. The discard of materials shows clear patterning and regularity of activity over a long period of time.

As an example of activity areas reflected by material patterns, we may consider the distribution of food-related artifacts—the array of items associated with food and beverage preparation and consumption—across the site. The full assemblage shows generalized activity along with two areas of material accumulation. When the subset of these artifacts associated with food preparation is considered, it shows a specific pattern of discard down the slope from the right side of the house, a pattern matched by the distribution of dietary faunal remains and less specifically food consumption. This pattern is consistent with descriptions of food preparation and cooking practices related to the author by Mr. Guy Benjamin, who was born in this house prior to the transfer of the Islands by the Danish. Mr. Benjamin indicated that food was prepared and cooked on mobile iron coal pots used as hearths located behind and to the left of the structure. Another subset of food-related artifacts, however—those associated with beverage consumption—shows a distinctly different pattern, with a concentration on the right downslope area, suggesting that consumption centered on the platform to the right of the house. These data illustrate the utility of detailed analyses of material culture as a means to gaining insight into the complexities of social interaction and the complex web of activities that took place within an East End household.

Conclusion

The archaeological and historical study of East End, St. John, provides perspective on the emergence of a community of free persons during a period of slavery. In the process it expands our perspective of the African Diaspora. The archaeological survey of abandoned house sites has already proven useful in illuminating changes in the orientation and spatial distribution of residences in the community over time. The integration of survey and archival data within the regional historical context has allowed us to begin to project trends and delineate changing social relations both within the community and beyond to its neighbors. Material analysis from house site excavations indicates that this type of investigation has considerable potential for expanding our understanding of the changing cultural landscape at the local site and household level. As the study progresses, we hope to be able to link individuals and families with specific house sites so that we may glimpse the daily life and routines of the village and explore the dynamic movement and interactions of the community over time.

The East End community was sustained through the residents' ability to contribute domestic commodities such as fish, charcoal, and basketry to the local market. In addition, residents were involved in boatbuilding, trade, and merchant marine labor. Together these elements provided East Enders with an uncontested basis for community formation and maintenance through the dramatic changes in the world around them in the nineteenth century.

7

"GETTING THE ESSENCE OF IT"
Galways Plantation, Montserrat, West Indies

Lydia M. Pulsipher and Conrad "Mac" Goodwin

One fine summer morning not too long ago, John "Montserrat" Carty, Junior Martin, Lydia Pulsipher, and James Howson stood on the roadside above Galways plantation. As they had been for several years now, they were talking about place names and meanings attached to them. One of these was Gadinge, a somewhat mysterious place beyond a high misty mountain ridge above them, a place where to this day skilled tropical horticulturists like to locate their gardens. On this day, they were trying to puzzle out the name's obscure meaning. Mr. Carty, despite having lived and worked on the mountain all his life, despite knowing Gadinge, the place, intimately, kept repeating in his Creole lilt, "Me jus' can't get the essence of it." The others agreed, and for the time being, all remained befuddled by this bit of the puzzle of Galways Mountain.

The Galways Project (1980–present) was funded by grants from the Earthwatch/Center for Field Research, the John Carter Brown Library Fellowship Program, the Skaggs Family Foundation, the Wenner-Gren Foundation, the Association of American Geographers, Boston University, the University of Tennessee, the Smithsonian Museum of Natural History, the Smithsonian Associates Program, the National Endowment for the Humanities Summer Fellowship Program, the Fulbright-Hays Program, and numerous private contributions. Colleagues from many disciplines have participated in this study, but the principal investigators have been Lydia Mihelic Pulsipher, a geographer, and Conrad McCall Goodwin, an archaeologist, both from the University of Tennessee. Archaeologist Jean Howson, of New York University, has been involved with documentary research and with the excavations in the Galways village.

Trying to "get the essence of it" rather accurately conveys the nature of our fifteen-year collective effort to learn about Galways Mountain—our probing to define the many material aspects of human history within the tropical mountain environment and especially our search for the meaning that the place and its material culture has held over the last some 300 years for the people of Galways Mountain. The complications of time and cultural distance have stood between us and our objective. Our colleagues on Galways Mountain and throughout Montserrat have educated us about many a material and cognitive detail, but even they have been stumped by some questions.

Prehistoric archaeological research indicates that at least the lower reaches of Galways Mountain were occupied long before Europeans arrived (Watters 1980b). The historic period began in the mid-seventeenth century, when at least one sugar works was constructed and managed or owned by David Galway. By 1673, the lower slopes south of Germans Ghaut were occupied by Irish and Scots indentured servants who worked for Galways (Pulsipher 1986a). This period of early colonization was a time of rapid change. By the early eighteenth century, the labor force was no longer European but primarily African in origin. From that time to the present, the majority of the people of Galways Mountain have been African-Caribbean. This statement holds true for Montserrat as a whole, although for several decades now it has been popular to emphasize Montserrat's Irish heritage rather than the African in much of the modern tourism literature (Donoghue 1995; Fergus 1983) and in academia (Fergus 1981; Lawrence 1956; Messenger 1975). Apart from residual family names, place names, possibly a few food customs, and some linguistic features, Irish cultural traditions seem to have disappeared rather early on the island.

The overwhelming influence on Montserratian culture—belief systems, family organization, subsistence activities (including resource management and other uses of the landscape), language spoken, and musical and oral traditions—is what we may call Creole. That is, it is a dynamic intermingling of strands from many sources, among which Africa was very important. But it is interesting to note that as we learn more about Galways specifically and about the larger phenomena of cultural diffusion and evolution in the Caribbean, those who look for specific items that may have derived from Africa or Ireland or elsewhere will probably be disappointed. Caribbean culture is now an amalgamation of many cultural themes that have been adapted and readapted to suit local needs. For the Galways Project, we have attempted to document and describe the evolving cultural complex found there today and in the past. We have concerned ourselves not with seeking the origins of the traits we note but rather with understanding how all of what we collectively learned fits together to form the culture of the place.

The Historical and Geographical Context of the Galways Project

Montserrat is a small mountainous volcanic island in the eastern Caribbean archipelago (figure 7.1). Just forty square miles contain a wide array of physical environments. Along the coast intermittent beaches, steep cliffs, and marshes grade inland toward grasslands and scrub woodlands, which, in turn, give way to dense tropical rain forests in the uplands and high mountains. Cloud forests adapted to wind, high moisture, and consistent cloud cover occupied the very highest peaks before the island's Soufrière volcano erupted in 1995 and dramatically changed Montserrat's physical and cultural landscapes (Williams 1997). All of Galways Mountain was obliterated by a massive pyroclastic flow on December 26, 1997.

Beginning in 1632, the island was settled by English and Irish colonists from the neighboring island of St. Kitts. At first the Europeans used Irish and Scots indentured labor on the plantations they established. Soon, however, they were importing enslaved Africans to work their indigo, cotton, tobacco, and sugar fields. In a few decades, probably by 1700, virtually all the original native inhabitants were gone. The conditions that had facilitated the use of Irish and Scots indentures had changed by this time. Now many thousands of enslaved Africans were transported to the West Indies to work the sugar in their stead (Pulsipher 1986a, 1991).

Sugar flourished as a cash crop in the eighteenth century throughout the eastern Caribbean. Almost all of the land that could possibly support cane was used, usually on a shifting basis. Many sugar works were constructed in Montserrat between 1650 and 1800, some on very marginal land. Throughout the plantation era, thousands of ordinary laborers lived out their lives on Montserrat sugar estates. By 1730, blacks outnumbered whites five to one, and near the end of the eighteenth century by nearly ten to one (Pulsipher 1986a).

During the nineteenth century some of the more successful sugar works were upgraded to take advantage of the emerging steam-powered technology, but by the mid-nineteenth century, sugar was no longer a viable cash crop in most of the eastern Caribbean (Galloway 1985). Soon many older, less efficient, plantations were in receivership but continued in operation mostly because the now emancipated laborers subsidized the failing system with their underpaid

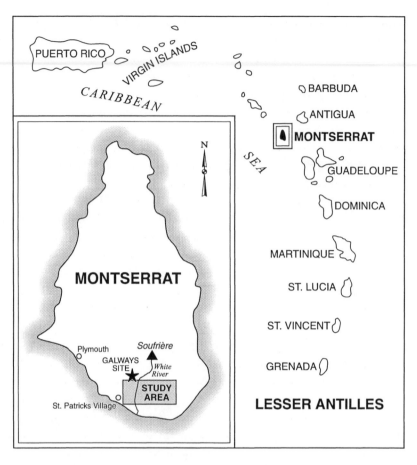

Fig. 7.1. Location of Montserrat and the Galways study area.

labor (Fergus 1983; Mintz 1985; Sheridan 1973; Smith 1987). In an effort to save the dying system, unproductive estates were combined, central cooperative factories were organized, sharecropping systems were established, and laborers were tied to particular estates by allowing only those who agreed to work at low wages for their home plantations to retain their houses and subsistence plots. On Montserrat, new or supplementary cash crops—cotton or lime juice— were also tried (unpublished oral history interviews with Paul Hollander 1986, owner and manager of Waterworks estate; James Hannum 1986, who grew up on Brodericks estate, managed by his father; and Kingsley Howes 1986, manager of Trants estate until it closed in c. 1950). By the twentieth century, only a few sugar estates in Montserrat were still in operation. Earthquakes and hurricanes helped to shut down all but two or three. The last one stopped production in 1965, reportedly for want of a small replacement part (personal communication, Paul Hollander 1986).

On Galways Mountain

The archaeological site known as Galways estate lies at 1100 feet above the sea on the flanks of the Soufrière Hills in southwest Montserrat; over the last fifteen years of regular research, this place has come to be known locally as Galways Mountain. The steep mountainside bounded by Germans Bay Ghaut on the northwest and the White River on the southeast (figure 7.2) rises from the sea to 3000 feet in just over two miles. The convoluted landforms of the entire mountain were created by volcanic deposition and subsequent erosion. At about 2000 feet, in a partial crater, is Galway's Soufrière, a sometimes active fumerole. The volcanic origin of the landforms, the complex wind patterns originating in the northeast trades, and the highly variable rainfall have conspired to create a complex mosaic of ecological zones further modified by humans (Pulsipher 1991).

The availability of moisture on Galways Mountain is directly reflected in the vegetation patterns and has had particular implications for the history of Galways plantation. Rain nearly always comes from the east, where the high mountains intercept the warm moist northeast trade winds, forcing them up into cooler elevations so that they drop their moisture on the peaks and on the leeward (western) slopes. Showers several times a day move from east to west across the higher slopes. The tropical rain forest is the natural vegetation. Shifting cultivation plots interrupt the forest cover here and there and have probably done so since prehistoric settlement and throughout the plantation era (Pulsipher 1990).

Rainfall tends to decrease as the air masses move downslope. At between 2000 and 1000 feet, enough rain falls to support tall trees and herbaceous plants characteristic of rain forests if the land is left undisturbed, but grasslands and scrub woodland are more common these days after hundreds of years of clearing, cultivation, and grazing. On this particular mountain, sugarcane thrived in this zone. Below 1000 feet the winds shift to the north, blowing any rain toward the central leeward coast, so that the lower elevations of Galways Mountain receive very little rainfall. Long years of cultivation, erosion, and goat grazing have exacerbated the natural aridity. There is much barren ground (Pulsipher 1991).

In this lower, drier region David Galway, an Irishman who seems to have had strong English sympathies, first placed his sugar works sometime in the 1660s.

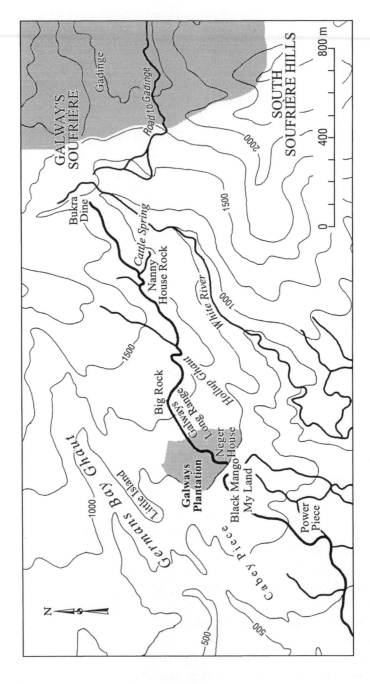

Fig. 7.2. Galways Mountain, a long volcanic finger on the southwest slope of Montserrat's Soufrière Hills, showing the location of Galways plantation in the eighteenth century.

This is also the place where hundreds of Irish indentures and smallholders lived during the same period. His estate, comprising 1300 acres, apparently stretched between Germans Bay Ghaut and White River Ghaut from the sea to the tops of the mountains in the east (Public Record Office 1729). There are at least three sugar works on the lower reaches of Galways Mountain. All were very likely associated with the Galways estate or with land hived off from the original land grant. Seventeenth-century documentary information and archaeological and geographical field data suggest that the earliest plantation buildings may have been those now in ruins on Mango Ghaut, just above the present village of St. Patricks. A very early cattle mill and boiling house are located here on what must have been a watercourse before extensive clearing and spring tapping changed the local hydrology. Architectural details of the buildings and the very sparse surface artifacts indicate an early date of construction and occupation. Slightly above these features and several hundred yards to the northwest are the undated ruins of a substantial house and other buildings.

The 1677 census lists seventy-four slaves at David Galway's estate. The census also lists 311 Irish as living in fifty-nine households on or near Galway's land (Oliver 1910). On the pictographic 1673 map of Montserrat, many small houses and fields are shown arrayed on the barren windswept slopes (figure 7.3). These people, if not actually indentured servants, probably provided seasonal labor to the plantation. Interestingly, the 1673 map also indicates that some of Galway's cleared fields were in wetter zones high above the settlement, perhaps where the now archaeologically documented plantation works were built in the mid-eighteenth century at 1100 feet above the sea (Pulsipher 1986a, 1987a, 1991).

This spatial organization on Galways Mountain—with both human settlement and agricultural activity located at the bottom of the mountain in land that today appears to be too impossibly dry and wasted for much beyond goat grazing—seems to have survived well into the eighteenth century. Only a few fields were located far above in the wetter zone. Between the 1670s and the 1730s, there is evidence that Galway's operation did not flourish as an economic enterprise, yet it still consisted of over 1300 acres of land, most of which must have lain in the wetter uplands (figure 7.3)(Public Record Office 1729). The lower slopes probably declined rapidly in productivity as radical clearing of vegetation created erosion and desiccation. Eventually this zone proved too difficult a venue for human habitation. As soon as they could, the Irish laborers left. Meanwhile, and for many decades to come, the high fields where rainfall was more abundant were regarded as too remote or too difficult to access.

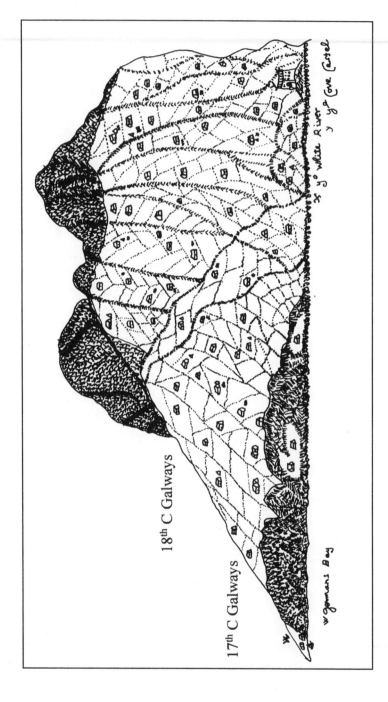

Fig. 7.3. The southern portion of the 1673 map of Montserrat showing numerous tiny houses on small plots with animal pens on Galways Mountain. The locations of both the first (seventeenth century) and second (eighteenth century) Galways plantations are approximate. Map redrafted in September 1996 from original in the J. Carter Brown Library, Brown University.

The 1729 census presents a picture of a colonial enterprise in decline: the Galway family, headed now by David Galway, the grandson of the founder, consisted of five men and a boy but no females. There were no white servants, just 40 enslaved adults and 22 enslaved children (later, in the mid-eighteenth and early nineteenth centuries, Galways regularly had about 160 enslaved workers). The census indicates that, in an era when many planters had added windmills for cane crushing, the Galways operation still used the older cattle-mill technology, and only 120 of the 1300 acres were cultivated. Patrick Roach, a neighbor with only 370 acres of land, appears to have been far more prosperous, with a windmill and two cattle mills, 159 slaves, and 200 acres in cane (Public Record Office 1729).

The estate passed in the 1740s to nephews of the second David Galway, who then leased the estate to Nicholas Tuite for £225 sterling per year. In 1765, the surviving nephew, Tobias Wall Galway, leased the estate to Henry and John Dyer of Montserrat for nine years at £500 a year. By this time, Galways had shrunk to just 500 acres in size, with only 12 acres of land in cane and still just the one cattle mill for crushing cane. The enslaved people included 36 adults and 26 children who lived on the estate. It was a very small operation for the period (Howson 1995). Though no records have yet been discovered to confirm exactly how the Galways tract of 1300 acres was reduced to 500 acres, sometime between 1729 and 1765 the estate was probably divided and other sugar works built by the new owners or lessees. Perhaps some of the sugar works with windmill towers now totally dismantled—one at 200 feet near Spring Ghaut and one at 700 feet on Power Piece (figure 7.2)—date from this period (Pulsipher 1995). The third sugar works (at 500 feet), now called Lower Galways, was built in the mid-nineteenth century (Pulsipher and Goodwin 1981).

Henry Dyer appears to have been the principal actor in the partnership formed in 1765. The archaeological and documentary evidence to date suggests that he decided to relocate the Galways sugar works to the present site at 1140 feet above the sea (Goodwin 1987). In the new, upland, more fertile and well-watered location, and with a loan from Neave and Willet of London, he built what for the time was a completely modern sugar agri-industrial complex. Dyer's 1771 lease stated that he had erected several new buildings at his own expense. The estate then included a boiling and curing house, a rum room, one copper and two furnaces, a still house, and other plantation implements (Montserrat Court Record Book 1771).

This new eighteenth-century plantation included a village for the enslaved African laborers, a great house, a windmill and backup cattle mill, a boiling house and curing house, and a large warehouse and stables. All but the workers' village were built of stone in the Georgian style. An extensive water management system including surface catchments and reservoirs, underground tunnels, and cisterns was installed to manage the increased water supply available at this higher elevation and to minimize the erosion damage that could be done by heavy rains. The village, consisting of a cluster of twenty or more small wood dwellings, was located just below the boiling house and was home to at least 155 or 160 enslaved people from the late eighteenth century until abolition in the 1830s.

That the lessees spared no expense to improve the efficiency of the plantation, and even invested in architectural aesthetics, reflects the prevailing European optimism concerning the sugar trade. Sugar, increasingly popular in the European diet, was a tremendously profitable crop in the West Indies. As a result, West Indian sugar planters controlled the Houses of Parliament. Although many new investors were eager to try their luck, those who had been in the business for some time were just as eager to keep out the competition. The negotiations at the Peace of Paris in 1763, which ended the Seven Years War, were dominated by old British sugar interests. They managed to squelch the possibility for new British investors to take over sugar lands in Guadeloupe and Martinique—a development that would have increased the amount of sugar available in the British markets, thus depressing the price—by seeing to it that Britain returned these islands to France in exchange for concessions in North America. Thwarted by this move to limit competition, the hopeful new sugar speculators sought to take over marginal plantations like Galways in the British sugar islands of Montserrat, St. Kitts, and Antigua.

Probably because of this rush to become sugar barons, we find evidence of what seems now to have been unwarranted investor optimism: beautiful new buildings on a difficult steep slope, uncertain supplies of water posing threats of both deficits and erosive overabundance, and rather inefficiently engineered sugar-processing facilities. Neave and Willet, a London firm, advanced more than £5000 to Dyer for the move and improvements (Howson 1995). Although investors, like the lessees of Galways, were eager to cash in on the sugar boom, older planter families, like the Galways, who by the eighteenth century had plantations elsewhere in the eastern Caribbean, were probably glad to relieve themselves of marginal, relatively unproductive holdings (Pulsipher 1991). In 1775, just ten years after he began his project, Dyer signed over the title to Galways to James Neave, a son of the firm's partner. Neave and his heirs owned the estate until 1836 (Howson 1995).

After the abolition of slavery in 1834, the former slaves still had to provide forty-five hours of free labor a week, after which they were paid four pence a day. Later the estate switched to a similarly oppressive system of sharecropping, which lasted well into the twentieth century. Under this system, the former slaves were allotted parcels of land that they cultivated independently, but they had to give the property manager the better part of both their subsistence and cash crops in order to live on estate land and cultivate it. As we walk the landscape of Galways Mountain today, we come across many small homesites scattered with the fragments of nineteenth-century plates, bowls, cups, and chamber pots, indicating that some people moved from the old slave village onto the lands they cultivated as sharecroppers (Goodwin 1987). Yet archaeological evidence indicates that the estate village remained the place that defined community even as people moved out onto the mountainside (Howson 1995). A core of people continued to live in the Galways village, and both a school and a cemetery were in active use until the late nineteenth century. In the first decades of the twentieth century, people began to make St. Patricks village at the base of Galways Mountain the center of community.

As a sugar enterprise, Galways began to fail in the 1840s. John Davy, who rode through the plantation in 1847, commented that by then it was only 300 acres in size and produced 200 hogsheads of sugar (approximately twelve tons). He further indicated that the estate had recently been sold for an amount equal to what it had once cost to build just the windmill (Davy 1854). This decline is probably related to several factors. Emancipation complicated labor relations, and the switch to sharecropping resulted in further loss of control over labor. The world market prices for sugar were dropping, too, partly because of the greater efficiency of steam-powered mills but also because sugar lands in the Pacific and Asia were opening up and employing the latest in technology. The sugar beet, which could be grown in mid-latitude zones, was also beginning to impact the market.

In the 1860s, possibly a little earlier, a new sugar-processing complex was constructed back down the mountain at what is now known as Lower Galways. Technologically, this was not an advanced installation, but it was closer to the main road and on more gently sloping land. This mill, affectionately called "Industrious Mary," operated until the 1930s. Many people now in their eighties and nineties remember seeing and hearing her crush sugarcane grown by their sharecropper parents. As a child, Nellie Dyer, now ninety-four, was occasionally given candylike chunks of black sugar as a reward for some task she performed for a mill worker (personal communication with authors

1983–1984). As late as 1981, remnants of the top wooden housing of the mill gears and sails as well as the long "tail" were visible.

The Upper Galways complex went through several stages of decline. Some Montserratians suggest that the boiling house was used as a school for a while, with the teacher living in the great house. If so, it was probably one of the mission-related schools established for slaves in the 1830s. Remarkably, people still remember that the teacher's name was Abraham Riley. When cotton became the chief cash crop, the boiling house became a cotton storage facility. Sometime in the late nineteenth century, perhaps after the earthquake and hurricane of the late 1890s, the buildings were abandoned, and the last descendants of the slaves moved down to St. Patricks, though many continued to cultivate Galways land.

Twentieth-century hurricanes and earthquakes, especially those in the 1920s and 1930s, hastened the deterioration. Sharecropping of cotton remained the land use system on Galways Mountain until the 1950s, when the price for cotton dropped and many hundreds of Montserratians migrated to Britain to work in the post–World War II industries (Pulsipher 1987b, 1989, 1992). In 1989, Hurricane Hugo, which hung over Montserrat for at least twelve hours, knocked down both the picturesque north gable end and the south end of the boiling house. It also cleared away many ancient trees, thus robbing the site of landmarks and valuable shade (Harden and Pulsipher 1992). Finally, in late 1997, a series of volcanic eruptions first destroyed the surface of Galways Mountain and then blanketed it with ash.

Galways estate, architecturally beautiful, spectacularly situated high on the flanks of the Soufrière Hills overlooking the sea far below, was actually quite an ordinary sugar plantation like hundreds throughout the Caribbean. The descendants of the enslaved Africans and the indentured Irish laborers at Galways lived nearby on the lower slopes—those first occupied in the seventeenth century—until they were evacuated in 1996. They chose this location to be near the road and schools, electricity, and piped water. Some, in return for minimal rents, used parts of the mountain for small tropical horticulture plots or for grazing goats and cattle. Much of the mountain was unused, however, and most of the villagers worked at professional or service jobs in town or in tourism. Many of the elderly depended on remittances from relatives abroad who began migrating in the 1950s.

THE GALWAYS PROJECT

The study of Galways Mountain began in 1980 at the behest of the Montserrat National Trust. By the 1980s, both the national trust and the government of Montserrat were promoting tourism as the island's primary economic development strategy. The trust thought Montserrat needed several properly researched and interpreted historic sites that would appeal to more educated, wealthy, and culturally sensitive tourists. One of the most intriguing possibilities was the dramatic ruins of the Georgian-style sugar estate built by Henry Dyer in the eighteenth century. In the late 1970s, historical geographer Lydia Pulsipher was invited to direct the Galways Project. Her mandate from the Montserrat National Trust was to learn what she could about the place and to write a report that would help in interpreting the site for visitors. The trust provided in-kind and logistical support, but all research funds were raised by Pulsipher and the colleagues who joined her in the study. Her research consortium was given the liberty to define the goals of the research to suit their academic needs.

The Research Perspective

In 1980, the ruins of Galways were heavily overgrown with dense vegetation, much of which was thorny acacia. All of the main features had been so long abandoned that they were swathed in tall trees and heavy vines. Reconnaissance revealed that the entire site had been covered over with a great deal of eroded sediment. Many of the features were buried, some rather deeply. The need for archaeology immediately became evident. Conrad "Mac" Goodwin, an archaeologist then affiliated with the College of William and Mary in Virginia, joined Lydia Pulsipher as codirector of the project in 1981. Together, they (we) formulated the following research goals and research strategies to achieve them.

RESEARCH GOALS

As directors of the project, we sought to accomplish the following:
1. To better understand the evolution of Galways plantation and, by extension, West Indian plantation society as a whole from the seventeenth century to the twentieth and thereby to gain a better comprehension of how all estate inhabitants (but especially those of African-Caribbean heritage) made a life for themselves, forming and transforming Caribbean culture through their adaptive strategies, their coping mechanisms, and their creative resistance.
2. To document the architectural and industrial details of sugar plantations in general and Galways in particular so as to interpret the local lifeways that emerged and evolved in such places.
3. To learn as much as possible about the daily lives of those who worked on

the plantation in the past—their material culture, their development and use of space on the mountain, their social institutions, and their cognitive frameworks.

4. To study the human ecology of this particular plantation, that is, the various ways in which the plantation was, or was not, integrated into its physical setting by its builders and managers and the ways in which both the managerial class and especially the laborers, who formed the great majority of residents, perceived and used the physical resources and adjusted to the liabilities of the entire mountain.

5. To place Galways plantation in the broader contexts of Montserrat, of the Caribbean region, and of the New World plantation systems and to better envision how, over time, Montserrat and Galways (as a local case study) became ever more integrated into, or marginalized by, the global economic system— a conflicting and contradictory process that continues to the present.

6. To interest all people in revisiting the plantation era, not to glorify it, but rather to learn how it influenced life in the Americas and to understand better the details of how enslaved African-Caribbean people and their descendants responded to the circumstances of plantation slavery and its aftermath.

Research Strategies

Archaeological field research included clearing the bush overburden from the entire site; surface collecting; selective test excavations; intensive areal excavations to sterile soil of several features in the plantation yard, the great house, the burying ground, and the slave village; mapping of the central complex; measured drawings of most features; and the processing of all artifacts (cleaning, labeling, and cataloging).

Geographical fieldwork consisted of studying all areal representations of Galways Mountain, including historic and modern maps and air photos; observing and describing the climatic and geological features of the mountain, especially the hydrologic, vegetative, and volcanic features; exploration of the entire landscape by foot and horseback accompanied by local informants who supplied place names, rationales for these names, stories about specific locations, and information on resource management activities; observing and describing the spatial and ecological features of current subsistence cultivation plots; and the mapping of all of the above.

Ethnographic research consisted of recording oral histories with the descendants of those once enslaved at Galways and documenting material culture practices such as food processing and preservation (of cassava, meat, cocoa, ginger, and coconut); recording the building, maintaining, and use of traditional stone ovens; documenting the making of nonceramic food-related tools and vessels (principally from coconut shells and calabash gourds); documenting the making of tools from a wide range of local products and the preparation for use of purchased tools such as cutlasses and hoes; documenting the making of rope and packaging from plant fiber; documenting boatbuilding, the building of wooden houses, daubing, thatching, the construction of an "underpin" house and rock-and-rubble masonry construction; recording the preparation of a donkey to carry a load, animal tending, and butchering; and recording all aspects of subsistence and market-oriented tropical small plot horticulture (Berleant-Schiller and Pulsipher 1986; Pulsipher 1994; Pulsipher and Goodwin field notes, 1982–1995).

Long-term ethno-archaeological research on Montserrat houseyards provided very specific information that aided in interpreting the signature of the Galways village per se. With the full participation and assistance of all residents, eleven yards were mapped and studied for information on the spatial arrangements of all structures and activity areas; methods of construction of the buildings and how they were anchored to the site; patterns of yard sweeping and waste disposal, both material and human or animal; and the uses of plants and animals on domestic sites. Information was also gathered on human relationships within the yard, especially including kinship and economic interaction (Pulsipher 1986b, 1987b, 1989, 1993a, 1993b, 1994).

Archival research comprised a major part of the Galways Project and was conducted independently at various repositories by Lydia Pulsipher, Mac Goodwin, and Jean Howson (whose work focused primarily on the Galways village). Many historical documents remain on the island, but the collection falls far short of a full complement of what was produced, and only a very few documents pertain to Galways specifically. Hence, most archival research was conducted in archives in Antigua and Jamaica; at the Library of Congress in Washington, D.C.; at the John Carter Brown Library in Providence, Rhode Island; at the Boston Public Library; at the University of Tennessee; at Southern Illinois University; and at the Public Record Office and other repositories in London. Helpful colleagues have provided further information from Irish and English collections.

Researchers as Actors

From the beginning of our work on Galways, we discussed how to position ourselves as scholars within the research enterprise. We decided not only that the Galways Project was to be a long-term, interdisciplinary study using as many sources of information as possible but also that our research process would involve Montserratians not as "informants" (though they certainly filled that role) but rather as colleagues who had the right to question or criticize and thereby influence the research process and results. Forming collegial relationships between rural subsistence farmers, agricultural laborers, craftspeople, homemakers, and scholars is not as difficult as it sounds, once the scholars drop their academic lingo and demeanor and acknowledge that spending long, unstructured hours as participants in the community is their part of the bargain. Only after years of association can the benefits of this sort of interaction be appreciated. Mutual trust is built, old techniques and skills are remembered and seen in a new light, personal histories are validated, insights are gained, and questions are raised that could never have found a context outside the effort involved in the mutual construction of knowledge.

This policy of inclusion in turn made it mandatory that our joint findings be interpreted, first of all, with and for the people of Galways Mountain, for the people of Montserrat, and for the many volunteers who came to Montserrat to work with us. Eventually our audiences also came to include academic colleagues and students, funding agencies, island visitors, and the interested general public—people of all ages, including hundreds of thousands of visitors to the Smithsonian Museum of Natural History, which featured the Galways research as part of the 1991–1993 "Seeds of Change" exhibit. This communication with our various audiences was, and is, the guiding principle that underlies our work. A fundamental axiom of such communication is that whenever possible we use the active voice. For the most part, when we write about our research, we use the first person, as we are largely doing in this case.

In this regard, we feel that there is a relationship, unverifiable but nonetheless valid, between our approach as actors in directing the project and reporting the results in the active voice and our view of the other players, past and present, as active decision makers in the course of their everyday lives and as creators of the vibrant Caribbean cultures of today. These players were not passive, formless recipients of action, never mind how dominating the plantation system may have been. Rather they were, for the most part, robust and inventive in their coping strategies.

Although, without question, our approach is humanistic, it in no way precludes us from employing rigorous scientific methodologies nor from using established theory to make verifiable observations about the landscape and the various natural and human impacts that affected it. Nor does it keep us from drawing from these observations reasonable inferences about the human behaviors that produced Galways Mountain the place. Nonetheless, other ways of knowing and depicting have also contributed significantly to our understanding and interpretation of this place. We have used historic maps and pictures and various forms of narrative—oral histories, folklore, printed historical accounts, correspondence, court records, legal texts, and other official documents, trade records, and church records—to gain a sense of the details of life. In presenting the work of the Galways collective, we, the directors, have written the standard academic treatises, have given slide-illustrated lectures in many venues, have written and illustrated newspaper and magazine articles, and have participated in the creation of the Smithsonian exhibit mentioned above. In an attempt to convey what E. V. Walter (1988) calls the "haptic" experience (the physical and emotional sensations) of life on Galways Mountain in the historic past, we have also written fiction and have commissioned (as well as produced ourselves) artists' renderings of life there in the eighteenth and nineteenth centuries.

Archaeologist James Deetz has spoken of the three hierarchical realms of knowledge available to the historical archaeologist: the material world, the behavioral world, and the cognitive or ideational world. We found all three worlds available to us at Galways. The material world was the most obvious and at first seemed the easiest to understand. This statement was especially true of the industrial part of the site, where it was not too difficult to decipher the main components of the sugar-processing system. The industrial site was still clearly inscribed on the landscape with stone ruins of massive proportions. The excavations almost always revealed rather clearly interpretable details—stone floors, sluices, and drains, all of which could be verified from historical sources or even from living memory.

But when we began to contemplate studying such things as the management of fresh water for human use, or subsistence gardening, which the work of Sidney Mintz and Douglas Hall (1960) had proven was enormously important in the local economy of eighteenth-century Jamaica, or of daily life in the plantation village (the last of which was one of our most important goals), we found that the material evidence was as ephemeral as a wisp because it was biodegradable. Without some prior understanding of the cognitive (ideational) and behavioral worlds of Galways people, we would very likely have missed or would at least have misinterpreted the material evidence. Oddly enough, it was necessary to understand the behavior that produced certain types of material evidence even before we were aware that the evidence existed archaeologically (this was especially true for the houseyard study, which in turn informed the slave village excavations and interpretations). And in many cases the cognitive (ideational) rationale for the behavior is only now revealed to us as, over the years, we gain greater familiarity with our Montserrat colleagues' lived experience, which in turn helps us imagine the possible ideational systems of past Galways people.

The Visible Ruins

In 1981, after the bush had been cleared from the property, the Galways Project research teams observed the remains of several buildings, ancillary structures, and landscape features that inhabitants had constructed in the latter part of the eighteenth century and then modified at later dates. During the course of several field seasons, the researchers mapped these features (figure 7.4), the principal elements of which were a cattle mill; a windmill; a boiling and curing house; a warehouse; two cistern complexes; a stone tunnel and various related passageways and retaining walls; the village (about a dozen houses were documented); and a great house with related features. Each of these is discussed briefly below and is located on the accompanying map (figure 7.4).

THE CATTLE MILL

Animal mills were the earliest type of device used to crush cane in the Caribbean. The remains of such mills are ubiquitous. Although David Galway's original lowland plantation had only a cattle mill, at least until sometime after 1729, the later, relocated complex had both a cattle mill and windmill. The cattle mill consists of a raised circular track built of earth, stone, and mortar, measuring forty feet in diameter (figure 7.5). The track passes over a wide arched passageway that affords easy access to the center of the structure. In the center of the track, on a recessed area twenty-one feet in diameter, was an upright three-roller mill. A tall post extended out of the center roller, reaching to twelve or more feet above the surface of the track. Two long sweeps were connected to the top of this post and were yoked to two teams of cattle. The cattle walked around the raised track, thereby turning the center post and the center roller, which was equipped with a band of gears around its top. As the center roller turned, its gears engaged those on the side rollers, which then turned in opposition to the center roller. Freshly cut cane was carried in through the archway and fed, a few stalks at a time, between the rollers. The cane juice collected in a pan below the rollers and flowed in a trough through the archway, down to the boiling house for processing.

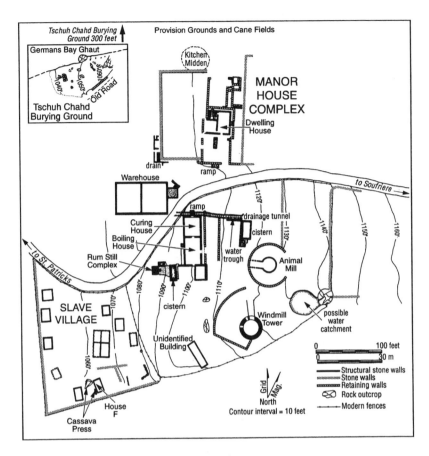

Fig. 7.4. Archaeological site plan of Galways plantation.

THE WINDMILL

The Galways windmill tower sits to the south of the cattle mill on a semicircular earthen platform supported by a thick stone retaining wall (figure 7.6). On the north side, where the retaining wall grades into the natural slope, a ramp leads to the elevated main entrance of the windmill. From this entrance, cane was fed through a three-roller mill similar to that in the cattle mill, though in this case the center post was rotated by wind-turned sails attached to a shaft and gear system located in a wooden housing at the top of the stone tower. The housing at the top of the tower and the wind sails could be rotated in and out of the wind by a long wooden "tail" attached to the opposite end of the

Fig. 7.5. The cattle mill at Galways.

Fig. 7.6. The windmill tower at Galways.

housing and extending at an angle to the semicircular earthen platform. Inside the circular mill tower, the massive wooden center post was braced by wooden beams that were set horizontally into the stone walls in a spiral pattern.

The expressed cane juice flowed down to the boiling house in a trough that fit through the smallest archway in the tower. The tall slender opening in the tower wall, which faced the earthen platform and the sea beyond, was used periodically to replace the center post that reached from the center roller to the top of the tower. Because of its length, the center post would not have fit through the main doorway. The crushed cane stalks, called bagasse, were tossed out of this narrow opening to dry in the sun on the earthworks. Once dried, these fibrous stalks were used as fuel in the sugar-boiling operation and/or as food for livestock.

The Boiling and Curing House

The Galways boiling house was the focal point of sugar processing and, as on most West Indian sugar estates in the eighteenth century, was the most impressive feature of the plantation in both form and function. The architectural design of the Galways building is classic Georgian, with nicely finished cut stone detail (figure 7.7). The building was originally roofed with red clay tiles and had a guttering system that fed rainwater into adjacent cisterns. For ventilation, the north and south gable ends of the building were pierced with circular openings fitted with wooden louvers. Like all the stone structures at Galways, the boiling house was constructed using the technique of compound masonry—mortared courses of cut, rectangular facing stones on the exterior and random-pattern facing stones on the interior, with the space in between filled with rocks and mortar (Bettesworth and Hitch 1981). The curved arches of the doors and windows of the top story, the arched vents and crawl spaces associated with the furnaces on the lower lever, and the flat arches of the curing house on the lower level north end were all constructed using mason's forms and were trimmed with matched curved or straight facing stones and centered keystones.

The builders set the boiling house into the mountain across the angle of slope in such a way that it has only one story on the upslope (east) side and two on the downslope (west) side. The south end, which is closest to the two mills, was equipped to boil the cane juice. The lower level of the south end contained the furnace and flue system that heated the boiling pots mortared along the west wall of the upper floor (figure 7.8). The north end of the building was used for storing and curing the crystallizing sugar and for collecting the byproduct, molasses.

Fig. 7.7. The boiling house is the south end (left) and the curing house the north end of this building at Galways.

Fig. 7.8. The furnace and flue vents are on the right in this west view of the sugar factory at Galways.

Off the southwest corner of the boiling house sits a series of large stone tubs arranged in irregular stair-step fashion (figure 7.9). Three are well preserved, and the remains of at least four others are visible. Although the cisterns could have been meant simply to store water drained off the red tile roof of the boiling house, we have inferred from archaeological evidence that at least part of the complex was also used in rum distilling (Goodwin 1987). In 1982, we excavated a large amount of ash from a stone-enclosed pit just upslope of the westernmost (lowest) tub. We think the ash came from fires used to heat a rum still. The water that was needed to cool the distillation coil was probably trapped on the roof of the boiling house and stored in the largest and highest cistern, where we found evidence of a stone rack for the coil. Like the rum made on Montserrat plantations in the early twentieth century (Hollander and Hannum, interviews, 1983), the rum produced at Galways was most likely relatively crude and was consumed locally, not marketed.

THE BARN/WAREHOUSE COMPLEX

About 25 feet west (downslope) of the northwest corner of the boiling house and at a right angle to it sit the remains of the largest structure on the estate. This building, some 48 × 80 feet in size, had two large rooms of equal size and was two stories in height, with its eastern end set into the slope so that the upper story was at ground level. This east end of the barn/warehouse was connected to the north entrance of the curing house by ramps set at right angles and linked by a wide stone walk. When the curing process was complete, workers could roll the large barrels from the curing room down the gently sloping stone path and into the warehouse, where they were stored until the time came for transport to the waterfront. The lower-level rooms of this building may have served as a barn for horses and storage for feed and other necessaries for the plantation (Zachs 1985).

THE GREAT HOUSE

About 100 feet to the northeast of the boiling house sits the Galways great house (figure 7.10). Because of the nearly constant wind from the east-northeast, this location protected the residence from both the fire hazards and the offensive odors that accompanied sugar processing. Furthermore, from this location the great house commanded a panoramic view of activity in the plantation yard and the Caribbean Sea far below. Although the great house is now in an advanced state of ruin, it is possible still to see that,

Fig. 7.9. The Galways cistern complex.

although it was never a grand structure, it did go through several revisions that
made it into a two-story (raised basement) stone edifice with attractive lines,
expansive galleries, and graceful staircases (Goodwin 1987:142–151). Eventually
earthquakes, hurricanes, trees, and vines destroyed it.

Initially, the great house was a modest rectangular raised-basement stone
structure with its long side set parallel to the slope. Although the second story
may have been wooden for a time, the residents eventually built a second story
of stone, with several windows facing in all four directions. At some point, the
inhabitants added a two-story stone wing extending to the west and covering
former exterior window openings. It is difficult to be sure how the wooden
gallery was configured, because the entire west wall has fallen (probably during
an earthquake either in 1899 or in the 1930s), but the second-story gallery
probably extended around the south and west sides and along the north face
of the ell created by the new wing.

The roof of the great house was probably two hipped roofs with narrow
eaves and covered with wooden shingles (no roofing tiles have been recovered).
Very likely the gallery roof was separate from, but tied into, the main roof.
This arrangement was a common strategy that kept the entire roof from being
lost if hurricane winds caught the vulnerable gallery overhang. The gallery,

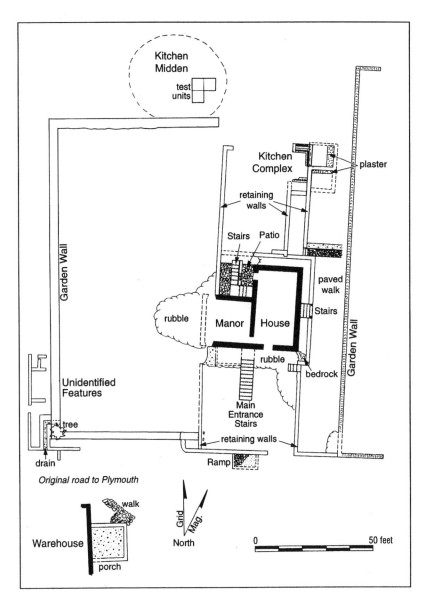

Fig. 7.10. Plan of the great house domestic complex.

which was probably supported by modest wooden columns, not only was an attractive architectural feature but also served to cool the house and provided an important vantage point from which to observe plantation activities and the sea traffic far below. On clear days, Guadeloupe was visible to the south, and Nevis and St. Kitts could be seen to the north.

The kitchen area lay about forty feet to the north of the residence (figure 7.10). It consisted of a cooking shed on a mortared stone platform, a stone oven, and several other unidentified small, mortared stone facilities. Because this area has been used as a subsistence garden for many years, the details of the site have been lost, but the area is littered with thousands of ceramic sherds from food preparation and serving vessels.

Immediately upslope of the kitchen and great house lies a road that probably led from the main road first to the great house and then across the slope to fields and a possible chapel. A burying ground lies downslope, along Germans Bay Ghaut, and the road may once have wound down to it as well. Behind the house, this road is bordered along the uphill side by a mortared and capped stone garden wall. It is likely that the great house vegetable and/or flower garden lay on the other side.

Water Management Strategies: Catchments,
Tanks, Tunnel System, and Retaining Walls

When the builders employed by Henry Dyer completed their installation of the new Galways complex on the steep, forested mountainside in the mid-eighteenth century, the natural hydrology of the environment was severely interrupted. As long as forests covered the land, the heavy rains common in the area did no special damage because the vegetation broke the force of the rain and absorbed considerable moisture through leaf, stem, and trunk surfaces. The detritus on the forest floor absorbed further moisture, storing it long enough for the plant roots to guide the droplets into the soil. Excess moisture slowly found its way into watercourses that were heavily shaded with vegetation and probably trickled with water most of the time.

After the workers cleared the land, frequent rains hit the unprotected soil hard, dislodging soil particles and lubricating their travel downslope. Erosion became a serious problem, and large volumes of water moved quickly through the system. Watercourses flowed heavily but briefly after a rainfall, carrying tons of sediment out to sea. With no protection from the sun, ground temperatures rose sharply, inhibiting the regrowth of many forest plants and greatly increasing evaporation rates. Hence, the Galways site became one that suffered in quick succession from too much water during and just after a rainstorm and then from too little moisture as stream flow stopped and the land rapidly dried out. Natural springs disappeared, and measures were needed both to protect the site and its buildings from rapidly flowing runoff and to save rainwater for future use.

Above the plantation industrial yard a walled catchment caught rainwater and channeled it into a deep stone and mortar cistern just to the north of the cattle mill. Water may also have been channeled across the present road to a large stone-walled holding tank still very evident just below the great house and known locally as the Old Dam or the Pond. The builders diverted overflow from the cistern north of the cattle mill into a tunnel (figure 7.4) that ran down just north of the boiling house under the north doorway entrance ramp. Between the cattle mill and the boiling house, there was also a series of contour stone walls to interrupt the flow of runoff and divert it into the tunnel. The tunnel discharged its flow into a watercourse running downhill along the south side of the barn/warehouse.

In the course of our investigations of the overall mountain landscape, we observed that a few small streams several hundred yards both to the north and south of the main plantation complex show distinct signs of having been modified to save water during peak periods of runoff. Someone before the modern period had constructed small stone and mud barricades (dams) across the watercourses, creating deep pools that still hold water long after a rain. We believe that the enslaved laborers created these numerous small catchments for their own use, because, first, most such features are within a short walk of the slave village and, second, none of our Montserratian colleagues/informants claimed to have known about or used, much less built, these catchments. It is not known whether the slaves had access to the more formally constructed stone reservoirs and cisterns described above, but on other plantations access to such water was sometimes strictly controlled (Smith 1987). It would therefore have been logical for slaves to have designed their own water systems.

Neaga House: The Galways Slave Village

At Galways, as on most plantations, the enslaved Africans lived in a settlement near the sugar works and within sight of the great house. On most plantations in Montserrat and on some other islands, the residents of the slave villages used the creole *Neaga House* (place where black people live) to denote their community. Although the remains of the village were no longer easily visible in 1981 when the Galways Project began, St. Patricks people knew from oral tradition where Neaga House had been and what it was called. Some specified that it was *Pond Neaga House;* in local parlance (especially in St. Patricks village), Galways estate was called Pond, probably because of the walled water catchment near the great house.

Throughout most of the eighteenth century, there were between 50 and 60 slaves at Galways, but after James Neave acquired title to the estate in 1775, the slave population seems to have begun increasing slowly. Between 1810 and 1834 (emancipation), the enslaved labor force had nearly tripled to between 151 and 158 (Howson 1995). The slaves lived in a cluster of wooden houses—we identified twelve archaeologically but believe that many more remain to be uncovered—on a tract of approximately two acres just below the boiling house and windmill (figure 7.4).

The houses were rectangular and varied in size from 8 × 16 feet to 10 × 20 feet. From the archaeological evidence, we have inferred that the houses were built of wood and were raised above ground level on notched *nogs* (slender wood posts) that were set in holes carved in the underlying volcanic bedrock (figure 7.11). The residents of several of these houses then trimmed up the spaces between the nogs with a course of unmortared stones laid under the walls around the structure's perimeter. This feature, called a *groundsel,* can still be seen under many older wooden houses throughout the eastern Caribbean and was apparently a mark of status or well-being. The houses in Neaga House were irregularly arranged on informal terraces across a sloped hillside. They were probably thatched with cane leaves and were undoubtedly surrounded by small gardens, useful trees, and animal pens.

In the areas around the houses, the people prepared and ate their meals, raised their children, made tools, repaired their clothes, and generally provided for their families. All these domestic activities had to be done early in the morning, late at night, and on Sundays, because most of their daylight hours were spent laboring for the plantation. Nevertheless, these Galways people were more fortunate than many of their counterparts elsewhere on Montserrat and in the West Indies. Despite the hardships of being enslaved, the Galways village inhabitants seem to have been able to provide for themselves a fairly high level of material well-being, especially for a slave population. As Jean Howson (1995) has shown, the people of Galways Neaga House owned a wide range of European ceramics of several different forms. Most notable are the decorative plates, which Howson argues were purchased primarily for display, since the local cuisine required bowls for serving (1995). We think the villagers earned the money for their dishes and other purchased items by growing gardens on land unsuitable for sugarcane, usually high in the mountains to the east of the

Fig. 7.11. Nog holes outside the groundsel at Galways house A.

plantation. As Mintz and Hall (1960) have argued for Jamaica, these gardens provided surpluses beyond subsistence that could be sold for cash or traded for other goods. Particular crops could be preserved and banked for future gain. Cassava, for example, could be made into bread that could be stored for as long as six months and then sold. Cocoa could be made into cocoa logs that had a relatively long shelf life, and ginger could be preserved as candy. Surplus sweet potatoes could be fed to pigs, which could be sold or butchered when the market was favorable. In 1986, our Montserratian colleagues found the archaeological remains of two cassava presses in the Galways village (figure 7.12) that are exactly like those still in use for similar community or family cassava-processing enterprises. We are all convinced that past Galways people had similar, possibly cooperative enterprises aimed at generating cash.

Jean Howson (1995) used the ceramics excavated at Galways to explore the possibility that people in this particular village engaged in the acquisition of specific types of ceramics for their symbolic value—that is, because of the meaning such pieces conveyed to the village community about the status of the households that displayed them. The assemblage recovered archaeologically included both imported ceramics and locally made earthenwares. The manufacturing dates for the imported ceramics, nearly all of which were European

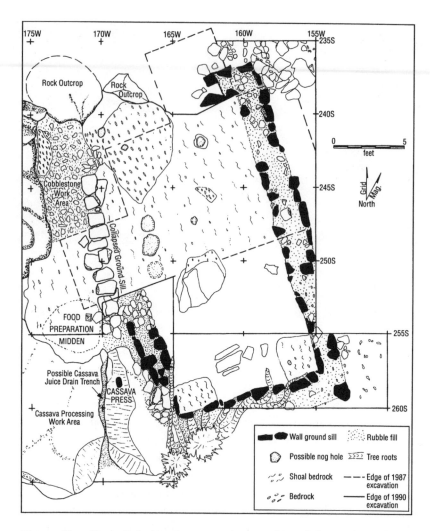

Fig. 7.12. Plan of house F, showing the cassava press located in rock faces to the southwest.

in origin, ranged between circa 1770 and circa 1870. Howson identified five principal decorative types of imported wares: plain or undecorated; shell-edged; transfer-printed and molded white-bodied; painted; and a category we might call banded (including dipped annular, sponged, cut-sponged, and lined decorations). When the collection as a whole was considered, she found that decorated vessels were more numerous than undecorated vessels and that printed wares predominated, with the percentage of this type increasing slightly during the nineteenth century (possibly reflecting the decrease in the price of printed whitewares relative to other types due to manufacturing efficiencies). Elsewhere in the Caribbean, archaeologists also have found high percentages (25 percent or more) of printed wares in slave ceramic assemblages, indicating that, like Galways people, they were able to acquire these goods well before they became wage earners (Howson 1995).

Howson's findings become yet more interesting when she assesses the significance of the relative numbers of plates and bowls and of the dominant decorations in the two categories. Imported ceramic bowls and plates were both popular items in the slave village. Inasmuch as locally made earthenware bowls were also very common in the archaeological record, it is safe to say that bowls were probably the more often used form. This statement fits with what we know about African West Indian foodways even in the recent past: namely, people cooked outside and ate in informal groupings in the houseyard, sitting on doorsteps and convenient boulders ("yard stones"). The most frequent fare was a vegetable stew seasoned with as much meat as people could afford. Hence, bowls were the chosen vessels for eating. The bowls tended to be rather plain: 50 percent were simply banded, and less than 15 percent were printed.

But what of the also numerous plates found at Galways? Unlike the bowls, these plates tended to have printed designs, usually idyllic scenes of life in Europe or Asia. Although it was possible to buy whole sets of such plates, there is no evidence that Galways people owned sets. They seem rather to have chosen a variety of printed designs in their holdings. Howson argues that slaves at Galways acquired printed plates, not for their function as part of the food service, but rather as display items. Printed plates were a visible symbol of success in the economic activities that were open to the Galways laborers—primarily the production of surpluses in their small plot cultivations and the making and selling of cassava bread and, possibly, other preserved foods as well as the raising and marketing of small animals like pigs, goats, and chickens. The ability to display ceramic plates not only indicated economic success but was also a Creole expression of household status within the village community (Howson 1995). In the village, then, the printed plates were for display to demonstrate household success, whereas at the great house, printed plates were for dining per se. As Deetz has suggested (1977), in Anglo-American culture there was a move away from older, more communal forms of serving food to increasing emphasis on the autonomy of the individual, each with his or her own place setting. This trend was not in evidence at the Galways Neaga House. Here plates served a symbolic role, whereas bowls had a dual purpose.

Howson argues that bowls were banded rather than printed like the plates because the bowls had both symbolic and practical uses. She suggests that people used the bowls both for food consumption and as an expression of the economic ability to acquire imported goods. There seems to be a third factor at work, however. Although printed bowls were available, the slaves chose mostly bowls with various kinds of banded decorations—stripes, mocha, stamped, sponged, and painted—bright multicolored designs against plain backgrounds. Howson believes that preferences for these graphically varied decorations on the bowls in everyday use may represent a remnant of an African aesthetic favoring bright, bold patterns that was transported to the New World. When similarly bright and bold patterns were encountered in European ceramics, they were chosen for everyday use (Howson 1995).

Tschuh-Chahd: The Burying Ground

A small burying ground lies in the bush right on the edge of Germans Bay Ghaut a little over 300 feet north and downhill from the great house ruins and completely out of sight of the slave village (figure 7.13). Three carved stones marked human interments, and piles of fieldstone extending from them seemingly defined the graves. Several other piles of fieldstone lay near at hand, possibly marking other burials. The relatively level area had long been abandoned, and in more recent times, cultivators had used it to grow vegetables and graze livestock.

The Galways team excavated a portion of this graveyard in 1987 and conducted additional limited testing in 1990. Our specific research goals were: (1) to define the boundaries of the burying ground; (2) to determine who was buried there (whether plantation owners and managers or enslaved Africans); and (3) to begin to gather comparative data on human nutrition on British Caribbean plantations during the period of slavery.

We recovered the remains of seventeen individuals; fourteen of them came from Grave Site 1 (figure 7.13) and the remaining three from Grave Site 3. The excavations revealed that specific sites within the burying ground were reused repeatedly, with little or no regard for previous burials. Apparently when the gravediggers encountered a previous interment, they simply collected the skeletal remains in nonarticulated assemblages and reburied them in the sidewalls of the burial shaft. Of the seventeen individuals, five were of African descent, six were either African, European, or of mixed ancestry, and the ethnicity or gender attributes of the remaining six could not be determined. We present a summary of statistics in table 7.1 (a more complete analysis appears in Goodwin et al. 1992).

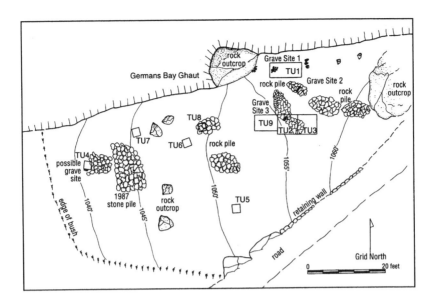

Fig. 7.13. Plan of the *Tschuh Chahd* burying ground.

The artifacts we recovered from the excavations provide a terminus post quem of circa 1830 for the burials. As a result—and since none of the individuals could be identified positively as being of European descent, whereas several of them were positively identified as being of African ethnicity—we inferred that the individuals interred here came from the Galways slave population. We recovered several different kinds of grave goods—fragments from clay pipes, wine glass and bottle glass fragments, white glass buttons, clothing fasteners of copper alloy, and ceramic sherds. The sherds came from nine locally made bowls and jars and eight imported vessels—four plates, three bowls, and one "Buckley-type" flat-bottomed pan.

Individual I0003, the sixty-plus-year-old woman, was the only fully articulated skeletal remains we recovered. She not only had a headstone marking her grave but also was buried in a coffin on which there was a badly deteriorated decorative iron plaque. She had been clothed in garments that fastened with white glass buttons and brass hooks and eyes. She had a number of kaolin clay pipes nearby that appeared to have been buried with her. It is not unusual to find pipes associated with women; some mature West Indian women smoked pipes in slavery days, and some smoke corncob pipes even today. Given the circumstances of her burial—a marked grave, a decorated

Table 7.1. Individuals from the *Tschuh Chahd* Burying Ground.

Individual	Ethnicity	Sex	Age	Pathology
I0001	African	Male	15-18	Cribra orbitalia
I0002	African	Female	18-25	None observed
I0003	African	Female	60+	Osteoarthritis, enthesophytes, osteophytosis, ectocranial porosis, periostitis of the feet, a well-healed skull fracture, tooth loss, and teeth grooves from pipe smoking
I0004	African	Male	20-25	Hyperstosis frontalis interna
I0005	Indeterminate	Indeterminate	Adult	None observed
I0006	Indeterminate	Female	20-30	None observed
I0007	African	Male	14-16	Cribra orbitalia
I0008	Indeterminate	Female	Adult	Teeth grooves from pipe smoking
I0009	Indeterminate	Female	Adult	None, only cranial bones remain
I0010	Indeterminate	Male	Adult	None, only cranial bones remain
I0011	Indeterminate	Indeterminate	Adult	None, only cranial bones remain
I0012	Can't be Determined	Can't be Determined	5	None, only deciduous teeth remain
I0013	Can't be Determined	Can't be Determined	5	None, only deciduous teeth remain
I0014	Can't be Determined	Can't be Determined	3-4	None, only deciduous teeth remain
I0015	Can't be Determined	Can't be Determined	3-4	None, only deciduous teeth remain
I0016	Can't be Determined	Can't be Determined	18-24 months	None, only deciduous teeth remain
I0017	Can't be Determined	Can't be Determined	12-18 months	None, only deciduous teeth remain

coffin, the garments that clothed her, and the artifactual remains—individual Io003 certainly appears to have attained a position of prominence within the Galways community. The particular role she played, however, will probably never be known.

NUTRITION AND HEALTH

The most interesting results came from the pathological examination of the human skeletal remains. The Galways slave population, as represented by this sample, was relatively healthy, especially by comparison with slaves found at the Seville site in Jamaica (Baker 1993; Fleischman and Armstrong 1990), the Bransby site in Montserrat (Mann et al. 1987; Watters 1987), or the Newton site in Barbados (Handler and Corruccini 1983; Handler and Lange 1978), where investigators reported significant signs of malnutrition. One Galways individual exhibited normal signs of aging, and three had minor to moderate indications of anemia, which may or may not have been nutritionally based. None of the individuals had significant signs of malnutrition. How do we explain the differences?

We argue that at Galways the slaves had a much better diet than was available in many other Caribbean locations, including the Bransby, Newton, and Seville sites (Goodwin et al. 1992). They not only grew food and raised animals in the village but also had access to many favorable garden locations relatively close to the village in high, well-watered environments where they could grow a multiplicity of nutritious crops.

Getting the Essence of It

Two recurring texts weave the tale of Galways plantation. One belongs to the owners and managers of the estate. The other is the narrative of the plantation workers. Each of these two groups had different goals: management sought to make money and achieve position and power; workers, to attain freedom, self-determination, and the ability to make a life for themselves. Their aims were often in conflict, yet sometimes they reached unspoken accommodation.

THE MANAGERS' TALE

Galways plantation, like all the other West Indian estates, in large part reflected its owner's desire to acquire wealth quickly. When Henry Dyer moved to better-watered, more fertile land, higher on the slopes of Galways Mountain in the 1760s and directed the building of his new sugar works, he installed the most current technological innovations and followed the newest management strategies to increase efficiency. He built a windmill but retained the slower, less efficient animal mill as a backup. He used the "Jamaica train" boiling system for sugar production because it was more efficient in the use of fuel and was better suited to mass production of muscovado sugar. This "black" sugar crystallized out in about half the time it took to make white sugar. Even though the price was lower for muscovado, then, he could make more of it faster and could therefore use it to turn greater profits—a capitalist expression of quantity over quality.

Many aspects of the plantation were managed for efficiency and sustainability. Bagasse, the by-product of cane crushing, had several uses. It could serve as silage for cattle feed. Sun-dried bagasse could be used as fuel to boil down the cane juice. Ash produced by the furnace in the boiling house was mixed with manure and applied to the fields as fertilizer. Water, always a matter for concern in any settlement, was managed carefully. As previously mentioned, Dyer instituted a sophisticated system to provide clean water for people and livestock. To protect his expensive structures against heavy rains and erosion, he built an elaborate system of retaining walls, cisterns, drains, and tunnels.

Spatially, the sugar industrial complex was arranged much like an assembly line that used gravity to ease the transportation of materials at several stages. The upslope mills sent the newly pressed juice downslope to the boiling house. The curing house was next in line, with the rack for storing the barrels of curing sugar at the same level as the boiling system. The molasses that dripped from these barrels was caught at the lower level near the rum still where the molasses was used to make strong drink. Meanwhile, the distillation tube of the rum works was cooled in a cistern just above the still by rainwater caught off the roof of the boiling house. The warehouse stood off to one side and slightly downslope of the sugar works so that the barrels could be rolled into it (Goodwin 1987:151–155). Throughout this operation, Dyer and his laborers took optimal advantage of the specific environmental setting and spatial relationships of Galways Mountain.

Eighteenth-century planters wrote treatises on how to run a sugar plantation efficiently. William Belgrove (1755) and Samuel Martin (1765 and 1773) are the best-known authors. On Montserrat, by the third quarter of the eighteenth century, Henry Dyer, James Neave, and other planters took these ideas of plantation management to heart. They had little fear of a crop failure due to poor management (Campbell 1774, v.II). Dyer, by implementing "plantership," was expressing his desire to acquire wealth. His ultimate failure, so that Galways went into receivership, mostly reflects declining world sugar prices and Montserrat's insignificance in the sugar system because of its small size and lack of a safe harbor. The abolition of slavery in 1834 probably also had little to do with the demise of Galways as an enterprise. In fact, the slow decline very likely began as soon as the first David Galway occupied the land in the 1660s. The steep terrain, the tropical environment, the monocrop agriculture system, the location of the estate on the island and of the island in the region, the slave-labor system, the transportation and marketing arrangements—all worked against the sustainability of the operation for more than a few decades.

The Workers' Tale

Does the demise of Galways as a sugar plantation mean that the people of Galways Mountain were failures? Clearly not! The image of the Galways community that emerges from our interdisciplinary study demonstrates that even under the harsh conditions of slavery, Galways people constructed a well-ordered family and community life for themselves (Pulsipher and Goodwin 1999). They became managers of their physical environment, skillfully using the natural resources of Galways Mountain to maximize their subsistence efforts. They brought horticultural gardening techniques from Africa and improved on them in the new environment. They successfully modified Amerindian methods of cultivating and processing crops like beans, corn, squash, cassava, cocoa, vanilla, pineapple, soursop, peanuts, sweet potatoes, and tannia. One of the most significant discoveries in the village at Galways was the area where people apparently had been processing cassava on a cooperative and possibly commercial basis.

Such entrepreneurial activities sometimes made it possible for slaves to save some money. Although slaves rarely amassed substantial sums, we know from the archaeology of the village at Galways that they regularly bought items in the market and stores of Plymouth, the capital. The many thousands of fragments of European and Asian bowls, plates, cups, and clay tobacco pipes that were found throughout the village were commonly sold in colonial market towns throughout the Americas. Those found in the slave village were not simply discards from the great house, because the patterns and shapes found there are quite different. Rather, in all likelihood, slaves used the money they earned in a wide variety of activities to buy these items for their homes.

There were even more fragments of various vessels made of red clay. These wares in many shapes and sizes were used to carry and store water, to store beans and flour and sugar, and to cook and to eat out of. A study, interrupted by the recent volcanic activity, was under way to determine whether these heavy red clay pots, bowls, jugs, and griddles were made locally or whether, perhaps, they were exchanged in a formal or informal trading network between islands.

THE END OF THE TALE

The history of Galways plantation can be seen as reflecting the long struggle against the dehumanizing aspects of slavery. Yet the slaves were able to gain some measure of independence, health, and self-determination. A range of factors came together to make their accomplishments possible. The mountainous location of the estate provided moist, fertile, and covert locations for "secret gardens." The apparent shift in management strategies in the late eighteenth century eased some conditions of everyday life for slaves. But most of all, the desire to improve their situation prompted Galways people to put virtually all free time to use in entrepreneurial activities such as gardening and other cooperative production—activities that provided a degree of physical health (as seen in the human skeletal remains) and material well-being (as reflected in the abundance of purchased items recovered archaeologically in the Galways village).

There is much yet to be learned about the lifeways of those who comprised the great laboring majority at Galways on Montserrat and on the scores of other plantations throughout the islands. Nevertheless, the insights already gained have demonstrated some of the many ways in which life then bore systemic connections with life today. In thousands of such villages across the islands, Caribbean people drew from many cultural strains to construct the present Creole culture: cuisine, architecture, belief systems, language, music, dance, literature, family organization, and economic relationships.

Epilogue

And what of the word *Gadinge?* Although much more study is required, it now seems possible that the word is one of those rare instances in which Gaelic may yet survive in Montserrat creole. Linguists tell us that, contrary to popular opinion, Montserratian is not the relic language of seventeenth-century Irish indentured servants who adopted English. Rather, like other English creoles in the islands, Montserratian, though it retains many influences of early English pronunciation and word usage, is in fact a language created in the West Indies from primarily European and African linguistic traditions that were then transformed by the New World experience.

We propose here, for the first time, that *Gadinge* derives from the Gaelic word *Garrdhanta,* meaning "gardens," and that it was an early place name first used by the Irish indentures who lived on the lower reaches of Galways Mountain in the 1670s to designate the place high up and across the ridge where the enslaved Africans and possibly surviving native Taino Indians were cultivating at the time. Montserratians today refer to their cultivation plots not as gardens but rather as "grounds." Hence the meaning of the Gaelic word did not survive the cultural and biological absorption of the Irish minority into the African-Montserratian population, but the place name did survive albeit slightly mispronounced.

PART 3
CARIBBEAN CULTURES

8

CREOLIZATION IN SEVENTEENTH-CENTURY BARBADOS
Two Case Studies

Thomas C. Loftfield

Deetz (1977), Reitz and Scarry (1985), and Faulkner and Faulkner (1987) were among the first of many to argue that once a colonist set foot on the new shore, a process began that ultimately transformed the cultural behavior of the colonist into something new and different from what it had been in the home country. This change was wrought by accommodation to new environments, both physical and social. The exact nature of the changes depended on the cultural origin of the settlers and the particular regions where they settled.

In addition to cultural changes attendant upon residence in a new physical environment, change occurred as a consequence of exposure to new cultures. In the Caribbean these new cultures were represented by Europeans, indigenous Amerindian populations, and African populations forcefully relocated to the New World because of the slave trade. In the Caribbean, this process of culture change has been called creolization.

No understanding of Caribbean culture can be attempted without an examination of the creolization process. Whereas many early investigations of postcontact Caribbean cultures assumed that European culture had been transplanted wholesale from the metropole, most recent attempts at understanding the development of local cultures in the Caribbean have focused on the search for African influences. Neither of these earlier approaches is sufficient. The best understanding of the development of culture in the historic-period Caribbean can come only from syntheses derived from study of transplanted European culture, indigenous Amerindian culture, transplanted African culture, and the changes that each of these underwent as a consequence of exposure to the others and to what was a new physical environment for two of them.

Historical archaeological work currently being conducted in Barbados, West Indies, has sought to examine the early stages of creolization in the seventeenth century. Specific cases studied include the development of a vernacular system of defense and fortification and the evolution of a local ceramics industry. Both case studies illustrate components of the creolization process as manifested in this particular island.

Vernacular Military Architecture in Seventeenth-Century Barbados

Barbados is the southeastern-most island in the Caribbean, although it is really an Atlantic island (figure 8.1). Its earliest discovery by Europeans is shrouded in some mystery, but the island was apparently given its name by Portuguese sailors in the sixteenth century. Other early landings by Europeans are uncertain, but some pigs were set free by the Portuguese, or others, in the late sixteenth century, and all of the Amerindian population had been removed by the time the English first noted the island in 1625.

Colonization began in 1627 with the arrival of four ships from England. The location of Barbados both to windward and upcurrent of all other Caribbean Islands placed it in a very important strategic position in the days of sailing ships. From Barbados, a force under sail could maneuver downwind to attack any other island. A return attacker, however, would be forced into a long and difficult beat to windward to reach Barbados. Even though the British had grasped this strategic fact by the middle of the seventeenth century, the local inhabitants were allowed to be almost entirely responsible for the defense of the island until the early eighteenth century.

To gain a perspective on the methods of defense employed in Barbados during the period of local responsibility, a systematic survey of fortifications was undertaken in 1992 and 1993. The survey employed a local ordnance survey map that identified the known or presumed locations of fortifications. Those forts that could be located were visited, photographed, and sketched. Inventories of ordnance known to be at each fort were then consulted to determine the extent to which individual forts were actually outfitted. The following discussion derives from the data produced during the systematic survey.

From the perspective of local defense, the island was vulnerable on its western and southern sides. The north and east coasts were protected naturally by reefs, vertical cliff faces with crashing surf at the bottom, and a general

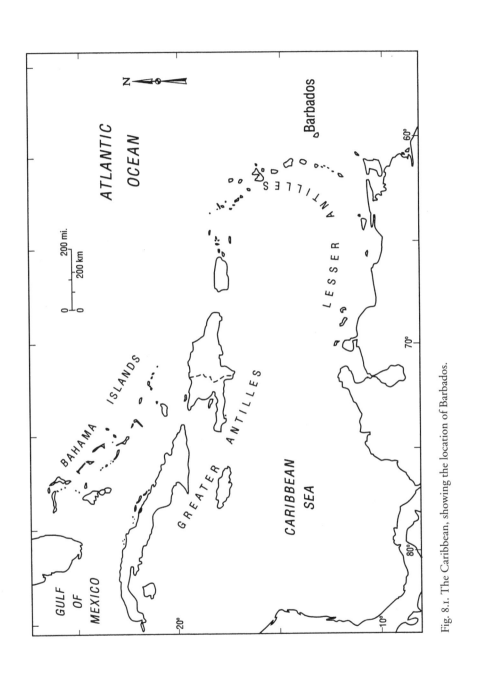

Fig. 8.1. The Caribbean, showing the location of Barbados.

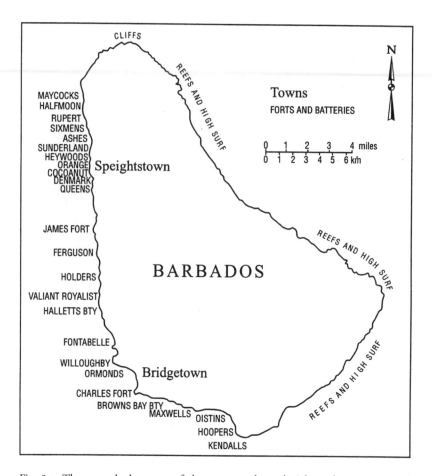

Fig. 8.2. The general placement of the seventeenth- and eighteenth-century coastal fortifications in Barbados. The map is derived from known locations of fortifications, from surviving place names, and from period maps.

lack of landing places. Landings could be effected, however, at numerous places on the southwest and western sides along a twenty-four-mile stretch of beach (figure 8.2). The seventeenth-century colonists set out to defend this vulnerable stretch of coastline. The system of defense that was adopted displays elements derived from defense systems then current in England but designed and implemented locally. Thus the system, though at heart English, was modified for the particulars in Barbados.

The seventeenth-century Barbados system of defense was ingenious in that it accommodated available manpower and financial resources, yet it was faulty in that it incorporated a number of potential military errors. The system was politically palatable in that it was predicated upon a strong sense of local government that dictated a distrust of professional soldiers.

SETTLEMENT AND EARLY DEVELOPMENT

From its beginning as an English colony, the island was fraught with troubles. The island had been claimed for James the First by Captain John Powell on May 14, 1625. Upon discovery by the English, two brothers, Sir Peter and Sir William Courteen, organized for settlement of the island. On February 17, 1627, four ships, under the command of Henry Powell, John's younger brother, landed eighty colonists at Holetown on the west coast. The constitutionality of this venture is unclear. Inconsistent and opposing documentary evidence suggests that the brothers Courteen had no patent from the king, so that their colonists were little more than squatters (Beckles 1990:7). As proprietor, Courteen made all rules and laws for land tenure. His policy dictated that settlers could not own land but would plant crops, give them to the resident agent, and be paid a labor wage of £100 per year. The island was, therefore, a company colony with the colonists as employees.

The Courteen regime was short lived. On July 22, 1627, Charles I granted letters of patent for the colonization of Barbados and the other "Caribee islands" to James Hay, the Earl of Carlisle (Beckles 1990:8; Harlow 1926:8). This patent led to political and economic tension on the island that was further exacerbated by the issuance of a patent to the Earl of Pembroke (acting for Courteen) that included Barbados and several other islands. Carlisle obtained a second patent on April 1, 1628, that clearly negated the Pembroke patent (Beckles 1990:8; Harlow 1926:9). During the interim, the Powell faction on the island maintained control by firmly resisting the newer contenders. After receiving his second patent, Carlisle issued land grants to a London merchant group that then invested £10,000 in the island's development. Charles Wolverton was dispatched to Barbados as agent and arrived in June 1628. By August, he had consolidated all factions under his control, and on September 4 he was selected governor of Barbados. Although Courteen's men were systematically excluded from government, the quarrel did not end. The ownership of land remained in dispute as well as land policy itself. Throughout the 1630s, continuing factionalism kept the island divided politically.

During the English civil war and parliamentary interregnum, Barbados attempted to be neutral. Richard Ligon (1657), visiting in the late 1640s, commented that royalists and parliamentarians were particularly friendly with each other and even avoided using the words "Roundhead" and "Cavalier." The friendship, however, merely masked deeper disputes, and after the execution of Charles I, intrigues in London affected politics on the island, culminating in the Cromwellian "invasion" of 1651.

The political and social divisions within the island population had two results that affected the means of island defenses. First, because there was always internal friction of relatively large proportion, neither side was willing to tolerate a strong military presence on the part of the other. Second, the island developed early a strong and abiding affection for local rule. This feature again thwarted the presence on the island of a strong professional military from the metropole. Island defenses centered on the militia, a local manifestation of the English system of "trained bands" established in 1573.

Although the militia rules and laws are cumbersome to enumerate, they can be distilled into the statement that every able-bodied white person participated, with certain large landowners being designated officers. The land defense of the island was thus primarily in the hands of amateurs. The militia did, however, suit local sentiments. An anonymous commentary written in 1667 or 1668, after or shortly before the end of England's war with France and Holland, alluded quite clearly to the controlling feeling on the island. According to this commentary, when the governor, Lord Willoughby, urged that a thousand troops be paid to man the forts in time of war, the local response was that it would be better to lose everything than to have veteran soldiers on the island (Handler and Shelby 1973:120).

The militia system was particularly effective in Barbados because of the island's large white population. By the 1660s, the militia could muster close to 10,000 men, including gunners for the forts and regiments of foot and horse supported by field artillery. The white population declined thereafter, but the militia numbers did not fall below 6,000. Despite the apparently large numbers, the quality of the Barbados trained bands is open to question. The same anonymous commentator noted above decried the ability of the militia to gather in defense of the island and suggested that there was, in fact, little substance to the island's defenses.

DEFENSIVE STRUCTURES

The defensive structures of seventeenth-century Barbados fell into two broad categories. Near Bridgetown, the major city, two formal fortifications were constructed in about the middle of the seventeenth century, Needham Fort (named Charles Fort after the restoration), the larger of the two (figure 8.3), and Fort Willoughby. These structures appear to have followed the then current "Italian" plan, with bastions and ditches. The two forts, supported by James Fort and Ormonds Battery, commanded Carlisle Bay, the anchorage and

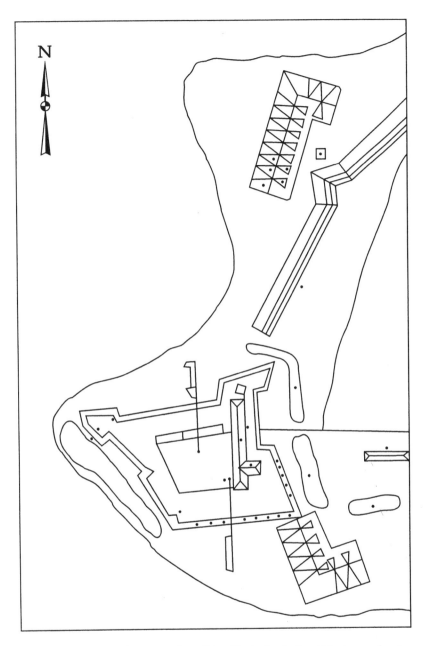

Fig. 8.3. Early nineteenth-century plan of Fort Charles by the Royal Engineers, showing the formal and professional design of the fort after European military models.

approach to Bridgetown. Given the prevailing winds and currents, the forts were located at the point on the island most easily attacked by square-rigged sailing ships (Trollope 1991, personal communication 1994). These two forts were designed by professional military engineers and are inherently different in concept from the locally designed forts described below.

The other category of defensive works consisted of a chain of "forts" that were, in effect, little more than barbettes, or gun platforms (figure 8.4). By the end of the seventeenth century, a line of these forts had been constructed along the leeward side of the island from Speightstown to Oistins (figure 8.2). With approximately twenty-four miles of vulnerable coastline to defend, these little gun emplacements were intended to drive off landing parties. Their placement, almost entirely on the littoral and eschewing the higher cliffs and rocks from which a downward fire could be directed, shows that their intended use was to prevent, or at least discourage, landings of enemy personnel on the shore.

Campbell (1975:3) has suggested that the plan of defense called for the forts to prevent landings, and if these forts were breached, for the militia, in line behind the forts, to force the enemy to retreat. This exact sequence was played out on November 22, 1651, during the attempt by Sir George Ayscue to overthrow the royalist government of Barbados. In this engagement, Captain Morris with 200 men attacked and captured James Fort at Holetown. Although Morris was able to force and bypass the fort quickly, his party was not strong enough to face the militia and was forced to retreat to the ships. Ayscue's success a few months later was due entirely to internal divisions within the ranks of the Barbadian defenders.

The only other test of the system came in 1665 when the Dutch Admiral De Ruyter attacked Bridgetown. In this event, the admiral chose a frontal assault. His ships fired upon the forts defending the town, but the return fire of cannon from the forts was so great that the admiral's own ship was disabled, and after a protracted series of attacks lasting the better part of a day, the admiral was compelled to abandon his attempt on Barbados. This attack, focused as it was on the major defenses of Bridgetown, clearly did not involve any of the small barbettes along the coast.

The same anonymous mid-seventeenth-century commentator noted above also describes the general condition of defense. He noted that there were many places where six or seven miles intervened between coast forts, and nowhere were they less than three or four miles apart (Handler and Shelby 1973:120). By the end of the seventeenth century, however, lines of trenches were in place to connect the forts together.

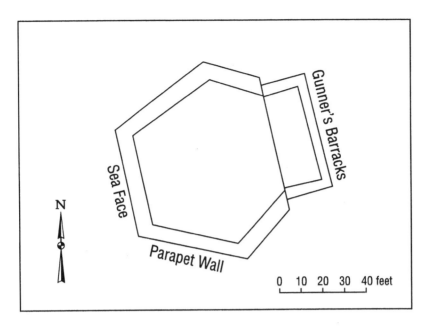

Fig. 8.4. Ruperts Battery, typical of the small gun platforms and barbettes designed and built by the local militia. The guns, on a five-sided platform backed by a gunners' barracks, fired over a low parapet wall along the sea face and the two sides attached thereto. From an early eighteenth-century plan by the Royal Engineers.

Antecedents to the coastal gun platform system of defense may be found in Europe prior to the establishment of the system in Barbados. By the beginning of the seventeenth century, European defenses had taken on several distinct forms. In the south, the Italians had perfected the bastion system of fortified defense, in which an attacking enemy was subjected to an enfilading fire from two different directions (Hughes 1991:88). This system relied on heavy stone and brick structures, with relatively few guns firing slowly and with short ranges. In contrast, the northern Europeans (primarily Germans and Poles) had developed a system that relied on massive firepower from well-developed gun platforms (Hughes 1991:88). At the same time the English, with a long coastline to defend, had developed a system of small bastion forts with connecting trenches for coastal defense.

In the abstract, then, the Barbadian system mimicked elements of the northern European defense plan, with an array of large guns designed to thwart an attack by means of massive frontal firepower. It had as well elements of the Italian system of forts with bastions, and it contained the small forts to be used with trenches for coastal defense. The design of the coastal batteries, however,

Fig. 8.5. Maycocks fort.

distinguished Barbados from contemporary Europe. These all appear to have been designed and constructed locally and benefited little, if at all, from formal military instruction. The forts have no apparent bastions or outer works for self-protection. Surviving examples and extant plans show that most had no landward-facing defenses, eschewing even loop holes for small arms fire toward the land (figure 8.5). Finally, the barracks for the gunners had massive walls located behind the guns that would have produced extensive ricochet and flying stone splinters from in-coming fire, exposing the gun crews within the forts to potentially extensive casualties (Trollope, personal communication 1994).

The closest European parallel to the Barbadian system appears in eighteenth-century coastal defenses in Malta. As the Knights sought to improve their coastal defenses in the mid-eighteenth century, they employed coastal defense batteries, which had been developed by the French at the end of the seventeenth century. Fort St. Louis (1692–1697) at Toulon is a typical example, according to Hughes (1991:133). These French-inspired batteries consisted of a semicircular sea face with embrasures for four to eight guns to fire through the parapet. The garrison was typically housed in two rooms located at the rear of the fort. More sophisticated than the Barbadian form, the French forts had loopholes for muskets and a redan with similar loopholes for defense of the land face (Hughes 1991:133).

In almost all cases, the Barbadian barbette forts stand immediately adjacent to the water. Today the sea is actually lapping at the bases of most of these forts, but eighteenth-century accounts suggest that they may have been a little farther from the water's edge. P. F. Campbell, quoting from the "Act for Better Security of Forts, Bays, and Batteries" (September 28, 1715), and the "Act for the Better Establishment of the Several Fortifications" (October 12, 1715), has found evidence that the forts had ditches full of cactus and thorns "in front" to assist in defense (Campbell 1975:3). People were fined if their domestic animals browsed these thorns and cacti to the detriment of the defense. Whether "in front" means on the land side or the sea side is unclear, but the sea side is strongly implied.

The siting of the forts so close to the sea made them vulnerable to gunfire from attacking ships. First noted in 1705 by Colonel Christian Lilly of the Royal Engineers (Lilly 1978), the bad placement of the forts was again noted by Governor Pinfold in his report of 1762 (Pinfold 1762). The governor commented that not only could the large guns of ships effectively batter the barbettes, but small arms fire from the ships' tops would have put the gunners at extreme risk. Although the governor was not a military man himself, his report probably passed on observations made by men with military training.

The siting, then, appears to have been dictated by a belief that the forts needed to be close to the sea to repel invaders. The locations seem rarely to have taken advantage of nearby rises or prominences. This is most clearly seen at Maycocks Fort, which was probably constructed in the 1690s. The two forts that compose this complex are located on the first terrace above the littoral, at an elevation less than 10 feet above sea level. Within one-quarter mile to the west, however, the land rises to an elevation over 100 feet above sea level with an almost vertical cliff face. Not only is the fort's location hot and sweltering because the cliff blocks the wind, but if the cliff top were taken by the enemy, the fort would be forced into immediate surrender. The report of Governor Pinfold spells out the conditions at Maycocks.

Maycocks Fort in a small semicircular Bay it is built on the strand surrounded by high cliffs, and the ascent so narrow and steep that a few men are able to keep down a thousand. The landing place is close by the fort, but no enemy could ever think of descent here, except he could suppose that everyone was asleep within two or three miles of it. It may be of service to cover a small vessel from a privateer, as it is on a point difficult to turn at some seasons, but can be of no other use. On the top of the cliff above the fort there is a small semicircular brest work which is likewise marked in the mapps by the name Maycocks Fort; it never has been finished, and it would be difficult to get guns up to it, but it is a proper brest work to fire into the other fort, and is every way a fitter place for a battery, not being commanded by the small arms of the ships tops which the fort must be, and even exposed to the fire from the decks. (Pinfold 1762)

The defensive value of upland locations was realized in the early eighteenth century when a series of "cliff forts" was established to protect the sea forts. Campbell notes that during the seventeenth century there were a few cliff forts located about a mile inland from the sea forts, but these served primarily as lookouts to alert the sea forts (Campbell 1975:3).

Finally, in a well-presented article on St. Ann's Castle, P. F. Campbell has pointed out that there was no refuge of last desperation (a Dos D'Asne or "Dod'ane") in Barbados during the seventeenth century to which the populace could retire in the event that a superior enemy gained a foothold on the island (Campbell 1975:1–16). Many other islands had such refuges at the time; they were intended to protect the island populace until additional forces could be mustered from other islands or from the metropole. The refuges were thus meant to withstand a siege of several months' duration.

The lack of a Dod'ane in Barbados again indicates an accommodation to local conditions. Although Dod'anes were common in other Caribbean islands, especially the Lesser Antilles, where populations were small, the population in Barbados was simply too great to be accommodated in a defensive shelter. Indeed, it has been argued that the very size of the population in Barbados was one of the greatest deterrents to enemy attack during the colonial period (Trollope, personal communication 1994).

By the middle of the seventeenth century, Barbados enjoyed relative security based on a large white population, a sizable militia, and its geographic position. Placed in the context of global geopolitics of the time, it was unlikely to suffer a successful attack, as indeed history has shown. An invasion large enough to carry the island could not be mounted from other islands but only from Spain, France, or Holland. That Holland alone tried during the seventeenth century attests to the effectiveness of the Barbadian security system within the global political setting of the time.

In its form, local defense in Barbados copied several European ideas but adapted them to local conditions, both geographical and political. Throughout the seventeenth century, England regularly expected its overseas possessions to provide for local land defense. The mother country provided the navy from its own purse but required the colony to pay for a local garrison if one was requested. The antipathy to a garrison of regular soldiers in Barbados was such that the House of Assembly regularly declined to provide the requisite pay for professional soldiers, preferring to rely on the militia. This approach was possible only because the population of the island could provide for a credible militia. The militia reinforced a series of small coastal gun batteries to prevent a landing by attempting to keep enemy ships away from shore. In this approach can be seen an amalgamation of older European forms, modified to accommodate local sentiments, resources, and competence.

The defensive system of Barbados in the seventeenth century can be seen as truly vernacular. The formulation of the defensive policy had military weaknesses not overcome until the eighteenth century with the arrival of formally trained military men. Seventeenth-century defensive preparations did, however, accommodate the local political climate as well as the real level of manpower and financial resources available for defense from local sources. The development of a local military architecture in Barbados can thus be seen as a classic example of a pragmatic response to the then existing political and economic milieu on the island.

Ceramic Evidence of Creolization

During archaeological reconnaissance of historic properties in Barbados, sherds of unglazed red earthenware were observed to be widely scattered across virtually every cane field. Handler (1963a) began the formal discussion of these wares with his examination of the historical evidence of local ceramic manufacture on the island. Handler and Lange (1978), Lange and Handler (1985), Lange and Carlson (1985), and Handler (1989) all include discussions of unglazed red earthenwares.

To date, the unglazed red earthenwares have not been formally described in detail. Lack of temporal control, lack of data ascribing cultural affiliation, and a woefully incomplete catalog of forms have all precluded a definitive study of the locally manufactured wares. Despite the incomplete description of unglazed red earthenwares in Barbados, there is evidence of creolization within the body of known forms.

CODRINGTON COLLEGE SITE

Archaeological excavations at Codrington College in St. John parish, on the eastern side of Barbados, have been ongoing since 1990. In addition to a prehistoric Amerindian occupation that is not the main focus of this chapter, the Codrington estate has been continuously occupied since the mid-seventeenth century, first as a sugar plantation and after 1710 as a sugar plantation supporting a college. The property entered sugar production in the 1640s as the Consett estate but was sold in the 1660s to the Codrington family. The first son of the second Codrington generation at the plantation, Christopher Codrington III, willed his two Barbados sugar estates to the Society for the Propagation of the Gospel in Foreign Parts (SPG, the developing missionary arm of the Church of England) upon his death in 1710.

The SPG reorganized the Codrington estates, employing the proceeds of the sugar plantation to fund a "college" for the purpose of training theologians and physicians who were intended to improve the lot of enslaved Africans in the island by promoting better health and by exposing them to the teachings of the Church of England (Harlow 1928). In 1714, Colonel Christian Lilly drew up plans for the college, but fluctuations in the price of sugar slowed the project. Although the fabric of the college was finished by 1723, the interior was not completed until the 1730s, and the school did not open until 1745 (Harlow 1928:215–216).

As part of its program of construction and teaching, which continued until the Codrington Trust was established in Barbados in 1983, the SPG kept meticulous and unparalleled records of each year's activities, providing a documentary history of not only the college but also the sugar plantation itself. Because Codrington was a college yard, the area around the original seventeenth-century sugar factory, mansion house, and slave lots has remained virtually untouched, with clearly stratified zones from the seventeenth century through the twentieth. The extraordinary remains of material culture, combined with the excellent records of the SPG, have made Codrington College a remarkably productive venue for the study of early Barbados and the beginning of the creolization process on this island.

Archaeological excavations at Codrington College have recovered a wide array of domestic ceramics in addition to the ubiquitous industrial ceramics associated with the sugar industry. Found in undisturbed contexts as old as the seventeenth century, these ceramics hold great potential for addressing questions of creolization, the development of the local ceramic industry, the socioeconomic status of the planter, indentured servant, free husbandman, and slave, and the role of sugar in forming the society of Barbados. The majority of finds to date have been derived from refuse deposits associated with domestic units, which are of greatest value in addressing socioeconomic questions. In 1993 the archaeological team learned the location of the Codrington estate pottery manufactory. Seen today as a great waster pile approximately 100 feet on a side, the top of the last kiln is visible above the wasters. Data obtained from the waster pile, used comparatively with data obtained from other industrial sites and from domestic areas on the Codrington estate, define the influence of industrial manufacturing on the creolization process.

LOCAL BARBADOS REDWARES

Although Handler (1963a:130–135) was unable to find any documentary evidence for a local ceramic industry prior to 1650, there is little doubt that ceramic manufacture in Barbados during the historic period began in the seventeenth century. The oldest piece of Barbadian manufactured pottery so far known archaeologically was found not in Barbados but at the site of Charles Towne on the Cape Fear River in Brunswick County, North Carolina (Smith, Loftfield, and Paulssen 1994). This site, occupied from 1664 to 1667, was a failed precursor of Charleston, South Carolina. It was founded and supplied by Barbadians as one of a number of extra-island colonial ventures that originated in this most densely populated island in the Caribbean.

Several pieces of pottery have been recovered from Charles Towne that have a constellation of attributes typical of ceramics manufactured in seventeenth-century Barbados. The paste is soft, laden with plagioclase feldspar, and the sherds exhibit a distinct reduced gray core within well-oxidized pink/red exterior surfaces (Smith et al. 1994). The sherds present in North Carolina are from typical flat-bottomed jars usually identified as molasses drip jars that were associated with the sugar industry. The few sherds found in North Carolina that fit this description are remarkably different from all other unglazed red earthenwares found at Charles Towne but could not be separated from the thousands of sherds of unglazed red earthenware recovered in Barbados. The finds in North Carolina demonstrate not only that there was a functional ceramic industry in Barbados by the mid-1660s but that at least some of the typical Barbadian forms had been established by the same date.

Unglazed red earthenware vessel forms recognized at early sites in Barbados can be identified as domestic, industrial, or architectural. Numerically, industrial and architectural forms predominate. Industrial forms include the sugar mold and the molasses drip jar. Architectural forms include tiles, flat in very early sites and S-shaped pantiles later. Although intact examples of both sugar molds and molasses drip jars are extant, they are rarely found intact in the field. Nonetheless, forms can be reconstructed from diagnostic elements.

Sugar molds are identifiable from both rims and bases. Crystallizing sugar from the boiling vats was packed into the molds and allowed to cool. The bases

Fig. 8.6. The bases of sugar molds.

of sugar molds typically have one perforation in which a plug was placed when the mold was filled with cooling syrup that would crystallize and harden into sugar (figure 8.6). After a few days, the bottom of the mold was unplugged and the molasses allowed to run out into the drip jar. After a few weeks of curing, the mold was tipped and the sugar cone removed to be packed in hogsheads for shipment to the metropole. The sherds are derived from wheel-thrown vessels. The wall thickness of the perforated mold bases is thinner than the jar bases. Vessel walls rarely reach 0.5 inch in thickness, with 0.25 inch being the most common. The bases have an inverted subconoidal that turns to a small flat on the bottom itself. The drip hole (usually 0.5 to 0.6 inch in diameter) is perforated through the center of the bottom flat.

Straight-sided vessels with absolutely plain, straight rims or with worked rims are identified as sugar molds (figure 8.7). Whereas the straight rims may be slightly thickened, worked rims are generally thickened and worked on the exterior surface. Worked rims generally have an everted rounded lip that in some specimens is enlarged into an annular band around the rim. Straight rims are slightly thickened but are essentially straight, on both the interior and the exterior. They generally have convex, rounded lips.

Fig. 8.7. A complete sugar mold.

The wall thickness of sugar mold vessels ranges from 0.2 inch to 0.6 inch close to the rim, with 0.4 inch being the average thickness. Vessel mouths range in diameter from 12 inches to over 20 inches.

Molasses drip jars were also wheel thrown. The bases are heavy, with flat bottoms and wall-to-base angles that approach 90 degrees. In thickness, vessel bottoms range from 0.5 to 0.75 inch, whereas vessel walls range from 0.5 to 0.66 inch. Base diameters are approximately 9.5 inches (figure 8.8). In most of the specimens examined, the wall thickness decreases dramatically within a short distance of the turn of the bottom, suggesting that the vessels were

Fig. 8.8. A molasses drip jar.

thin walled and probably not too large. The vessels were wheel thrown, but the paste in the base angles is generally poorly made, with visible contortions. The bottom of the base is essentially flat and constructed so that the vessel would have stood securely on a flat surface.

Typical molasses drip jar rims are tightly constricted, with such narrow openings that the rims are worked from what is essentially a horizontal surface. Mouth openings range in diameter from 4 inches to 7 inches. Typically, the rims consist of a bead of clay 0.75 to 1.2 inches in diameter and almost circular in cross section. Rolled to stand up perpendicular to the top of the vessel, the clay in the rim bead is contorted. This general pattern encompasses a variety of rim treatments, and with further study, a temporal seriation by form may be possible.

Architectural ceramics include flat tiles and pantiles. In thickness, flat tiles are all very close to 0.75 inch, and many pieces have a raised edge or lip along one side. There are no clear indicators of method of manufacture. These tiles can be recognized from body sections because they are flat in all dimensions. These tiles were used for roofing, paving, covering storage pits, and lining chimney flues. Use may occasionally be determined by the presence and alignment of punched holes for nailing or from burn marks if they lined flues.

Pantiles are identified as roofing tiles with a typical S-shaped cross section. Tile thickness ranges from 0.55 inch to 0.6 inch. Scrape marks indicate that these tiles were made in molds. These tiles can be identified from body sections of large vessels because, perpendicular to the curved dimension, the tiles are flat and lack the compound curvature of vessels. Many pantile edge sherds have raised lugs that were used in the installation of the tiles on roofs.

Unglazed red earthenwares were both made locally and imported from England. Relying on documentary sources, Handler (1963a) and Handler and Lange (1978:139–144) have detailed the origin of earthenware manufacture in Barbados and have demonstrated the importation of sugar molds from the mother country. The ability to differentiate between imported and local wares thus becomes a critical diagnostic tool for evaluating the economic dynamics at various plantations.

With the exception of the tiles, most of the unglazed red earthenwares suspected of having originated in Barbados are rather poorly made. The ceramics were fired at low temperatures for inadequate periods of time, producing sherd surfaces that are chalky and friable. Despite thorough washing of the sherds, one cannot handle them without getting one's fingers red with eroding ceramic. Voids in some of the sherds, plus the contorted paste visible in many others, indicate poor control of the manufacturing processes. The gray core with many particles of carbon suggests incomplete firing.

The inept manufacture of the vessels argues for local production. During the later seventeenth century and most of the eighteenth (when earthenware molds were most in use), loss of forest had produced a fuel shortage on the island. As a result, bagasse (the cane from which the sugar juice has been expressed) came to be the primary fuel burned in the sugar boilers (Galloway 1989:96–98; Sloane 1707). By extension, it can be assumed that the pottery kilns were also fired with bagasse. In a Barbados short on fuel, there would have been an economic incentive to skimp on the length of the firing in the kiln, which would account for the poor firing evidenced on most Barbadian-made vessels. Such poorly made earthenware vessels from England would hardly have survived transportation. English ceramics are almost never seen to be so poorly made, and after 1655, the Navigation Acts would have precluded, or at least limited, importation of such vessels from any other source.

CERAMICS IN THE SUGAR INDUSTRY

The majority of unglazed red earthenware sherds recovered from fields and from excavations in Barbados are associated with the sugar industry. Ligon (1657:84) indicates that in the middle seventeenth century, sugar was cured in wooden or "board" molds. Handler (1963a:131–133, 135) has shown that by the end of the seventeenth century, unglazed earthenware molds had been introduced and were becoming the mold of choice for the island. The Barbadian sherds from North Carolina suggest that the transition to ceramic molds and drips was under way by the 1660s. At the end of the seventeenth century, both wood and ceramic sugar molds were in use, but by the mid-eighteenth century wood had been almost entirely supplanted by ceramic for sugar production. The use of ceramic vessels in the sugar industry declined through the early nineteenth century and had ceased by the mid-nineteenth century with the introduction of steam machinery, vacuum evaporation, and centrifugal drying (Handler 1963a:147). From beginning to end, then, ceramic molds and molasses jars were in use in Barbados for less than 200 years.

The identity of seventeenth-century potters as individuals is uncertain, but documents suggest that the technology was introduced by potters from England who then taught enslaved Africans (Handler 1963a; Handler and Lange 1978). Most ceramic vessels were probably manufactured on plantations, although an independent cottage industry certainly contributed. Workable clay deposits in Barbados are limited to a small section of the island's east coast, called the Scotland District, where, from the mid-nineteenth century to the mid-twentieth, there was a thriving cottage ceramic industry. Producing a variety of traditional forms, this industry has fallen on hard times as technological progress has rendered its products impractical.

Handler (1963a) explored the origin of the pottery industry in the Scotland District with special emphasis on the origin of the traditional forms. Some of the traditional forms (braziers, also called coal pots, gurglets, and pitchers) have great antiquity in European forms. The "monkey," an unglazed, spouted water jug with a strap handle that resembles a large teapot, has no certain origin and is probably an indigenous development. The final traditional form, the conaree, a lidded pot that is cylindrical to slightly convex-sided and glazed on the interior, could have been derived from several older European forms (figure 8.9). Its use in Barbados, however, is most likely associated with African foodways. Although some writers have placed the earliest appearance of forms usually associated with the cottage ceramic industry at the middle eighteenth to early nineteenth century, Handler (1963a) and Handler and Lange (1978) were unable to determine the temporal origin of these local domestic ceramic forms primarily because there was a dearth of excavated materials and a lack of documentary sources.

Although archaeological excavations in Barbados to date have produced no recognizable examples of monkeys, one lid and a small rim fragment

Fig. 8.9. A modern monkey, conaree, and coal pot.

found in a seventeenth-century context at Codrington College suggest an early appearance of the conaree. Excavated materials from Codrington College also indicate that coal pots were manufactured in the seventeenth century (figure 8.10), as was, most importantly, a small bowl with an incurving rim that has no known English antecedent.

Of crucial importance to the thesis developed herein is the idea that English potters taught English ceramic technology to Africans. Handler has demonstrated this educational relationship with some certainty, although relative numbers of English and African potters have not been determined (Handler 1963a). The significance of the relationships among the plantation-based ceramic industry, English potters, and enslaved Africans lies in the quest for evidence of creolization in the ceramics of Barbados.

Because pottery is formed from a fluid medium and is fragile yet virtually indestructible, it provides excellent evidence of cultural preferences in manufacture and use. Evidence of African and European cultural preferences should be most apparent in a medium such as clay, which, once formed, retains the ideas of its maker.

Fig. 8.10. A seventeenth-century conaree lid and coal pot.

African Influences in New World Ceramics

Examination of patterns of production of red earthenwares from the Caribbean and North America has revealed several distinct patterns of creolization. Recognizing the role of Colono and English redwares in the market for cheap, readily available ceramics, Turnbaugh (1985:22) states that "for the eastern United States, Colono ware seems to occur in ceramic samples in inverse proportion to English colonial redware." With the exception of some Colono ware, presumed by Deetz to be imported from the West Indies (Deetz 1976, 1977), at the Parting Ways site in Massachusetts, no Colono or Native American tradition of red earthenware production is recognized in the Northeast (Turnbaugh 1985:22). Excavations at several sites where African potters were known to have worked have produced no clear evidence of forms other than those typical of English production (Turnbaugh 1985:22). African potters north of Delaware appear to have produced ceramic forms indistinguishable from those of the English with no apparent Africanisms employed.

In contrast to the evidence for creolization in the northeast, the ceramic record for the southeast indicates strong survival of African ceramic traditions in Colono wares. Colono wares known to have been produced by Africans were handmade, fired in open fires, and exhibit some vessel forms atypical of English design. Colono ware fulfilled the need for cheap and readily available domestic pottery and found its way not only into the huts of enslaved Africans but into the kitchens of whites as well (Ferguson 1992). Southeastern Colono wares seem to have been replaced by cheaper European wares by the middle of the nineteenth century, although the percentage of Colono ware had been decreasing prior to that time (Ferguson 1992). In the southeastern United States, Colono wares are most common in tidewater and low country settings where the English plantation system was operating. They are virtually absent from interior upland locations (Turnbaugh 1985:23). Ferguson (1992) has suggested that the development of Colono wares in the plantation areas of the American Southeast was influenced by the nature of the plantation system itself, with villages of enslaved Africans living in virtual isolation on the plantations and the importation of slaves directly from Africa who would have kept alive the traditions of the homeland.

A similar development is noted in Jamaica. Excavations at Drax Hall plantation have revealed local manufacture of Afro-Jamaican pottery. These vessels were made by coiling and were fired in open fires. Vessel forms tended to consist of open orifice bowls and two forms with simple, restricted orifices that were probably cooking vessels (Armstrong 1990:147, 151). These vessels resemble the Colono wares of the North American Southeast and are probably the product of African potters reproducing forms remembered from the homeland. Afro-Jamaican wares show evidence of syncretism, however, indicating local adaptations (Armstrong 1990:150).

After declining in popularity during the late eighteenth and early nineteenth centuries, the Afro-Jamaican forms (called yabbas) experienced a resurgence at the time of emancipation. The reduction during the late eighteenth and early nineteenth centuries has been seen as a response to the importation of cheap English ceramics and cast iron pots, whereas the resurgence has been ascribed to a revitalization of Africanisms and to economic exigencies that probably attended emancipation. Recently freed slaves were unable to afford imported ceramic or iron vessels and resorted to home manufacture of familiar forms (Armstrong 1990:157–158).

Unlike Jamaica or the southeastern region of North America, Barbados has no tradition of local hand-coiled ceramic manufacture and no tradition of African-inspired vessel forms. In contrast to the areas to the north, the utilitarian ceramic of seventeenth- and eighteenth-century Barbados is red-ware, wheel thrown and kiln fired, usually unglazed, almost always English in form but indeed locally manufactured. In this regard, Barbados more closely resembles New England, where locally made redwares of English form satisfied the need for cheap domestic items.

A comparison of the four areas discussed herein suggests that in New England the pattern of slavery placed small numbers of Africans on small farms and in small shops where unity with other Africans would have been reduced. A local redware industry provided inexpensive domestic items and precluded survival of African technology and vessel form. On the tidewater plantations of the Southeast, the presence of large communities of enslaved Africans combined with the absence of well-established or widespread local ceramic industries encouraged local handicraft manufacture and the survival of African forms. The same factors influenced Jamaica, where local manufacture of coil-constructed and open-fired vessels with African forms continued well into the nineteenth century. Although a similar plantation system in Barbados should have produced a similar expression of African forms in ceramics, different economic and environmental factors led to a unique ceramic expression. A comparison with the economic and environmental system in Jamaica is perhaps most illuminating.

In Jamaica, the sugar industry employed wooden molds for crystallization. In 1722, the Drax estate recorded only 60 ceramic sugar molds in contrast to 1100 wooden molds (Armstrong 1990:151). From these figures, it can be inferred that Jamaica did not enjoy the development of a local industrial ceramic productive capacity. The preference for wooden molds may reflect the much larger landmass of Jamaica, with an attendant survival of exploitable forests. In Barbados, by comparison, the smaller land mass and more gentle terrain resulted in total deforestation and an attendant need to find replacements for the wooden molds that had, indeed, been used in the beginning of the sugar industry (Handler 1963a:131).

The early development of an industrial ceramic capacity in Barbados meant that enslaved Africans learned European ceramic technology. It can be suggested that the presence of a well-established and widespread ceramic industry led to the submergence of African traits in domestic wares produced on the island. The need for handmade, coiled, open-fired vessels would have been greatly reduced, since the enslaved population could have thrown and then fired vessels for domestic use in the local potteries. At the same time, the English ceramic "tutors" would have created great cultural pressure to produce, and then use, English forms.

Although it is apparent that English forms soon predominated in Barbados, there is evidence from excavations at Codrington College to indicate some creolization of African ceramists. From one late seventeenth-century context and one early eighteenth-century context, several sherds of a black (deeply reduced body and surface), coiled, open-fired ware have been recovered. These sherds appear to represent a totally unaltered African ceramic form. One of the vessels is a small cooking pot, whereas the other is a small cup, probably for drinking. This ware is seen in very limited numbers on other sites, notably from Springhead plantation in St. James Parish (Loftfield and Legg 1997). Although coiled, open-fired vessels are present on the island, they are conspicuously rare. Since Amerindian production in the historic period can be all but ruled out in Barbados, an African origin remains most plausible.

Two vessel fragments recovered from seventeenth-century levels at the college show presumed "Africanisms" in form but not in manufacture. The first sherd, a small fragment of a rim, has a rim band with punctations that are distinctly not European in inspiration. The second piece, a large fragment of a vessel including the entire base and about one-quarter of the body with a segment of rim, shows an open orifice bowl with a slightly constricting rim that is also very atypical of European vessels of the period. Although these two vessel fragments indicate probable African design inspiration, they are both made on a wheel and fired in a kiln. Clearly evincing creolization, they, like the traditional African sherds, are the more noteworthy because they are the only sherds discovered on the island to date that are so clearly African in inspiration.

From a similar early eighteenth-century deposit has come the base of a wheel-thrown, kiln-fired vessel that is decorated with crosshatch marks. The vessel form is probably English, and the marks are probably decoration of an African origin.

Finally, one intriguing sherd was recovered from Springhead plantation that was handmade but fired in a kiln (Loftfield and Legg 1997). These few sherds indicate the initial directions taken by the creolization process. African potters quickly abandoned the use of traditional technologies for the manufacture of traditional forms. At first they shifted to the employment of English technology to produce remembered forms, but they seem quickly to have abandoned traditional forms in favor of an entirely learned repertoire of English forms made with learned English technology.

In Barbados, the development of an industrial ceramic manufactory apparently overpowered the effects of the plantation system to preclude the manufacture of coiled vessels, open firing, and the survival of African ceramic forms. Although some African ceramic traits may have appeared in vessels produced during the early stages of the development of the ceramic industry, and some newly arrived Africans may have attempted to produce traditional vessel forms, cheap wares, locally made with English technology and in English form, soon predominated in Barbados.

Both Armstrong (1990) and Ferguson (1992) have alluded to the survival of an African foodway as an inspiration for vessel forms identified in Jamaica and the southeastern United States. This foodway requires a large vessel for cooking a starch; a smaller vessel for cooking a stew containing vegetables, meat, or fish; and a small personal bowl into which the starch and stew may be placed for consumption or from which the savory stews are dipped. In Barbados, these cultural foodway functions employed vessels of English form with some local modifications. The Barbadian conaree jar clearly satisfied the function of a stew pot. Its continued modern use for "pepper pot," an ongoing protein-rich stew, clearly extends into the present day its original function in the African foodway. The vessels for cooking the starch are less apparent, as are the individual bowls. Although their function in Barbados was probably assumed by imported European forms, early, locally made examples may emerge from excavations of domestic refuse now under way at Codrington College.

Summary

Although the two case studies detailed above are specific to Barbados, they broaden the available models of the creolization process. In each case, it is possible to discern social, economic, and political forces that influenced the course of fairly rapid cultural change within the groups under study.

The form of military defense created in seventeenth-century Barbados almost entirely within the domain of English settlers reflected an evolving sense of local autonomy and fear of encroachment by political and military power from the metropole. Motivated by fear of a loss of local authority and control, the form of military defense exhibited signs of local inspiration, with limited reference to known military practices in Europe. The local military defense responded to local perceptions of need but ultimately exhibited significant flaws when it was examined by professionals from the metropole.

The development of the local ceramic industry in Barbados was driven by economic considerations attendant upon the sugar industry and deforestation. Although the original potters were almost certainly English, enslaved Africans were quickly taught the craft. The development of the local ceramic industry operated by enslaved Africans significantly reduced the survival of African ceramic technology and African vessel forms in Barbados. Although the plantation system has been credited with the survival of African technology and vessel form in Jamaica and the southeastern United States, an industrial ceramic manufactory in Barbados overwhelmed the effects of the plantation system. The study of ceramics from Codrington College not only shows that Africans in Barbados experienced a greater degree of creolization (at least in ceramic manufacture) than in Jamaica or the American Southeast but also illuminates the process by which first manufacturing techniques, then vessel shape, and finally vessel decoration were lost.

Colonies and colonial settlers cannot be viewed simply as extensions of their places of origin. Rather, to fully understand and explain colonial culture, it is necessary to appreciate the changes in culture that always attended residence in the new physical and social environment. The two case studies do not purport to present creolization as a new discovery but rather to shed light on deep structural values operating within the two dominant cultural groups in Barbados. It is possible to see how these values developed and changed very quickly to produce a new culture different in significant ways from that of the homelands left behind.

9

"NEGROE HOUSES BUILT OF STONE BESIDES OTHERS WATL'D + PLAISTERED"
The Creation of a Bahamian Tradition

Paul Farnsworth

Africans and Europeans brought their own ideas and cultural backgrounds to a dynamic cultural context in the Caribbean. One result was the negotiation of new cultural expressions that reflected an amalgamation and melding of traditional ideas to satisfy the needs of the physical, biological, and cultural environment that they now shared. The negotiation was not so much verbal as it was one of actions and reactions by individuals, day after day, in common situations and places. As each individual tested the new environment, consensus was reached on what was, and was not, successful or acceptable.

The fieldwork that produced the data used in this chapter was performed over a decade from 1989 to 1999. It is almost impossible, therefore, to thank individually everyone who helped and/or participated at different times. First, I am grateful to the people of the Bahamas and Turks and Caicos Islands for their hospitality. I also thank the many students and volunteers who carried out all the hard work in the field. The students came from many universities across the United States to participate in field schools sponsored by the University of California, Los Angeles; Louisiana State University; and the University of California, Berkeley. Volunteers from the Bahamas and the Turks and Caicos Islands also participated in the various excavations. None of this research could have been completed successfully without the assistance of the staff of the Department of Archives, Commonwealth of the Bahamas, and the Pompey Museum Nassau. All excavations in the Commonwealth of the Bahamas were carried out with the full permission and cooperation of the government of the Bahamas. I thank the government of the Turks and Caicos Islands for their cooperation with the Wade's Green research project. I also thank the Bahamas National Trust for sponsoring the excavations at Marine Farm and Great Hope and for providing assistance with the research at Promised Land and Clifton. In particular, I am grateful to Pericles Maillis, Lynn Gape, and the members of the Historic Preservation Committee. I spent many hours

These negotiations were not necessarily between individuals of equal power, particularly on the plantation. In many instances, the negotiation was extremely one-sided, but even enslaved people drew on a certain amount of symbolic cultural capital when dealing with their enslaver. One area in which planters generally accepted more African control was in the "hearth and home" of the enslaved. Although planters held ultimate control over the housing of enslaved people, the extent to which they exercised it varied considerably at different times and places.

Until the late seventeenth century in the Caribbean, Africans built their traditional African-style houses with minimal interference from most planters (Debien 1974:220–221; Edwards 1980:305, 1994:176). During the eighteenth century, planters, especially those on larger plantations, increasingly imposed restrictions, particularly on the layout and organization of the slave settlements (Debien 1974:221–224). In the late eighteenth and nineteenth centuries, many planters further imposed their ideas about the size, plan, materials, and methods of construction of the houses themselves (Chapman 1991; Debien 1974:224226). Although these general trends can be discerned, however, there was tremendous variation from colony to colony, island to island, and even plantation to plantation throughout the Caribbean.

With the end of slavery, African-Caribbean peoples were now free to choose the form of housing they preferred although within the new limits imposed by colonial governments and by almost universal economic hardship. In some places, people could choose to stay in the houses they occupied during enslavement; in others, they were evicted without ceremony. The structures themselves continued as elements of the cultural landscape, occupied or not. To what extent did these structures influence the development of subsequent folk housing?

The question can have no single answer, but for the Bahamas, the house type recognized by modern Bahamians as their ancestral house form clearly resembles the stone-built slave houses on the plantations (Craton and Saunders 1992:303–305, 341; Kozy 1983:147; Saunders 1983:57–58, 1985:38, 153–155, 230). Examples of the traditional Bahamian house type can be found throughout the Family Islands today. Some are still occupied, but many have now been abandoned. By the same token, stone-built slave houses can be found among

in the Department of Archives, Nassau; the Department of Lands and Surveys, Nassau; the Registrar General's Office, Nassau; the offices of Maillis and Maillis, Nassau; and the Public Record Office at Kew, England. I thank the staff members of each institution for their assistance. The figures in this chapter were all drafted by Mary Lee Eggart of the Cartographic Section of the Department of Geography and Anthropology, Louisiana State University. Finally, I thank Laurie Wilkie for her many and varied contributions to my research.

the ruined buildings still standing on many of the plantations. The similarities between the two are striking, although there have yet to be detailed architectural and archaeological surveys of the islands that can be used to substantiate the evolutionary connection between them. If the connection is presumed to exist, however, as it is by most Bahamians, then why would people of African ancestry adopt, adapt, and continue to build houses resembling those stone-built slave houses that appear so European in design, even though they stand as symbols of their enslavement? The answer to this question lies in two further questions: (1) were the stone-built slave houses typical of slave housing in the Bahamas? and (2) are the stone-built slave houses on the plantations a European type imposed on the enslaved population?

Historical Overview

British Loyalists fleeing the American colonies after the Revolution were primarily resettled in England, Canada, Jamaica, and the Bahamas between 1784 and 1785. Over 6,000 settled in the Bahamas, where they were compensated for lost property with Bahamian land grants (Peters 1960; Siebert 1975). The Loyalists were predominantly American by birth, most being members of planter families established in the Carolinas and Georgia. They brought with them enslaved people at least two-thirds of whom were American-born (Craton 1986). The Loyalists established a cotton plantation economy with racially based slavery, largely supplanting the original Anglo-Bahamian Creole population. Therefore, it was as a new but nonetheless Creole population that the Loyalists and their slaves entered the Bahamas (Craton 1986; Craton and Saunders 1992; Johnson 1991; Saunders 1983, 1985).

In addition to the Creoles, thousands of African-born slaves were imported directly to the Bahamas prior to 1807. More Africans liberated from foreign slave vessels were "apprenticed" to Bahamian planters after that date. British-born fortune seekers and merchants turned planters also entered Bahamian society at this time, some fleeing from Georgia, the Carolinas, and East Florida, others coming directly from Britain. Each of these groups brought new ideas and identities to the islands (Craton 1986; Craton and Saunders 1992; Johnson 1991; Saunders 1983, 1985).

After a brief period of prosperity during which cotton was the principal cash crop, the combination of poor soils and insect attack led many plantations to decline in the early years of the nineteenth century. By clearing new land for cotton, experimenting with sugar production, changing to mixed farming strategies, and raking salt (where possible), some of the Bahamian plantations survived and expanded. Most, however, were abandoned. By the 1820s, cotton production in the Bahamas was minimal, the surviving plantations practiced mixed agriculture, and salt was the islands' primary economic resource. Emancipation in 1834 largely ended the plantation system (Craton 1986; Craton and Saunders 1992; Johnson 1991; Saunders 1983, 1985).

The Loyalists transformed the landscape of the Bahamas, especially New Providence and the islands to the south, such as the Caicos Islands, Cat Island, Crooked Island, Exuma, and San Salvador. Most of these islands had not been permanently settled before. What settlement there had been was based on salt raking, fishing, and wrecking. Settlement was small-scale and relatively impermanent. The plantations transformed these islands, creating a Loyalist landscape of fields and buildings, including numerous houses built by the thousands of enslaved people who became the new resident population of the Bahamas.

Housing Bahamian Slavery

In view of the documentary evidence, architectural studies, and excavations by archaeologists, it might seem to be relatively simple to describe "typical" Bahamian slave housing and the range of variability that existed. This task has never before been attempted, however, and it is not easy to accomplish. Only two published architectural studies have dealt specifically with the Bahamas. One focused on Long Bay Cays on southern Andros (Otterbein 1975), an area that was not settled until the second half of the nineteenth century, after the end of slavery. In this study, no structures dating before the twentieth century were recorded. The other focused on Nassau (Saunders and Cartwright 1979) and paid minimal attention to slave dwellings in that city. Saunders and Cartwright (1979) did provide a brief discussion of "Black Dwellings" in the Loyalist period:

> the houses of the blacks and coloured population were mostly built of wood, but some had limestone walls, probably of wattle and plaster made of sand and lime. A cottage was usually about 15 to 20 feet in length and 14 feet wide and usually had one or two rooms. The rooms would be divided by a wooden partition. The roofs were covered, some with shingles, others with thatching of palmetto leaves. . . . it was rare to see a house with glass windows; board shutters took their place and fireplaces and chimneys were unknown . . . . the floor could be of natural earth. (Saunders and Cartwright 1979:21–23)

Unfortunately, as the book is intended for a popular audience, no sources for this description are provided, no extant structures are mentioned, and the only illustration is an undated photograph.

In his *Historic Architecture of the Caribbean,* David Buisseret (1980) very briefly discusses slave housing. He refers to, and includes photographs of, huts made of "freestanding stone. Such are the walls of the slave huts of Bonaire, of the little estate-houses at Alleynedale in Barbados, of the cottages of West Caicos" (Buisseret 1980:2). The Caicos were part of the Bahama Island colony during the period of slavery, and the accompanying photograph shows a stone-and-mortar, gabled, thatched house with a substantial chimney that is still being occupied and completely contradicts Saunders and Cartwright's (1979) description in both the method of construction and the presence of the chimney.

Historians have been equally contradictory in their descriptions of slave housing in the Bahamas. The focus has shifted from buildings constructed of wood and thatch in publications prior to 1983 (Craton 1962:193; Peters 1960:186) to stone-built, two-room structures with thatched roofs since that time (Craton and Saunders 1992:303–305, 341; Kozy 1983:147; Saunders 1983:57–58, 1985:38, 153–155, 230). Other writers have not addressed the subject (e.g., Albury 1975; Johnson 1991; Riley 1983).

Craton and Saunders (1992) provide the most comprehensive description of slave housing in the Bahamas. They suggest that, although wattle and daub structures existed on poorer estates, the standard slave housing on the majority of Bahamian plantations (as opposed to that for slaves working salt ponds or laboring in Nassau) was a stone-built, two-room structure with a thatched roof. This hypothesis appears to derive largely from four sources: (1) surviving ruined slave houses on San Salvador studied by Gerace between 1973 and 1976 (Gerace 1982, 1987); (2) surviving ruined houses at Clifton plantation on New Providence; (3) entries in Farquharson's plantation journal for 1831–1832 (Peggs 1957); and (4) William Wylly's regulations for running his plantations (Colonial Office Records [CO] 1815). There is no reference to other contemporary historical documentation in the discussion by Craton and Saunders (1992) and no citations of such documentation. Equally, the descriptions by Craton (1962), Peters (1960), and Saunders (1983, 1985) of plantation slave housing in the Bahamas refer solely to Farquharson's journal or William Wylly's regulations.

Kozy (1983) does not elaborate on slave housing but includes a transcript of an estate inventory with the entry "thirteen large stone houses for Negroes" (Kozy 1983:147), a third contemporary description of Bahamian slave housing. Taken together, however, the documentation cited to date is not an adequate basis for an accurate description of slave housing in the Bahamas. The subject requires more detailed research in the contemporary historical records. In addition, careful consideration of the results of archaeological research should be incorporated into any reconstruction. The present chapter is a preliminary attempt at this goal.

The Documentary Evidence

There is very little contemporary documentation of slave housing in the Bahamas, and most of it has already been mentioned in the preceding discussion! Furthermore, although they have been frequently cited in this regard, William Wylly's 1815 regulations for running his plantations are a unique code written by a man who was radically different from the "typical" planter in the Bahamas. As attorney general of the islands, he worked fervently to ameliorate the conditions endured by Bahamian slaves, prosecuted planters for mistreatment of their slaves, and suffered the wrath of the planters' elected legislature for his efforts. Becuse he was an ardent reformer, Wylly's regulations, and the ruins of his plantation's slave houses, are very unlikely to indicate conditions on other plantations. As a result, unless other documentary sources or archaeological research at other plantations show that this pattern was typical, it would be misleading to base a general description on Wylly's plantations.

Farquharson's Journal from 1831–1832 (Peggs 1957), mentioned above, was used by Craton (1962) to infer that slave houses were made of wood, yet Gerace's archaeological research at the Farquharson estate in the 1970s revealed evidence of stone-built slave cabins. There are a number of entries in the journal about the slave houses, all of them brief. The dozen entries listed in table 9.1 are those related either explicitly or implicitly to slave housing. From these references, it is clear that the slave houses were thatched, but the material composition of the rest of the house remains ambiguous. The inside walls of one house were mortared, but whether over walls of stone, wood, or wattle is not recorded. Similarly, floors are laid, but how or of what material is not recorded. References to sand, lime, and mixing mortar on the same week imply, perhaps, that the floors were of mortar, but the entries were made on different days. Men are employed "ridging" the main house and other houses of the yard, but the meaning is not clear. Finally, the journal at one point notes that men were fetching leaves and wattles, but the purpose or the subsequent use of these materials is not mentioned.

There are also numerous references to "jack [sic] at carpenter's work," but this tells us little. In short, there is nothing to suggest that slave houses were

Table 9.1. References to Construction Activities related possibly to Slave Houses in Farquharson's Journal for 1831-32 (Peggs 1957).

1. "Denis. C.Charles and Harry priming up the inside wall of William's House with Mortar . . ." (Peggs 1957:1);

2. "Employed 6 men cutting Thatch 2 laying the floor in Tina's House." (Peggs 1957:1);

3. "Employed the men Thatching C.Charles House . . ." (Peggs 1957:1);

4. "Employed 6 men to bring lime, sand and. Mixing Mortar 3 ridging the Dwelling House and other Houses about the yard . . ." (Peggs 1957:2);

5. "Employed 2 men laying the floor in William's House." (Peggs 1957:2);

6. "2 hands geting leaves and wattles . . ." (Peggs 1957:8);

7. "Employed the men thatching Mistreses shad and one side of the roof which the Hurricane tore up a good deal last year . . ." (Peggs 1957:38);

8. "Employed the men thatching one side of Maria's house . . ." (Peggs 1957:40);

9. "Employed the men thatching the Negro House at Kerr Mount . . ." (Peggs 1957:46);

10. "7 Men gone over the Creek to cut thatch for Dennis' house . . ." (Peggs 1957:78);

11. "Employed the men thatching. Dennis' house . . ." (Peggs 1957:78);

12. "Employed 2 hands cuting thatch over the Creek, . . ." (Peggs 1957:83)

of wood, as Craton (1962) suggests, or that any slave houses were actually constructed in 1831–1832 (it would not be surprising if there was no new construction at this late date). All the activities appear to relate to the repair of existing houses. Beyond the fact that the houses were thatched, we can glean little from this source alone.

Daniel McKinnen (1804) confirms that slave houses were usually thatched in his description of the Bahamas in 1803. McKinnen wrote, "The small palmetto . . . supplied them [the Loyalists] with an abundant and convenient thatching for their houses, still generally used as a covering for the negro huts" (McKinnen 1804:168). Although he refers to "negro huts" elsewhere (McKinnen 1804:18, 57, 153), McKinnen does not describe them further.

Estate inventories compiled at the death of a planter are another source to be consulted. At this time, I have not undertaken a complete study, but I have reviewed all Bahamian inventories—more than 350 manuscript pages—from the Loyalist period registered prior to April 1802 and most between 1802 and 1834. Unfortunately, most do not include the slave houses or their contents. Others briefly list the buildings (including "Negro houses"), "improvements," the amount of land and a value but supply no details. A very small number list "Negro Houses," the number, and a combined value. The inventory of Archibald Campbell's estate on Long Island, for example, includes "18 Negro houses @ £15," with a total value of £270, and "4 ditto houses @ £13," with a total value of £52 (Registrar General's Department [RGD] 1798). There is no explanation of the difference in value assigned.

The estate inventory for William Moss (RGD 1797), one of the wealthiest planters in the Bahamas at the time of his death, lists four plantations on Crooked Island and includes the following descriptions: "17 Negro houses 100," "6 Negro Houses 50," "13 Negro houses 40," and "6 Negro houses 20." This shorthand contrasts with quite detailed descriptions of other structures. We can extract the average cost of the slave houses from this inventory, but it is not quite as easy to do so as might be supposed. The three men making the inventory gave valuations usually in Bahamian pounds but occasionally in dollars, only converting the page total to pounds. In fact, given the page layout, I suspect that at least one of them made his part of the inventory in dollars, and someone else subsequently converted the totals. Thus, although the main buildings are valued in Bahamian pounds, the slave houses vary. The first two entries listed are valued in dollars and the second two in Bahamian pounds, a difference that explains the large disparity in values assigned in this document. The document uses a conversion rate of two and one-half dollars to the Bahamian pound. At this rate, the average valuation of the slave houses at each estate comes to £2.4, £3.3, £3.1, and £3.3, so that they are much more similar in value than cursory examination of the document suggested.

The Moss inventory also has more detailed descriptions of the plantations' main buildings, including the following: "A wooden frame building boarded and shingled roofed and two stories high with a cellar 1000; A stone built kitchen 34 feet by 17 and shingled with a piazza 100; A barn framed and shingled 30 feet by 10 feet, underpinned 100; Four office houses 40" (RGD 1797). With values given in pounds, these give us some measure of the slave cabins' value of approximately £3, or about 3 percent of the value of the 34 × 17 foot, stone-built kitchen. The kitchen is approximately half as large again as most of the stone-built slave cabins I have recorded (see below) and is a more complex structure presumably including a chimney, but the large difference in value strongly suggests that these slave cabins were not made of stone and were far less substantial. If the cabins on the estates of one of the wealthiest planters on the Islands were not stone, the vast majority of cabins on other estates in 1797 were probably not stone.

Further confirmation comes from the inventory of John Moultrie's estates, also on Crooked Island, taken in early 1799 (RGD 1799a). One of these estates included "10 Negro houses compleat [*sic*] @ £30 ea framed and with stone chimneys." Based on this value, the houses at the Moss estates at only 10 percent of this value must have been quite insubstantial. Moultrie's other Crooked Island estates must also have had less substantial slave housing, as one had "15 Negro houses at 25 dollars each" and the other had "12 Negro houses and a barn @ 20 dollars each." At £10 and £8, respectively, these houses were presumably more substantial than the Moss houses, more like those on the Campbell estate on Long Island, and less substantial than Moultrie's framed houses with stone chimneys.

The inventory of one of George Gray's estates on Crooked Island taken later in 1799 (RGD 1799b) describes cabins valued at £10 each as "1 wattled and plastered house 20 feet by 12" and "1 ditto ditto 24 feet by 13." This description suggests a variation of wattle-and-daub construction using plaster rather than mud over the wattles as described by Saunders and Cartwright (1979). It could, however, imply the more traditional mud daub plastered over the wattles, perhaps with a lime plaster coating, as has been noted elsewhere in the Caribbean (e.g., Debien 1974:228). Whichever was the case, as a method of construction for "Negro houses" it was certainly common enough that the men making the Moultrie and Campbell inventories did not think it worthy of note compared to the framed houses.

An exception that illustrates the lack of interest in, and relative value of, wattle and plaster houses comes from the 1801 estate inventory of Dr. John Bell on Middle Caicos quoted earlier (Kozy 1983:147), but the entire entry reads "13 large Negroe [*sic*] houses built of stone besides others watl'd + plaistered [*sic*]" (RGD 1801). Presumably at least some of the "Negro houses" included in other estate inventories without further description or separate valuation must have been of this construction also. The fact, however, that there existed an even less substantial form of housing not described in any of the inventories but valued at one-third of a wattle and plaster house hints that the majority of the "Negro houses" in the inventories were probably these structures that were almost worthless and so common as not to need further description.

Equally important is the absence of any mention of stone slave houses in the estate inventories prior to Bell's in 1801 (RGD 1801). According to Kozy (1983:116), Dr. John Bell owned ninety slaves and was "a man of great wealth." Unfortunately, no separate value had been assigned to these houses, which would provide an interesting benchmark to compare with the other valuations from the same time period. There is no reason to suppose, however, that Bell's cabins were typical of those generally found on plantations, given his wealth and perhaps his background as a medical doctor. The fact that the inventory explicitly describes "Negroe [*sic*] houses built of stone" when no other inventories do so suggests that stone was a very unusual construction material for slave housing in the Bahamas at the time.

Another source that might provide some contemporary information on slave housing is the advertisements in the newspapers for plantations being sold. Again, however, in most cases where any mention is made at all, the term "Negro houses" is the extent of the description. One exception is an ad for Bellefield estate on North Caicos in 1805, which notes "thirty commodious Negro houses wattled and plastered" (*Royal Gazette and Bahama Advertiser* [*RGBA*] 1805). As with the reference in the estate inventories to stone houses, the fact that this ad specifically describes the houses as wattle and plaster may indicate that even this method of construction was atypical for slave houses on most estates prior to 1805.

In summary, the contemporary documentary record yields some useful information. Slave houses were thatched, often with palmetto; some were constructed of stone, although very few prior to 1802; and some were framed with stone chimneys, although again there is only one mention of this method of construction prior to 1802 (table 9.2). Others were constructed of wattle and plaster, but most are simply not described in any detail. The Moss estate inventory indicates that they were very cheap at approximately three pounds, costing less than a mahogany dining table (four pounds) and more than a wheelbarrow (two pounds) (RGD 1797). To judge from the documentary sources, therefore, it is highly unlikely that slave houses were built of stone on most estates in the Bahamas at any time and certainly not prior to 1802. Unfortunately, I have yet to find any contemporary Bahamian document that describes the most common type of slave house.

The Archaeological Evidence

Unfortunately, a relatively small number of plantations have been excavated in the Bahamas to date: three by Kathy Gerace on San Salvador; three by George Anthony Aarons on New Providence, and five by me (two on New Providence, two on Crooked Island, and one on North Caicos; figure 9.1). Of these projects, only Gerace's projects at Sandy Point and Farquharson's, and my project at Clifton, considered the slave villages in detail. Of Aaron's work, only Southwest Bay included any slave houses, and it will be discussed further.

Gerace's research on San Salvador is described in two publications (Gerace 1982, 1987) that give a limited overview of the slave villages. At Sandy Point, the slave quarters were located east of the main house approximately 300 feet

Table 9.2. Examples of Slave Houses described in Bahamian Estate Inventories prior to 1802 (Registrar General's Department 1797, 1798, 1799a, 1799b, 1801).

Description	Value Each	Inventory of	Date
Negro Houses	£3.3-2.4	William Moss	1797
Wattled and plastered	£10	George Gray	1799
Watl'd + plaistered	n/a	John Bell	1801
Negro Houses	£10-8	John Moultrie	1799
Negro Houses	£15-13	Archibald Campbell	1798
Framed and with stone chimneys	£30	John Moultrie	1799
Houses built of stone	n/a	John Bell	1801

Fig. 9.1. The Bahamas archipelago.

along the same ridge. Twelve houses were located and mapped. These were constructed of piled-up rocks, neither cut nor mortared but simply plastered on the inside to keep them partially bonded together. Each of the buildings had a single room, and there was evidence of neither fireplaces nor chimneys. The buildings were arranged along the ridge east to west but with varying distances between them and no apparent order imposed. Sandy Point was first granted in 1803, but we do not know when the quarters were built. According to Gerace (1987:17), the artifacts recovered from the quarters date from the early nineteenth century through to the present.

The quarters at Farquharson's plantation (Gerace 1982, 1987) were located approximately 800 feet north of the main house and at a much lower elevation. Fifteen buildings were uncovered and mapped, with stone walls connecting many of them. Most of the houses were built in a row along a stone fence line, which served as one wall for several of the houses. Stone walls also formed yard areas around several houses. Most of the buildings were of cut stone plastered inside and out, with at least one door and often two, with as many as four windows. Four of the buildings contained fireplaces, and two of those had two rooms, the other two having just one. Two other two-roomed buildings were found, whereas one had three rooms. The remaining ten buildings were one-room structures. Near three of the houses were small, poorly built structures that according to Gerace may have been pens for animals or storage buildings. The plantation was first granted to Charles Farquharson in 1803, but no documentary evidence for the construction of the quarters has been recovered. The artifacts dated from the late eighteenth century through to the present century (Gerace 1987:18).

The Fortune Hill quarters were not excavated, but Gerace (1982, 1987) and Gerace and Shaklee (1991) describe them in some detail. They are located approximately 400 meters northwest from the main house, along a ridge, but at a lower elevation than the main house. The quarters consist of thirty buildings arranged in two east-west rows with a "road" in between that is twenty meters wide. Eleven buildings were interpreted as residential, because a fireplace chimney was present at one end. All of the residential structures are large (approximately 8 × 4.5 meters), rectangular, cut limestone buildings covered with mortar inside and out. One of them lies centered between the two rows, oriented north-south at the east end of the quarters, and is thought to be the house of the taskmaster or overseer.

Buildings without chimneys were assumed to be nonresidential. These structures varied in construction materials and methods, surface finish, and size. Gerace and Shakley (1991) interpret all of these as ancillary buildings used for storage and other purposes. It seems likely, however, given their location in the quarters, their size, and description by comparison with slave houses on other plantations, that some of the "nonresidential" structures were also residences. According to the documentary evidence, Fortune Hill was granted in 1789, but there is no reason to believe that the plantation was developed until after the land had been purchased by Burton Williams in 1804.

Comparing the three sets of quarters, Gerace (1987:20) suggests that the varying wealth of the estate owners is reflected in the size and quality of the slave houses. The haphazard piled-stone houses of Sandy Point she attributes to Prince Storr, whom Charles Farquharson mentions as the owner in his journal of 1831/-1832. Storr was a black man who owned two estates, according to Gerace (1987:15), and was the poorest of the owners. The well-constructed quarters in two neat rows at Fortune Hill are attributed to Burton Williams, who was a wealthy Loyalist. Charles Farquharson, Gerace argues, fell between these two men in both wealth and the construction of his quarters (Gerace 1987:20). Gerace supports her model with reference to the main houses, which followed the same pattern, and the quality of the artifacts recovered from each.

Gerace's model is both logical and appealing in its correlation of planter wealth with quality of construction of the slave housing. Closer examination, however, suggests that the model may be an oversimplification. Sandy Point was first granted in 1803 (Gerace 1987), and Turner (1992:35) notes that Sandy Point actually belonged to John Storr, who passed it to his son, John Storr, Jr., a Nassau merchant, by 1822. Prince, a slave belonging to John, Jr., was sent to San Salvador around 1825 to manage his plantations and was emancipated by John Storr, Jr., in 1833. Storr subsequently gave the estates on San Salvador to Prince. As Turner points out (Turner 1992:36), the artifacts from the quarters at Sandy Point mostly date to the period of ownership by John Storr, Sr. There is no reason to believe that Storr was less wealthy than Charles Farquharson; if anything, the reverse is more likely.

At Fortune Hill, the assumption that only structures with chimneys could be residential biases the impression of the quarters there. The buildings with chimneys are all well built, cut-stone structures evincing considerable time and trouble (and hence cost) in their construction. If the other buildings located directly adjacent to the "road" were also slave residences, however, then they conflict with the model too. Therefore, without further evidence we must treat Gerace's model with caution.

Four stone-built structures were investigated by Aarons at South West Bay plantation on New Providence (Aarons 1991). One unit was excavated in structure D. A few nails and other iron objects were recovered. This structure was located 754 feet northwest of the main house complex and at a lower elevation (Turner 1992:34). A similar structure was found nearby (Aarons, Outten, and Turner 1990:57). Aarons et al. (1990) interpret structure D as a possible cotton house (Aarons et al. 1990:64). They describe it as one story, constructed of stone, and measuring 25 feet × 16 feet (Aarons et al. 1990:59). The plan (Aarons et al. 1990:plan 1) shows only one doorway. Aarons et al. (1990:56) date the majority of the artifacts recovered to the period 1800–1825.

Turner (1992:35), however, suggests that the two stone-built structures northwest of the main house complex are probably slave houses, given their size, location, and construction. The floor was plastered, but neither structure had a fireplace (Turner 1992:34–35). Given that the only excavation was within the cabin and that the cabin had a solid plaster floor, the lack of domestic artifacts does not preclude Turner's interpretation, especially in view of our work at nearby Clifton.

At Clifton between 1996 and 1999 we recorded and excavated in and around seven slave houses (figure 9.2), although the extent of the excavations at each house varies from a minimum of five square meters to a maximum of fifty square meters (Farnsworth 1999; Wilkie and Farnsworth 1996, 1997, 1999a, 1999b). The property was originally granted in three separate parcels to Lewis Johnston, John Wood, and Thomas Ross in 1788 and 1789 (RGD 1799c). William Wylly purchased two of the three parcels as early as 1799 (RGD 1799c), but by 1806 they belonged to another owner (*RGBA* 1806). After a series of land transactions, all three parcels were purchased in 1809 by William Wylly (RGD 1809), who then developed Clifton as his main estate. In 1821, he was transferred to St. Vincent (Department of Archives [DA] 1821b).

As mentioned previously, Wylly was a very controversial figure. As attorney general, he prosecuted several prominent planters on charges of cruelty and underprovisioning of slaves (CO 1818a). A convert to Methodism (Peggs 1960: 61–61, 73–74), Wylly advocated a strong paternalistic approach to the management of enslaved people and imposed laws regarding morality, family life, and religion on his slaves (CO 1815). The artifacts excavated from the cabins largely correspond to the period of Wylly's ownership (see Wilkie this volume, table 10.1) and an 1806 advertisement for the property (*RGBA* 1806) describes only a stone-built main house (and no other stone-built structures). Therefore, it is reasonable to conclude that the cabins were constructed under Wylly's tenure after 1809.

The seven slave houses (G-M) are arranged in a row along the road leading to the main house complex, approximately 300 meters (about 1000 feet) to the south (figure 9.2). All of the buildings are constructed of unshaped limestone

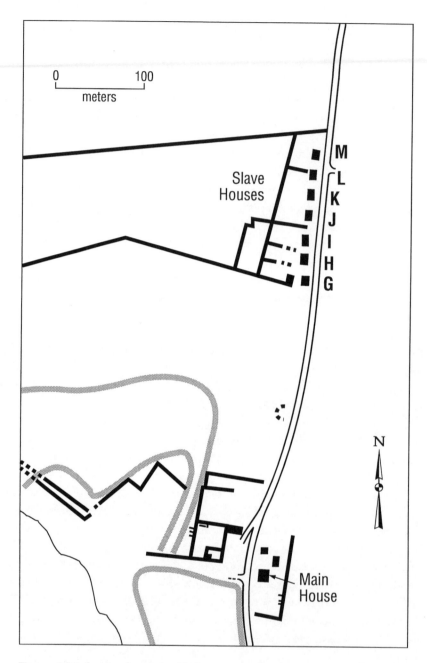

Fig. 9.2. Map showing the relationship between the slave houses (G–M) and the main house complex of Clifton plantation, New Providence.

blocks mortared in place. The corners feature cut-stone quoins, and cut stone frames the doors and windows. The majority of the ruins still stand to the eaves, with only the roofs missing, and one building still has remnants of roof framing. Presumably, the roofs were originally thatched, but we have no direct evidence of thatching. The buildings' walls are coated in mortar inside and out. The insides sometimes bear traces of plaster. None of the buildings has a chimney, and surprisingly, given Wylly's claim that married slaves at Clifton were to be given a stone-built house with two rooms, none of the buildings shows evidence of partitions, even though at least three are large enough to have been divided into two rooms. Most of the houses, however, have been reoccupied since the period of slavery, and subsequent modifications may have removed or obliterated evidence of earlier partition walls.

At first glance, the houses all appear similar, but closer examination reveals that no two are exactly alike (table 9.3). All of the buildings have two doors, one each front (east) and back (west) at the midpoint of the long walls. All feature a window facing south, toward the main house (figure 9.3). Roof lines, however, vary along the row. The first house at the southern end of the row (G) had a hipped roof, as did the fifth down the row going north (K) (figure 9.4). The others had gabled roofs with lofts. The northernmost house (M) had a small window opening in its north gable for the loft (figure 9.5), whereas the house immediately to the south (L) of it had a window in its east wall, north of the doorway (figure 9.6). Sizes also varied. The third building in the row (I) was the largest, followed by the two houses closest to the main house (G and

Table 9.3. Variation in Slave Houses at Clifton Plantation.

House	Dimensions		Roof Style	Windows
	Meters	Feet		
G	8.3 x 5.3	27 x 17.5	Hipped	One to South
H	8.3 x 5.3	27 x 17.5	Gabled	One to South
I	8.65 x 5.3	28.5 x 17.2	Gabled	One to South
J	6.35 x 4.6	20 x 15	Gabled	One to South
K	6.35 x 4.6	20 x 15	Hipped	One to South
L	6.35 x 4.6	20 x 15	Gabled	Two, South & East (to north of door)
M	6.35 x 4.6	20 x 15	Gabled	Two, South & North (in upper Gable)

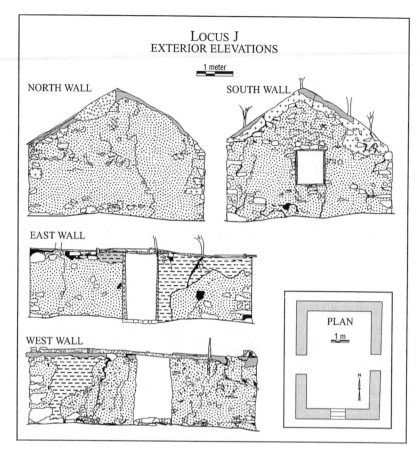

LOCUS J
EXTERIOR ELEVATIONS

1 meter

NORTH WALL

SOUTH WALL

EAST WALL

WEST WALL

PLAN
1 m

Fig. 9.3. Ground plan and exterior elevations of house J at Clifton plantation, New Providence.

H). The other four (J–M) were smaller. Overall, the houses appear regular in construction and layout, but each one varies in specific details.

Another plantation that appears to have had a separate slave quarter is Great Hope on Crooked Island. James Menzies developed the plantation after 1792 (RGD 1792). His executors sold the plantation in 1817, and it eventually became the property of Henry Moss (RGD 1817, 1818). Henry Moss owned Great Hope through 1847 (Department of Lands and Surveys [DLS] 1847).

Our research on Crooked Island was sponsored by the Bahamas National Trust, to which the central complex at Great Hope had been donated. As a result, the central complex was the focus of our research (Farnsworth 1999; Farnsworth and Wilkie 1998; Wilkie 1996a; Wilkie and Farnsworth 1995,

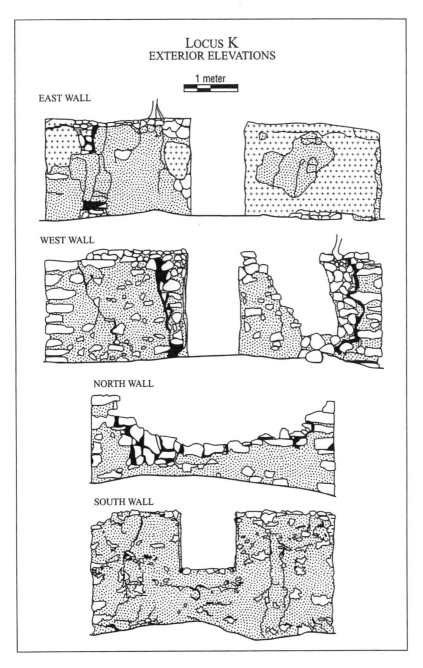

Fig. 9.4. Exterior wall elevations of house K at Clifton plantation, New Providence.

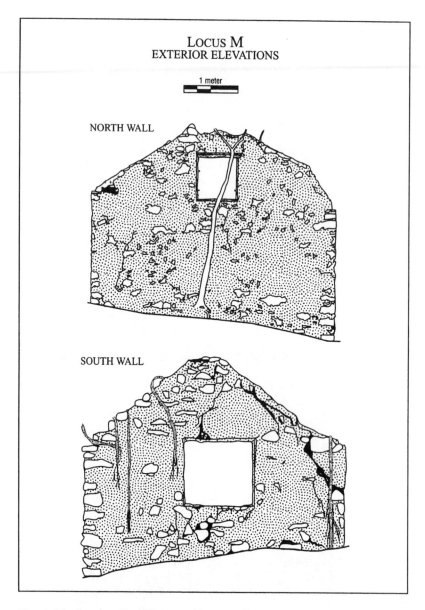

Fig. 9.5. North and south wall exterior elevations of house M at Clifton plantation, New Providence.

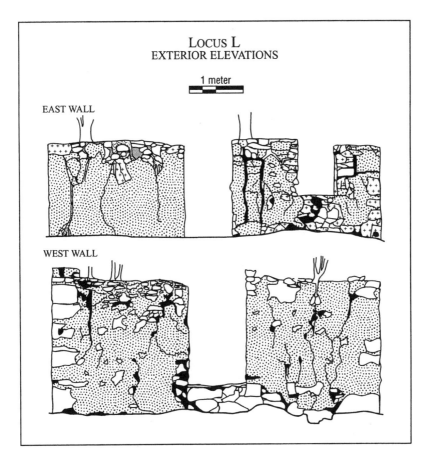

Fig. 9.6. East and west wall exterior elevations of house L at Clifton plantation, New Providence.

1999a). A brief survey north of the trust's property, however, revealed what is probably the ruins of the slave village approximately 100 meters north of the main house. At least part of the village appears to consist of four stone-built houses along a field wall running northwest, away from the central compound. Two structures were located slightly closer to the main house. One had a chimney. At the farther end of the row lie two other buildings, apparently at right angles to the main row. Additional survey and mapping were carried out by Christopher Lee of Louisiana State University in June 1999, but until his results are available, little more can be said of the complex at this time.

The central complex at Great Hope consists of twelve structures enclosed by dry-stone walls. One of these, located 20 meters north of the main house, may have been home to an enslaved family, although it may also have served as a kitchen, bakehouse, or laundry in addition (Farnsworth 1999; Wilkie 1996a). The structure consists of a substantial standing, stone-built chimney, 2.85 meters (over 9 feet) high. Excavation revealed evidence of a mortar floor ending at the south and east wall foundations, which were relatively insubstantial and were made of limestone rubble and mortar. The chimney formed the west end of the structure. The building appears to have measured 5.2 × 2.8 meters (approximately 17 × 9 feet), which is small, compared with most of the other buildings we have recorded. Not surprisingly, our limited excavation inside the building found no evidence of any partition. The evidence of impressions of vertical, round posts in the chimney and the recovery of mortar with impressions of round poles, and smaller sticks in it, suggests that the building was constructed of wood post framing with wattles in between daubed with lime mortar.

Approximately 25 percent of the building's ceramic vessel count dates prior to 1820, and James Menzies apparently erected the structure sometime after 1792. If so, then this building is probably earlier than either the Clifton cabins or any of those studied on San Salvador. It might have served as the first kitchen for the main house until a larger one was built, or it could simply have been an early house for domestic slaves, built by a man whose background in the cold and damp of Scotland led him to suggest that a chimney should be included in the cabin. The artifacts recovered certainly suggest domestic activities. The construction methods used in this early structure are reminiscent of the description of George Gray's two wattled and plastered houses, also on Crooked Island in 1799 (RGD 1799b), and the 1805 advertisement for Bellefield estate's thirty "houses wattled and plastered" (*RGBA* 1805). These houses must also have been constructed earlier than either the Clifton or the San Salvador stone-built cabins.

Bellefield estate was on North Caicos. Englishman Wade Stubbs, a Loyalist refugee from British East Florida (Siebert 1972b:281), was granted Bellefield in 1789 (RGD 1789). At some point the property was purchased by land speculators, whose eventual bankruptcy led to the advertisement just mentioned (*RGBA* 1805). The estate was then purchased in 1806 by Wade Stubbs (DA 1806). At some point after regaining the estate, Stubbs renamed it Wade's Green plantation (DA 1821a). Wade Stubbs lived on the Caicos Islands until his death in 1822 (*RGBA* 1822).

The 1805 ad makes plain that the estate was well established by that time. Most of the buildings described were probably erected in the early 1790s. Our survey of the main complex of the plantation in 1989 revealed twelve stone-built structures, most arranged around a sub-rectangular compound enclosed by a dry-stone wall (Farnsworth 1993, 1996, 1999; Wilkie and Farnsworth 1999a). Unfortunately, time permitted us to record and excavate only five of the structures: the main house, the kitchen, the overseer's house, a storage building, and one structure that was probably a slave cabin. The ad does not list any stone-built cabins at Bellefield, but we identified three of the stone-built structures as slave cabins. Domestic artifacts were found on the surface associated with all three. Excavation of the most unusual of the three also recovered artifacts indicating that a range of domestic activities took place in it. We were therefore convinced that all three structures were stone-built slave cabins. If so, they must have been constructed after Wade Stubbs purchased the estate in 1805.

All three cabins have most of their walls standing to full height, and all three are similar in size. There is no evidence of partitions. All three cabins were built of limestone blocks mortared together, and all formed part of the wall defining the yard area. One cabin, however, was on the east side of the yard almost at the midpoint of the east wall, whereas the other two cabins lay on the west wall of the yard toward its northwest corner.

The excavated cabin was located farthest north along the wall (figure 9.7). Although this cabin had two doors, neither opened into the yard. One door opened west toward the fields; the other opened south toward the other cabin. Strangely, both doors were located close to the southwest corner of the building, each being approximately one meter from the corner! The structure measured 6.3 × 4.7 meters (20.7 × 15.4 feet), had a hipped roof, and featured one window slightly to the north of the center of the east wall, facing the yard. Three ventilation slots also pierce this wall, two north of the window, one to the south. These slots are commonly found in storage rooms and buildings in the Bahamas. Excavation revealed no evidence of flooring, and so a dirt floor is likely. Artifacts from inside and out were domestic in nature. The majority of the ceramics appear to be from the nineteenth century, with a mean ceramic date of 1819.

Our survey revealed no trace of the thirty "wattled and plastered" slave houses described in the newspaper (*RGBA* 1805). The survey was a visual inspection and surface collection, however, and was not designed to reveal structures that left no trace on the surface. In addition, there is no reason

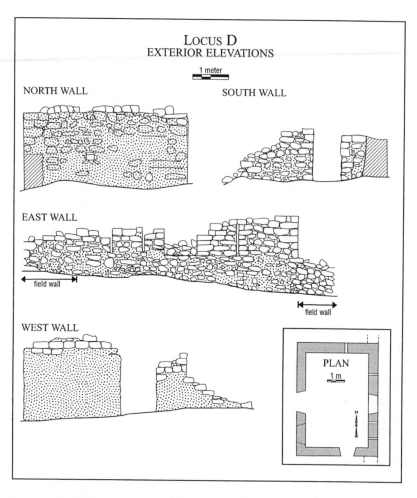

Fig. 9.7. Ground plan and exterior wall elevations of house D at Wade's Green/Bellefield plantation, North Caicos.

to expect that these houses would be in the central yard area where our research was focused. Maps of the area reveal two other clusters of ruins in the vicinity of the main house that would have been part of the original estate, one approximately 200 meters northwest of the main house and the other 250 meters southwest. Dense brush prevented us from visiting them, but it is possible that they represent the wattle-and-plaster houses described in the newspaper or, more likely, stone-built replacements.

The three stone-built cabins at Wade's Green differ from the stone-built cabin we recorded at Marine Farm on Crooked Island (Farnsworth 1999;

Farnsworth and Wilkie 1998; Wilkie and Farnsworth 1995, 1999a). The Marine Farm cabin (figure 9.8) is slightly larger at 7.1 × 5.1 meters (23.4 × 16.6 feet), and falls between the sizes recorded at Clifton. It had walls constructed of unshaped limestone blocks and mortar, all heavily coated in mortar, and a mortar floor. It originally had a hipped roof. The structure has its long axis oriented east-west in contrast to the stone-built cabins at Clifton and Wade's Green. The house has doors in both long sides. The door to the north, which opens into the yard area of the plantation, is centered. The door in the south wall is west of center and is balanced by a window opening to the east. Both the east and west walls also had windows at their midpoints. The ceramics recovered indicate occupation during the first and second decades of the nineteenth century.

Marine Farm was granted to Joseph Hunter in January 1791 (RGD 1791), but his ownership of Marine Farm had definitely ended by 1808 at the latest (*Bahama Gazette* [*BG*] 1815; CO 1818a) and may have ended, we believe, by 1796 (RGD n.d.). By 1808 Marine Farm belonged to James Moss, who was a merchant in Nassau and had been the principal slave importer to the Bahamas (*BG* 1786–1800). He became one of the wealthiest and most powerful men in the colony and president of the council, second only to the governor in rank. By the time of his death in 1820 (*RGBA* 1820), he owned 840 slaves in the Bahamas (DA 1822), making him the largest slave owner in the colony. He also owned slaves in Demerara (CO 1828) and possibly other colonies.

The Marine Farm plantation complex consists of a main house, a kitchen building just behind, a privy to the west, and the slave cabin some twenty-five meters to the east (Farnsworth 1999; Farnsworth and Wilkie 1998; Wilkie and Farnsworth 1995, 1999a). A group of ruined slave cabins are mentioned in a 1940s description of the property a half a mile or more to the north (Rees 1944), but we did not attempt to relocate them because the Bahamas National Trust was sponsoring our project and the structures were not on trust property. In the summer of 1999, Christopher Lee of Louisiana State University located and mapped several clusters of ruined cabins in this vicinity. The 1940s document describes the quarters as "practically gone," possibly suggesting that they were foundations of wattle-and-plaster slave houses like the structure at nearby Great Hope. Lee (personal communication 1999) found low stone walls. Some had postholes for a wood-framed superstructure; others were represented by low ridges of limestone rubble that give no hint as to the building's method of construction. At some houses, Lee reported finding limestone mortar from the walls, but he did not mention the presence of wattle impressions.

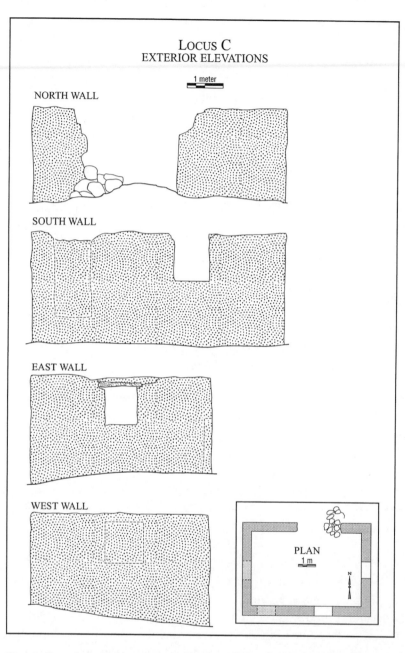

Fig. 9.8. Ground plan and exterior wall elevations of house C at Marine Farm plantation, Crooked Island.

Given Gerace's hypothesis that the wealth of the planter was reflected in the construction of the slave cabins, we might expect the cabins at Marine Farm, owned by one of the wealthiest men in the Bahamas, to be made not of wattle and plaster, or even of wood, but of stone. The evidence from Promised Land plantation on New Providence, however, clearly shows that James Moss built wattle-and-plaster slave houses on his plantations.

Promised Land was granted in 1785 to William Moss, but upon his death in 1796, the plantation passed to his brother, James Moss, and the plantation was developed after 1796 by James (Aarons et al. 1990:4; *BG* 1796; DLS 1785). In addition to excavations at the main house, a systematic survey was made of twenty-eight hectares roughly centered on the main house, and systematic shovel testing was carried out over the two-hectare area encompassing the main house ruins and field walls. The shovel testing located the remains of what appear to be two structures with a yard area between them approximately fifty meters south of the main house. Relatively large quantities of domestic artifacts were recovered from the excavation units in the area around and between these structures. The ceramics suggest a late eighteenth- to early nineteenth-century occupation ending around 1820 (Farnsworth 1994, 1996, 1999; Wilkie and Farnsworth 1999a).

Rather than being stone built, these structures used a lime and sand mortar to coat wattle walls supported on round poles and in some cases square-cut lumber, of which the mortar preserved impressions. Some of the mortar fragments show that the outer surface was scored, with a layer of lime plaster applied, which was then painted yellow.

Unfortunately, time did not allow us to excavate either structure completely. For the eastern house, although the more extensively excavated, we found no evidence of floors, foundations, or postholes. Each building, however, was represented by heavy concentrations of mortar fragments whose distribution suggests the structure's size. Given the lack of structural features in the excavation units and the higher mortar concentrations in some units, the house appears to have been at least 5 × 4 meters (16 × 13 feet), with the longer side oriented north-south. The other structure, though less intensively excavated, is partly defined by the surviving dry-stone field wall that once abutted its north end and possibly the south end as well. Excavation at the northern end of the gap in the wall uncovered a lime mortar foundation running east-west. A large boulder in the unit at the south end of the gap may have served the same purpose. The gap in the wall suggests a maximum north-south dimension of 7.6 meters (25 feet), whereas the distribution of mortar fragments in the units to east and west suggests a width of less than 6 meters (about 19 feet). Thus both cabins fall within the approximate size range suggested by the stone-built cabins elsewhere, the wattle-and-plaster structure at Great Hope, and the wattle-and-plaster houses listed in George Gray's 1799 inventory. No further details regarding door or window placement can be derived from the excavations, and both cabins presumably had thatched roofs.

Finally, in this survey of the archaeological evidence for slave housing in the Bahamas, mention must be made of the most recent excavations at Clifton plantation on New Providence. Although the quarters, main house, and various other structures are located inland, there are two stone-built structures by the beach. Excavations at these structures in 1998 revealed that a large prehistoric site lay beneath them and that the southern-most structure was built earlier than the main plantation complex, probably in the mid to late eighteenth century (either before the Loyalist period in the Bahamas or in its early stages). During systematic testing of the underlying prehistoric site in 1999, evidence of two additional historic structures was found. One was approximately twenty-five meters south of the southern-most stone-built house, and excavation recovered mortar and plaster with wattle impressions. The ceramics again indicated a mid- to late-eighteenth-century occupation. The similarities to the Promised Land cabins in method of construction and artifacts recovered, combined with the location relative to the stone-built structure, suggest that this may be a slave cabin. The ceramics recovered clearly indicate that the structure predates Wylly's 1799 ownership (Wilkie and Farnsworth 1999b, 1999c, 2000).

The overall picture of slave housing painted by archaeological studies is predominantly one of stone-built cabins, mostly with only one room, some with chimneys, and probably with thatched roofs. Dimensions range from approximately 28–20 feet in length by 17–15 feet in width. In every case, however, these structures appear to date after 1800. Promised Land, Great Hope, and now Clifton also suggest the existence of wattle and plaster houses measuring approximately 16–17 feet in length by 9–13 feet in width. In each case the evidence suggests they were constructed before 1800 and match those described for George Gray's Crooked Island estate and Bellefield plantation in the historical record.

The archaeological record is biased, because preservation favors stone buildings over wattle and plaster, wood frame, or wattle-and-daub structures. Furthermore, most archaeological reconnaissance on Bahamian plantations has relied on visual inspection, which would not locate the remains of less substantial structures. Only the Promised Land and Clifton projects have employed any form of extensive systematic, subsurface testing strategy, and both projects located evidence of less substantial slave houses.

The references to "Negro houses" in the inventories and other documents that do not mention the construction material, together with the values assigned to them in the Moss inventory, lead me to conclude that the majority of slave houses built by the slaves of incoming Loyalist planters between 1783 and 1800 were single-room, wattle-and-daub structures that have yet to be identified in the archaeological record. Archaeologists must change their research strategies in order to identify these structures if archaeology is to clarify the nature and development of slave housing further in the Bahamas. The wattle-and-plaster cabins recorded for George Gray and at Bellefield plantation and excavated at Promised Land, Great Hope, and Clifton represent a 1780s and 1790s elaboration on an as yet unrecorded building tradition, with stone-built cabins only appearing on Bahamian plantations after 1800.

Negotiating Acceptable Housing

The preceding discussion suggests that slave housing in the Bahamas was neither uniform nor static over time. Wattle and daub may have given way to wattle and plaster and then to stone, but only on some estates. Even among the stone-built houses, there was considerable variation in construction methods, door and window placement, and roof design. I believe that all of these variations reflect changes in the cultural negotiation between planters and enslaved peoples regarding acceptable housing.

Although the Loyalists came to the Bahamas from East Florida, they were originally from South Carolina and Georgia (Kozy 1983; Peters 1960; Siebert 1975). What was the nature of slave housing in those areas prior to the Revolution? Given that few slave houses survive from that time period, research by architectural historians has been limited to documentary sources. Vlach (1986a:155) describes slave houses in South Carolina as typically small, rectangular, one-room huts with mud walls and thatched roofs that were essentially African-style houses. Ferguson (1992:63–82) uses archaeological evidence from a series of sites in South Carolina to demonstrate that slave houses prior to 1800 were typically mud-walled, either cob or wattle and daub, with a thatched roof. He suggests they were single- or double-unit buildings, each unit consisting of one room.

Ferguson (1992:66) suggests that in the second half of the eighteenth century, cob walling declined in popularity and was replaced by wattle and daub or planks infilling post-built structures. Chimneys also appear in the second half of the century on some slave houses but not before. Dirt floors were the rule for most of the century, although raised floors appear toward the end of the century, probably after the Loyalists had left (Ferguson 1992:73).

Archaeological evidence for eighteenth-century slave housing in Georgia is harder to find, as most plantation excavations have focused on the nineteenth century. At Kings Bay, in southern coastal Georgia, Adams (1987) excavated three adjacent plantations that must have been contemporary with the Loyalist plantations in the Bahamas, as they date from 1791, 1793, and 1801. At two of the sites no clear architectural features were found; only architectural materials were recovered. These led Adams to suggest a cabin of tabby-plastered lathing with a brick hearth at one site. It must be noted here that in Georgia the term "tabby" generally refers to plaster made of crushed shells, sand, and shell lime (Otto 1984:129) and so has a slightly different sense from the Bahamian use of the same term. At Kings Bay plantation, features representing four cabins were uncovered, two being represented by postholes, the other two by postholes and a wall trench. Tabby chunks and tabby mortar are mentioned at three of the four cabins. All had combinations of square and round postholes outlining double pen houses (i.e., two units, each consisting of one room). Adams (1987) doesn't discuss these structures further, but wattle and daub, wattle and tabby, or lath and tabby seem likely for the infilling of the structures.

Therefore, when the Loyalist planters and their enslaved workers first arrived in the Bahamas, it seems likely that they were used to wattle-and-daub, and wattle-and-tabby-plaster, one-room single- or double-pen houses with thatch roofs. Thomas Ross, Lewis Johnston, and John Wood, the original grantees of Clifton, together with William Wylly, the subsequent owner, all came to the Bahamas from Georgia (Siebert 1972a:48, 1972b:361). William Moss, although English born, came from Georgia via East Florida, bringing eighty-one slaves with him (Siebert 1972b:100, 244, 361). His brother James may have come via East Florida, if not Georgia (*RGBA* 1820). The discovery of wattle-and-plaster houses at Clifton and Promised Land (originally William's property but developed by his brother James) supports the argument that the Loyalists built wattle-and-daub or wattle-and-plaster houses for their enslaved workers when they first established their plantations in the Bahamas. The newspaper advertisement for Wade Stubbs's Bellefield estate describing thirty wattle-and-plaster houses can also be cited in this regard, since Stubbs came via East Florida (Siebert 1972b:281).

To newly arrived enslaved Africans, these one-room wattle-and-daub houses with thatched roofs would not necessarily be unusual. The origins of the enslaved Africans brought directly to the Bahamas, however, are uncertain and mixed. Craton and Saunders (1992:436) found advertisements for runaways mentioning Angolas, Congoes, Fulani, Senegal, Ebo, Quaqua and "Guinea born." Dalleo (1982) names at least thirty different African groups as being represented in the slave and free black population of the Bahamas, and points out that the vague nature of many of the terms applied by Europeans means that they often encompassed several ethnic groups at least. Most of the newspaper ads for slaves imported by William and James Moss (*BG* 1786–1800), for example, simply refer to "Windward Coast Negroes," a group that, Higman (1984:128) suggests, would be dominated by Canga and Kwakwa ethnicities. One ad by James Moss, Jr., describes a shipment of slaves from Angola (*RGBA* 1804).

Therefore, it is difficult, if not impossible, to look to one West African group for specific ancestral Bahamian house types. That said, post-in-ground, wattle-and-daub, thatched houses seem to be common to many West African traditions, although they do not necessarily predominate (Agorsah 1983; Anthony 1976a, 1976b; Armstrong 1990:10–11; Haviser 1997e; Jones 1985:199–200; McIntosh 1974; Vlach 1986b). According to Edwards (1980:304, figure 4), rectangular, hipped and gabled roof houses were typical of much of the area of West Africa where slaves were obtained. The frequency of one- and two-room or multiroom structures also varies (Armstrong 1990; Fletcher 1977; Prussin 1969), although two-room houses have tended to predominate in discussions of West African housing (e.g., Agorsah 1983; Edwards 1980:304; Haviser 1997e; Vlach 1986b). Finally, it has been suggested (Edwards 1980:305; Vlach 1975 in Edwards 1980:figure 7; Vlach 1986a:165, 1986b:74–76) that few African houses measured more than approximately fourteen feet wide in their outside dimensions, whereas British houses rarely measure less than about fourteen feet wide in their inside dimensions.

Documentary sources and archaeological excavations combine to suggest that wattle-and-daub, one- or, more commonly, two-room (not double-pen) thatched houses were the norm on plantations throughout the Caribbean in the eighteenth century (e.g., Armstrong 1990; Armstrong and Kelly 1992; Chapman 1991; Debien 1974; Handler and Lange 1978; Haviser 1997e; Kelly 1989). Since throughout the Caribbean, slaves usually built their own houses from locally available materials (Debien 1974; Lange and Handler 1985:18), the resulting structures are attributed to African traditions. A West African arriving on a Bahamian plantation would not be particularly surprised to see a wattle-and-daub thatched house. Only the lack of a partition creating two rooms (if the South Carolina single-room pattern was brought to the Bahamas with the

Loyalists) might conflict with their experience. Since we know nothing about Bahamian wattle-and-daub houses, however, the discussion must focus on the reasons for the prevalence of one-room structures in South Carolina, a topic that lies beyond the scope of this chapter.

Many Bahamian planters such as William Wylly and Burton Williams were American born, and William Moss, James Moss, and Wade Stubbs were born in northwest England but spent time in Georgia and/or East Florida before coming to the Bahamas. As a result, they would have been familiar with wattle-and-daub houses from the Southeast. But what of James Menzies and Charles Farquharson, who were Scottish, and other planters who were British born and did not come via the Southeast? How common was wattle-and-daub thatched housing in mid- to late-eighteenth-century Britain?

This question is harder to answer. Certainly thatch was the prevalent roofing material until the mid-eighteenth century (Brunskill 1971:199), and it continues in use to the present day, but the use of wattle and daub is more questionable. Although it was common in the medieval period (e.g., Aslet and Powers 1985:54; Brunskill 1971:58; Clarke 1984:35–38; Steane 1985:179, 190; West 1971:119–120), there is little discussion of it in postmedieval archaeological (e.g., Crossley 1990:34–43) or architectural studies (e.g., Mercer 1975; Muir 1980; Royal Commission on Historical Monuments of England 1986). In part, this omission reflects a lack of preservation in standing structures (Mercer 1975:113) and comparatively little excavation of rural, postmedieval cottages (Crossley 1990:41). In addition, however, it may reflect a change in building practice in the late medieval period. Steane (1985:190), for example, states that "a changeover from turf, clay or timber to stone-walled buildings occurred all over the country [England] during the late twelfth and early thirteenth centuries." Clarke (1984:37, 180) confirms that stone began to be used as a building material in much of England in the thirteenth century.

According to Michael Reed, brick became the usual building material during the seventeenth century: "The wattle and daub technique used in many timber-framed houses and cottages was replaced by brick nogging," and "by the end of the seventeenth century house builders had learnt to use brick on its own" (1983:81). Reed adds, however, that "the one- or two-roomed cabins . . . which were the homes of the very poorest sections of the community . . . were far removed from the comfort of the newly built farmhouse. . . . They persisted in some districts of Lowland Britain until well into the nineteenth century" (Reed 1983:82). West notes that wattle and daub "persisted for centuries and was so satisfactory that the rural builders stuck to it long after more sophisticated ways had been introduced" (1971:120).

Mercer (1975:136) notes that unbaked earth was used by the poor as a building material for a long time in most areas of England until mass-produced bricks became cheap in the nineteenth century. The same was probably true for much of Scotland, where Reed states that, in the eighteenth century, "the farmhouses of Scottish tenant farmers and the cottages of their subtenants were . . . occasionally of stake and rise (wattle and daub). Walls were rarely more than six feet high and upper storeys almost entirely unknown. . . . The roof itself was . . . thatched with straw, rushes or heather" (1983:72).

Thus, although wattle-and-daub construction was not the fashion in Britain in the eighteenth century, men such as Moss, Stubbs, Menzies, and Farquharson would probably have been familiar with the use of wattle and daub with thatched roofs and would probably have found it appropriate for housing their slaves, the poorest members of society. Clearly, then, the adoption of wattle-and-daub structures from the Carolinas to the Caribbean reflected the negotiation of a common building tradition between Europeans and Africans and one that the Loyalists continued in the Bahamas.

Lime mortar appears to have replaced mud daub in Georgia (Adams 1987) as well as in the Bahamas (e.g., Clifton, Promised Land, Bellefield) and at about the same time. The use of lime mortar for construction had been established throughout Europe from Roman times (Anderson and Spiers 1927; Boon 1974; Wheeler 1964), and its use as a coating over wattle-and-daub walls is of similar antiquity (Boon 1974:198–200; Richmond 1969:51). Lath and plaster infilling for walls, along with extensive plasterwork in houses, emerged in the sixteenth and early seventeenth centuries (Aslet and Powers 1985: 56–58; Brunskill 1971:66; Platt 1978:235; Steane 1985:203; Warmington 1976:136; West 1971:120) and had spread throughout England by the late seventeenth century (Brunskill 1971:66; Mercer 1975:120).

The addition of lime to the outer layers of clay daub to protect walls was also a well-established tradition in medieval and postmedieval Britain (e.g., Brunskill 1971:58; Mercer 1975:133–136; Taylor 1974:77; West 1971:120). This technique, however, was also known in West Africa. Ethnographic research among the Konkomba of northern Ghana, for example, records that ground shells from the nearby Oti River were used to make a lime powder that was added to the cow dung that was applied to the surfaces of house walls and floors. The result is described as a smooth, hard, near-white surface that was impervious to rain (Prussin 1969:42–43). On the basis of his ethnographic research, Jones (1985:199) notes that the prototype for tabby, consisting of burnt lime with seashells used as a reinforcing agent, is used throughout the Guinea Coast region of West Africa. As a result, to West Africans familiar with mud daub, and possibly coating it with a hard lime outer layer, or the use of tabby as described by Jones (1985:199), changing to a more durable lime mortar over wattles would not have required any radical shift in mental templates. It should also be noted that the two wattle-and-plaster houses we have excavated in the Bahamas thus far, measured approximately nine and thirteen feet wide, respectively, well within the width of the African house module suggested by Edwards (1980:305) and Vlach (1975 in Edwards 1980:figure 5; Vlach 1986a:165, 1986b:74–76). Therefore, the use of lime mortar probably met with little resistance in the negotiation between planter and enslaved and again represents a common ground in the architectural traditions of each group. Only the technology of burning lime and shells for mortar may have been introduced to the enslaved people.

The sudden appearance of stone-built cabins after 1800 in the Bahamas and other Caribbean islands (Chapman 1991; Handler and Lange 1978), however, must have involved more cultural negotiation. Although wattle-and-daub houses predominate in much of West Africa, stone construction may not have been unknown to Africans brought to the Bahamas. According to DeCorse (1992:185) stone foundations and walls were in use in some areas of West Africa prior to European contact. Furthermore, there were many stone-built European trading stations on the West African coast from which the slave trade was conducted (DeCorse 1992; Posnansky and DeCorse 1986). As a result, Africans arriving in the Bahamas probably had some familiarity with stone-built structures and, perhaps, a little experience in their construction.

Since there is little evidence to suggest that stone-built cabins were common in the Southeast prior to the Revolution, and no significant tradition of stone construction in West Africa, the change to stone-built cabins presumably originated in Europe. Chapman (1991) has addressed this issue for the Danish West Indies, where, in the last decade of the eighteenth century and first two decades of the nineteenth, slave houses changed from single-unit, two-room wattle-and-daub cottages to multiple-unit, multiple-room masonry buildings. Chapman (1991:108) states that similar changes took place in Barbados, Jamaica, and other sugar-producing islands around the same time. It would appear that the Bahamas, though not a "sugar island," can be added to the list.

On St. Croix, Chapman (1991:112) suggests that the change occurred after 1790. He states that the earliest buildings were little more than masonry versions of wattle-and-daub structures. He describes a surviving example as a two-room structure with exterior dimensions of sixteen by twenty-six feet, with walls of rubble masonry and cut stone and coral blocks used to reinforce corners and window openings. The roofs are hipped and were originally thatched. The description parallels the Bahamian cabins except for the partition into two rooms that we have yet to find in most of our cabins. On St. Croix, at a slightly later date, beginning between 1795 and 1810 and continuing through the 1820s, a new slave house form appears consisting of masonry cottages with two units, each consisting of two rooms, arranged along a row, or masonry row houses with four or more two-room units (Chapman 1991:113). Thus far, we have not found any parallels to these houses on Bahamian plantations.

Chapman (1991) ascribes these changes to the influence of the agricultural reform movement in Britain in the late eighteenth century and particularly the improvements in estate workers' housing there. This movement was accompanied by published treatises that included appropriate designs for agricultural housing, beginning in 1775 with Nathaniel Kent's *Hints to Gentlemen of Landed Property*, with other publications appearing in 1789 by John Miller and in 1790 by John Plaw (Chapman 1991:116). According to Chapman (1991:116), the most important publication for West Indian buildings was John Wood's *A Series of Plans for Cottages or Habitations of the Labourer either in Husbandry or the Mechanical Arts*, published in 1781, reprinted in 1792, and reissued in a new edition in 1806. Wood recommended that housing be built of masonry, with lime mortar and plaster, although roofs could be thatched, tiled, or covered with slate (Chapman 1991:116).

Slavery was already under attack in Britain by the 1780s and 1790s, and planters feared that the importation of slaves from Africa would soon come to an end. Improved housing was seen by West Indian planters in the sugar islands as a way to halt and help reverse the population decline that they were all experiencing (Chapman 1991). Besides, by providing improved housing, the planters hoped to combat the criticisms of the abolitionists. In *Practical Rules for the Management and Medical Treatment of Negro Slaves in the Sugar Colonies*, published in London in 1803, Dr. Collins, a planter from St. Kitts, recommended improved housing as one measure to be taken; he noted, for one thing, that houses should ideally be constructed of stone (Chapman 1991:118).

Estate inventories show that at least some Bahamian planters maintained extensive libraries, and the Nassau newspapers frequently republished articles from newspapers they received from Europe, North America, and the Caribbean. In addition, many of the planters frequently visited Britain and other Caribbean islands. Because the official mail boat as well as many vessels carrying goods and passengers from London came to Nassau via Kingston, Jamaica, Bahamians were particularly well informed on Jamaican events and trends. It is therefore almost inconceivable that Bahamian planters did not know of these publications or lacked access to them. The idea for the relatively sudden appearance of stone-built cabins in the Bahamas, therefore, may be traced in large part to the British agricultural reform movement.

A change in the planter population may also have influenced the adoption of stone-built cabins. By the turn of the century, the cotton plantations in the Bahamas were already in decline, and planters looking for quick profits were moving on, leaving a core of planters who were perhaps more dedicated and more determined to adapt to the changing economic and environmental circumstances. These men may well have taken a more long-term and professional approach than the "get-rich-quick" Loyalists, who abandoned their lands once cotton appeared doomed. Furthermore, by the early nineteenth century there was a core of enslaved men trained in limestone rubble-and-mortar construction, because stone-built kitchens and other major plantation buildings were common by the late 1790s. These factors—the emergence of professional planters with a long-term outlook and the training of stonemasons—coincide with the introduction of the idea of housing reform from Britain around the turn of the century.

That said, although the idea may have come from Britain, the execution was Bahamian, producing a truly Creole house form. Dr. Collins and John Wood included several other specific recommendations of which we have yet to find evidence in the Bahamas. Wood proposed, for example, that buildings be elevated fifteen to eighteen inches above the ground, with separate rooms for parents and children (Chapman 1991:116). Wood recommended that the building have an internal width of twelve feet or less, and that units be built in pairs or multiple units, with plans provided for two-, three-, and four-unit cottages. Dr. Collins suggested elevating houses six to eight inches above grade and placing at least two, and ideally three, two-room units in one building with internal dimensions of twelve by sixty-six feet (Chapman 1991:116–118). Buildings following these guidelines have been documented by Chapman (1991) in St. Croix, so why aren't they in the Bahamas?

Part of the answer probably lies in the relatively small size of most Bahamian plantation slave populations. James Moss and Wade Stubbs were exceptional in the numbers of slaves they owned, and even they divided their workforce between a number of estates. According to Craton and Saunders (1992:278), only 25 percent of Bahamian slaves belonged to owners with more than fifty slaves, as compared with over 80 percent in Jamaica. The majority of Bahamian slaveholders owned fewer than thirty slaves (Craton and Saunders 1992:278). As a result, there was little need for extensive, large-scale slave housing comparable to that in the sugar islands.

The answer also lies, in part, in the cultural negotiations between planters and slaves. As in St. Croix, the first masonry slave houses built on Bahamian plantations resembled the wattle-and-daub houses but were built of stone. In the Bahamas, however, unlike St. Croix, the typical house, perhaps reflecting southeastern ancestry, consisted of only one room, not two, and two-unit dwellings were not typical. The result was that most Bahamian cabins are one-room structures made of limestone rubble and lime mortar with cut stone reinforcing corners, doors, and windows with thatched roofs. Houses recorded thus far are fifteen feet or more wide, in accordance with the typical British house module discussed by Edwards (1980:305), but do not exhibit the twelve-foot width recommended by Wood or Dr. Collins (Chapman 1991:116–118). There is otherwise little standardization between plantations. The cabins at Wade's Green, Marine Farm, and Clifton all differ significantly in detail from each other. Only at Clifton does there seem to be internal standardization of size and the placement of the two east-west doors, with the one window in the southern wall, although, even here, as previously mentioned, each cabin also differs significantly from the others.

There was no long tradition of stone construction in the African and Creole slaves' past. Given limited supervision, the slaves used stone to build houses that resembled their familiar wattle-and-daub houses, as happened on St. Croix, but they were unwilling to build the raised, multiroom, multiunit structures recommended by the British reform literature, which the planters may ideally have wanted. At this time, too, however, cotton was failing in the Bahamas, and the economic future of the colony was in doubt (Craton and Saunders 1992). Furthermore, the slave population of the Bahamas was already increasing naturally, and planters often had more slaves than they knew what to do with (Craton and Saunders 1992). As a result, the pressure to promote a natural increase in the enslaved population that prompted planters on St. Croix, Barbados, St. Kitts, and Jamaica to add multiple-unit, improved houses was absent in the Bahamas. Therefore, most planters had no impetus to build anything more complex than the simple stone-built cabins that could be regarded as improved housing and that might address the concerns of the abolitionist movement, and the slaves had no desire for more elaborate construction either. As a result, the larger, improved housing units were not built in the Bahamas.

Only a resident reforming planter like William Wylly cared enough to impose more uniformity on his slaves. Even so, all of the Clifton houses feature minor variations—from hipped roofs to extra windows—that individualized the buildings and subverted the orderly appearance Wylly probably desired.

In negotiation, Wylly may have imposed his will to a greater degree than other planters, but the enslaved people were still able to negotiate some elements of compromise.

Summary

The majority of enslaved people on Bahamian plantations probably lived in one-room, wattle-and-daub, thatched houses. These houses were part of the cultural heritage shared by both West African and Creole slaves, as well as British- and American-born planters. We have, however, no contemporary descriptions of these structures, no surviving examples, and none have been found archaeologically! The closest we have come is archaeological evidence for wattle-and-plaster houses, for which we also have limited documentary evidence. Although these houses attest to the introduction of a commonly used European construction material, they represent only a minor shift in the cultural negotiation between peoples of West African and European ancestry.

The majority of the archaeologically recorded slave cabins are stone-built, one-room structures that had hipped, thatched roofs. Again, we have limited documentary evidence for these structures, but their origins probably lie in the publications on improved housing produced by the British agrarian reform movement. Most of the masonry houses recorded so far resemble the African-style wattle-and-daub houses built in limestone and mortar more than the raised, multiroom, multiunit structures proposed by the British reformers. With no West African tradition of stone-built housing, Bahamian slaves were probably unwilling to stray too far from their traditional houses in their cultural negotiation with the Loyalist planters. For their part, the Loyalist planters had little to gain by forcing the issue. In the Bahamas, only ardent reformers of slavery, like William Wylly, who were willing to supervise construction strictly were able to impose more European-inspired houses on their enslaved people. Even here, the enslaved people were able to negotiate design changes that subverted the orderly, planned appearance that the reformers desired.

The stone-built, hipped-roof house recorded archaeologically on the plantations was a successful cultural compromise between African and European peoples that established a Bahamian architectural tradition. Despite their superficial European appearance, these houses are as much African in their heritage as they are European. Equally, the majority of enslaved people did not live in these stone-built houses. Most enslaved people in the Bahamas lived in wattle-and-daub or wattle-and-plaster houses that probably closely resembled the stone houses in their general form. The wattle-and-daub or wattle-and-plaster houses also represent the results of a negotiation between Africans and Europeans, but the use of perishable materials makes their African ancestry more apparent. When confronted by reformist planters wanting the enslaved people in the Bahamas to build "improved" stone housing, the laborers simply used stone to reproduce the perishable houses. After the end of slavery, they further developed the style into the traditional Bahamian house built throughout the islands during the rest of the nineteenth century and the first half of the twentieth century (e.g., Cottman 1963:58; Malone and Roberts 1991:20–21; Otterbein 1975).

Previous research on Bahamian architecture has failed to capture the complexities of the diachronic cultural negotiation between Africans and Europeans that resulted in the creation of a unique architectural heritage. Through the analysis of multiple lines of evidence derived from documentary, architectural, and archaeological sources, it has been possible both to reconstruct a more accurate model of slave housing and to derive a more sophisticated understanding of the process of creolization in the Bahamas.

METHODIST INTENTIONS AND AFRICAN SENSIBILITIES

The Victory of African Consumerism over Planter Paternalism at a Bahamian Plantation

Laurie A. Wilkie

[William Wylly] addressed himself at least indirectly to a number of Blacks then among the numerous bystanders, declaring them an oppressed people and himself their protector, abused the House of Assembly in the most contemptuous and scurrilous manner; menaced all his opponents with some secret but powerful influence that he had with his Majesty's Government; talked of his son's [*sic*] being his Ambassador at home; and in short spoke and committed so many furious extravagances that we might have been charitably inclined to overlook them as the melancholly ravings of a disordered mind, were we not too well assured that the paroxysm was that of wounded pride, and not of mental imbecillity, the writhings of a haughty domineering spirit. (CO 1817)

So an exasperated committee from the Bahamian General Assembly wrote of their attorney general, William Wylly, in 1817, shortly after arresting him for treason. The reasons for Wylly's arrest were as numerous as his enemies, but the charges against him had mainly to do with his interactions with the British African Institute, which was pushing for reform in the conditions of enslavement (Craton and Saunders 1992:223). As part of their reform efforts, the African Institute supported the adoption of a registry system for slaves held in British colonies. The Caribbean and its sugar industry were notorious for cruelty and the waste of human life, as evidenced by high mortality rates. In addition, although Britain had outlawed the further importation of African slaves to its colonies in 1807, the African Institute, and other observers, claimed that an illegal trade continued to flourish in the Caribbean. The institution of a slave registry system, it was believed, would help regulate planters' behavior and treatment of slaves while also permitting individual slaves to be tracked over time (Craton and Saunders 1992; Higman 1984).

The slave registry system, which was to be conducted on a triennial basis, would completely and accurately account for all enslaved people in the colonies. Individuals would be listed by name, age, sex, origin (whether African or Creole, meaning island-born), and, depending upon the individual island, the economic activities in which they were engaged. In addition, the registry would enumerate any infirmities and would indicate whether a slave had died or had been sold or manumitted in the time between registers. The Bahamas General Assembly resented the imposition of the registry system and actively strove not to adopt one. The Bahamas were one of the last colonies to adopt a registry system in 1821 (Higman 1984:8). William Wylly, however, supported the system, and was rumored to have written a letter in 1817 to the African Institute condemning the behavior of the Bahamian General Assembly and the overall treatment of enslaved people in the Bahamas. The rumored existence of this letter led to Wylly's two arrests and to his horsewhipping on a public street in Nassau (CO 1817).

The competing letters written by Wylly and the General Assembly to the Colonial Office show that both sides had a dramatic flair for presenting their case and that the "truth" depended much upon the writer's political affiliation. The "Wylly Affair," as it came to be known, however, indicates how much Wylly's views differed from those of the rest of the Bahamian planter population. Wylly, a midlife convert to Methodism, considered himself a reformer of slavery but not an abolitionist. He owned three major plantations on New Providence Island, where he housed at least sixty-seven slaves (DA 1821b). His explicit list of rules for slaves on his plantations encouraged literacy, attendance of Methodist religious services, and participation in the local markets as both vendors and purchasers. Wylly encouraged his enslaved population to work plots of land for themselves, leaving them entitled to their own produce (CO 1818b). Yet in his apparent "lenience," Wylly wanted to demonstrate that enslaved Africans and their descendants could be productive, educated, religious individuals in the proper English manner. Wylly essentially embraced a paternalistic attitude toward his slaves, which, although common throughout the American South by this time, was rare in the Bahamas.

The documentary record of William Wylly's life portrays a conflicted man who wanted to adopt the tenets of his newly embraced religion but at the same time could not distance himself completely from the racism and oppression of his time. What distinguishes Wylly from other planters in the Bahamas is the clear evidence that he sincerely considered himself to be a reformer and a humanist. Still, although Wylly acknowledged the humanity of his enslaved people, he viewed this humanity solely from a European colonial perspective. The best interests of his slaves, so thought Wylly, would be served only if they adopted his culture and his faith.

Wylly was a complicated individual whose views, attitudes, and actions are available to us through the documentary record. Outspoken, opinionated, and powerful, Wylly pushed his reform agenda through his appointment as attorney general. He used his office to prosecute other planters for cruelty to their slaves and to clarify the rights of the large population of free Africans who lived in the Bahamian capital of Nassau (CO 1816; Craton and Saunders 1992; Saunders 1985). Wylly constantly held up his own plantations as models for how slavery should be. Yet within his own "household," he did not always practice what he preached.

When Boatswain, a trusted enslaved mason, and his wife and children attempted to flee enslavement, Wylly offered a reward for their return (*BG* 1821). Upon their capture, he sold the family in 1823 to Henry Moss, one of the Bahamas' more notoriously cruel planters (CO 1827; DA 1825). Boatswain and his family went from lives as domestic servants and craftsmen to workers in the salt ponds of Crooked Island and Long Cay (DA 1831), which afforded the worst working conditions in the Bahamas. From the period between 1784 and 1821, Wylly is recorded as having manumitted six of his slaves (DA 1784), including a woman and her two young children. The woman was the daughter of one of his deceased enslaved nurses who had saved Wylly's daughter's life when she was ill in 1805. Rather than manumit Lusty, Wylly repaid the nurse by promising to manumit Lusty's infant daughter Sarah, and Sarah's produce, once Sarah turned twenty-one in 1826, long after Lusty had died (RGD 1805).

Wylly did not manumit any enslaved people in his will. After Wylly's death in 1828, the provisions of his will split long-established families and couples, separating elderly husbands and wives (DA 1821b, 1822, 1825, 1827, 1828; Hughes 1997). This harsh behavior contrasts sharply with the concern for reform that he had expressed earlier. It is clear from the documentary record that Wylly grew increasingly disenchanted with, and frustrated by, his enslaved population. The cause of Wylly's frustration may be found within the archaeological record of enslaved life at Clifton plantation.

The rich historical record documenting the deeds and ideas of William Wylly provides a rare archaeological opportunity. Not only can we compare the public and private realms of Wylly's life to learn whether he acted on his words of reform, but we can also begin to understand the lives of those denied a voice in the historical record: the enslaved population of Wylly's plantations who lived within the framework of Wylly's social experiment. Wylly's enslaved population did not passively participate in Wylly's social engineering. Instead, as the archaeological record makes plain, the opportunities and freedoms permitted by Wylly's "reforms" allowed the enslaved population greater opportunities to maintain a sense of African cultural identity. Rather than becoming more Europeanized, more Methodist, and more loyal, Wylly's enslaved population remained strongly and defiantly African, through both their creative and consumer culture.

William Wylly and the Economics of Clifton Plantation

Part of Clifton plantation was purchased by Wylly around 1799 (RGD 1799c), but he did not own the entire property until 1809 (Wilkie and Farnsworth 1999a, 1999b). Clifton served as Wylly's main plantation until he moved to St. Vincent in 1821. By the time Wylly left the Bahamas, he owned sixty-seven slaves, most of whom resided at Clifton (CO 1818b; DA 1828).

Wylly's highly public and controversial persona makes him a highly visible figure in the Colonial Office correspondence of his time. After the "Wylly Affair," Wylly's enemies in the assembly sought to drive him out of the attorney general's seat through a series of charges against him, including the allegation that he had failed to properly feed his enslaved population. In answering these charges, Wylly drew together a collection of letters and ledgers documenting the treatment of slaves on his plantation, their rations, his rules of conduct, and their economic activities (CO 1818b). These documents provide valuable insight into the boundaries within which the slaves of Clifton lived.

Wylly's rules of Clifton plantation sought to outline and define proper slave behavior on the plantation as well as to delineate what Wylly regarded as his responsibilities toward the slaves. The published rules of Clifton plantation bear an 1815 date (CO 1815), but it is impossible to know how early or late they may have been employed. On August 31, 1818, Wylly wrote of the economic arrangements on Clifton:

> I believe it is the practice in much of the West Indies, as well as in some parts of this colony to allow certain descriptions of slaves one day in each week, for the purpose of enabling them to raise or purchase their own provisions, and I perceived soon after I had made my present establishment at Clifton, which is at the west end of this island, that it would be necessary for me to adopt some practice of that sort, in order

to enable the Negroes to bring their own pigs, poultry, etc., to market. I therefore consented to give Saturday to those slaves whose services could be despenced [*sic*] with on that day. And I have no doubt but they would all (most gladly) have accepted it, in lieu of their established allowance of Provisions. But not choosing to let them entirely dependent upon their own industry for their subsistence, I continued to give them one half of the usual allowance of corn; which with what they received for the use of their children (all of whom from the time of birth are entitled to half allowances) was perhaps, in general, sufficient for their support. (CO 1818b)

In a letter to his overseer James Rutherford (CO 1818b) dated November 1, 1817, Wylly stated:

Each man and his wife must plant two acres of provisions: (which the woman alone will be able to attend): and when they have potatoes or other bulky articles to carry to market, they may use my boat: only taking care to return her, in safety, to her moorings. . . . whenever I may have occasion to employ any of the tradesmen or labourers, I shall allow them half a dollar, a day wages. The price of building walls has been fixed at one shilling a yard.

If any of the people would prefer being furnished with provisions out of the barn, they have only to give their name to the Driver, and they will receive their weekly allowance of eight quarts of corn: but they must in that case do full tasks both the Friday and Saturday.

Summaries of ledger books provided by Wylly demonstrated that at least twenty-two men had taken the opportunity to earn cash by building walls on the plantation, with one man earning over four pounds for his efforts (CO 1818b). Likewise, accounts showed that slave families at Clifton were raising "guinea corn" [sorghum], "Indian corn" [maize], "yams," "potatoes," "pumpkins," "squashes," "peas," "beans," "ocre" [okra], "benny" [sesame], "ground nuts" [peanuts], "eddies" [taro], "plantains," "bannanas," "water melon," "musk melon," "dung hill fowls," and "hogs" in their provisioning grounds (CO 1818c).

Wylly's rules of Clifton plantation also established that he would purchase hogs from the slaves at market price. The excess produce, animals, fowl, and even provisioned corn were all goods that could be sold at market. By granting slaves permission to use his boat, Wylly facilitated their access to Nassau's thriving marketplace. In addition, currency that the slaves earned by building walls could be spent in the town of Nassau.

It is clear from the documentary record that the enslaved African-Bahamians of Clifton had not only access to the market but also the means to be active consumers in the marketplace. The archaeological record of Clifton offers the greatest opportunity for understanding how Wylly's slaves exercised their consumer power.

The African and African-Bahamian Population of Clifton

The island of New Providence was home to a large, thriving African community. After the formal abolition of the African slave trade, Britain seized large numbers of Africans bound for Cuba as contraband. Many of these individuals were conscripted into the British West India Regiments; others were "apprenticed" to planters on different islands (CO 1811; Craton and Saunders 1992). Free African settlements grew in the "Over the Hill" section of Nassau and on the western end of the island. Some of these settlements retained distinctive African ethnic identities. Baintown residents, for instance, maintain that they are descendants of the Yoruban peoples (from modern Nigeria), whereas their neighbors, in Contabutta, are Congoes (from modern Zaire) (Eneas 1976:7–8). Eneas, in a synthesis of oral histories from Baintown, reported that, throughout the late nineteenth and early twentieth centuries, the two groups maintained distinct communities and had minimal social interaction (Eneas 1976:36).

A relatively large African population appears to have lived and worked at Clifton. In 1821, at the time of the first Bahamas slave register (DA 1821b), Wylly was documented as owning sixty-seven slaves, who were spread across Wylly's three plantations. Fifteen of these individuals were registered as having been born in Africa, representing slightly more than 20 percent of the enslaved population. Based upon an 1818 record of families with provisioning grounds (CO 1818c), forty-four of the enslaved individuals lived at Clifton, of whom ten or more were Africans.

Africans held positions of prestige within the plantation population, both as the heads of families and as workers. Eight of the twelve families known to have lived on Clifton in 1818 were headed by at least one African parent (CO 1818c; DA 1821b). In other words, the Creole population on Clifton consisted mostly of the children of enslaved Africans. The underdriver, Jack, was the highest ranked slave on Clifton. Jack and his wife, Sue Eve, a cook, were both Africans (CO 1818c; DA 1821b). In addition to this core of enslaved Africans living at Clifton, Wylly acquired five "liberated African" apprentices in 1811 (CO 1811). In 1818, four of these men and their free wives (places of birth unknown) are listed as working provisioning grounds at Clifton along with the enslaved families (CO 1818c). At least one "liberated African" and his enslaved wife lived on Clifton.

The Africans living within Clifton were a visibly distinctive subgroup of the plantation population distinguished by their native body art and, often, their names. The apprenticed Africans maintained their African names. "Cudjoe," "Appea," "Adon," "Teracoo," and "Abuka" were apprenticed to Wylly on September 2, 1811 (CO 1811). In addition to their African names, each of the apprentices was described as having "country marks." Cudjoe bore scars on his temples and belly; Appea on his temples, Adon on the side of his belly; Teracoo on his body; and Abuka, on his face (CO 1811). With the exception of Adon, all of the men were still apprenticed to Wylly in 1818 (CO 1818b). Although clothing may have covered the body art on the chest and abdomen at least part of the time, the scarring present on temples and face would always be visible, serving as a potent cultural symbol. Unfortunately, the documentary record for Clifton does not provide any insight into the art that may have adorned the bodies of the enslaved Africans and even Creoles, although advertisements for runaways often do.

The position of the enslaved Africans within Clifton's community, as heads of families and as distinguished individuals in the plantation hierarchy, probably enabled them to wield a great deal of cultural influence over the Creole population. The population's demographic profile makes it appropriate to study the material culture of Clifton's enslaved community for evidence of African continuities. Furthermore, although we do not know the origins of the Clifton slaves, given the strong Yoruban and Congo sense of identity that seems to have survived elsewhere on New Providence into the current century, it seems appropriate to focus in particular upon potential continuities in Yoruban and Bakongo (Congo) cultural ideals and practices.

According to Higman (1984:127, table 5.10), as many as 30.8 percent of the African slaves brought to the British Caribbean between 1790 and 1807 were from the region of Central Africa, with a majority being Bakongo peoples. Slave registers from the Bahamas as well as advertisements for runaways mention names such as "Congo Jim" or otherwise specify individuals of Congo background (DA 1825; Saunders 1985:82). The documentary record suggests that enslaved and free Congo peoples lived in the Bahamas. Less clear is how much of the Yoruban population was free rather than enslaved. Yoruban influences continue in modern-day New Providence, most strikingly perhaps in the traditions of Junkanoo (Bethel 1991). Saunders (1991:22–23) describes the Congo, Ibo, Mandingo, and Yoruba as the most represented African ethnic groups brought to the Bahamas as slaves. A survey of names found on slave registers also indicates the presence of Akan peoples (Wilkie 1993). Saunders (1991:22–23) further states, "Most of these [African] tribes had maintained the separate identity down to 1960 in the form of the Congo Lodges I and II and the Yoruba Lodge."

Expressions of African Sensibilities through Material Culture

Enslaved Africans and African-Americans are among the muted peoples of history. Through the study of the materials discarded at slave quarters, archaeologists working in the American South, Caribbean, and Brazil have enhanced our understanding of the experiences of enslaved people. Archaeologists have studied the quality of life under enslavement, the power relationships within plantations, the slaves' foodways, and their socioeconomic status. Perhaps the most elusive and most highly sought archaeological evidence, however, is that which can enlighten us regarding African cultural continuities in the New World.

The degree to which African cultural practices survived the Middle Passage and the brutality of slavery has long interested anthropologists and historians (e.g., Herskovits 1941; Mintz and Price 1992; Thompson 1983). Since European-American planters were likely to discourage continuities in African culture, and were themselves cultural outsiders who may not have recognized African traditions, the documentary record has limited potential for identifying evidence of continuities. Persisting African traditions would most likely be masked and disguised from planters, again contributing to documentary invisibility. For this reason, archaeology provides the most promising way of researching African continuities during the period of enslavement.

Archaeologists in the Caribbean have been successful in identifying objects that were either African in origin or African in their style of manufacture. In excavating the slave cemetery of Newton plantation in Barbados, for example, Jerome Handler and Frederick Lange (1978) recovered the skeleton of an individual who wore two copper bracelets on his left arm, two metal rings, a copper ring, and a necklace consisting of seven cowry shells, twenty-one drilled dog canines, fourteen glass beads, five frilled fish vertebrae, and one large agate bead. Handler and Lange argued that these were likely to be materials of extremely high status that had been brought from Africa. Working in Jamaica, Roderick Ebanks (1995) and Douglas Armstrong (1990) identified, in the material form of Yabba wares, a ceramic manufacturing tradition that grew from West African pottery traditions. Similar pottery traditions are reported in the American South under the name "Colono wares" (Ferguson 1992). Candice Goucher (1999), working in Trinidad and Tobago, has uncovered archaeological evidence of West African ironworking traditions.

In addition to finding materials that reflect a West African heritage, archaeologists have identified behaviors that reflect West African traditions. Grace Turner (1993:116), for instance, has noted the recovery of human teeth near the rooflines of houses in the Bahamas. Turner, drawing upon oral traditions, ties this practice to the contemporary practice of throwing lost teeth over the shoulder and onto the roof to bring good luck. Herskovits (1941:195) also noted this tradition in other parts of the New World and believed that it originated in Dahomey.

Handler (1996) has recently argued that one of the individuals buried at Newton plantation was a witch or other negatively viewed person, based upon burial in the prone position. Matthew Reeves (1996), working in Jamaica, discovered two bottles near the doorway of an enslaved person's house that he has interpreted as Obeah bottles, intended to harm the occupants of the house. The use of bottles as containers for conjure is well documented in the Caribbean and throughout the American South (e.g., Eneas 1976; Hurston 1938; Puckett 1926; Thompson 1983; Wilkie 1997). Again, this magical practice appears to have a West African basis. Lydia Pulsipher (1993a), working in Montserrat, has found continuities in the formation and use of houseyard compounds on that island with house gardens in West Africa.

AFRICAN AMERICANS AS CONSUMERS

Although these and other studies have clearly demonstrated that material evidence of African continuities is available throughout the Caribbean, less attention has been paid to the potential meanings of the non-African materials recovered from enslaved houses. Many enslaved people would have had little time or opportunity to create and manufacture their own material culture. Ceramics and iron objects were produced by a limited number of craftspeople. African-style basketry and mats were probably widely manufactured, but these materials rarely survive in the archaeological record. The vast majority of the materials recovered archaeologically from enslaved peoples' houses in the Caribbean were made in England or other parts of Europe.

Although owners may have made available to the enslaved people many of the European-manufactured materials recovered from plantation sites, the enslaved people themselves are likely to have procured some of the materials through internal marketing systems (Howson 1995; Wilkie 1999). If enslaved people maintained a sense of African identity through magical practices, burial practices, the ways that they organized their house space, and in their pottery and iron traditions, why wouldn't they actively select those European-manufactured goods that also enhanced their sense of Africanness? Research conducted on later African-American sites in the American South has demonstrated that African-American consumers expressed ethnic preferences and ideals through their selection of mass-produced goods (e.g., Wilkie 1994a, 1994b, 1996b, 1996c, 1999, 2000a).

In most instances, it is very difficult, if not impossible, to determine archaeologically which materials reflect the consumer preferences of planters versus those of slaves. The archaeological assemblages from Clifton plantation, however, offer a rare opportunity to study enslaved people's consumer choices. The analysis of materials from these cabins illustrates that African-inspired aesthetic and religious traditions influenced the consumer choices of Clifton's African-Bahamian plantation.

The Archaeology of Clifton

Clifton plantation is one of the best-preserved plantation complexes in the Bahamas. The complex of buildings and features at Clifton consisted of a planter's residence (A), kitchen (B), storeroom/office (C), chapel/barn (D), stable (E), slave kitchen/storeroom (F), seven slave cabins (G–M), at least two other related outbuildings (N, P), and a number of walled fields, corrals and compounds (figure 10.1).

During the summer of 1996, a joint team of archaeologists from the University of California, Berkeley, Louisiana State University, and the Bahamas Department of Archives began excavations at Clifton plantation (Wilkie and Farnsworth 1996, 1997, 1999a). Fifteen standing structures were identified during a field survey. Each structure was tested with at least one interior and four exterior excavation units. All units measured one meter square and were dug using trowel and brush. Larger-scale block excavations were undertaken at the driver's cabin (G) and the slave kitchen (F). Twenty-two and twenty-four units, respectively, were excavated at these two structures, which thus provided the greatest abundance of materials.

The assemblage from the driver's cabin (Locus G) is particularly important for this study. The house has been designated as the driver's cabin because of its position at the head of the row and its obvious connection with, and probable control over, the slave kitchen (Locus F). It has been possible, based on this attribution, to narrow the potential occupants of the house to one of two families. Clifton is known to have had a free black overseer, James Rutherford,

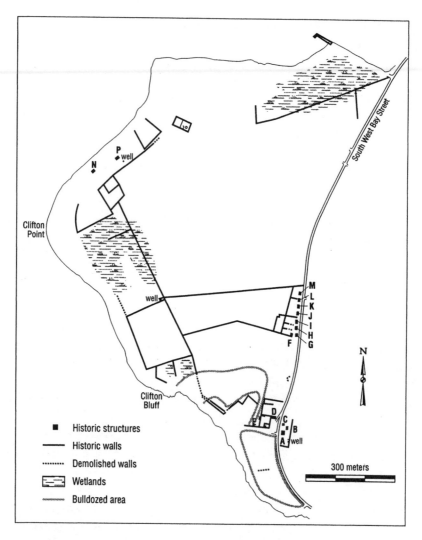

Fig. 10.1. Location of structures on Clifton plantation. The function of buildings A–P are given in Table 10.1.

who managed all three of Wylly's west-side plantations. In correspondence, Rutherford refers to himself as "Overseer," and legal documents gathered in Wylly's defense also refer to Rutherford as "overseer." Wylly, however, refers to Rutherford in one document as his "driver." Ledgers kept by Rutherford refer to Jack as the plantation driver. The question becomes: which of these two individuals is likely to have occupied the house?

Although the cabin at Locus G is slightly larger than most of the others in the row, it is not significantly different from the other slave cabins. Overseer houses on other Bahamian plantations are significantly larger than slave cabins and are not located in the quarters (e.g., Farnsworth and Wilkie Farnsworth 1990). In addition, it appears to have been common practice on Bahamian plantations to have the driver live in the quarters as an internal monitor of slave behavior (e.g., CO 1827). Finally, the driver's wife, Sue Eve, is listed in plantation ledgers as a "cook." If the family of Jack and Sue Eve were the occupants of the house, the proximity of the driver's cabin to the slave kitchen would not only allow the driver to control provisions that were distributed from the kitchen but would also give his wife easy access for food preparation. The issue is of relevance, because both Jack and his wife, Sue Eve, are recorded as having been Africans.

The date for each structure was determined using a technique developed by Stanley South (1977) known as mean ceramic dating. The technique uses the dates of peaks of ceramic style popularity to establish a site date. Mean ceramic dates (MCD) were calculated based upon minimum number of vessel counts rather than sherd counts. An MCD was calculated for every structure where more than two ceramic vessels were recovered. Although this dating technique has proven very reliable in the United States, in the Bahamas, ceramic popularity seems to lag slightly behind the continental mainland. This lag may reflect market conditions unique to the West Indies (Farnsworth 1996). As a result, Clifton's MCDs are earlier than would be suggested by the established documentary chronology of the site, but they remain useful for determining the relative age of occupation of structures within the site (Wilkie and Farnsworth 1997, 1999a). The dates and functions for the structures are summarized in table 10.1.

Artifact Analysis

A wide range of materials was recovered from the excavations at Clifton. Ceramics, glass, tobacco pipe, metal, fish bone, and marine shell artifacts and ecofacts were recovered throughout the planter house compound and the slave quarters. With the possible exception of one ceramic, all of the artifacts were mass-produced artifacts of European origin. Although other Caribbean archaeologists have tended to equate the use of European-produced goods with assimilation (e.g., Armstrong 1983; Haviser 1997e), I would argue that if the materials are analyzed with the needs, desires, and preferences of an

Table 10.1. Locus Designation, Possible Function and Mean Ceramic Date.

Locus Designation	Possible Function	Mean Ceramic Date
A	Wylly's House	1805
B	Planter kitchen	1808
F	Slave kitchen	1808
G	Driver's cabin	1807
H	Slave cabin	1810
I	Slave cabin	1804
J	Slave cabin	1819
K	Slave cabin	1817
L	Slave cabin	1816
M	Slave cabin	1804

enslaved African consumer, an African sensibility and aesthetic may be seen to have guided purchasing decisions.

The archaeological research from Clifton plantation is still in its earliest stages, with additional field seasons planned. Therefore, this analysis represents preliminary interpretations. The results of ceramic, tobacco pipe, and button analysis, however, strongly suggest the presence of distinct African-rooted consumer behaviors in the past.

CERAMIC ANALYSIS

Archaeologists studying ceramics from enslaved people's households must constantly attempt to determine whether the ceramics patterns they are studying represent the preferences and economics of the planter or those of the enslaved people. Enslaved people may gain access to ceramics through allotments provided by the planter, through gifts of secondhand ceramics from the planter, through theft from the planter, or through their own purchasing or bartering practices. I will argue, given comparisons between the Clifton planter and slave assemblages, and comparisons of Clifton assemblages with other Bahamian and U.S. plantations, that the composition of the enslaved ceramic assemblages at Clifton reflects African aesthetic and cultural practices (see also Wilkie 1999, 2000b).

For this discussion, I focus upon three characteristics of the ceramic assemblage: the selection of decorative type and its socioeconomic implications;

the selection of decoration color; and the potential cultural connotations of design motifs found on the ceramics.

Decoration selection. To study socioeconomic class and consumer purchasing decisions, historical archaeologists employ ceramic price indexing. George Miller (1980, 1991) developed Miller's Ceramic Index on the basis of the relative prices of different English earthenware ceramic decorative types common throughout the late eighteenth and nineteenth centuries. Miller found that four classes of decorative types maintain the same ranking relative to one another through time and could therefore be used to look at the relative expense of different ceramic assemblages.

"Plain" ceramics were always the cheapest on the market, followed by "minimally decorated" ceramics, which included banded, mocha, sponged, and shell-edged ceramics. "Hand-painted" ceramics, which were more labor intensive to manufacture, were the second most expensive category, and "transfer-printed" wares were the most expensive earthenware. Miller's index does not include some of the other expensive ceramics available at this time, such as porcelains, basalt wares and other fine stonewares. By comparing the abundance within an assemblage of ceramics at each price level, an archaeologist can begin to study the consumer choices that shaped a family's ceramic purchases.

For Clifton, the relative abundance of each ceramic decorative type was calculated for each locus (table 10.2). As would be expected, the Wylly planter assemblage contains the highest percentage of transfer-printed ceramics, and some of the lowest incidences of plain ceramics. The slave assemblages, however, contain large numbers of ceramics in the hand-painted category and a significant number of ceramics in the transfer-printed category. In the cases of Loci G and I, 40 percent or more of the ceramics are from the highest two price categories, and from Loci F, H and L, over 50 percent of the ceramics are from the highest price categories.

The results from the Clifton analysis contrast sharply with a similar analysis of the slave assemblage at Promised Land plantation, New Providence (Farnsworth 1996). At Promised Land, the slave assemblage contains 88 percent plain, 0 percent minimally decorated, 11.8 percent hand-painted, and 0 percent transfer-printed ceramics. Similar studies in the southeastern United States typically have only 20–30 percent of the ceramics in the highest two categories for assemblages associated with enslaved people (Farnsworth 1996). It is important to note that this analysis should not be interpreted as meaning that the enslaved people at Clifton were wealthy. In terms of abundance of ceramics, the slave quarters contained a much lower density of ceramic vessels

Table 10.2. Distribution of Ceramics (%) from Clifton Plantation by Price Level (includes earthenwares only).

Locus	Plain	Minimally Decorated	Hand-Painted	Transfer-Prints	Minimum Number of Vessels
A Wylly House	18.8	31.3	18.8	31.3	16
B Wylly Kitchen	11.3	35.2	14.1	39.4	71
F Slave Kitchen	19.5	26.8	39.0	14.6	41
G Driver's Cabin	17.0	33.9	32.1	17.0	53
H Slave Cabin	30.0	10.0	50.0	10.0	10
I Slave Cabin	20.0	40.0	20.0	20.0	10
J Slave Cabin	*	*	*	*	*
K Slave Cabin	25.0	37.5	37.5	0	8
L Slave Cabin	15.8	26.3	36.8	21.1	19
M Slave Cabin	50.0	33.3	16.6	0	6

* indicates that too few ceramics were recovered from this locus for this analysis

than the planter residence and kitchen. Instead, this analysis demonstrates that the slaves had access to more expensive ceramics than enslaved people did at Promised Land or in the southeastern United States.

Hand-painted ceramics seem to be the most popular decorative type recovered from the slave quarters, accounting for over 30 percent of the ceramic vessels in five of the eight slave assemblages. Hand-painted ceramics are less popular in the Wylly planter assemblages, where they account for less than 20 percent of the ceramic vessels.

Superficially, the relative percentages of minimally decorated ceramics seen in the planter and slave assemblages seem to be more comparable. The minimally decorated ceramic category, however, includes a range of very different-looking ceramics, including molded/embossed, shell-edged, and annular/mocha wares. When the planter and slave assemblages are compared, it becomes evident that although the two planter assemblages contain a greater percentage of shell-edged wares than annular wares, the slave assemblages generally demonstrate a preference for annular wares over shell-edged (table 10.3). Since these decorative types fall within the same price category, I suggest that the different distribution between slave and planter households represented a difference in consumer preference between the two groups.

Color selection. Comparison of the relative incidence of certain colors

Table 10.3. Distribution (%) of Minimally Decorated Ceramics by Type.

Locus	Shell	Sponge/Spatter	Annular	Minimum Number of Vessels
A Wylly House	80.0	0	20.0	5
B Wylly Kitchen	56.0	0	44.0	25
F Slave Kitchen	36.4	0	63.6	11
G Driver's Cabin	33.3	5.5	61.1	17
H Slave Cabin	*	*	*	1
I Slave Cabin	*	*	*	4
J Slave Cabin	*	*	*	2
K Slave Cabin	*	*	*	3
L Slave Cabin	20.0	0	80.0	5
M Slave Cabin	*	*	*	2

* indicates that too few ceramics were recovered from this locus for this analysis

further illuminates differences between the planter and enslaved peoples' assemblages. During the period of the site's occupation, underglazed transfer-printed ceramics were limited to the color blue, and shell-edged ceramics were mainly available in blue or green. In contrast, banded/mocha wares and hand-painted wares could be found in the full range of colors, including blues, yellows, oranges, reds, greens, and browns, as both monochromes and polychromes.

Upon initially analyzing the planter and enslaved peoples' ceramics from Clifton, I was struck, on a qualitative level, by how different the color schemes of the assemblages seemed to be. I decided to look at the incidence of different colors in the assemblages to see whether I could substantiate my perception quantitatively. Using only the hand-painted and banded/mocha wares, I calculated for each assemblage the percentage of vessels on which each color occurred. I found that there were significant differences (table 10.4). In the Wylly house assemblage, the most popular color, blue, occurred on 60 percent of the vessels, followed by orange, on 40 percent of the vessels, and brown, on 20 percent. In the Wylly kitchen assemblage, blue was again the most popular, occurring on 50 percent of the vessels, followed by brown at 45 percent. In both cases, blue was the most common color.

In the enslaved families' assemblages, however, a different pattern was evident. In six of the eight assemblages, brown was the most popular color. Green was the most prevalent color in the other two. Blue was clearly the

Table 10.4. Percentage of Vessels Decorated with a given Color[+].

Locus	Brown	Blue	Orange	Yellow	Green	Red	Black
A Wylly House	20.0	60.0	40.0	0	20.0	0	0
B Wylly Kitchen	45.0	50.0	5.0	25.0	30.0	0	10.0
F Slave Kitchen	50.0	40.0	25.0	0	25.0	0	5.0
G Driver's Cabin	63.0	29.6	44.4	18.5	18.5	0	0
H Slave Cabin	40.0	40.0	40.0	0	80.0	0	0
I Slave Cabin	75.0	25.0	50.0	50.0	0	0	0
J Slave Cabin	*	*	*	*	*	*	*
K Slave Cabin	33.3	33.3	33.3	50.0	66.6	0	16.6
L Slave Cabin	75.0	62.5	37.5	12.5	37.5	0	12.5
M Slave Cabin	100.0	50.0	0	0	0	0	0

* indicates sample size was too small to justify this analysis.
[+] since many vessels were polychrome, total percentages for each structure exceed 100%

second most common in three assemblages, orange in two assemblages, and yellow in one assemblage. Although the sample size for this analysis is admittedly small at this point, the differences are still striking.

The difference in color selection between the enslaved families' assemblages and the planter family assemblage cannot be attributed to socioeconomic factors, because the ceramics being compared come from the same relative price category. Instead, as I will argue below, these differences may be attributable to cultural differences in assessing a ceramic's aesthetic value.

Design motifs. Finally, I will consider the ceramic design motifs within the enslaved assemblages that may suggest African aesthetic or cultural traditions. As noted above, the African/African-Bahamian ceramic assemblages suggest a preference for annular or mocha wares over shell-edged, as well as a preference for hand-painted ceramics over other ceramics, even though they were relatively expensive. Brief consideration of traditions in West African art may provide some insight into these patterns.

Important West African craft traditions include the production of ceramics, wood carving, and cloth production. Personal and ethnic aesthetics were also commonly expressed through body art such as scarification, tattooing, hair braiding, or the wearing of ornamental art such as beads and piercings. Geometric lines, chevrons, bands, and lines of dots are commonly used as artistic elements to adorn crafts and bodies.

Yoruban pots are decorated using a variety of techniques, including incising, molding, rouletting, stamping and applied clay decorations (figure 10.2). Shells, corncobs, carved wood, and pebbles are all used to incise pots (Fatunsin 1992:33–34). Painted pottery is not commonly found. Concentric circles, bands, and zagging lines are all commonly found both incised and embossed on Yoruban pots. Concentric bands can often serve as visual dividers between different design elements of the pots.

Bakongo pottery is decorated in many of the same ways as Yoruban pots, with incised and applied decorations and little use of paint (Thompson 1981). Like the Yoruban pots, a number of different decorations may occur along the horizontal axis of the pot and are visually separated from one another by solid incised lines or raised clay bands (figure 10.2).

Chevrons, bands, and dots, all common elements on Yoruban and Bakongo pottery (Thompson 1983), are also commonly found on the engine-turned annular/mocha wares produced by the English potters (figure 10.2). English hand-painted wares also often include these elements. Although annular and mocha wares are predominantly glazed, many vessels also include incised decorations. In addition, mocha wares often consist of several different bands of decoration that are distinguished from one another on the vessel through the use of dark or different colored annular rings. Hand-painted wares also often contain different bands of design (figure 10.2).

Although the vessel forms and decoration method used in the production of the English pots are very different, the design elements and the organization of the designs do conform to Yoruban and Bakongo decorative expectations for pots. The annular/mocha ceramics are certainly not the equivalents of the African pots, but to an African consumer faced with an array of English pots to choose from, the annular/mocha wares might have seemed the most appropriate selection.

Some surprising support for this argument that the selection of annular/mocha wares may have reflected African design sensibilities comes from Africa itself. Robert Ferris Thompson (1981:183–187, figures 165 and 170) illustrates his discussion of Bakongo grave treatment with two early twentieth-century photographs of chiefs' graves in Zaire. Each grave is decorated with large numbers of European-produced ceramics and bottles whose dates of manufacture and decoration seem to place them in the mid-nineteenth century. The majority of ceramics in each of these photographs are annular and mocha decorated mugs and bowls. Two different groups, sharing a common ancestral heritage but separated by an ocean and at least thirty years, seem to have selected the same kinds of British ceramics.

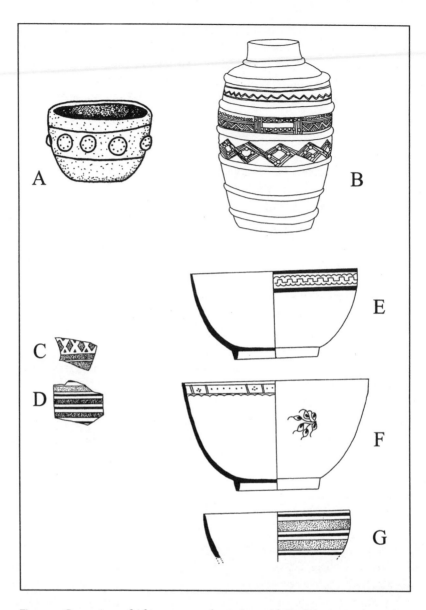

Fig. 10.2. Comparison of African pottery decorations with English pottery decorations found at Clifton plantation. (A) Yoruban pot (after Fatunsin 1992); (B) Bakongo funerary pot (after Thompson 1981); (C) Incised factory slip ware from Locus G, note the similarity to embossed decoration on the Bakongo pot; (D & E) Factory slip ware from Locus G; (F) Hand-painted pearlware recovered from Locus G, note the similarity of the border design to the depiction of the cosmogram on the Bakongo pot; (G) Factory slip ware.

In addition to the organization of the decorative elements of the ceramics, the color palette chosen in Clifton's quarters may also reflect cultural preferences. The fact that the browns, oranges, yellows, and greens found on both banded and hand-painted ceramics can be commonly found in West African cloth (Thompson 1983) perhaps suggests another reason why these ceramics may have been selected. Although painted ceramics were not typically used by Bakongo and Yoruban peoples, when faced with ceramics decorated with colors, they selected colors that were commonly used in a different artistic medium, again, to appease their aesthetic sensibilities.

We also need to consider the specific designs on hand-painted English ceramics that may have held additional cultural meanings for African and African-Bahamian users. Although many of the hand-painted patterns were geometric designs and floral patterns, portions of birds were represented on at least three vessels. In each instance, the birds portrayed are peacocks, or at least peacock feathers (figure 10.2).

Birds, commonly found in West African sculpture, are often associated with deities, witchcraft, and wisdom (Thompson 1983). Among the Bakongo, birds represent souls in flight or spirits, because their wings fan the air, like spirits or witches (MacGaffey 1986:131). Thompson (1983:76, plate 48) illustrates a fan from Cuba that was made for the Yoruban orisha Yemayá and was adorned with peacock feathers, which he states insinuate witchcraft. In other contexts, African-styled pipes decorated with animal and bird imagery have been recovered archaeologically from slave quarters throughout the Chesapeake region (Emerson 1988, 1994). Although these pipes were manufactured by African or African-American craftsman, we should not discount the potential importance of such imagery when found on English-made pottery in the households of enslaved Africans.

African Colono ware pottery found in South Carolina has been discovered with X marks, some of which crosscut circles and are carved on the exterior and interior bases of bowls. Leland Ferguson (1992) has convincingly argued that these marks may represent New World versions of the Bakongo cosmogram, like those identified by Robert Ferris Thompson in Haiti (Thompson 1981, 1983). In its original form, the Bakongo cosmogram is a circle, quartered by an X, with smaller circles on the end of each X representing the four movements of the sun. The cosmogram represents the circle of life and death and the progression of the seasons.

When placed on the base of a bowl, whether the interior or the exterior, the cosmogram signifies a bowl used to create *nkisi*, or sacred medicine. *Nkisi* can take many forms, including statuettes, bowls and their contents, and bundles of magical ingredients tied in cloth (MacGaffey 1991). Magical bundles of herbs and cloth can commonly be seen hanging from or immediately outside the houses of older Bahamians and are believed to serve as protective medicine for the house's occupants. Although such charms are currently considered to belong to the realm of Obeah in the Bahamas, their use may be Bakongo in origin.

The ceramic assemblage from the driver's cabin (Locus G) may provide archaeological evidence of *Nkisi* (Wilkie 1999). Two of the hand-painted ceramic sherds recovered from the slave quarters at Clifton bear a design remarkably similar to the Bakongo cosmogram (figure 10.3). One came from Locus G, and a second example was found at the neighboring house, Locus H. When the design formed part of a complete vessel, it would have been located on the interior base of the bowl, much as are the South Carolina Colono ware designs. On the broken sherd from Locus G, the design is nearly centered and was perhaps curated after the bowl broke. Although we can never know what function or meaning this bowl and its decoration may have had for its user, it seems more than coincidental that a ceramic bearing a powerful African symbol just happened to be found at a site occupied by people of African origin or ancestry. Imagine the surprise and pleasure of an African consumer at the Nassau market upon seeing this ceramic, which, though European made, bore a significant African design.

Tobacco Pipes

At Clifton plantation, tobacco was popularly used by planter and enslaved person alike. The greatest densities of pipe fragments were found at the planter residence and kitchen (Wilkie and Farnsworth 1997). Although lower densities of pipes were recovered from the slave quarters, the pipe types recovered from the cabins were more diverse than those recovered from the planter complex (table 10.5). Wylly is known to have distributed tobacco to his enslaved population at Christmas. He stated in his rules of Clifton plantation, "An ox (or a competent number of hogs) is to be killed for the Christmas dinner of the people; and Rum, Sugar, Pipes and Tobacco are served out on that day" (Saunders 1985:231). It seems unlikely, however, that Wylly was the source of all pipes found in the quarters. In addition, it seems unlikely that Wylly would purchase ornate and decorated pipes for his enslaved population when he used only plain pipes himself. Like the ceramics, the diverse pipe styles recovered from the quarters may reflect the consumer choices of the enslaved population.

As mentioned briefly above, African tobacco pipes have been recovered from the Chesapeake area of the southern United States. The pipes were

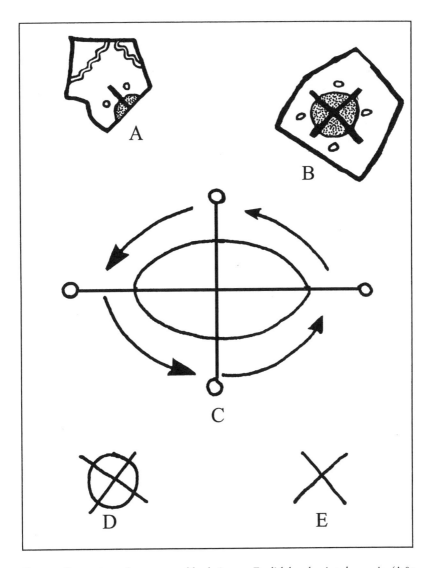

Fig. 10.3. Comparison of cosmogram-like designs on English hand-painted ceramics (A & B) from Clifton plantation with cosmograms recorded in Haiti (C) and South Carolina (D & E). (A) English design from Locus H; (B) English design from Locus G; (C) Bakongo cosmogram recorded by Thompson (1983) in Haiti; (D & E) Examples of cosmograms found on Colono ware pots, South Carolina (after Ferguson 1992).

Table 10.5. Distribution of Kaolin Tobacco Pipes at Clifton Plantation.

Locus	# Stem Fragments	# Bowl Fragments	# of Decoration Types	Minimum Number of Pipes
A Wylly House	4	1	1	2
B Wylly Kitchen	28	18	2	3
F Slave Kitchen	24	13	2	3
G Driver's Cabin	24	15	4	5
H Slave Cabin	2	0	1	1
I Slave Cabin	3	6	1	2
J Slave Cabin	3	3	2	2
K Slave Cabin	7	7	2	2
L Slave Cabin	5	8	1	3
M Slave Cabin	1	2	1	1

incised with significant motifs, including a Nigerian *kwardata* motif, which symbolized the transition to adulthood among the Ga'anda; a cattle motif found throughout West and Central Africa; and a lozenge with surrounding circlets, which has also been found on Ashanti vessels from Ghana (Emerson 1988:148–152). Tobacco pipes, in other American settings, have obviously been manufactured and used to express ethnic affiliation and ritual practice.

The majority of the decorated pipes from the quarters of Clifton plantation are rouletted or minimally embossed. The banded rouletting found on the pipes is comparable to that found on both Yoruban and Bakongo pottery, again suggesting continuity in preferences regarding decorative motifs.

Three pipes recovered from the driver's cabin (Locus G) and Locus J were highly embossed with a prominent beehive surrounded by flying bees and were in addition decorated with flowering vines (figure 10.4). At this point, the manufacturer of these pipes has not been identified. The distinctiveness of this pipe design combined with its presence at two of the cabins led me to explore whether these motifs could have had any additional meanings for an African user (see also Wilkie 2000b).

I first sought to determine whether or not any important folkloric, spiritual, or iconographic imagery was associated with bees. Bees do not seem to play an important role in African-Bahamian folklore (e.g., Crowley 1966)

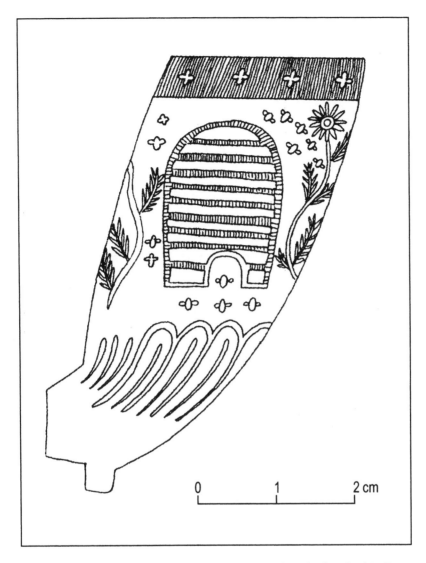

Fig. 10.4. Tobacco pipe decorated with beehive, recovered from the driver's cabin (Locus G) at Clifton plantation.

or, more broadly, in African-American folklore. I was able to locate only one story related to "Brer Wasp" (Abrahams 1985:119–121). Working in the 1920s American South, Puckett (1926) recorded the meanings of bees that appeared in dreams. Interestingly enough, bees associated with beehives in dreams were interpreted as bringing the dreamer great dignity (Puckett 1926).

The recovery of one of these pipes from the driver's cabin, which was occupied by an individual of high rank within the slave community, might be cited as evidence that the pipe had this meaning for the user. I am not completely comfortable, however, with using an early twentieth-century ethnographic analogy drawn from a highly creolized population to interpret an artifact from, essentially, an African household.

The beehive pipes were certainly of European manufacture, probably English. Large dome-shaped basketry beehives were a common element in scenes of agricultural and rural life and were depicted in lithographs and on transfer-printed ceramics (e.g., Coysh and Henrywood 1982:37–38). As someone accustomed to seeing beehives depicted on Staffordshire ceramics, I quickly recognized the pipe design as a beehive and noticed the surrounding bees. For me, identification had been easy, because I was not completely an outsider to nineteenth-century English rural life and its imagery.

Upon reconsideration, however, I realized that the student who excavated the most complete pipe had no similar background and did not recognize the design as depicting a beehive. I decided to reevaluate the pipe and its design without drawing upon my own European-American ethnocentric biases. What could this scene have meant to someone whose life experiences were based upon life in Africa and the Bahamas rather than in England?

Since one of the pipes had been recovered from the driver's cabin, where the ceramic with the "Bakongo cosmogram" had been recovered, I further explored Bakongo imagery and discovered that ant/termite hills are powerful physical and metaphysical objects within Bakongo cosmology. MacGaffey (1986:74) cites termite hills as locations inhabited by the dead: "The dead go to the land of the ancestors (bimbindi). No one knows how long they stay there, but eventually they fall asleep leaning against a n'senga tree. They sink into the earth and become termite hills" (Brittremieux 1922, in McGaffey 1986:74). Termite hills are important parts of the spiritual landscape, and people passing by them may be expected to make small offerings (MacGaffey 1986:80). "Termites are like the dead in that they fly, like souls and spirits, but live 'underground,' in a gravelike mound. A magician knocks over a termite hill in order to see the dead" (MacGaffey 1986:263). Like birds, flying insects often symbolize divination, or spiritual revelation, within Bakongo belief systems (MacGaffey 1986:133).

Mound-building termites are not limited to West Africa; termites that build large, dome-shaped mounds, sometimes as high as four or five feet (but more typically two to three feet), are commonly found throughout the Bahamas, including the site of Clifton plantation. The presence of these mounds in the

Bahamas could signal a continuity in the spiritual landscape to an enslaved Bakongo person. On New Providence, it is still considered unlucky to move or disturb a termite mound. Importantly, graves are also associated with mounds in the Bahamas and Turks and Caicos (formerly part of the Bahamas). On the island of North Caicos, local residents asked us not to excavate two mounds on Wade's Green plantation because they were grave mounds and excavation would disturb the spirits housed there.

If we step back and allow ourselves to recognize that an image manufactured with a European in mind could mean something very different to a person of Bakongo descent, we can see that the tobacco pipes from Clifton could depict powerful religious beliefs. What someone of Anglo descent saw as a beehive surrounded by bees could, to a viewer of Bakongo descent, signify a termite hill surrounded by flying insects. Like the Bakongo cosmogram, which emphasizes the relationship between life and death, and the interrelationship of each in the life cycle, the tobacco pipe could represent the same juxtaposition between the living and the dead. The dead (termite hill) exist among the living (the flying insects); one stage of existence always balances the other.

Could the tobacco pipe have been selected by the families that used it merely because it was attractive and ornamental? Yes, this possibility always exists. Still, at this point several artifacts have been recovered from the driver's cabin (Locus G) that could be interpreted as having Bakongo meanings. The presence of a ceramic bearing a likeness of the Bakongo cosmogram and a ceramic vessel depicting birds, with their Bakongo symbolic implications, found in association with a tobacco pipe bearing another potentially significant Bakongo iconographic image, seems more than coincidental. Jack and Sue Eve may be recorded in the documentary record of the Bahamas as "African," but the archaeological record seems more explicitly to suggest that they were Bakongo (Wilkie 2000b).

Personal Adornment

Personal adornment can take many forms. Cultural attitudes can be expressed through the way one's hair is styled, through body art, such as tattooing, scarification, and piercings, or through clothing and ornaments worn on the body. As already discussed, body scarification was reportedly present on some of the Clifton population. Mass-produced artifacts provided additional opportunities to express body and personal aesthetic ideals. Personal adornment artifacts dating to the period of enslavement in the quarters were also exclusively buttons, with the exception of one blue glass bead (recovered from Locus L). Although beads have commonly been recovered from other African-

American contexts in the Caribbean and the southern United States (e.g., Handler and Lange 1978; Stine, Caback, and Groover 1996), they are only rarely recovered in the Bahamas, probably because of conditions associated with the Bahamian regional market (Farnsworth 1996; Wilkie and Farnsworth 1996, 1997).

Buttons of many forms and materials were found throughout the site, with the highest concentrations being recovered from the slave quarters. Although cloth and clothing of high quality were expensive to purchase, buttons could be more cheaply acquired and could be used to ornament otherwise drab clothing. Wylly claimed to have furnished his slaves with the following clothing: "2 suits of Oznaburgs, or some other coarse linen; and one suit of woolen, are to be allowed annually to each slave, of whatever Age" (Saunders 1985:230). Buttons could not only serve as fasteners, but, like beads, could also be strung together on a cord or sewn directly onto clothing in decorative patterns.

Consideration of button distribution by type clearly illustrates that the most expensive buttons were recovered from the slave quarters rather than the planter's complex (table 10.6). All of the gilt (gold-plated buttons) were recovered from the slave quarters, and all but one of the brass buttons were recovered from the quarters. Five gilt buttons were recovered from the driver's cabin alone. It is possible that buttons were used as visual symbols of status, much as beads and scarification were used to denote status, gender, and stage of life among many West African groups. As this research continues, the potential significance of the composition and color of buttons will be further explored.

Buttons could have additional, perhaps spiritual meanings, to African consumers as well. As mentioned above, the Bakongo cosmogram is closely associated with the creation of sacred medicines, as are the herb bundles currently found in the Bahamas. In the American South, buttons have been found in caches in association with other potentially sacred artifacts in archaeological contexts in Maryland and Virginia (Wilkie 1997). In these areas, archaeologists have interpreted buttons as being components of *nkisi* charms. The circular shape of buttons could be seen as yet another symbol of the cycle of life and death so central to Bakongo ideology. Both glass and shell beads and buttons are common components in modern Bakongo nkisi charms (MacGaffey 1991). It is interesting to note that shell buttons, which closely resemble flat shell disk beads found adorning nkisi bundles, were found in greatest abundance at the slave kitchen (Locus F) and the driver's cabin (Locus G).

The significance of buttons, either as expressions of personal beauty and ornamentation or as religious metaphors, remains unclear at this time. The differences in the distribution, frequency, and types of buttons recovered from

Table 10.6. Buttons Recovered from Clifton by Locus and Material of Manufacture.

Locus	Gilt	Brass	Pewter	Bone	Shell	Ceramic	Modern	Total
A Wylly House			1				1	2
B Wylly Kitchen								0
F Slave Kitchen	2	1	1	1	7		3	16
G Driver's Cabin	3	4		1	3	1	2	14
H Slave Cabin			2				3	5
I Slave Cabin								0
J Slave Cabin							3	3
K Slave Cabin					1			1
L Slave Cabin	1	2			2		2	7
M Slave Cabin								0

the quarters at Clifton, however, suggests that African consumer preferences, rather than planter distribution, may have shaped the archaeological assemblages of personal adornment.

Conclusion

William Wylly saw himself as a reformer of slavery who sought to introduce his enslaved population to the "civilized" Anglo influences of Christianity, literacy, and industry. Never did Wylly, like most of his peers among the English planters, consider the possibility that the enslaved Africans would not consider his culture superior to their own. He made the mistaken assumption that the enslaved people of his plantations would also want to be English. Instead, the enslaved people of Clifton, left to build new lives in a strange land, held onto their own cultural values, using whatever opportunities became available to express and maintain those values.

William Wylly, in an effort to minimize his plantation overhead, came to encourage his enslaved population to produce foodstuffs for trade both with him and in the market in Nassau. He also provided employment opportunities to the men of his plantation so that they could earn cash wages. Wylly fully encouraged the participation of his enslaved people in the Bahamian market economy. It seems to have been Wylly's intention to minimize his economic expenses while also encouraging a "European" style of peasant living among his enslaved people. In fact, Wylly's practices seem to have encouraged continuities in African aesthetic and, possibly, religious traditions.

Although the materials that the people of Clifton bought were European in origin, the *assemblage* of European-manufactured artifacts that they selected and collected were African in construction. Color palettes, decorative types, and motifs were selected according to West African cultural standards, not European ones. In this chapter I have drawn my analogies predominantly using the Yoruban and Bakongo cultures because of evidence that the Yoruban and Bakongo groups were populous on the island of New Providence. This approach has proven useful in identifying artifacts with potentially significant imagery, motifs, or decorative elements. In particular, the driver's cabin assemblage (Locus G) seems to have a number of Bakongo influences represented. As archaeologists delve more deeply into the ethnographic and documentary records relating to the original African populations who were brought to the New World, perhaps it will become increasingly possible to recognize not just African-inspired consumer practices but the consumer practices of specific African ethnic groups. The intent of such research would not be to develop particularistic or deterministic models of consumerism to be replicated from one site to another but to recognize the diverse voices of African peoples whose imaginations and experiences have shaped contemporary American and Caribbean identities.

BIBLIOGRAPHY

Aarons, G. A. 1984. Sevilla la Nueva: Microcosm of Spain in Jamaica. Part II: Unearthing the past. *Jamaica Journal* 17(1):28–37.

Aarons, G. A. 1991. The South West Bay plantation, New Providence: Over two centuries of history on the Divi Golf Course. In *Aspects of Bahamian history: Bahamian history through archaeology*, edited by D. G. Saunders, pp. 15–19. Nassau: Department of Archives, Ministry of Education.

Aarons, G. A., K. Outten, and G. S. R. Turner. 1990. Historical-archaeological research at an eighteenth-century plantation: South Ocean Beach, Divi Bahamas, Ltd. February 12–23 and April 19–23. Ms. on file, Department of Archives, Nassau, Bahamas.

Abrahams, R. D. 1985. *Afro-American folktales*. New York: Pantheon Books.

Adams, W. H. 1987. *Historical archaeology of plantations at Kings Bay, Camden County, Georgia*. Reports of Investigations 5. Gainesville: Department of Anthropology, University of Florida.

Agorsah, E. K. 1983. *An archaeological study of settlement and behavior: Patterns of a West African traditional society: The Nehumuru of Banda-Wiae in Ghana*. Ph.D. dissertation, University of California, Los Angeles. Ann Arbor: University Microfilms.

Agorsah, E. K. 1992. Archaeology and the Maroon heritage in Jamaica. *Jamaica Journal* 24(2):2–9.

Agorsah, E. K., ed. 1994. *Maroon heritage: Archaeological, ethnographic, and historical perspectives*. Kingston: Canoe Press.

Albury, P. 1975. *The story of the Bahamas*. London: Macmillan Caribbean.

Alegría, R. E., ed. 1993. *Indice analítico de las actas de los congresos de la Asociación de Arqueología del Caribe, 1963–1993*. San Juan: Centro de Estudios Avanzados de Puerto Rico y el Caribe.

Allaire, L. 1980. On the historicity of Carib migrations in the Lesser Antilles. *American Antiquity* 45:238–245.

Allaire, L. 1994. Historic Carib site discovered! *University of Manitoba–St. Vincent Archaeological Project Newsletter* 1:1–3.

Allaire, L. 1996. Visions of cannibals: Distant islands and distant lands. In *The Lesser Antilles in the age of European expansion,* edited by R. L. Paquette and S. L. Engerman, pp. 33–49. Gainesville: University Press of Florida.

Allaire, L. 1997. The Caribs of the Lesser Antilles. In *The indigenous people of the Caribbean,* edited by S. M. Wilson, pp. 177–185. Gainesville: University Press of Florida.

Allen, R. 1991. The folk material culture related to food quest and food production in Curaçao culture. In *Proceedings of the Thirteenth International Congress for Caribbean Archaeology,* edited by E. N. Ayubi and J. B. Haviser, pp. 462–476. Report No. 9. Curaçao: Archaeological-Anthropological Institute of the Netherlands Antilles.

Alleyne, W., and J. Sheppard. 1990. *The Barbados garrison and its buildings.* London: Macmillan Caribbean.

Anderson, W. J., and R. P. Spiers. 1927. *The architecture of ancient Rome.* London: B. T. Batsford.

Anthony, C. 1976a. The big house and the slave quarters: Part 1, Prelude to New World architecture. *Landscape* 20(3):8–19.

Anthony, C. 1976b. The big house and the slave quarters: Part 2, African contributions to the New World. *Landscape* 21(1):9–15.

Armstrong, D. V. 1983. *The old village at Drax Hall plantation: An archaeological examination of an Afro-Jamaican settlement.* Ph.D. dissertation, Department of Anthropology, University of California, Los Angeles. Ann Arbor: University Microfilms.

Armstrong, D. V. 1985. Afro-Jamaican slave settlement: Archaeological investigations at Drax Hall. In *The archaeology of slavery and plantation life,* edited by T. Singleton, pp. 261–287. New York: Academic Press.

Armstrong, D. V. 1990. *The old village and the great house: An archaeological and historical examination of Drax Hall plantation, St. Ann's Bay, Jamaica.* Urbana: University of Illinois Press.

Armstrong, D. V. 1991. An archaeological study of the Afro-Jamaican community at Drax Hall. *Jamaica Journal* 24(1):3–8.

Armstrong, D. V. 1992. Spatial transformations in African Jamaican housing at Seville plantation. *Archaeology Jamaica* 6:51–63.

Armstrong, D. V. 1998. Cultural transformation among Caribbean slave communities. In *Studies in culture contact: Interaction, culture change, and archaeology,* edited by James Cusick, pp. 378–401. Occasional Paper No. 25. Carbondale: Center for Archaeological Investigations, Southern Illinois University.

Armstrong, D. V., and M. L. Fleischman. 1993. Summary report: Analysis of four house-area burials from the African Jamaican settlement at Seville. *Syracuse University Archaeological Report* 6(5):1–119.

Armstrong, D. V., and K. Kelly. 1992. Spatial transformations in African Jamaican housing at Seville plantation. Paper presented at the Twenty-fifth Annual Meeting of the Society for Historical Archaeology, Kingston, Jamaica.

Arnold, J. B. III, and R. Weddle. 1978. *The nautical archaeology of Padre Island.* New York: Academic Press.

Arrom, J. J., and M. A. García Arévalo. 1986. *Cimarrón.* Serie Monográfica 18. Tallahassee: University Press of Florida; Santo Domingo: Fundación Garcia Arévalo.

Ashmore, W., ed. 1981. *Lowland Maya settlement patterns.* Albuquerque: University of New Mexico Press.

Aslet, C., and A. Powers. 1985. *The National Trust book of the English house.* Harmondsworth, Middlesex: Viking.

Attema, Y. 1976. *St. Eustatius: A short history of the island and its monuments.* Zutphen, The Netherlands: De Walburg Pers.

Ayubi, E., ed. 1996. *Papers of the Third Seminar on Latin American and Caribbean Folklore.* Report No. 12. Curaçao: Archaeological-Anthropological Institute of the Netherlands Antilles.

Ayubi, E., E. Boerstra, and A. Versteeg. 1985. Archeologie. In *Encyclopedie van de Nederlandse Antillen II,* edited by J. de Palm, pp. 31–32. Zutphen, The Netherlands: De Walburg Pers.

Ayubi, E. N., and J. B. Haviser, eds. 1991. In *Proceedings of the Thirteenth International Congress for Caribbean Archaeology.* Report No. 9. Curaçao: Archaeological-Anthropological Institute of the Netherlands Antilles.

Baart, J. 1990. Fort Amsterdam op Sint Maarten, de oudste Europese vesting in West-Indie. *Ons Amsterdam* 4:86.

Baart, J. 1992. The archaeology of Fort Amsterdam. Paper presented at the Twenty-fifth Annual Meeting of the Society for Historical Archaeology, Kingston, Jamaica.

Baart, J., W. Knook, and A. Lagerwey. 1988. Fort Amsterdam: Archeologisch onderzoek op Sint Maarten, Nederlandse Antillen. *KNOB Bulletin* 87(6):15.

Bahama Gazette (BG). 1796. Death. *Bahama Gazette* 13 (1000), December 9, 1796.

Bahama Gazette (BG). 1786–1800. Advertisements placed by William and James Moss. *Bahama Gazette,* various dates.

Bahama Gazette (BG). 1815. Explanations of Mr. Thomas Whewell. *Supplement to the Bahama Gazette* 5(472), 20 April.

Bahama Gazette (BG). 1821. Advertisement for reward for runaway slaves, placed by William Wylly. January 24.

Baker, H. 1968. Archaeological investigations at Panama la Vieja. Master's thesis, Department of Anthropology, University of Florida, Gainesville.

Baker, J. E. 1993. An osteological survey of Caribbean slave health. Master's thesis, Department of Anthropology, Syracuse University, Syracuse, New York.

Barbotin, M. 1975. *Les moulins de Marie-Galante.* Basse-Terre, Guadeloupe: Société d'Histoire de la Guadeloupe.

Barbotin, M. 1978. Découverte de crânes, fémurs, et autres os. *Bulletin de la Société d'Histoire de la Guadeloupe* 38 (4):3–37.

Barka, N. F. 1982. Historical archaeology of St. Eustatius, 1981. Paper presented at the Fifteenth Annual Meeting of the Society for Historical Archaeology, Philadelphia.

Barka, N. F. 1983. The archaeology of St. Eustatius, season two. Paper presented at the Sixteenth Annual Meeting of the Society for Historical Archaeology, Denver.

Barka, N. F. 1985. *Archaeology of St. Eustatius, Netherlands Antilles: An interim report on the 1981–1984 seasons.* St. Eustatius Archaeological Research Series No. 1. Williamsburg, Va.: Department of Anthropology, College of William and Mary.

Barka, N. F. 1986. *Archaeology of the Government Guest House, St. Eustatius, Netherlands Antilles: An interim report.* St. Eustatius Archaeological Research Series No. 2. Williamsburg, Va.: Department of Anthropology, College of William and Mary.

Barka, N. F. 1987a. *Archaeological investigation of Princess Estate, St. Eustatius, Netherlands Antilles: An interim report on the supposed Jewish mikve.* St. Eustatius Archaeological Research Series No. 3. Williamsburg, Va.: Department of Anthropology, College of William and Mary.

Barka, N. F. 1987b. *The potential for historical archaeology research in the Netherlands Antilles.* Report No. 4. Curaçao: Archaeological-Anthropological Institute of the Netherlands Antilles.

Barka, N. F. 1988. *Archaeology of the Jewish Synagogue Honen Dalim, St. Eustatius, Netherlands Antilles.* St. Eustatius Archaeological Research Series No. 4. Williamsburg, Va.: Department of Anthropology, College of William and Mary.

Barka, N. F. 1989. *A progress report on the structural aspects of the Government Guest House complex, St. Eustatius, Netherlands Antilles.* St. Eustatius Archaeological Research Series No. 5. Williamsburg, Va.: Department of Anthropology, College of William and Mary.

Barka, N. F. 1990. *Archaeological investigations of Structure 4, Government Guest House complex, St. Eustatius, Netherlands Antilles.* St. Eustatius Archaeological Research Series No. 6. Williamsburg, Va.: Department of Anthropology, College of William and Mary.

Barka, N. F. 1991a. *Ebenezer plantation: A preliminary archaeological survey, St. Maarten, Netherlands Antilles.* St. Maarten Archaeological Research Series No. 2. Williamsburg, Va.: Department of Anthropology, College of William and Mary.

Barka, N. F. 1991b. The merchants of St. Eustatius: An archaeological and historical analysis. In *Proceedings of the Thirteenth International Congress for Caribbean Archaeology,* edited by E. N. Ayubi and J. B. Haviser, pp. 384–392. Report No. 9. Curaçao: Archaeological-Anthropological Institute of the Netherlands Antilles.

Barka, N. F. 1991c. *Archaeological investigations of Battery Concordia, St. Eustatius, Netherlands Antilles.* St. Eustatius Archaeological Research Series No. 7. Williamsburg, Va.: Department of Anthropology, College of William and Mary.

Barka, N. F. 1992. A cultural resources survey of St. Maarten. Paper presented at the Twenty-fifth Annual Meeting of the Society for Historical Archaeology, Kingston, Jamaica.

Barka, N. F. 1993. *Archaeological survey of sites and buildings, St. Maarten, Netherlands Antilles I.* St. Maarten Archaeological Research Series No. 3. Williamsburg, Va.: Department of Anthropology, College of William and Mary.

Barka, N. F. 1996a. *Archaeology of the Dutch elite: The country estate of Johannes de Graaff.* St. Eustatius Archaeological Research Series No. 8. Williamsburg, Va.: Department of Anthropology, College of William and Mary.

Barka, N. F. 1996b. Citizens of St. Eustatius, 1781: A historical and archaeological study. In *The Lesser Antilles in the age of European expansion,* edited by R. Paquette and S. Engerman, pp. 223–238. Gainesville: University Press of Florida.

Barka, N., and S. Sanders. 1990. *A preliminary study of Welgelegen, St. Maarten, Netherlands Antilles.* St. Maarten Archaeological Research Series No. 1. Williamsburg, Va.: College of William and Mary.

Barrett, W. 1965. Caribbean sugar-production standards in the seventeenth and eighteenth centuries. In *Merchants and scholars,* pp. 148–168. Minneapolis: University of Minnesota Press.

Bass, G. F. 1972. *A history of seafaring based on underwater archaeology.* New York: Walker.

Beckford, W. 1790. *A descriptive account of the island of Jamaica.* London: T. & G. Egerton.

Beckles, H. 1990. *A history of Barbados from Amerindian settlement to nation-state.* Cambridge: Cambridge University Press.

Bégot, D. 1991. Les habitations-sucreries du littoral guadeloupéen et leur évolution. *Caribena: Cahiers d'études américanistes de la Caraïbe* 1:149–190.

Bégot, D. 1992. Villes et urbanismes. In *Voyage aux îles d'Amérique: Archives Nationales, Hôtel de Rohan, avril-juillet 1992,* pp. 259–265. Paris: Archives Nationales.

Belgrove, W. 1755. *A treatise upon husbandry or planting—Barbados.* Boston: D. Fowles.

Bequette, K. 1991. Shipwrecks of St. Eustatius: A preliminary study. In *Proceedings of the Thirteenth International Congress for Caribbean Archaeology,* edited by E. N. Ayubi and J. B. Haviser, pp. 787–790. Report No. 9. Curaçao: Archaeological-Anthropological Institute of the Netherlands Antilles.

Bequette, K. 1995. Report of 1994 maritime archaeology and research of the HMS *Proselyte,* St. Maarten. Report submitted to the Executive Council of St. Maarten, Philipsburg, and the Archaeological-Anthropological Institute of the Netherlands Antilles, Curaçao.

Bequette, K., and S. Sanders. 1995. Report of a 1994 emergency soil profile drawing conducted at the Bishop Hill cemetery, St. Maarten. Report submitted to the Executive Council of St. Maarten, Philipsburg, and the Archaeological-Anthropological Institute of the Netherlands Antilles, Curaçao.

Berleant-Schiller, R., and L. M. Pulsipher. 1986. Subsistence cultivation in the Caribbean. *New West Indian Guide* 60 (1&2):1–40.

Bethel, E. 1991. *Junkanoo: Festival of the Bahamas.* London: Macmillan Caribbean.

Bettesworth, A., and C. Hitch. 1981. *The builder's dictionary; or, Gentleman architect's companion.* Reprint of the original 1734 edition. Washington, D.C.: Association of Preservation Technology.

Boomert, A. 1986. The Cayo complex of St. Vincent: Ethnohistorical and archaeological aspects of the island Carib problem. *Antropológica* 66:3–68.

Boomert, A., O. R. Ortiz-Troncoso, and H. H. van Regteren Altena. 1987. Archaeological-historical survey of Tobago, West Indies. *Journal de la Société des Américanistes* 73:246–258.

Boon, G. C. 1974. *Silchester: The Roman town of Calleva*. Newton Abbot, Devon: David & Charles.

Boone, J. 1980. *Artifact deposition and demographic change: An archaeological case study of medieval colonialism in the Age of Expansion*. Ph.D. dissertation, State University of New York, Binghamton. Ann Arbor: University Microfilms.

Borrell, P. 1979. El rescate del galeón *Concepción* en aguas Dominicanas. *Geomundo* 3:384–403.

Borrell, P. 1983a. *Historia y rescate del Galeon Nuestra Senora de Conception*. Santo Domingo: Museo Casa Reales.

Borrell, P. 1983b. *The Quicksilver Galleons*. Santo Domingo: Museo Casas Reales.

Bosch, G. 1836. *Reizen in West Indie, Vol. 2*. Utrecht: N. van der Monde.

Boucher, P. P. 1992. *Cannibal encounters: Europeans and island Caribs, 1492–1763*. Baltimore: Johns Hopkins University Press.

Braudel, F. 1979. *Civilization and capitalism, fifteenth–eighteenth century: Vol. 1, The structures of everyday life*. New York: Harper & Row.

Brenneker, P. 1969–1975. *Sambubu: Volkskunde van Curaçao, Aruba, en Bonaire*. Vols. 1–10. Curaçao: Verenigde Antilliaanse Drukkerijen.

Breton, Père R. 1978. *Relations de l'île de la Guadeloupe,* vol. 1. Bibliothèque d'histoire antillaise 3. Basse-Terre, Guadeloupe: Société d'histoire de la Guadeloupe.

Brill, R., I. L. Barnes, S. C. Tong, E. C. Joel, and M. J. Murtaugh. 1986. Laboratory studies of some European artifacts excavated on San Salvador Island. In *Proceedings of the First San Salvador Conference: Columbus and his world,* edited by D. Gerace, pp. 247–292. San Salvador, Bahamas: Bahamian Field Station of the College of the Finger Lakes.

Brill, R., I. L. Barnes, S. C. Tong, E. C. Joel, and M. J. Murtaugh. 1992. Preliminary remarks on the analysis of glasses from La Isabela, Dominican Republic. Paper presented at the annual meeting of the American Association for the Advancement of Science, Chicago.

Brito, N. 1989. Merchants of Curaçao in the early eighteenth Century. Master's thesis, Department of Anthropology, College of William and Mary, Williamsburg, Virginia.

Brito, N. 1991. The revelation of Willemstad as a historic center. In *Proceedings of the Thirteenth International Congress for Caribbean Archaeology,* edited by E. N. Ayubi and J. B. Haviser, pp. 393–414. Report No. 9. Curaçao: Archaeological-Anthropological Institute of the Netherlands Antilles.

Bro-Jorgensen, M. 1966. *Dansk Vestindien indtil 1755: Kolonisation og kompagnistryre, Bind I of vore gamle tropekolonier under redaktion af Johannes Brondsted*. Copenhagen: Fremad.

Brown, R. S. 1979. The vernacular architecture of Frederiksted. *Journal of the Virgin Islands Archaeological Society* 8:3–43.

Brugman, F. 1994. The monuments of Saba. Ph.D. dissertation, Architecture Department, University of Delft, The Netherlands.

Brunskill, R. W. 1971. *Illustrated handbook of vernacular architecture.* London: Faber & Faber.

Buckley, R. N. 1979. *Slaves in red coats: The British West India Regiments, 1795–1815.* New Haven: Yale University Press.

Buddingh', B. 1994. *Van Punt en Snoa.* 's-Hertogenbosch, The Netherlands: Aldus Uitgevers.

Buisseret, D. 1980. *Historic architecture of the Caribbean.* London: Heinemann.

Bush, B. 1990. *Slave women in Caribbean society, 1650–1838.* Bloomington: Indiana University Press.

Campbell, J. 1774. *A political survey of Britain.* Vol. 2. London: By the Author.

Campbell, P. F. 1975. St. Ann's Fort and the garrison. *Journal of the Barbados Museum and Historical Society* 35(1).

Campos Carrasco, J., F. Pozo Blázquez, B. Calero Ramos, and F. Diaz de Olmo. 1992. *La Isabela, umbral de América: Guia de interpretación.* Santo Domingo: Agencia Española de Cooperción Internacional.

Caro, J. A. 1973. La Isabela, Santo Domingo, R. D. *Boletín del Museo del Hombre Dominicano* 3:48–52.

Caron, A. P., and A. R. Highfield. 1981. *The French intervention in the St. John slave revolt of 1733–34.* Occasional Paper 7. St. Croix: Bureau of Libraries, Museums, and Archaeological Services, Department of Conservation and Cultural Affairs.

Carrington, S. H. H. 1988. *The British West Indies during the American Revolution.* Leiden: Koninklijk Instituut voor Taal-, Land-, en Volkenkunde.

Carstensen, B. 1993. *Betty's Hope: An Antiguan sugar plantation.* Betty's Hope Trust, St. John's, Antigua.

Chang, K. C., ed. 1968. *Settlement archaeology.* Palo Alto, Calif.: National Press Books.

Chanlatte Baik, L. 1978. Arqueología colonial. *Boletín del Museo del Hombre Dominicano* 7(10):133–138.

Chapman, W. 1991. Slave villages in the Danish West Indies: Changes of the late eighteenth and early nineteenth centuries. In *Perspectives in vernacular architecture, IV,* edited by T. Carter and B. L. Herman, pp. 108–120. Columbia: University of Missouri Press.

Chiarelli, B., ed. 1987. La Isabela. *International Journal of Anthropology* 2(3):195–253.

Clarke, H. 1984. *The archaeology of medieval England.* London: Colonnade Books.

Clausen, C. 1965. *A 1715 treasure ship.* Gainesville: Florida State Museum.

Clement, C. O. 1997. Settlement patterning on the British Caribbean island of Tobago. *Historical Archaeology* 31(2):93–106.

Cloyd, P. C. 1984. *Historic architecture: Design guidelines for a historic district in St. John's, Antigua.* St. John's, Antigua: Original Printery.

Cody Holdren, A. 1998. Raiders and traders: Caraïbe social and political networks at the time of European contact and colonization in the eastern Caribbean. Ph.D. dissertation, University of California, Los Angeles.

Colonial Office Records [CO]. 1811. African list on service of the customs, Port of Nassau. Colonial Office Records, CO23/63:292–307. Department of Archives, Nassau, Bahamas.

Colonial Office Records [CO]. 1815. Regulations for the government of the slaves at Clifton and Tusculum in New Providence, printed at the office of the *Royal Gazette*. Colonial Office Records, CO 23/67:153. Public Record Office, Kew, Richmond, Surrey, England.

Colonial Office Records [CO]. 1816. Transcript of Dick and Richard Evans cruelty case. Colonial Office Records, CO23/67:115–116. Department of Archives, Nassau, Bahamas.

Colonial Office Records [CO]. 1817. S. Kerr, W. Kerr, H. M. Williams, W. MacKie, and others to Earl Bathurst. Colonial Office Records, CO23/64:114. Department of Archives, Nassau, Bahamas.

Colonial Office Records [CO]. 1818a. William V. Munnings to Earl Bathurst, August 10, 1818. Colonial Office Records, CO 23/67:103–115. Public Record Office, Kew, Richmond, Surrey, England.

Colonial Office Records [CO]. 1818b. Letters from Wylly defending management of Clifton plantation, enclosed in William V. Munnings to Bathurst, September 9, 1818. Colonial Office Records, CO 23/67:147–153. Department of Archives, Nassau, Bahamas.

Colonial Office Records [CO]. 1818c. Account of Provisioning Grounds at Clifton Plantation, enclosed in Williams V. Munnings to Earl Bathurst, September 9, 1818. Colonial Office Records, CO 23/67:164–165. Department of Archives, Nassau, Bahamas.

Colonial Office Records [CO]. 1827. Transcript of the Henry and Helen Moss cruelty case. Colonial Office Records, CO23/76:275–289. Department of Archives, Nassau, Bahamas.

Colonial Office Records [CO]. 1828. Justice Balley to Horace Twiss, October 23, 1828. Colonial Office Records, CO 23/78:232–250. Public Record Office, Kew, Richmond, Surrey, England.

Congregation Mikvé Israel-Emanuel. 1982. *Our Snoa: 5492–5742.* Curaçao: Congregation.

Cook, J., ed. 1992. *Columbus and the land of Ayllón.* Darien: Carl Vinson Institute of Government, University of Georgia.

Coomans, H., M. Newton, and M. Coomans-Eustatia, eds. 1990. *Building up the future from the past.* UNA Publications No. 34. Zutphen, The Netherlands: De Walburg Pers.

Corruccini, R. S., J. S. Handler, R. J. Mutaw, and F. W. Lange. 1982. Osteology of a slave burial population from Barbados, West Indies. *American Journal of Physical Anthropology* 59:443–459.

Cotter, C. S. 1948. The discovery of Spanish carvings at Seville. *Jamaican Historical Review* 1(3):227–233.

Cotter, C. S. 1964. The Jamaica of Columbus. *Jamaican Historical Review* 3(16):252–259.

Cotter, C. S. 1970. Sevilla Nueva: The story of an excavation. *Jamaica Journal* 4(2):15–22.

Cottman, E. W. 1963. *Out-island doctor.* London: Hodder & Stoughton.

Courtaud, P. 1997. *Anse Sainte Marguerite, Grande-Terre, Commune du Moule.* Rapports de fouille inédits, Service Régional de l'Archéologie. Basse-Terre, Guadeloupe: Direction Régionale des Affaires Culturelles (DRAC).

Courtaud, P. 1998. *Anse Sainte Marguerite, Grande-Terre, Commune du Moule.* Rapports de fouille inédits, Service Régional de l'Archéologie. Basse-Terre, Guadeloupe: Direction Régionale des Affaires Culturelles (DRAC).

Courtaud P., A. Delpuech, and T. Romon. 1999. Archaeological investigations at colonial cemeteries on Guadeloupe: African slave sites or not? In *African sites archaeology in the Caribbean,* edited by J. B. Haviser, pp. 277–290. Princeton: Markus Wiener; Kingston: Ian Randle.

Coysh, A. W., and R. K. Henrywood. 1982. *The dictionary of blue and white printed pottery, 1780–1880.* Vol. 1. Woodbridge, Suffolk: Antique Collectors' Club.

Crandall, D. R., and B. S. Dyde. 1989. *The fortification of St. George's Hill, Montserrat.* Plymouth: Montserrat National Trust.

Crane, B. 1990. Patterns of consumption in nineteenth-century San Juan, Puerto Rico. Paper presented at the Twenty-third Annual Meeting of the Society for Historical Archaeology, Tucson, Arizona.

Crane, J. 1971. *Educated to emigrate: The social organization of Saba.* Assen, The Netherlands: Van Gorcum.

Craton, M. 1962. *A history of the Bahamas.* London: Collins.

Craton, M. 1986. *A history of the Bahamas.* 3d ed. Waterloo, Ontario: San Salvador Press.

Craton, M., and G. Saunders. 1992. *Islanders in the stream: A history of the Bahamian people.* Athens: University of Georgia Press.

Crespo, E., and J. B. Guisti. 1992. Primera evidencia de mutilación dentaria en la población negroide de Puerto Rico. *Revista Salud y Cultura* año 4, 1(5):95–105.

Crespo, E., and J. B. Guisti. 1995. Análisis osteológico de dos restos esqueléticos humanos descubriertos durante las excavaciones del Cuartel de Ballajá, San Juan. In *Proceedings of the Fifteenth International Congress for Caribbean Archaeology,* edited by R. E. Alegría and M. Rodríguez, pp. 533–543. San Juan: Centro de Estudios Avanzados de Puerto Rico y el Caribe.

Crossley, D. 1990. *Post-medieval archaeology in Britain.* Leicester: Leicester University Press.

Crouse, N. M. 1943. *The French struggle for the West Indies, 1665–1713.* New York: Columbia University Press.

Crowley, D. J. 1966. *I could talk old story good.* Berkeley: University of California Press.

Cruxent, J. 1965. IVIC-241. *American Journal of Science, Radiocarbon* 9:243.

Cruxent, J. 1989. Relación y noticias cerca de Isabela. *Ysabela* 1(1):12–18.

Cruxent, J. 1990. The origin of La Isabela: First Spanish colony in the New World. In *Columbian consequences,* vol. 2, edited by D. H. Thomas, pp. 251–260. Washington, D.C.: Smithsonian Institution Press.

Cruxent, J. M., and K. A. Deagan. 1992. New insights from the first Euro-American town, La Isabela. Paper presented at the annual meeting of the American Association for the Advancement of Science, Chicago.

Cruxent, J. M., K. A. Deagan, and M. Arevalo. 1993. Aspectos arqueologicos de la Isabela: Primera ciudad Europa de las Indias. Three papers presented at the Fifteenth International Congress for Caribbean Archaeology, San Juan, Puerto Rico.

Cruxent, J., and I. Rouse. 1969. Archaeologie. In *Encyclopedie van de Nederlandse Antillen,* edited by H. Hoetink, pp. 29–39. Amsterdam: Elsevier.

Cruxent, J. M., and J. E. Vaz. 1980. Hidroceramos Mexicanos en la Republica Dominicana. *Casas Reales* 11:71–85.

Cummins, A. 1989. The history and development of museums in the English-speaking Caribbean. Master's thesis, University of Leicester.

Cummins, A. 1993. *Report on the Status of Caribbean Museums and Recommendations for Upgrading Museums to ICOM standards.* CARICOM/UNDP/UNESCO Regional Museum Development Project RLA/88/028. Barbados Museum and Historical Society, Bridgetown, Barbados.

Cummins, A. 1994a. The "Caribbeanization" of the West Indies: The museum's role in the development of national identity. In *Museums and the making of "ourselves": The role of objects in national identity,* edited by Flora E. S. Kaplan, pp. 192–220. London: Leicester University Press.

Cummins, A. 1994b. *Directory of Caribbean museums.* Museums Association of the Caribbean, Bridgetown, Barbados.

Cusick, J. 1989. Change in pottery as a reflection of social change: A study of Taino pottery before and after contact at the site of En Bas Saline, Haiti. Master's thesis, Department of Anthropology, University of Florida, Gainesville.

Dalleo, P. T. 1982. African-Bahamian origins. *Journal of the Bahamas Historical Society* 4(1):17–19.

Davis, D. 1974. The strategy of early Spanish ecosystem management on Cuba. *Journal of Anthropological Research* 30:294–314.

Davis, D. 1996. Revolutionary archaeology in Cuba. *Journal of Archaeological Method and Theory* 3(3):159–188.

Davis, D. D., and R. C. Goodwin. 1990. Island Carib origins: Evidence and non-evidence. *American Antiquity* 54:37–48.

Davy, J. 1854. *The West Indies before and since slave emancipation.* London: W. & F. G. Cash.

Deagan, K. A. 1983a. *Spanish St. Augustine: The archaeology of a colonial Creole community.* New York: Academic Press.

Deagan, K. A. 1983b. Spanish Florida as part of the Caribbean colonial sphere. In *Proceedings of the Ninth International Congress for the Study of Pre-Columbian Cultures of the Lesser Antilles,* edited by L. Allaire and F.-M. Mayer, pp. 419–429. Montreal: Centre de Recherches Caraïbes, Université de Montréal.

Deagan, K. A. 1985. Spanish-Indian interaction in sixteenth-century Florida and Hispaniola. In *Cultures in contact: The European impact on native cultural institutions in Eastern North America, A.D. 1000–1800,* edited by W. Fitzhugh, pp. 281–318. Washington, D.C.: Smithsonian Institution Press.

Deagan, K. A. 1986. First colony, lost colony. *National Geographic* 172(5):672–676.

Deagan, K. A. 1987a. *Artifacts of the Spanish colonies of Florida and the Caribbean, 1500–1800,* Vol. 1. Washington, D.C.: Smithsonian Institution Press.

Deagan, K. A. 1987b. El impacto de la presencia European en la Navidad (La Española). *Revista de Indías* 47(181):713–732.

Deagan, K. A. 1987c. Searching for Columbus' lost colony. *National Geographic* 172(5):672–675.

Deagan, K. A. 1988. The archaeology of the Spanish contact period in the Caribbean. *Journal of World Prehistory* 2(2):187–233.

Deagan, K. A. 1989a. Report on the 1989 sub-surface test program at La Isabela, Dominican Republic. Gainesville: Florida Museum of Natural History.

Deagan, K. A. 1989b. The search for La Navidad, Columbus's 1492 settlement. In *First encounters,* edited by J. T. Milanich &. S. Milbrath, pp. 41–54. Gainesville: University Press of Florida.

Deagan, K. A. 1990a. Accommodation and resistance: The process and impact of Spanish colonization in the Southeast. In *Columbian consequences,* vol. 2, edited by D. H. Thomas, pp. 297–314. Washington, D.C.: Smithsonian Institution Press.

Deagan, K. A. 1990b. Sixteenth-century Spanish-American colonization in the southeastern United States and the Caribbean. In *Columbian consequences,* vol. 2, edited by D. H. Thomas, pp. 225–250. Washington, D.C.: Smithsonian Institution Press.

Deagan, K. A. 1995. *Puerto Real: The archaeology of a sixteenth-century Spanish town in Hispaniola.* Gainesville: University Press of Florida.

Deagan, K. A. 1997. Transculturation and Spanish American ethnogenesis: The archaeological legacy of the Quincentenary. In *Studies in culture contact: Interaction, culture change, and archaeology,* edited by J. G. Cusick, pp. 23–43. Center for Archaeological Investigations, Occasional Paper No. 25. Carbondale: Southern Illinois University.

Deagan, K. A., and J. M. Cruxent. 1992. The first European artifacts in the Americas: La Isabela, 1493–1498. Paper presented at "Trade and Discovery: The Scientific Analysis of Artifacts from Europe and Beyond, 1500–1800." London: British Museum.

Deagan, K. A., and J. M. Cruxent. 1993. From contact to Criollos: The archaeology of Spanish Colonization in Hispaniola. In *Proceedings of the British Academy* 81:67–104.

Deagan, K. A., and Williams, M. 1990. The search for La Navidad in a contact period Arawak town on Haiti's north coast. In *Proceedings of the Eleventh International Congress for Caribbean Archaeology,* edited by A. G. Pantel, I. Vargas Arenas, and M. Sanoja Obediente, pp. 453–458. San Juan: Fundación Arqueológica, Antropológica, e Histórica de Puerto Rico.

Debien, Gabriel. 1974. *Les esclaves aux Antilles françaises: Dix-septième–dix-huitième siècles.* Basse-Terre, Guadeloupe: Société d'histoire de la Guadeloupe; Fort-de-France: Société d'histoire de la Martinique. (Translation courtesy of J. D. Edwards.)

DeBoyrie, M. E. 1964. *La casa de Piedra de Ponce de León en Higuey.* Santo Domingo: Academia Dominicana de la Historia.

DeCorse, C. R. 1992. Culture contact, continuity, and change on the Gold Coast, A.D. 1400–1900. *African Archaeological Review* 10:163–196.

Deerr, N. 1950. *The history of sugar.* 2 vols. London: Chapman & Hall.

Deetz, J. 1976. Black settlement at Plymouth. *Archaeology* 29:207.

Deetz, J. 1977. *In small things forgotten.* Garden City, N.Y.: Anchor Press/Doubleday.

de Haseth, E. 1984. De Keuken van de "Kas di pali maishi." Master's thesis, Department of Cultural Anthropology, Leiden University, The Netherlands.

de Hostos, A. 1938. Investigaciones historicas. Ms. on file, Castillo de San Marcos National Monument, St. Augustine, Florida.

de Josselin de Jong, J. P. B. 1923. *Verslag van de Deensch-Nederlandse expeditie naar de Antillen.* Bulletin 79. Leiden: Van het Rijksmuseum voor Volkenkunde.

Delatour, P. 1984. Monuments and sites in the Caribbean. *Technical Report* PP/1981–1983/4/7.6/04. Paris: UNESCO.

Delle, J. A. 1989. A spatial analysis of sugar plantations on St. Eustatius, Netherlands Antilles. Master's thesis, Department of Anthropology, College of William and Mary, Williamsburg, Virginia.

Delle, J. A. 1994. The settlement pattern of sugar plantations on St. Eustatius, Netherlands Antilles. In *Spatial patterning in historical archaeology: Selected studies of settlement,* edited by D. Linebaugh and G. Robinson, pp. 33–62. Occasional Papers in Archaeology No. 2. Williamsburg, Va.: William and Mary Center for Archaeological Research.

Delle, J. A. 1998. *An archaeology of social space: Analyzing coffee plantations in Jamaica's Blue Mountains.* New York: Plenum Press.

Delpuech, A. 1996a. Le service régional d'archéologie de la DRAC de Guadeloupe: Bilan et perspectives, 1992–1994. In *Les musées des départements français d'Amérique: Actes du congrès,* pp. 38–46. Fort-de-France, Martinique: Association des Amis du Musée Régional d'Histoire et d'Ethnographie.

Delpuech, A., ed. 1996b. *Bilan scientifique de la région Guadeloupe, 1995.* Basse-Terre: Service Régional de l'Archéologie, Direction Régionale des Affaires Culturelles de la Guadeloupe.

Delpuech, A., ed. 1998. *Bilan scientifique de la région Guadeloupe, 1996.* Basse-Terre: Service Régional de l'Archéologie, Direction Régionale des Affaires Culturelles de la Guadeloupe.

Delpuech, A., ed. 1999a. *Bilan scientifique de la région Guadeloupe, 1997.* Basse-Terre: Service Régional de l'Archéologie, Direction Régionale des Affaires Culturelles de la Guadeloupe.

Delpuech, A., ed. 1999b. *Bilan scientifique de la région Guadeloupe, 1998.* Basse-Terre: Service Régional de l'Archéologie, Direction Régionale des Affaires Culturelles de la Guadeloupe.

Denters, M. 1979. Woonhuizen op Aruba. Thesis, Architecture Department, Technical University of Delft, The Netherlands.

Department of Archives [DA], Nassau, Bahamas. 1784. Register of Manumissions from 1784–1834.

Department of Archives [DA], Nassau, Bahamas. 1806. Indenture between James

Moss and John McIntosh, and Wade Stubbs, December 30. Indentures, April 6 1825–October 3 1826, pp. 193–197.

Department of Archives [DA], Nassau, Bahamas. 1821a. Last will and testament of Wade Stubbs, October 17.

Department of Archives [DA], Nassau, Bahamas. 1821b. Register of slaves, October 8.

Department of Archives [DA], Nassau, Bahamas. 1822. Register of slaves, January 1.

Department of Archives [DA], Nassau, Bahamas. 1825. Register of slaves, January 1.

Department of Archives [DA], Nassau, Bahamas. 1827. Last will and testament of William Wylly. Supreme Court Wills, W–Y, March 18.

Department of Archives [DA], Nassau, Bahamas. 1828. Register of slaves, January 1, 1828.

Department of Archives [DA], Nassau, Bahamas. 1831. Register of slaves, January 1.

Department of Lands and Surveys [DLS], Nassau, Bahamas. 1785. Grant Book A, p. 21.

Department of Lands and Surveys [DLS], Nassau, Bahamas. 1847. Grant Book B2, p. 255.

de Passalacqua, J. L. A. 1987. The sea walls of St. Eustatius. In *Underwater archaeology proceedings from the Society for Historical Archaeology Conference,* edited by A. B. Albright, pp. 142–144. Tucson: Society for Historical Archaeology.

de Paula, A. 1967. *From objective to subjective social barriers.* Curaçao: De Curaçaosche Courant.

Derrow, S. 1995. Preliminary analysis of faunal remains from the Emanuel Point shipwreck. Paper presented at the Twenty-eighth Annual Meeting of the Society for Historical Archaeology, Washington D.C.

Dethlefsen, E. 1982. What were the questions? Historical summary and archaeological implications. Paper presented at the Fifteenth Annual Meeting of the Society for Historical Archaeology, Philadelphia.

Dethlefsen, E., S. Gluckman, R. Mathewson, and N. Barka. 1979. *A preliminary report on the historical archaeology and cultural resources of St. Eustatius, Netherlands Antilles.* Contributions to the Historical Archaeology of St. Eustatius, vol. 1. Williamsburg, Va.: Department of Anthropology, College of William and Mary.

Devas, R. P. 1974. *A history of the island of Grenada, 1498–1796.* St. George's, Grenada: Carenage Press.

Devaux, R. J. 1975. *Saint Lucia historic sites.* Castries, St. Lucia: Saint Lucia National Trust.

de Vos, G. 1975. Ethnic pluralism: Conflict and accommodation. In *Ethnic identity: Cultural continuities and change,* edited by G. de Vos and L. Komanucci-Ross, pp. 5–41. Palo Alto, Calif.: Mayfield.

Dick, K. C. 1977. Aboriginal and early Spanish names of some Caribbean, circum-Caribbean islands and cays. *Journal of the Virgin Islands Archaeological Society* 4:17–41.

Domínguez, L. 1978. La transculturacíon en Cuba (s. XVI–XVII). In *Cuba arqueología I,* pp. 33–50. Santiago de Cuba: Editorial Oriente.

Domínguez, L. 1980. Cerámica de transculturacíon del sitio colonial casa de la obrapia. In *Cuba arqueología II*. Santiago de Cuba: Editorial Oriente.

Domínguez, L. 1981. Arqueología del sitio colonial casa de la obrapia o de calvo de la puerta, Habana Vieja. *Santiago* 41:63–82.

Domínguez, L. 1984. *Arqueología colonial cubana: Dos estudios*. Havana: Editorial de Ciencias Sociales.

Domínguez, L. S., and A. Rives. 1995. Supervivencia o transculturación en el siglo XVI Antillano. In *Proceedings of the Fifteenth International Congress for Caribbean Archaeology*, edited by R. E. Alegría and M. Rodríguez, pp. 393–399. San Juan: Centro de Estudios Avanzados de Puerto Rico y el Caribe.

Donoghue, E. 1995. The black Irish of the Caribbean. *The St. Croix Avis*, No. 110:2. Friday, May 12.

Douglas, N., ed. 1986. *Anguilla Archaeological and Historical Society Review, 1981–1985*. The Valley: Anguilla Archaeological and Historical Society.

DROV. 1989. *Het monumentenplan*. Curaçao: Department of Urban Planning, Island Government of Curaçao.

DROV. 1990. *Monumentenplan voor Willemstad Curaçao*. Curaçao: Department of Urban Planning, Island Government of Curaçao.

Durden, C. J. 1978. Fossil cockroaches from a 1554 Spanish shipwreck. In *The nautical archaeology of Padre Island*, edited by J. B. Arnold and R. S. Weddle, pp. 407–416. New York: Academic Press.

Durlacher-Wolper, R. G. 1982. Columbus' landfall and the Indian settlement of San Salvador. *Florida Anthropologist* 35:203–207.

Du Tertre, R. P. J. B. 1978. *Histoire générale des Antilles: Habitées par les Français*. 4 vols. Fort-de-France, Martinique: E. Kolodziej.

Ebanks, R. 1995. A history of Jamaican ceramics, 1655–1840: Indigenization or creolization? Paper presented at the Twenty-eighth Annual Meeting of the Society for Historical Archaeology, Washington, D.C.

Edwards, J. D. 1980. The evolution of vernacular architecture in the western Caribbean. In *Cultural traditions and Caribbean identity: The question of patrimony*, edited by S. J. Wilkerson, pp. 291–339. Gainesville: Center for Latin American Studies, University of Florida.

Edwards, J. D. 1994. The origins of Creole architecture. *Winterthur Portfolio* 29(2/3): 155–189.

Effert, F. 1992. J. P. B. de Josselin de Jong, curator and archaeologist: A study of his career (1910–1935). Publication No. 7. Leiden: Centre of Non-Western Studies.

Eichholz, J. C. 1983. A Spanish colonial lime kiln. In *Proceedings of the Ninth International Congress for the Study of Pre-Columbian Cultures of the Lesser Antilles*, edited by L. Allaire and F.-M. Mayer, pp. 451–457. Montreal: Centre de Recherches Caraïbes, Université de Montréal.

Elia, R. 1992. The ethics of collaboration: Archaeologists and the Whydah Project. *Historical Archaeology* 26(4):105–117.

Emerson, M. C. 1988. Decorated clay pipes from the Chesapeake. Ph.D. dissertation, Department of Anthropology, University of California, Berkeley.

Emerson, M. C. 1994. Decorated clay tobacco pipes from the Chesapeake: An African connection. In *Historical archaeology of the Chesapeake,* edited by P. A. Shackel and B. J. Little, pp. 35–39. Washington, D.C.: Smithsonian Institution Press.

Eneas, C. W. 1976. *Bain Town.* Nassau: Cleveland and Muriel Eneas.

England, S. 1994. Acculturation in the Creole context: A case study of La Poterie, Martinique. Ph.D. dissertation, Department of Archaeology, Cambridge University, Cambridge, England.

Ericson, J. E. n.d. Report on analysis of stable isotopes from fauna at the En Bas Saline site, Haiti. Ms. on file, Florida Museum of Natural History, Gainesville, and Program in Social Ecology, University of California, Irvine.

Eubanks, T. H. 1992. *Sugar, slavery, and emancipation: The industrial archaeology of the West Indian island of Tobago.* Ph.D. dissertation, Department of Anthropology, University of Florida, Gainesville. Ann Arbor: University Microfilms.

Euwens, P. 1907. Historisch overzicht van het eiland Bonaire. *Neerlandia* 2:193–197.

Ewen, C. R. 1985. *Spanish colonial adaptation to the New World: Current research at Puerto Real, Haiti.* Bulletin No. 2. Port-au-Prince: Bureau National d'Ethnologie.

Ewen, C. R. 1987. From Spaniard to Creole: The archaeology of cultural formation at Puerto Real, Haiti. Ph.D. dissertation, Department of Anthropology, University of Florida, Gainesville.

Ewen, C. R. 1988. The short, unhappy life of a maverick Caribbean colony. *Archaeology* 41(4):41–46.

Ewen, C. R. 1990a. *The archaeology of Spanish colonialism in the Southeastern United States and the Caribbean.* Guides to the Archaeological Literature of the Immigrant Experience in America No. 1. Ann Arbor: Society for Historical Archaeology.

Ewen, C. R. 1990b. The rise and fall of Puerto Real. In *Columbian consequences,* vol. 2, edited by D. H. Thomas, pp. 261–268. Washington, D.C.: Smithsonian Institution Press.

Ewen, C. R. 1990c. Spanish colonial adaptation to the New World: Current research at Puerto Real, Haiti. In *Proceedings of the Eleventh International Congress for Caribbean Archaeology,* edited by A. G. Pantel, I. Vargas Arenas, and M. Sanoja Obediente, pp. 448–452. San Juan: Fundación Arqueológica, Antropológica, e Histórica de Puerto Rico.

Ewen, C. R. 1991. *From Spaniard to Creole: The archaeology of cultural formation at Puerto Real, Haiti.* Tuscaloosa: University of Alabama Press.

Fairbanks, C. H., and R. A. Marrinan. 1983. The Puerto Real Project, Haiti. In *Proceedings of the Ninth International Congress for the Study of Pre-Columbian Cultures of the Lesser Antilles,* edited by L. Allaire and F.-M. Mayer, pp. 409–417. Montreal: Centre de Recherches Caraïbes, Université de Montréal.

Fairbanks, C. H., R. A. Marrinan, G. Shapiro, B. McEwan, and A. Kemper. 1981. Collected papers from the Puerto Real Project, 1981 Season. Ms. on file, Florida State Museum, University of Florida, Gainesville.

Farnsworth, P. 1992. Comparative analysis in plantation archaeology: The application of a functional classification. Paper presented at the Twenty-fifth Annual Meeting of the Society for Historical Archaeology, Kingston, Jamaica.

Farnsworth, P. 1993. Archaeological excavations at Wade's Green plantation, North Caicos. *Journal of the Bahamas Historical Society* 15(1):2–10.

Farnsworth, P. 1994. Archaeological excavations at Promised Land plantation, New Providence. *Journal of the Bahamas Historical Society* 16(1):21–29.

Farnsworth, P. 1996. The influence of trade on Bahamian slave culture. *Historical Archaeology* 30(4):1–23.

Farnsworth, P. 1997. Isolation and the development of Bahamian culture. Paper presented at the Seventeenth International Congress for Caribbean Archaeology, Nassau, Bahamas.

Farnsworth, P. 1999. From the past to the present: An exploration of the formation of African-Bahamian identity during enslavement. In *African Sites Archaeology in the Caribbean,* edited by J. B. Haviser, pp. 94–130. Princeton: Markus Weiner; Kingston: Ian Randle.

Farnsworth, P., and L. A. Wilkie. 1998. Excavations at Marine Farm and Great Hope plantations, Crooked Island, Bahamas. *Journal of the Bahamas Historical Society* 20:19–25.

Farnsworth, P., and L. A. Wilkie Farnsworth. 1990. A preliminary report on the 1989 excavations at Wade's Green plantation, North Caicos. Report on file, Department of Education, Grand Turk, Turk and Caicos Islands, British West Indies.

Farnsworth, P., and J. S. Williams. 1992. The archaeology of the Spanish colonial and Mexican republican periods: Introduction. *Historical Archaeology* 26(1):1–6.

Farr, S. 1995. Gender and ethnogenesis in the early colonial Lesser Antilles. In *Caribbean archaeology,* edited by R. E. Alegría and M. Rodríguez, pp. 367–375. San Juan: Centro de Estudios Avanzados de Puerto Rico y el Caribe.

Fatunsin, A. K. 1992. *Yoruban pottery.* Lagos, Nigeria: National Commission for Museums and Monuments.

Faulkner, A., and G. Faulkner. 1987. *The French at Pentagoet, 1635–1674: An archaeological portrait of the Acadian frontier.* Augusta, Maine: Archaeological Society of Maine.

Felice Cardot, C. 1973. *Curazao hispánico.* Caracas, Venezuela: Academia Nacional de la Hostoria 115.

Ferbel, P. 1995. When a canoe means more than a water trough: The politics of Taino cultural heritage in the post-Quincentennial Dominican Republic. Ph.D. dissertation, Department of Anthropology, University of Minnesota, Minneapolis.

Fergus, H. A. 1981. Montserrat, "Colony of Ireland": The myth and the reality. *Studies* Winter 1981:325–340.

Fergus, H. A. 1983. *Montserrat, emerald isle of the Caribbean.* London: Macmillan Caribbean.

Fergus, H. A. 1994. *Montserrat: History of a Caribbean colony.* London: Macmillan Caribbean.

Ferguson, L. 1992. *Uncommon ground: Archaeology and early African America, 1650–1800.* Washington, D.C.: Smithsonian Institution Press.

Fernández Pequeno, J. M., and J. L. Hernández, eds. 1996. *El Caribe arqueológico.*

Annuario publicado por la Casa del Caribe como extensión de la revista Del Caribe No. 1. Casa del Caribe, Santiago de Cuba, Cuba.

Fleischman, M. L., and D. V. Armstrong. 1990. *Preliminary report: Analysis of Burial SAJ-B1 recovered from House-Area 16, Seville Afro-Jamaican settlement.* Report submitted to the Jamaica National Heritage Trust. Archaeological Report No. 6. Syracuse, N.Y.: Syracuse University.

Fletcher, R. 1977. Settlement studies (micro and semi-micro). In *Spatial archaeology,* edited by D. L. Clarke, pp. 47–162. New York: Academic Press.

Floore, P., J. Gawronski, and O. Ortiz-Troncoso, eds. 1995. *Nederlanders in Amerika: Een historisch-archeologische inventarisatie van de nederlandse trans-atlantische expansie.* Amsterdam: Ultramarine Foundation Press.

Foster, G. 1960. *Culture and conquest.* Chicago: Quadrangle Books.

Fournier-Garcia, P., and F. Miranda-Flores. 1992. Historic sites archaeology in Mexico. *Historical Archaeology* 26(1):75–83.

France, L. 1984. Sugar manufacturing in the West Indies: A study of innovation and variation. Master's thesis, Department of Anthropology, College of William and Mary, Williamsburg, Virginia.

Friends of English Harbour. 1972. *The romance of English Harbour.* 6th ed. Antigua: Friends of English Harbour.

Fuentes, Carlos. 1992. *The buried mirror.* New York: Houghton Mifflin.

Galloway, J. H. 1985. Tradition and innovation in the American sugar industry, c. 1500–1800: An explanation. *Annals of the Association of American Geographers* 75:334–351.

Galloway, J. H. 1989. *The sugar cane industry: An historical geography from its origins to 1914.* Cambridge: Cambridge University Press.

Gansemans, J. 1989. *Volksmuziekinstrumenten: Getuigen en resultaat van een interetnische samenleving: Een organologische studie met betrekking tot Aruba, Bonaire, en Curaçao.* Annalen Reeks In-8, Menswetenschappen No. 128. Tervuren, Belgium: Koninklijk Museum voor Midden-Afrika.

Garcia, O., and M. Garcia. 1993. Excavaciones arqueologicas en el Districto Historico de San German, Puerto Rico. Paper presented at the Fifteenth International Congress for Caribbean Archaeology, San Juan, Puerto Rico.

García Arévalo, M. A. 1977. Influencias de la dieta Indo-Hispanica en la cerámica Taina. Paper presented at the Seventh International Congress for the Study of the Pre-Columbian Cultures of the Lesser Antilles, Caracas, Venezuela.

García Arévalo, M. A. 1978. La arqueología Indo-Hispano en Santo Domingo. In *Unidades y variedades, ensavos, en homenaje a Jose M. Cruxent,* pp. 77–127. Caracas, Venezuela: Centro de Estudios Avanzados.

García Arévalo, M. A. 1990. Transculturation in contact period and contemporary Hispaniola. In *Columbian consequences,* vol. 2, edited by D. H. Thomas, pp. 269–280. Washington, D.C.: Smithsonian Institution Press.

García Arévalo, M. A. 1991. Influencias hispanicas en la alfareria Taina. In *Proceedings of the Thirteenth International Congress for Caribbean Archaeology,* edited by E. N. Ayubi and J. B. Haviser, pp. 363–383. Report No. 9. Curaçao: Archaeological-Anthropological Institute of the Netherlands Antilles.

García Castañeda, J. 1938. Asiento yayal. *Revista de Arqueología* 1(1):44–58.

Garland, A. 1982. The systematics of Dutch trade with the English in the Leewards, 1669–1700: An historical aid for predictive modeling. Paper presented at the Fifteenth Annual Meeting of the Society for Historical Archaeology, Philadelphia.

Gartley, R. T. 1979. Afro-Cruzan pottery: A new style of colonial earthenware from St. Croix. *Journal of the Virgin Islands Archaeological Society* 8:47–61.

Gaspar, D. B. 1985. *Bondmen and rebels: A study of the master-slave relations in Antigua.* Baltimore: Johns Hopkins University Press.

Geddes III, D. 1992. Archival research: The search for the Columbus Caravel at St. Ann's Bay, Jamaica. In *Underwater archaeology proceedings from the Society for Historical Archaeology Conference,* edited by D. Keith and T. Carrell, pp. 148–151. Tucson: Society for Historical Archaeology.

Gerace, K. 1982. Three Loyalist plantations on San Salvador Island, Bahamas. *Florida Anthropologist* 35(4):216–222.

Gerace, K. 1987. Early nineteenth century plantations on San Salvador, Bahamas: The archaeological record. *Journal of the Bahamas Historical Society* 9(1):14–21.

Gerace, K., and R. V. Shaklee. 1991. Fortune Hill Estate slave quarters site map. Ms. on file, Department of Archives, Nassau, Bahamas.

Gerace, K., and R. V. Shaklee. 1995. Fortune Hill Estate manor house complex. Ms. on file, Department of Archives, Nassau, Bahamas.

Gjessing, F. 1974. Reef Bay great house. *Journal of the Virgin Islands Archaeological Society* 1:7–12.

Glasscock, J. 1985. *Sint Maarten-Saint Martin: The making of an island.* Wellesley, Mass.: Windsor Press.

Glazier, S. D. 1993. Notes on transculturation and Amerindian religious traditions. In *Proceedings of the Fourteenth International Congress for Caribbean Archaeology,* edited by A. Cummins and P. King, pp. 232. Barbados: Barbados Museum and Historical Society.

Goggin, J. 1960. *The Spanish olive jar: An introductory study.* Yale University Publications in Anthropology 62. New Haven: Yale University Press.

Goggin, J. 1968. *Spanish majolica in the New World.* Yale University Publications in Anthropology 72. New Haven: Yale University Press.

Gonzales, J. 1980. Conferencia del Arq. José Gonzales. In *Objectos y ambientes de la Concepción de la Vega,* edited by A. Poladura, pp. 34–50. Santo Domingo: Museo Casas Reales.

Gonzalez, N. L. 1988. *Sojourners of the Caribbean: Ethnogenesis and ethnohistory of the Garifuna.* Urbana: University of Illinois Press.

Goodwin, C. M. 1982. Archaeology of Galways plantation. *Florida Anthropologist* 34(4):251–53.

Goodwin, C. M. 1987. Sugar, time, and Englishmen: A study of management strategies on Caribbean plantations. Ph.D. dissertation, Department of Archaeology, Boston University, Boston.

Goodwin, C. M. 1994. Betty's Hope windmill: An unexpected problem. *Historical Archaeology* 28(1):99–110.

Goodwin, C., and A. Pantel. 1978. A selected bibliography of physical anthropology in the Caribbean area. *Revista Interamericana* 8(3):531–540.

Goodwin, C. M., L. M. Pulsipher, D. G. Jones, M. R. Domurad, and W. M. Bass. 1992. The *Tschuh Chahd* burying ground at Galways plantation, Montserrat, West Indies. Ms. in the possession of the authors, Knoxville, Tennessee.

Goodwin, W. B. 1946. *Spanish and English ruins in Jamaica.* Boston: Meador.

Goslinga, C. C. 1971. *The Dutch in the Caribbean and on the wild coast, 1580–1680.* Assen, The Netherlands: Van Gorcum Pers; Gainesville: University Press of Florida.

Goslinga, C. C. 1979. *A Short History of the Netherlands Antilles and Suriname.* The Hague, The Netherlands: Nijhoff Pers.

Goslinga, C. C. 1985. *The Dutch in the Caribbean and in the Guianas, 1680–1791.* Assen, The Netherlands: Van Gorcum Pers.

Goucher, C. 1999. African-Caribbean metal technology: Forging cultural survivals in the Atlantic world. In *African sites archaeology in the Caribbean,* edited by J. Haviser, pp. 143–156. Princeton: Markus Wiener; Kingston: Ian Randle.

Goveia, E. 1965. *Slave society in the British Leeward Islands at the end of the eighteenth century.* New Haven: Yale University Press.

Graham, E., and A. Mills. 1990. Ethics and archaeology abroad. Paper presented at the 1990 Annual Meeting of the Society of American Archaeology, Las Vegas.

Granberry, J. 1980. A brief history of Bahamian archaeology. *Florida Anthropologist* 33:83–93.

Green-Pedersen, S. E. 1979. The economic considerations behind the Danish abolition of the Negro slave trade. In *The uncommon market: Essays in the economic history of the Atlantic slave trade,* edited by H. A. Gemery and J. S. Hogendorn, pp. 399–418. New York: Academic Press.

Guerrero, J. G., and E. Ortega. 1983. La Isabela, primera ciudad del Nuevo Mundo aun no ha mundo. *Hoy* 117:6–9.

Guzman, A. P. 1993. La contribucion de la arqueologia en el reconstrucion ethno-historico del Caribe. Paper presented at the Fifteenth International Congress for Caribbean Archaeology, San Juan, Puerto Rico.

Hall, D. 1989. *In Miserable Slavery: Thomas Thistlewood in Jamaica, 1750–86.* London: Macmillan.

Hall, J. L. 1992. A brief history of underwater salvage in the Dominican Republic. In *Underwater archaeology proceedings from the Society for Historical Archaeology Conference,* edited by D. Keith and T. Carrell, pp. 35–40. Tucson: Society for Historical Archaeology.

Hall, J. L. 1993. Across an indigo sea: A seventeenth-century shipwreck in Monte Cristo Bay, Dominican Republic. Paper presented at the Fifteenth International Congress for Caribbean Archaeology, San Juan, Puerto Rico.

Hall, N. A. T. 1992. *Slave society in the Danish West Indies: St. Thomas, St. John, and St. Croix,* edited by B. Higman. Kingston: Canoe Press.

Hamelberg, J. 1899. Historische schets van de Nederlandse Bovenwindse eilanden tot op het einde van de 17e eeuw. In *Geschied-, Taal-, Land-, en Volkenkundig Genootschap,* vol. 2. Amsterdam: Emmering.

Hamelberg, J. 1901–1909. *De Nederlanders op de West-Indische Eilanden*. 2 vols. Amsterdam: De Bussy.

Hamilton, J., and W. Hodges. 1982. Bayaha: A preliminary report. Ms. on file, Musée de Guahaba, Limbe, Haiti.

Hammond, P. 1970. Stratigraphic and electron survey of New Seville. Ms. on file, Jamaica National Trust Commission, Kingston, Jamaica.

Hamshere, C. 1972. *The British in the Caribbean*. Cambridge, Mass.: Harvard University Press.

Handler, J. S. 1963a. A historical sketch of pottery manufacture in Barbados. *Journal of the Barbados Museum and Historical Society* 30(3):129–153.

Handler, J. S. 1963b. Pottery making in rural Barbados. *Southwestern Journal of Anthropology* 19:314–334.

Handler, J. S. 1964. Notes on pottery-making in Antigua. *Man* 64:150–151.

Handler, J. S. 1972. An archaeological investigation of the domestic life of plantation slaves in Barbados. *Journal of the Barbados Museum and Historical Society* 34:64–72.

Handler, J. S. 1974. *The unappropriated people: Freedmen in the slave society of Barbados*. Baltimore: Johns Hopkins University Press.

Handler, J. S. 1989. *Searching for a slave cemetery in Barbados, West Indies: A bio-archaeological and ethnohistorical investigation*. Research Paper No. 59. Carbondale: Center for Archaeological Investigations, Southern Illinois University.

Handler, J. S. 1996. A prone burial from a plantation slave cemetery in Barbados, West Indies: Possible evidence for an African-type witch or other negatively viewed person. *Historical Archaeology* 30(3):76–86.

Handler, J. S., and R. S. Corruccini. 1983. Plantation slave life in Barbados: A physical anthropological analysis. *Journal of Interdisciplinary History* 14(1):65–90.

Handler, J. S., and J. Jacoby. 1993. Slave medicine and plant use in Barbados. *Journal of the Barbados Museum and Historical Society* 41:72–98.

Handler, J. S., and F. W. Lange. 1978. *Plantation slavery in Barbados: An archaeological and historical investigation*. Cambridge, Mass.: Harvard University Press.

Handler, J. S., and L. Shelby. 1973. A seventeenth century commentary on labor and military problems in Barbados. *Journal of the Barbados Museum and Historical Society* 34(3):117–121.

Hannon, T., and A. Hannon. 1976. Bottles found in St. Thomas, Virgin Islands, waters. *Journal of the Virgin Islands Archaeological Society* 3:29–45.

Hanrahan, P. 1990. Old bottles with British Guiana commercial markings. *Journal of Archaeology and Anthropology of the Walter Roth Museum of Anthropology* 7:5–18.

Hanrahan, P. 1993. The CS/Ostrich wine bottle. *Journal of Archaeology and Anthropology of the Walter Roth Museum of Anthropology* 9:35–39.

Harden, C., and L. M. Pulsipher. 1992. "Come a nasty gale": The physical and sociocultural response to Hurricane Hugo in Montserrat, West Indies. *Focus* 42(2):9–14.

Hardin, K., and S. Gluckman. 1982. The underwater survey of St. Eustatius, Netherlands Antilles. Paper presented at the Fifteenth Annual Meeting of the Society for Historical Archaeology, Philadelphia.

Harlow, V. T. 1926. *A history of Barbados, 1625–1685*. Oxford: Clarendon Press.

Harlow, V. T. 1928. *Christopher Codrington, 1668–1710.* London: Hurst.

Harper, R. K. 1990. An ethnoarchaeological study of the cisterns in Oranjestad, Sint Eustatius, Netherlands Antilles. Master's thesis, Department of Anthropology, College of William and Mary, Williamsburg, Virginia.

Hartog, J. 1953–1964. *Gesheidendenis van de Nederlandse Antillen.* 4 vols. Aruba: De Wit.

Hartog, J. 1964. *De Bovenwindse Eilanden.* Aruba: De Wit.

Hartog, J. 1965. *St. Maarten, Saba, and St. Eustatius.* Aruba: De Wit.

Hartog, J. 1968. *Curaçao: From colonial dependence to autonomy.* Aruba: De Wit.

Hartog, J. 1975. *History of Saba.* Saba: Saban Artisan Foundation.

Hartog, J. 1976a. *History of St. Eustatius.* Aruba: De Wit.

Hartog, J. 1976b. *The Jews of St. Eustatius.* St. Maarten: Windward Islands Bank.

Hartog, J. 1978. *A short history of Bonaire.* Aruba: De Wit.

Hartog, J. 1981. *History of Sint Maarten and Saint Martin.* Philipsburg: Sint Maarten Jaycees.

Hartog, J. 1988. *Aruba: Short history.* Aruba: Van Dorp.

Hartog, J. 1994. *The Forts of Sint Maarten and Saint Martin.* Zutphen, The Netherlands: Walburg Pers.

Hartog, J. 1996. *Het fort op de berg.* Assen, The Netherlands: Van Gorcum Pers.

Hartog, J. 1997a. *De forten, verdedingswerken, en geschutstellingen van Curaçao en Bonaire.* Zaltbommel, The Netherlands: Europese Bibliotheek.

Hartog, J. 1997b. *De forten, verdedingswerken, en geschutstellingen van Sint Maarten en Saint Martin.* Zaltbommel, The Netherlands: Europese Bibliotheek.

Hartog, J. 1997c. *De forten, verdedingswerken, en geschutstellingen van Sint Eustatius en Saba.* Zaltbommel, The Netherlands: Europese Bibliotheek.

Haviser, J. 1982. A preliminary archaeological survey and assessment of the land resources of St. Eustatius, Netherlands Antilles. Paper presented to the Fifteenth Annual Meeting of the Society for Historical Archaeology, Philadelphia.

Haviser, J. 1983. The Netherlands Antilles and America. Paper presented to the Sixteenth Annual Meeting of the Society for Historical Archaeology, Denver.

Haviser, J. 1984. Cultural polarization among the Netherlands Antilles, as seen through architecture. Paper presented to the Seventeenth Annual Meeting of the Society for Historical Archaeology, Williamsburg, Virginia.

Haviser, J. 1985. The conservation of cultural resources: Public interpretation and education. Paper presented at "Partners for Livable Places: A Symposium on Conservation of Natural and Cultural Resources in the Caribbean," Washington, D.C.

Haviser, J. 1987. *Amerindian cultural geography on Curaçao.* Natuurwetenscapellijke studiekring voor Suriname en de Nederlandse Antillen No. 120. Amsterdam.

Haviser, J. 1988. An archaeological survey of St. Maarten–St. Martin. Report No. 7. Curaçao: Archaeological-Anthropological Institute of the Netherlands Antilles.

Haviser, J. 1989a. A comparison of Amerindian insular adaptive strategies on Curaçao. In *Early ceramic population lifeways and adaptive strategies in the Caribbean,* edited by P. Siegel, pp. 3–28. BAR International Series 506. Oxford, England.

Haviser, J. 1989b. Legislation and archaeological preservation. In *Proceedings of the 1989 Annual Meeting of the Caribbean Conservation Association*. Curaçao: Caribbean Conservation Association.

Haviser, J. 1989c. Letter from Curaçao. *Archaeology Magazine* 42(2):54–55.

Haviser, J. 1990. *Archaeology of St. Maarten–St. Martin*. Middle school textbook, OKSNA, St. Maarten.

Haviser, J. 1991. *The first Bonaireans*. Report No. 10. Curaçao: Archaeological-Anthropological Institute of the Netherlands Antilles.

Haviser, J. 1992. Preliminary investigations at Zuurzak, a seventeenth century Dutch slave camp on Curaçao. Paper presented at the Twenty-fifth Annual Meeting of the Society for Historical Archaeology, Kingston, Jamaica.

Haviser, J. 1993a. Developers and archaeologists can work together. *Imagine Ambiental Magazine* 12(4):6–9.

Haviser, J. 1993b. Proposed contracts for archaeological investigations on Curaçao. Report submitted by the Archaeological-Anthropological Institute of the Netherlands Antilles to the Monumentenraad as advisers to the Island Government of Curaçao, Willemstad.

Haviser, J. 1993c. Proposed contracts for archaeological investigations on St. Maarten. Report submitted by the Archaeological-Anthropological Institute of the Netherlands Antilles to the Island Government of Sint Maarten, Philipsburg.

Haviser, J. 1993d. Using the past to develop the future. *Special Edition Expo Newspaper*, 5. Curaçao: Tourism Expo.

Haviser, J. 1995a. An archaeological investigation of community development in the Kenepa area of Curaçao. Report submitted by the Archaeological-Anthropological Institute of the Netherlands Antilles to the Fundashon Landhuis Knip, Curaçao.

Haviser, J. 1995b. Archaeological testing at optical telegraph sites on Curaçao, Netherlands Antilles. Paper presented at the Twenty-eighth Annual Meeting of the Society for Historical Archaeology, Washington, D.C.

Haviser, J. 1995c. The trend towards romanticized Amerindian identities among Caribbean peoples: A case study from Bonaire, Netherlands Antilles. In *Wolves from the sea*, edited by N. Whitehead, pp. 139–146. Leiden: Royal Institute of Linguistics and Anthropology.

Haviser, J. 1996a. An archaeological survey of the Belvedere plantation parcels I, II, and III, St. Maarten. Report submitted by the Archaeological-Anthropological Institute of the Netherlands Antilles to the St. Maarten Island Government, Curaçao.

Haviser, J. 1996b. Archaeological testing at optical telegraph sites on Curaçao. In *Proceedings of a Symposium on the Optical Telegraph held in Stockholm, June 21–23, 1994*, pp. 25–31. Stockholm: Telemuseum Press.

Haviser, J. 1997a. Social repercussions of slavery as evident in the African-Curaçaoan Kunuku house. Paper presented at the symposium "West Africa and the Americas: Repercussions of the Slave Trade," University of the West Indies at Mona, Jamaica.

Haviser, J. 1997b. Archaeological reconnaissance and limited test excavations at

Daai Booi Bay, Curaçao. Report submitted by the Archaeological-Anthropological Institute of the Netherlands Antilles to the development company Plan D-2, Curaçao.

Haviser, J. 1997c. Archaeological testing at Fort Oranje, Bonaire. Paper presented at the Seventeenth International Congress for Caribbean Archaeology, Nassau, Bahamas.

Haviser, J. 1997d. Curaçao. In *Encyclopedia of underwater and maritime archaeology,* edited by J. Delgado, pp. 121. London: British Museum Press.

Haviser, J. 1997e. Social repercussions of slavery as evident in African-Curaçaoan "Kunuku" houses. Paper presented at the Seventeenth International Congress for Caribbean Archaeology, Nassau, Bahamas.

Haviser, J. 1998a. First contact from the discoverer's view: The Native American role 500 years ago. In *Now, Curaçao.* Curaçao: Jonckheer and Hagens.

Haviser, J. 1998b. Lecture series/training course on diagnostic Dutch artifacts from the Netherlands Antilles, November 23–28. Ms. prepared for the Instituto del Patrimonio Cultural de Venezuela, Caracas, Venezuela.

Haviser, J. 1999. Identifying a post-emancipation (1863–1940) African-Curaçaoan material culture assemblage. In *African sites archaeology in the Caribbean,* edited by J. Haviser, pp. 221–263. Princeton: Markus Wiener; Kingston: Ian Randle.

Haviser, J. 2000. Archaeological investigations at African- Curaçaoan Kunuku houses. In *Proceedings of the Seventeenth International Congress for Caribbean Archaeology,* edited by J. Winter. Rockville Center, N.Y.: Molloy College.

Haviser, J. 2001a. Emancipation as a continuing process. In *Freedom in black history,* edited by E. K. Agorsah. Portland, Ore.: Arrow Press, in press. Ms. 1996.

Haviser, J. 2001b. An ethno-archaeological study of wood and other organic materials used by African-Curaçaoan peoples during the post-emancipation period. In *Proceedings of the Eighteenth International Congress for Caribbean Archaeology,* edited by L. Sutty. Grenada, in press.

Haviser, J. B., ed. 1999. *African sites archaeology in the Caribbean.* Princeton: Marcus Wiener; Kingston: Ian Randle.

Haviser, J., and R. Ansano. 1993. Algemene selectiecriteria voor archeologische monumenten op Curaçao. Report submitted to the Monumentenraad Curaçao for approval by the Curaçao Island Council, Curaçao.

Haviser, J., F. Brugman, and M. Newton. 1989. UNDP-UNESCO Training, Conservation, and Documentation Center for the Caribbean Region: A project proposal. Report submitted to the UNESCO Interregional Workgroup for "Actie Willemstad" Curaçao, Curaçao.

Haviser, J., and C. DeCorse. 1991. African-Caribbean interaction: A research plan for Curaçao Creole culture. In *Proceedings of the Thirteenth International Congress for Caribbean Archaeology,* edited by E. N. Ayubi and J. B. Haviser, pp. 326–337. Report No. 9. Curaçao: Archaeological-Anthropological Institute of the Netherlands Antilles.

Haviser, J., M. R. Khudabux, and E. van Langerfeld. 2001. History, archaeology, and physical anthropology of Dutch Protestant skeletal remains from the "De Tempel" site, Curaçao. In *Proceedings of the Eighteenth International Congress for Caribbean Archaeology,* edited by L. Sutty. Grenada, in press.

Haviser, J., and E. Maduro. 1990. Locating the sixteenth century Spanish village of "Puebla de la Madre de Dios de la Ascension." *Journal of Caribbean History* 23(1):51–61.

Haviser, J., and A. Sealy. 2000. Archaeological testing at Fort Oranje, Bonaire. In *Proceedings of the Seventeenth International Congress for Caribbean Archaeology,* edited by J. Winter. Rockville Center, N.Y.: Molloy College.

Haviser, J., R. Sillé, and W. Garcia. 1995. *Met ogen van toen.* Curaçao: Fundashon Material pa Skol.

Haviser, J. B., and N. Simmons-Brito. 1991. Sub-surface archaeological testing in the Punda area of Curaçao, Netherlands Antilles. In *Proceedings of the Fourteenth International Congress for Caribbean Archaeology,* edited by A. Cummins and P. King, pp. 380–407. Barbados: Barbados Museum and Historical Society.

Haviser, J. B., and N. Simmons-Brito. 1993. Archaeological testing in the Punda area of Curaçao. *Kristof* 8(2):23–38.

Haviser, J. B., and N. Simmons-Brito. 1995. Excavations at the Zuurzak site: A possible seventeenth century Dutch slave camp on Curaçao, Netherlands Antilles. In *Proceedings of the Fifteenth International Congress for Caribbean Archaeology,* edited by R. E. Alegría and M. Rodríguez, pp. 71–81. San Juan: Centro de Estudios Avanzados de Puerto Rico y el Caribe.

Hayward, Michele. 1995. Military life at Castillo de San Filipe del Morro, Puerto Rico, during the Spanish colonial period. Paper presented at the Sixteenth International Congress for Caribbean Archaeology, Basse-Terre, Guadeloupe.

Heath, B. J. 1988. *Afro-Caribbean ware: A study of ethnicity on St. Eustatius.* Ph.D. dissertation, Department of Anthropology, University of Pennsylvania, Philadelphia. Ann Arbor: University Microfilms.

Heath, B. J. 1991. Afro-Caribbean ware on St. Eustatius: A preliminary typology. In *Proceedings of the Thirteenth International Congress for Caribbean Archaeology,* edited by E. N. Ayubi and J. B. Haviser, pp. 338–343. Report No. 9. Curaçao: Archaeological-Anthropological Institute of the Netherlands Antilles.

Heath, B. J. 1999. Yabbas, monkeys, jugs, and jars: An historical context for African-Caribbean pottery on St. Eustatius. In *African Sites Archaeology in the Caribbean,* edited by J. Haviser, pp. 196–220. Princeton: Markus Wiener; Kingston: Ian Randle.

Henriquez, P. 1990. What future for Curaçao's architectural monuments? In *Building up the future from the past,* edited by H. Coomans, M. Newton, and M. Eustatia, pp. 165–171. Zutphen, The Netherlands: De Walburg Pers.

Hernéandez, M. 1868–1882. *Colección de documentos inéditos relativos al descubrimiento, conquista, y organización de las Antiguas posesiones espannñolas de América y Oceania sacados de los Archivos del Reino y muy especialmente del de Indias.* Madrid: Imprenta de M. Hernéandez.

Herskovits, M. 1941. *Myth of the Negro past.* 1962. Reprint. Boston: Beacon Press.

Higman, B. W. 1984. *Slave populations of the British Caribbean, 1807–1834*. Baltimore: Johns Hopkins University Press.

Higman, B. W. 1988. *Jamaica surveyed: Plantation maps and plans of the eighteenth and nineteenth centuries*. Kingston: Institute of Jamaica Publications.

Higman, B. W. 1998. *Montpelier, Jamaica: A plantation community in slavery and freedom, 1739–1912*. Kingston: University Press of the West Indies.

Hinote, R. 1981. Preliminary report on summer test excavations at Crook's Castle. Report submitted to the Department of Anthropology, College of William and Mary, Williamsburg, Virginia.

Hobson, D. 1989. An inventory of the historic structures of Nevis. Master's thesis, Department of History, University of Vermont, Burlington.

Hodges, W. 1979. How we found Puerto Real. Ms. on file, Musée de Guahaba, Limbe, Haiti.

Hodges, W. 1980. Puerto Real sources. Ms. on file, Musée de Guahaba, Limbe, Haiti.

Hodges, W. 1983. The search for La Navidad. Ms. on file, Musée de Guahaba, Limbe, Haiti.

Hodges, W. 1984. The search for La Navidad. Ms. on file, Musée de Guahaba, Limbe, Haiti.

Hodges, W. 1986. La forteleza de La Navidad. Ms. on file, Musée de Guahaba, Limbe, Haiti.

Hoetink, H. 1966. *Het patron van de oude Curaçaose samenleving: Een sociologische studie*. Aruba: De Wit.

Hoffman, C. A., Jr. 1985. Archaeological investigations at the Long Bay site, San Salvador, Bahamas. Paper presented at the First San Salvador Conference, "Columbus and His World," San Salvador, Bahamas.

Hoffman, P. 1980. *The Spanish crown and the defense of the Indies*. Baton Rouge: Louisiana State University Press.

Hofman, C. L. 1987. Historische beschrijving van de Bovenwindse Eilanden. *Sticusa Journal* 110:8–10.

Hofman, C. L. 1993. In search of the native population of pre-Columbian Saba. Ph.D. dissertation, Pre-History Department, University of Leiden, The Netherlands.

Hofman, C. L. 1995. Three late prehistoric sites in the periphery of Guadeloupe: Grande Anse, Terre de Bas, and Morne Cybèle 1 and 2, la Désirade. Paper presented at the Sixteenth International Congress for Caribbean Archaeology, Basse-Terre, Guadeloupe.

Honychurch, L. 1983. *The Cabrits and Prince Rupert's Bay*. Roseau: Dominica Institute.

Honychurch, L. 1984. *The Dominica story: A history of the island*. 2d ed. Roseau: Dominica Institute.

Honychurch, L. 1997. Crossroads in the Caribbean: A site of encounter and exchange on Dominica. *World Archaeology* 28:291–304.

Hoogland, M. 1996. In search of the native population of pre-Columbian Saba, Part II. Ph.D. dissertation, Pre-History Department, Leiden University, The Netherlands.

Hoover, G. N. 1974. *The elegant Royalls of colonial New England*. New York: Vantage Press.

Howard, B. P. 1991. Fortifications of St. Eustatius: An archaeological and historical study of defense in the Caribbean. Master's thesis, Department of Anthropology, College of William and Mary, Williamsburg, Virginia.

Howard, R. A., and E. S. Howard, eds. 1983. *Alexander Anderson's geography and history of St. Vincent, West Indies*. Cambridge, Mass.: President and Fellows of Harvard College and the Linnean Society of London.

Howson, J. 1990. Social relations and material culture: A critique of the archaeology of plantation slavery. *Historical Archaeology* 23:(1)78–91.

Howson, J. 1995. Colonial goods and the plantation village: Consumption and the internal economy in Montserrat from slavery to freedom. Ph.D. dissertation, Department of Anthropology, New York University, New York.

Hoyt, S. D. 1984. The archaeological survey of Pedro Bank, Jamaica, 1981–1983. *International Journal of Nautical Archaeology and Underwater Exploration* 13(2):99–111.

Hubbard, V. K. 1990. The Newcastle redoubt: The oldest standing structure in the English speaking Caribbean? *Nevis Historical and Conservation Society Newsletter* 17:13–17.

Hubbard, V. K. 1994. 1689 and 1690: War, pestilence, and earthquake. *Nevis Historical and Conservation Society Newsletter* 34:8–10.

Hudson, B. J. 1989. Waterfront development and redevelopment in the West Indies. *Caribbean Geography* 2:229–240.

Hughes, G. R. 1997. "A full perfect and faithful return": An anthropological reanalysis of Bahamian slave registers. Senior thesis, Department of Anthropology, University of California, Berkeley.

Hughes, Q. 1991. *Military architecture*. Liphook, Hampshire: Beaufort Publishing.

Hulme, P. 1992. *Colonial encounters: Europe and the native Caribbean, 1492–1797*. London: Routledge.

Hulme, P., and N. D. Whitehead, eds. 1992. *Wild majesty: Encounters with Caribs from Columbus to the present day*. Oxford: Clarendon Press.

Hurston, Z. N. 1938. *Tell my horse: Voodoo and life in Haiti and Jamaica*. Reprint. 1991. New York: Harper & Row.

Innis, P. 1985. *Historic Basseterre: The story of a West Indian town*. St. John's, Antigua: Island Resources Foundation.

Innis, P. 1991–93. *Country environmental profile*. [Individual monographic profiles completed for Anguilla, Antigua and Barbuda, Dominica, Grenada, Montserrat, St. Kitts and Nevis, St. Lucia, and St. Vincent and the Grenadines]. Barbados: Caribbean Conservation Association and Island Resources Foundation.

Irion, J. 1990. A survey of shipwrecks in Belize, Central America. In *Underwater archaeology proceedings from the Society for Historical Archaeology Conference*, edited by T. Carrell, pp. 70–74. Tucson: Society for Historical Archaeology.

Jamaica National Trust Commission. 1970. Future prospects for Sevilla Nueva. *Jamaica Journal* 4(2):13–14.

James, S. 1985. The analysis of the Conde de Tolosa and the Nuestra Señora de Guadalupe olive jar assemblage. Master's thesis, Department of Anthropology, Texas A&M University, College Station, Texas.

James, S. 1988. A reassessment of the chronological and typological framework of the Spanish olive jar. *Historical Archaeology* 22(1):43–66.

Jameson, J. F. 1903. St. Eustatius and the American Revolution. *American Historical Review* 8:683–708.

Jane, C. W. E. 1982. *Shirley Heights: The story of the Redcoats in Antigua.* English Harbour, Antigua: Nelson's Dockyard National Park Foundation.

Jesse, Rev. C. J. 1970. *Outlines of St. Lucia's history.* 3d ed. Castries: St. Lucia Archaeological and Historical Society.

Johnson, H. 1991. *The Bahamas in slavery and freedom.* Kingston: Ian Randle.

Johnson, W. 1979. *Saban lore.* Saba: By the author.

Johnson, W. 1987. *For the love of St. Maarten.* New York: Carlton Press.

Jones, S. L. 1985. The African-American tradition in vernacular architecture. In *The archaeology of slavery and plantation life,* edited by T. A. Singleton, pp. 195–213. Orlando, Fla.: Academic Press.

Joseph, J. W. 1987. Ballajá archaeological testing project: Management summary and data recovery plan. Report prepared by Garrow & Associates, Inc., and submitted to the U.S. Army Corps of Engineers, Jacksonville, Florida.

Joseph, J. W., and S. C. Bryne. 1992. Socio-economics and trade in Viejo San Juan, Puerto Rico: Observations from the Ballaja archaeological project. *Historical Archaeology* 26(1):45–58.

Joseph, J. W., and H. Rodríguez. 1987. An archaeological reconnaissance of proposed flood control corridors, Caguas and Gurabo, Puerto Rico. Report prepared by Garrow & Associates, Inc., and submitted to the U.S. Army Corps of Engineers, Jacksonville, Florida.

Judge, J. 1986. Where Columbus found the New World. *National Geographic* 170(5): 566–572, 578–599.

Juliana, E. 1976–78. *Guia etnologiko 1–3.* Curaçao: By the author.

Juliana, E. 1988. *Matrimonio i parto.* Report No. 5. Curaçao: Archaeological-Anthropological Institute of the Netherlands Antilles.

Kandle, P. L. 1985. St. Eustatius: Acculturation in a Dutch Caribbean colony. Master's thesis, Department of Anthropology, College of William and Mary, Williamsburg, Virginia.

Keegan, W. F. 1984. West Indian Archaeology 2. After Columbus. *Journal of Archaeological Research* 2(3):265–294.

Keegan, W. F. 1989. Columbus's 1492 voyage and the search for his landfall. In *First encounters,* edited by J. T. Milanich and S. Milbrath, pp. 27–40. Gainesville: University Press of Florida.

Keegan, W. F. 1992. *The people who discovered Columbus: The prehistory of the Bahamas.* Gainesville: University Press of Florida.

Keegan, W. F. 1996. Columbus was a cannibal: Myth and the first encounters. In *The*

Lesser Antilles in the age of European expansion, edited by R. L. Paquette and S. L. Engerman, pp. 18–32. Gainesville: University Press of Florida.

Keegan, W. F., and S. W. Mitchell. 1987. The archaeology of Christopher Columbus's voyage through the Bahamas. *American Archaeology* 6:102–108.

Keegan, W., A. Stokes, and L. Newsom. 1990. *Bullen Research Library Bibliography of Caribbean Archaeology 1.* Gainesville: Florida Museum of Natural History.

Keith, D. H. 1980. A report on treasure hunting activities in Berwick, Louisiana. Ms. on file, Department of Anthropology, East Carolina University, Greenville, North Carolina.

Keith, D. H. 1985. Analysis of hull remains, ballast, and artifact distribution of a sixteenth-century shipwreck, Molasses Reef, British West Indies. *Journal of Field Archaeology* 12:411–424.

Keith, D. H. 1987. The Molasses Reef wreck. Ph.D. dissertation, Department of Anthropology, Texas A&M University, College Station, Texas.

Keith, D. H. 1988. Shipwrecks of the explorers. In *Ships and shipwrecks of the Americas: A history based on underwater archaeology,* edited by George Bass, pp. 45–68. London: Thames & Hudson.

Keith, D. H. 1989. Ships of exploration and discovery: General projects. *SHA Newsletter* 22(4):41.

Keith, D., D. Lakey, J. Simmons III, and M. Myers. 1989. Ships of exploration and discovery research. In *Underwater archaeology proceedings from the Society for Historical Archaeology,* edited by J. B. Arnold III, pp. 87–99. Tucson: Society for Historical Archaeology.

Keith, D., and B. F. Thompson. 1985. An archaeological survey of La Isabela, Dominican Republic. Ms. on file, Institute of Nautical Archaeology, Texas A&M University, College Station, Texas.

Kelly, K. G. 1988. A bibliography of Caribbean archaeology. Ms. on file, Department of Anthropology, College of William & Mary, Williamsburg, Virginia.

Kelly, K. G. 1989. Historic archaeology of Jamaican tenant-manager relations: A case study from Drax Hall and Seville Estates, St. Ann, Jamaica. Master's thesis, Department of Anthropology, College of William and Mary, Williamsburg, Virginia.

Kelly, K. G., and D. V. Armstrong. 1991. Archaeological investigations of a nineteenth century free laborer house, Seville Estate, St. Ann's, Jamaica. In *Proceedings of the Thirteenth International Congress for Caribbean Archaeology,* edited by E. N. Ayubi and J. B. Haviser, pp. 429–435. Report No. 9. Curaçao: Archaeological-Anthropological Institute of the Netherlands Antilles.

Kemp, B. 1990. Basketmaking on the island of St. John. *Clarion* 15(3):52–59.

Keur, J. Y., and D. Keur. 1960. *Windward Island children: A study in the human ecology of the three Dutch Windward Islands in the Caribbean.* Assen, The Netherlands: Van Gorcum Pers.

Khudabux, M. R. 1991. Effects of life conditions on the health of a Negro slave community in Suriname. Ph.D. dissertation, Department of Anatomy and Embryology, Leiden University, The Netherlands.

Khudabux, M. R. 1999. Effects of life conditions on the health of a Negro slave community in Suriname. In *African sites archaeology in the Caribbean*, edited by J. B. Haviser, pp. 291–312. Princeton: Markus Wiener; Kingston: Ian Randle.

Kiple, K. F., and K. C. Ornelas. 1996. After the encounter: Disease and demographics in the Lesser Antilles. In *The Lesser Antilles in the age of European expansion*, edited by R. L. Paquette and S. L. Engerman, pp. 50–67. Gainesville: University Press of Florida.

Kirby, I. A. E. 1973. *The sugar mills of St. Vincent: Their sites, 172- to 1962.* Kingstown: St. Vincent Archaeological and Historical Society.

Klomp, A. 1980. *Politiek op Bonaire.* ICAU Mededelingen No. 18. Utrecht: Instituut voor Culturele Antropologie.

Klomp, A. 1983. Het "oude" Bonairiaanse woonhuis. *New West Indian Guide* 54(3/4): 155–213.

Knappert, L. 1932. *Geschediedenis van de Nederlandse Bovenwindsche Eilanden in de 18de eeuw.* The Hague: Martinus Nijhoff.

Knox, J. P. 1852. *A historical account of St. Thomas in the Danish West Indies.* New York: Charles Scribner.

Kochan, J. 1982. Archaeological and architectural investigations at Fort de Windt, St. Eustatius. Report submitted to the Department of Anthropology, College of William and Mary, Williamsburg, Virginia.

Kozy, C. J. 1983. A history of the Georgia Loyalists and the plantation period in the Turks and Caicos Islands. D.A. dissertation, Middle Tennessee State University, Murfreesboro, Tennessee.

Kraai, E. 1992. Multi-disciplinary approach towards conservation on Sint Maarten and St. Eustatius. Paper presented at the Twenty-fifth Annual Meeting of the Society for Historical Archaeology, Kingston, Jamaica.

Labat, R. P. J. B. 1979. *Nouveau voyage aux isles de l'Amérique.* 5 vols. Saint-Joseph, France: Courtinard.

Lafleur, G. 1992. *Les Caraïbes des Petites Antilles.* Paris: Karthala.

Lakey, D. 1990. Spain in the Indies: The process of discovery. In *Underwater archaeology proceedings from the Society for Historical Archaeology Conference*, edited by T. Carrell, pp. 66–69. Tucson: Society for Historical Archaeology.

Landers, J. 1990. African presence in early Spanish colonization of the Caribbean and southeastern borderlands. In *Columbian consequences,* vol. 2, edited by D. H. Thomas, pp. 315–328. Washington, D.C.: Smithsonian Institution Press.

Lange, F. W., and S. B. Carlson. 1985. Distributions of European earthenwares on Barbados, West Indies. In *The archaeology of slavery and plantation life*, edited by T. A. Singleton, pp. 97–120. Orlando, Fla.: Academic Press.

Lange, F. W., and J. S. Handler. 1985. The ethnohistorical approach to slavery. In *The archaeology of slavery and plantation life*, edited by T. A. Singleton, pp. 15–32. Orlando, Fla.: Academic Press.

La Rosa Corzo, G. 1983. *Arqueologia en sitios de contrabandistas.* Havana: Editorial Academia.

La Rosa Corzo, G. 1989. Armas y tácticas defensivas de los cimarrones en Cuba. *Reporte de Investigacion del Instituto de Ciencias Históricas* 2:1–28.

La Rosa Corzo, G. 1991. *Los palenques del oriente de Cuba: Resistencia y acoso.* Havana: Editorial Academia.

Larsen, C., M. Schoeninger, D. Hutchinson, K. Russell, and C. Ruff. 1990. Beyond demographic collapse: Biological adaptation and change in native populations of La Florida. In *Columbian consequences,* vol. 2, edited by D. H. Thomas, pp. 409–428. Washington, D.C.: Smithsonian Institution Press.

Lawrence, G. E. 1956. *Thomas O'Garra: A West Indian local preacher.* London: Epworth Press.

Leal, E. 1993. Habana Vieja project. *SHA Newsletter* 26(1):33.

Leemans, C. 1904. *Altertümer von Curaçao, Bonaire, und Aruba.* Mitteilungen, Veröffentliche Serie 2(9). Leiden: Niederländisches Reichsmuseum für Völkerkunde.

Ligon, R. 1657. *A true and exact history of the iland of Barbados.* London.

Lilly, C. 1978. Report upon the fortifications of Barbados. Presented to Governor Sir B. Grenville. [1705]. *Journal of the Barbados Museum and Historical Society* 35(4).

Lister, F., and R. Lister. 1974. Maiolica in colonial Spanish America. *Historical Archaeology* 8:17–52.

Lister, F., and R. Lister. 1976. *A descriptive dictionary for 500 years of Spanish tradition ceramics, thirteenth through eighteenth centuries.* Special Publication Series No. 1. Society for Historical Archaeology.

Lister, F., and R. Lister. 1984. The potter's quarter of colonial Puebla, Mexico. *Historical archaeology* 18(1):87–102.

Lister, F., and R. Lister. 1987. *Andalusian ceramics in Spain and New Spain.* Tucson: University of Arizona Press.

Loftfield, T. 1991. The Bendeshe/Byde sugar factory in Barbados: The ceramic evidence. In *Proceedings of the Fourteenth International Congress for Caribbean Archaeology,* edited by A. Cummins and P. King, pp. 408–415. Barbados: Barbados Museum and Historical Society.

Loftfield, T. 1992. Unglazed red earthenware from Barbados: A preliminary analysis. *Journal of the Barbados Museum and Historical Society* 40:19–36.

Loftfield, T. C., and J. B. Legg. 1997. Archaeological evidence of Afro-Barbadian life at Springhead plantation, St. James Parish, Barbados. *Journal of the Barbados Museum and Historical Society* 43:32–49.

Long, G. A. 1967. Archaeological investigations at Panama Vieja. Master's thesis, Department of Anthropology, University of Florida, Gainesville.

Lopez Perez, A., and C. Sanson. 1993. Excavacion y extraccion de una nao del siglo XVI "Nuestra Senora del Rosario," Cuba. Paper presented at the Fifteenth International Congress for Caribbean Archaeology, San Juan, Puerto Rico.

Lopez y Sebastian, L. E. 1982. Arqueología de Jamaica: Sevilla la Nueva. *Revista de Indias* 167–168:223–242.

Lopez y Sebastian, L. E. 1986. Sevilla la Nueva, arqueología. Ms. on file, Jamaica National Trust, Kingston, Jamaica.

Low, R. H., and Valls, R. 1991. *St. John backtime: Eyewitness accounts from 1718 to 1956.* St. John: Edin Hill Press.

Luna Calderón, F. 1983. Los esqueletos de La Isabela: Testigos mudos de una gran hazana. *Hoy* 117:10–11.

Luna Calderón, F. 1993. La Isabela, primer cemeterio indo- hispanico del Nueva Mundo. Paper presented at the Fifteenth International Congress for Caribbean Archaeology, San Juan, Puerto Rico.

Lyon, E. 1981. Puerto Real: Research on a Spanish town on Hispaniola's north coast. Ms. on file, Florida State Museum, University of Florida, Gainesville.

Lyon, E. 1989. *Niña,* ship of discovery. In *First encounters,* edited by J. T. Milanich and S. Milbrath, pp. 55–65. Gainesville: University Press of Florida.

MacGaffey, W. 1986. *Religion and society in central Africa.* Chicago: University of Chicago Press.

MacGaffey, W. 1991. *The art and healing of the Bakongo.* Stockholm: Folkens museumetnografiska.

Maduro, A. 1961. *Documenten uit de jaren 1639 en 1640, welke zich in de "Archivo General de Indias" te Sevilla bevinden en betrekking hebben op de door de Spanjaarden beraamde plannen om het Eiland Curaçao op de Nederlanders to heroveren.* Curaçao: Scherpenheuvel.

Magana, C. S., G. Tyson, and B. N. Driskell. 1989. Cultural resources survey Phases IA and IB of the proposed Long Bay Estates, St. John, U.S. Virgin Islands. Manuscript No. CZM-J2789L, on file at the U.S. Virgin Island SHPO, Department of Planning and Natural Resources, Division for Archaeology and Historic Preservation.

Malone, S. B., and R. C. Roberts. 1991. *Nostalgic Nassau.* Nassau: Nassau Nostalgia.

Mann, R. W., L. Meadows, W. M. Bass, and D. R. Watters. 1987. Description of skeletal remains from a black slave cemetery from Montserrat, West Indies. *Annals of Carnegie Museum* 56:319–336.

Mañon Arredondo, M. 1978. Importancia arqueología de los ingenios indo-hispanicos de las Antillas. *Boletín del Museo del Hombre Dominicano* 7(10):139–164.

Mansur, J. 1989. *Historia di Aruba.* Aruba: Clasico Diario, Aruba.

Marken, M. 1994. *Pottery from Spanish shipwrecks, 1500–1800.* Gainesville: University Press of Florida.

Marrinan, R. 1982. Test excavations at Building B (Area 2), Puerto Real, Haiti. Ms. on file, Florida State Museum, University of Florida, Gainesville.

Martin, S. 1765. *An essay upon plantership.* 4th ed. Antigua: Samuel Clapham.

Martin, S. 1773. *An essay upon plantership.* 5th ed. London: T. Cadell.

Marx, R. F. 1968. Discovery of two ships of Columbus. *Jamaica Journal* 2(4):13–17.

Marx, R. F. 1975. *Shipwrecks of the Western Hemisphere, 1492–1825.* New York: D. McKay.

Matheson, L. 1982. St. Kitts commemorates bicentennial of the siege of Brimstone Hill in 1782. *Caribbean Conservation News* 3:6–9.

Matheson, L. 1987. *The Brimstone Hill fortress: Brief history and story of the development of a "restoration society" to "national park" status, 1965–1987.* Basseterre, St. Kitts: Brimstone Hill Fortress National Park Society.

Mathewson, R. D. 1972a. History from the earth: Archaeological investigations at Old King's House. *Jamaica Journal* 6(1):3–11.

Mathewson, R. D. 1972b. Jamaican ceramics: An introduction to eighteenth century folk pottery in West African tradition. *Jamaica Journal* 6(2):54–56.

Mathewson, R. D. 1973. Archaeological analysis of material culture as a reflection of sub-cultural differentiation in eighteenth century Jamaica. *Jamaica Journal* 7(1–2):25–29.

Mathewson, R. D. 1983. *Archaeological treasure: The search for the "Nuestra Señora de Atocha."* Woodstock, Vt.: Seafarers Heritage Library.

Mathewson, R. D. 1986. *Treasure of the "Atocha": Sixteen dramatic years in search of the historic wreck.* New York: Dutton.

Mathurin, L. 1975. The arrivals of black women. *Jamaica Journal* 9(2–3):2–7, 49.

Mathurin Mair, L. 1986. Women field workers in Jamaica during slavery. *The 1986 Elsa Goveia Memorial Lecture.* Department of History, University of the West Indies, Mona, Jamaica.

McAlister, L. 1984. *Spain and Portugal in the New World, 1492–1700.* Minneapolis: University of Minnesota Press.

McEwan, B. G. 1983. Spanish colonial adaptation on Hispaniola. Master's thesis, Department of Anthropology, University of Florida, Gainesville.

McEwan, B. G. 1984. Faunal remains from Sevilla Nueva. *Archaeology Jamaica* 3d Qtr:21–29.

McEwan, B. G. 1986. Domestic architecture at Puerto Real, Haiti. *Historical Archaeology* 20(1):44–49.

McEwan, B. G. 1988. An archaeological perspective on sixteenth-century Spanish life in the Old World and the Americas. Ph.D. dissertation, Department of Anthropology, University of Florida, Gainesville.

McEwan, B. G. 1991. The archaeology of women in the Spanish New World. *Historical Archaeology* 25(4):33–41.

McEwan, B. G. 1992. The role of ceramics in Spain and Spanish America during the sixteenth century. *Historical Archaeology* 26(1):92–108.

McIntosh, R. J. 1974. Archaeology and mud wall decay in a West African village. *World Archaeology* 6(2):154–171.

McIntyre, K. 1983. Analysis of olive jar rims from the *Nuestra Señora de Atocha* and the *Santa Margarita:* A step towards detecting change through time in olive jar rim forms. Ms. on file, Florida State Museum, University of Florida, Gainesville.

McKinnen, D. 1804. *A tour through the British West Indies, in the years 1802 and 1803 giving a particular account of the Bahama Islands.* London: J. White.

Mendoza, L. 1957. Ceramica de las Ruinas de la Vega Vieja. *Casas Reales* 11:101–113.

Mercer, E. 1975. *English vernacular houses: A study of traditional farmhouses and cottages.* London: Royal Commission on Historical Monuments England, Her Majesty's Stationery Office.

Messenger, J. 1975. Montserrat: The most distinctively Irish settlement in the New World. *Ethnicity* 2:281–303.

Milanich, J. T., and S. Milbrath, eds. 1989. *First encounters: Spanish explorations in the Caribbean and the United States, 1492–1570.* Gainesville: University Press of Florida.

Miller, G. 1980. Classification and economic scaling of nineteenth century ceramics. *Historical Archaeology* 14(1):1–42.

Miller, G. 1991. A revised set of CC index values for classification and economic scaling of English ceramics from 1787 to 1880. *Historical Archaeology* 25(1):1–25.

Mintz, S. 1974. *Caribbean transformations.* Baltimore: Johns Hopkins University Press.

Mintz, S. 1979. Time, sugar, and sweetness. *Marxist perspectives* 8:56–72.

Mintz, S. 1985. *Sweetness and power.* New York: Viking Penguin.

Mintz, S. W., and D. Hall. 1960. *The origins of the Jamaican internal marketing system.* Yale University Publications in Anthropology No. 57. New Haven: Yale University Press.

Mintz, S. W., and R. Price. 1976. *An anthropological approach to the Afro-American past: A Caribbean perspective.* Occasional Papers No. 2. Philadelphia: Institute for the Study of Human Issues.

Mintz, S. W., and R. Price. 1992. *The birth of African-American culture.* Reprint of 1976 publication. New York: Beacon Press.

Monsanto, A., and C. Monsanto. 1991. *E Kas ta Bon Traha.* UNA Publications No. 34. Curaçao: University of the Netherlands Antilles.

Monteiro, M. M. 1990. The stone ovens of St. Eustatius: A study of material culture. Master's thesis, Department of Anthropology, College of William and Mary, Williamsburg, Virginia.

Montserrat Court Record Book. 1771. Court House, Plymouth, Montserrat.

Morales Padron, F. 1952. *Jamaica Española.* Publicación No. 67. Seville: Escuela de Estudios Hispano-Americanos.

Morales Patino, O., and R. P. D. Acevado. 1946. El período de tranculturación Indo-hispanica. *Revista de arquelogía y etnología* 1:5–20.

Moreau, J.-P. 1988. *Guide des trésors archéologiques sous-marins des Petites Antilles: D'après les archives anglaises, espagnoles, et françaises des XVI, XVII, et XVIII siècles.* Clamart, France: J.-P. Moreau.

Moreau, J.-P. 1991. Les Caraïbes insulaires et la mer aux seizième et dix-septième siècles d'aprés les sources ethnohistoriques. *Journal de la Société des Américanistes* 77:63–75.

Moreau, J.-P. 1992. *Les Petites Antilles de Christophe Colomb à Richelieu (1493–1635).* Paris: Karthala.

Morris, K. 1990. The "1577 Shipwreck" project: A preliminary report. In *Underwater archaeology proceedings from the Society for Historical Archaeology Conference,* edited by T. Carrell, pp. 63–65. Tucson: Society for Historical Archaeology.

Muir, R. 1980. *The English village.* London: Thames & Hudson.

Murphy, R. 1989. Betty's Hope Old North Mill excavated. *Antigua Historical and Archaeological Society Newsletter* 27:1, 5.

Murphy, R. 1993. The importance of Betty's Hope in a Caribbean historical perspective. *Antigua Historical and Archaeological Society Newsletter* 42:3.

Myers, J. E., F. D. A. Carredano, J. S. Olin, and A. P. Hernandez. 1992. Compositional identification of Seville majolica at overseas sites. *Historical Archaeology* 26(1): 131–147.

Myers, J. E., K. Deagan, J. Cruxent, and J. Olin. 1992. Characterization of the first European pottery in America: La Isabela, 1493–1498. Paper presented at "Trade and Discovery: The Scientific Analysis of Artifacts from Europe and Beyond, 1500–1800." London: British Museum.

Myers, J. E., and J. Olin. 1992. Analysis of the earliest Euro-American ceramics in the Americas: La Isabela. Paper presented at the annual meeting of the American Association for the Advancement of Science, Chicago.

Nagelkerken, W. 1985. *Preliminary report of the determination of the location of the historical anchorage at Orange Bay, St. Eustatius, Netherlands Antilles.* Report No. 1. Curaçao: Archaeological-Anthropological Institute of the Netherlands Antilles.

Nagelkerken, W. 1986. Preliminary report on the determination of the location of the historical anchorage at Orange Bay, St. Eustatius, Netherlands Antilles. In *Proceedings of the Sixteenth Conference on Underwater Archaeology,* edited by P. F. Johnston, pp. 60–76. Special Publication Series No. 4. Society for Historical Archaeology.

Nagelkerken, W. 1987. Preliminary report on the wine bottles of Oranje Bay, St. Eustatius. In *Collected papers on Netherlands Antilles archaeology at the Eleventh International Congress for Caribbean Archaeology,* Report No. 4, pp. 93–122. Curaçao: Archaeological-Anthropological Institute of the Netherlands Antilles.

Nagelkerken, W. 1988a. Ceramics of Orange Bay, St. Eustatius, Netherlands Antilles. In *Underwater archaeology proceedings from the Society for Historical Archaeology Conference,* edited by J. P. Delgado, pp. 141–144. Tucson: Society for Historical Archaeology.

Nagelkerken, W. 1988b. Test excavations on shipwrecks in St. Eustatius. In *Underwater archaeology proceedings from the Society for Historical Archaeology Conference,* edited by J. P. Delgado, pp. 105–107. Tucson: Society for Historical Archaeology.

Nagelkerken, W. 1990. Opgraving van het Hollandse fregat *Alphen* geexplodeerd in Curaçao in 1778. Report submitted to the Archaeological-Anthropological Institute of the Netherlands Antilles, Curaçao.

Nagelkerken, W. 1991. 1989 survey of the Dutch frigate *Alphen* which exploded and sank in 1778 in the harbour of Curaçao. In *Proceedings of the Thirteenth International Congress for Caribbean Archaeology,* edited by E. N. Ayubi and J. B. Haviser, pp. 771–787. Report No. 9. Curaçao: Archaeological-Anthropological Institute of the Netherlands Antilles.

Nagelkerken, W. 1993a. 1990–1991 underwater archaeological excavations in Orange Bay, St. Eustatius. Report submitted to the Archaeological-Anthropological Institute of the Netherlands Antilles, Curaçao.

Nagelkerken, W. 1993b. Onderwaterarcheologisch onderzoek van de historische vuilstortplaats langs de Handlekade in de St. Annabaai, Curaçao, Netherlands Antilles. Report submitted by the Archaeological-Anthropological Institute of the Netherlands Antilles to the Curaçao Ports Authority, Curaçao.

Nagelkerken, W. 1994. Archaeological research of the Handelkade. Lanternu no. 14, Central Historical Archives of the Netherlands Antilles, Curaçao.

Nagelkerken, W. 1997. 19de Eeuws Maastricht's aardewerk opgegraven in de haven van Curaçao. Report on file at the Archaeological-Anthropological Institute of the Netherlands Antilles, Curaçao.

Nagelkerken, W. 1998a. Nineteenth century Dutch pearlware recovered in the harbour of Curaçao, Netherlands Antilles. In *Underwater archaeology*, edited by L. E. Babbits, C. Fach, and R. Harris, pp. 104–110. Tucson: Society for Historical Archaeology.

Nagelkerken, W. 1998b. Mineraalwater kruiken en Jenever kruiken opgegraven in de St. Annabaai te Curaçao, Nederlandse Antillen. Report on file at the Archaeological-Anthropological Institute of the Netherlands Antilles, Curaçao.

Nash, D. 1977. Tourism as a form of imperialism. In *Hosts and guests: The anthropology of tourism*, edited by V. Smith, pp. 33–47. Philadelphia: University of Pennsylvania Press.

Nash, D. 1981. Tourism as an anthropological subject. *Current Anthropology* 22:361–468.

Neville, J., R. Neyland, and J. Parrent. 1992. The search for Columbus's lost ships: The 1991 field season. Ms. on file, Joyner Library, East Carolina University, Greenville, N.C.

Newson, L. 1976. *Aboriginal and Spanish colonial Trinidad.* New York: Academic Press.

Newton, M. 1986. *Architektuur en bouwwijze van het Curaçaose landhuis.* Delft, The Netherlands: Universitaire Pers.

Newton, M. 1988. De Willemstoren op Bonaire. In *De stenen droom: Opstellen over bouwkunst en monumentenzorg*, edited by C. L. Temmick-Grol, pp. 158–166. Zutphen, The Netherlands: De Walburg Pers.

Nicholson, D. V. 1979. The dating of West Indian historical sites by the analysis of ceramic sherds. *Journal of the Virgin Islands Archaeological Society* 7:52–74.

Nicholson, D. V. 1980. *Naval sheaves from under English Harbour.* St. John's: Antigua Historical and Conservation Commission.

Nicholson, D. V. 1983a. *English Harbour, Antigua: An historical and archaeological sketch.* English Harbour, Antigua: Nelson's Dockyard National Park.

Nicholson, D. V. 1983b. *The story of the Arawaks of Antigua and Barbuda.* St. John's: Antigua Archaeological and Historical Society.

Nicholson, D. V. 1990. Afro-Antiguan folk pottery and emancipation. In *Proceedings of the Eleventh Congress of the International Association for Caribbean Archaeology*, edited by A. G. Pantel, I. Vargas Arenas, and M. Sanoja Obediente, pp. 433–437. San Juan: Fundación Arqueológica, Antropológica, e Histórica de Puerto Rico.

Nicholson, D. V. 1991. *The Story of English Harbour, Antigua, West Indies.* Museum of Antigua and Barbuda, St. John's, Antigua.

Nicholson, D. V. 1992. *Antigua, Barbuda, and Redonda: A historical sketch.* St. John's: Museum of Antigua and Barbuda.

Nicholson, D. V. 1993a. *The archaeology of Antigua and Barbuda.* St. John's: Museum of Antigua and Barbuda.

Nicholson, D. V. 1993b. *Mud and blood: Artifacts from harbour dredging and the naval hospital site at English Harbour, Antigua.* St. John's: Museum of Antigua and Barbuda.

Nicholson, D. V. 1994a. *Heritage landmarks: Antigua and Barbuda.* St. John's: Museum of Antigua and Barbuda.

Nicholson, D. V. 1994b. *Antigua and Barbuda forts.* St. John's: Museum of Antigua and Barbuda.

Nicholson, D. V. 1994c. Vandalism of our historic environment. *Antigua Historical and Archaeological Society Newsletter* 47:1.

Nieves Sicart, M. 1980. Piezas cerámicas conservadas en los depósitos de Departmento de Ceramologia Historica del Museo Casas Reales. *Casas Reales* 11:87–98.

Nissen. 1792–1837. *Reminiscences by one NISSEN, 1792–1837.* Typewriter copy made from original manuscript by Miss Edith C. Moon, Supervising Librarian, 1933. Public Library, St. Thomas.

Oldendorp, C. G. A. 1987. *A Caribbean mission: History of the mission of the Evangelical Brethren on the Caribbean Islands of St. Thomas, St. Croix, and St. John.* Edited by Johann Jakob Bossard. English translation by A. R. Highfield and V. Barac. Ann Arbor: Karoma.

Olds, D. L. 1976. *Texas legacy from the Gulf: A report on the sixteenth-century shipwreck materials from the Texas tidelands.* Texas Memorial Museum, Miscellaneous Paper No. 5. Austin: Texas Memorial Museum, Texas Antiquities Committee.

Olin, J. S., and M. J. Blackman. 1989. Compositional classification of Spanish colonial majolica. In *Archaeological chemistry 4,* edited by R. O. Allen, pp. 87–112. Washington, D.C.: American Chemical Society.

Oliver, V. L., ed. 1910. Montserrat, 1677–78: A census. In *Caribbeana: Miscellaneous papers relating to the history, genealogy, topography, and antiquities of the British West Indies,* vol. 2, pp. 316–320, 342–347. London: Mitchell, Hughes, and Clarke.

Olwig, K. F. 1978. *Households, exchange, and social reproduction: The development of a Caribbean society.* Ph.D. dissertation, Department of Anthropology, University of Minnesota. Ann Arbor: University Microfilms.

Olwig, K. F. 1985. *Cultural adaptation and resistance on St. John: Three centuries of Afro-Caribbean life.* Gainesville: University Press of Florida.

Olwig, K. F. 1990. Cultural identity and material culture: Afro-Caribbean pottery. *Folk* 32:5–22.

Olwig, K. F. 1993. Defining the national in the transnational: Cultural identity in the Afro-Caribbean diaspora. *Ethnos* 58(3/4):361–376.

Olwig, K. F. 1994. *The land is the heritage: Land and community on St. John.* St. John Oral History Association Monograph Number 1. Copenhagen: Reproduction Center of the Division of Social Sciences, University of Copenhagen.

Olwig, K. F., ed. 1995. *Small islands, large questions: Society, culture, and resistance in the post-emancipation Caribbean.* London: F. Cass.

Ortega, E. 1971. Informe de las excavaciones arqueológicas realizadas en la Plazoleta y en la Calle Juan Baron. *Revista Dominicana de Arqueología y Antropología* 1(1):25–37.

Ortega, E. 1980. *Introducción a la loza comun a alfarería en el periodo colonial de Sto. Domingo.* Serie Científica 3. Santo Domingo: Fundacíon Ortega Alvarez.

Ortega, E. 1982. *Arqueología colonial de Santo Domingo.* Serie Científica 4. Santo Domingo: Fundacíon Ortega Alvarez.

Ortega, E. 1988. *La Isabela y la arqueologia en la ruta de colon.* San Pedro de Macorís, Dominican Republic: Fundación Ortega Alvarez.

Ortega, E., and J. Cruxent. 1976. Informe preliminar sobre las excavaciones en las rutas del Convento de San Francisco. *Actas del XLI Congreso Internacional de Americanistas* 3:674–689.

Ortega, E., and C. Fondeur. 1978a. *La arqueología de los monumentos historicos de Sto. Domingo.* San Pedro de Macorís, Dominican Republic: Universidad del Este.

Ortega, E., and C. Fondeur. 1978b. *Estudio de la cerámica del período indo-hispano de la antigua Concepción de la Vega.* Serie Científica 1. Santo Domingo: Fundacíon Ortega Alvarez.

Ortega, E., and C. Fondeur. 1979. *Arqueología de la Casa del Cordon.* Serie Científica 2. Santo Domingo: Fundacíon Ortega Alvarez.

Ortega, E., and M. L. Valdez. 1979. *Informe de las excavaciones arqueológicas de la Casa de Gorjon.* Boletín 12. Santo Domingo: Museo del Hombre Dominicano.

Osborne, F. J. 1974. Spanish Church, St. Ann's Bay. *Jamaica Journal* 8(2–3):33–35.

Otterbein, K. F. 1975. *Changing house types in Long Bay Cays.* New Haven: HRAFlex Books.

Otto, J. S. 1984. *Cannon's Point plantation, 1794–1860.* Orlando, Fla.: Academic Press.

Ozinga, M. 1959. *De monumenten van Curaçao in woord en beeld.* The Hague: De Stichting Monumentenzorg Curaçao.

Palm, E. 1945. Excavations at La Isabela, white man's first town in the Americas. *Acta Americana* 3:298–303.

Palm, E. 1952. La forteleza de la Concepción de la Vega. *Memoria del V Congreso Historico Municipal Interamericano* 2:115–118.

Pannet, P. 1994. Report on the conspiracy by the Aminas on St. John in 1733. In *The Kamina folk: Slavery and slave life in the Danish West Indies,* edited by G. F. Tyson and A. R. Highfield, pp. 19–23. Virgin Islands Humanities Council, St. Thomas, United States Virgin Islands.

Pantel, A. G., J. Sued-Badillo, A. S. Rivera, and B. Pantel. 1986. Archaeological investigations into the history, urbanism, and architecture of barrio Ballaja from pre-Columbian times through the twentieth century. Ms. on file, Foundation for Archaeology, Anthropology, and History of Puerto Rico, San Juan, Puerto Rico.

Paonessa, L. J. 1990. The cemeteries of St. Eustatius, N.A.: Status in a Caribbean community. Master's thesis, Department of Anthropology, College of William and Mary, Williamsburg, Virginia.

Paquette, R. L., and S. L. Engerman. 1995. *The Lesser Antilles in the age of European expansion.* Gainesville: University Press of Florida.

Parrent, J. 1990. Management of historic ship archaeological sites in the Caribbean. Ms. on microfiche, Joyner Library, East Carolina University, Greenville, North Carolina.

Parry, J. H., and P. Sherlock. 1971. *A short history of the West Indies.* 3d ed. New York: St. Martin's Press.

Paynter, R. 1982. *Models of spatial inequality: Settlement patterns in historical archaeology.* New York: Academic Press.

Pearson, C. 1981. Ceramics from *El Nuevo Constante.* Ms. on file, Coastal Environments, Inc., Baton Rouge, Louisiana.

Pearson, C. E., and P. Hoffman. 1994. *The last voyage of El Nuevo Constante.* Baton Rouge: Louisiana State University Press.

Peggs, A. D. 1957. *A relic of slavery: Farquharson's journal for 1831–32.* Nassau: Deans Peggs Research Fund.

Peggs, A. D. 1960. *A mission to the West India Islands: Dowson's journal for 1810–17.* Nassau: Deans Peggs Research Fund.

Peguero Guzmán, L. A. 1989. Algunas consideraciones sobre la arqueología del cimarronaje. *Boletín del Museo del Hombre Dominicano* 22:163–177.

Peniston, Captain W. 1966. St. Eustatius as seen in the 1850's. *Bermuda Historical Quarterly* 23(2):60–63.

Peters, T. P. 1960. *The American Loyalists and the plantation period in the Bahama Islands.* Ph.D. dissertation, Department of History, University of Florida, Gainesville. Ann Arbor: University Microfilms.

Petersen, J. B., and D. R. Watters. 1988. Afro-Montserratian ceramics from the Harney site slave cemetery, Montserrat, West Indies. *Annals of Carnegie Museum* 57:167–187.

Petersen, J. B., D. R. Watters, and D. V. Nicholson. 1999. Continuity and syncretism in Afro-Caribbean ceramics from the northern Lesser Antilles. In *African Sites Archaeology in the Caribbean,* edited by J. B. Haviser, pp. 157–195. Princeton: Markus Wiener; Kingston: Ian Randle.

Peterson, M. L. 1972. Traders and privateers across the Atlantic. In *A history of seafaring based on underwater archaeology,* edited by G. F. Bass, pp. 253–280. New York: Walker.

Peterson, M. L. 1974. The exploration of a sixteenth-century Bahamian shipwreck. In *National Geographic research reports: 1967 projects,* pp. 231–244. Washington, D.C.: National Geographic.

Peterson, T. 1985. Goudsmelterij te balashi, Aruba. Master's thesis, Architecture Department, Technical University of Delft, The Netherlands.

Petitjean Roget, H. 1990. Archéologie de l'imaginaire: 12 octobre 1942–16 janvier 1493: Les Tainos, les Espagnols, et les "Cannibales." *Bulletin de la Société d'Histoire de la Guadeloupe* 83–86:53–69.

Pichon, M., and Y. Vragar. 1997. *Le cimetière de l'anse du Vieux Fort, Sainte Rose "plage de Clugny" (Guadeloupe).* Rapport de sondage inédit, Service régional de l'archéologie. Basse-Terre, Guadeloupe: Direction Régionale des Affaires Culturelles (DRAC).

Pinfold, C. 1762. Answers of Charles Pinfold, governor of Barbados, to the queries proposed by the lords of trade and plantations. Copy in Harley Manuscripts, 205 fols. 456–73, British Museum, London.

Plan D'2. 1989. Oranjestad historic core renovation inventory, vol. 1, Survey report, November. St. Maarten.

Plan D'2. 1990. Oranjestad historic core renovation policy, vol. 1, Draft policy, May. St. Maarten.

Plan D'2. 1991. Oranjestad historic core renovation policy, vol. 1, January. St. Maarten.

Plan D'2. 1992. Oranjestad historic core renovation, Master plan (Draft), June. St. Maarten.

Platt, C. 1978. *Medieval England: A social history and archaeology from the Conquest to 1600 A.D.* New York: Charles Scribner's Sons.

Poladura, A., ed. 1980. *Objectos y ambientes de la Concepción de la Vega (exposición).* Santo Domingo: Museo Casas Reales.

Posnansky, M., and C. R. DeCorse. 1986. Historical archaeology in sub-Saharan Africa: A review. *Historical Archaeology* 20(1):1–14.

Prat Puig, F. 1980. *Significado de conjuto cerámico de siglo XVI de Santiago de Cuba.* Santiago de Cuba: Editorial Oriente.

Price, R. S., ed. 1973. *Maroon societies: Rebel slave communities in the Americas.* New York: Anchor.

Prunetti, P. 1987. *Scharloo, a nineteenth century quarter of Willemstad, Curaçao: Historical architecture and its background.* Florence: Edizioni Pligrafico Florentino.

Prussin, L. 1969. *Architecture in northern Ghana: A study of forms and functions.* Berkeley: University of California Press.

Public Record Office. 1729. List of Inhabitants, whites and blacks, of Montserrat, 1729, referred to in Col. Matthew's letter of 29th May, 1730. PRO B. T. Leeward Islands, Vol. 21. London.

Puckett, N. N. 1926. *Folk beliefs of the southern Negro.* Chapel Hill: University of North Carolina Press.

Puig Ortiz, J. A. 1973. *Por la valorización histórica de las ruinas de la Isabela, primera ciudad del Nuevo Mundo.* Santo Domingo: Editora del Caribe.

Pulsipher, L. M. 1986a. *Seventeenth century Montserrat: An environmental impact statement.* Historical Geography Research Series 17. Norwich, England: Geo Books.

Pulsipher, L. M. 1986b. Ethnoarchaeology for the study of Caribbean slave villages. Paper presented at "Ethnohistory and Historical Archaeology in the Caribbean," a symposium and workshop sponsored by the Program in Atlantic History, Culture, and Society, Johns Hopkins University, Baltimore.

Pulsipher, L. M. 1987a. Assessing the usefulness of a cartographic curiosity: The 1673 map of a sugar island. *Annals of the Association of American Geographers* 77(3):408–422.

Pulsipher, L. M. 1987b. Galways Mountain folk geography. Field notes on file, Department of Geography, University of Tennessee, Knoxville.

Pulsipher, L. M. 1989. Galways material culture study. Field notes on file, Department of Geography, University of Tennessee, Knoxville.

Pulsipher, L. M. 1990. They have Saturdays and Sundays to feed themselves. *Expedition* 32 (2):24–33.

Pulsipher, L. M. 1991. Galways Plantation, Montserrat. In *Seeds of change,* edited by H. J. Viola and C. Margolis, pp. 139–159. Washington, D.C.: Smithsonian Institution Press.

Pulsipher, L. M. 1992. The folk geography of Galways Mountain. Field notes on file, Department of Geography, University of Tennessee, Knoxville.

Pulsipher, L. M. 1993a. Changing roles in the life cycles of women in traditional West Indian houseyards. In *Women and change in the Caribbean,* edited by J. H. Momsen, pp. 50–64. Kingston: Ian Randle; Bloomington: Indiana University Press.

Pulsipher, L. M. 1993b. He won't let she stretch she foot. In *Full circles: Geographies of women over the life course,* edited by C. Katz and J. Monk, pp. 107–121. London: Routledge.

Pulsipher, L. M. 1994. The landscapes and ideational roles of Caribbean slave gardens. In *The archaeology of garden and field,* edited by N. Miller and K. Gleason, pp. 202–221. Philadelphia: University of Pennsylvania Press.

Pulsipher, L. M. 1995. Survey of lower Galways Mountain. Field notes on file, Department of Geography, University of Tennessee, Knoxville.

Pulsipher, L. M., and C. M. Goodwin. 1981. Galways Plantation, Montserrat West Indies. 1981 field report. Ms. on file, Department of Geography, University of Tennessee, Knoxville.

Pulsipher, L. M., and C. M. Goodwin. 1982. Galways: A Caribbean [Montserrat] sugar plantation. A report on the 1981 field season. Ms. on file, Department of Geography, University of Tennessee, Knoxville.

Pulsipher, L. M., and C. M. Goodwin. 1982–1995. Field notes and tape recorded interviews on the Galways Project, on file, Department of Geography, University of Tennessee, Knoxville.

Pulsipher, L. M., and C. M. Goodwin. 1999. Here where the old time people be: Reconstructing the landscapes of the slavery and post-slavery era in Montserrat, West Indies. In *African sites archaeology in the Caribbean,* edited by J. B. Haviser, pp. 9–37. Princeton: Markus Wiener; Kingston: Ian Randle.

Ramos, A., and R. Ramos. 1993. La Habana vieja: Experiencas y consideraciones en arqueologia urbana. Paper presented at the Fifteenth International Congress for Caribbean Archaeology, San Juan, Puerto Rico.

Reales, M. C. 1980. *Objectos y ambientes de la Concepción de la Vega.* Santo Domingo: Museo Casas Reales.

Recio, H. 1993. Conservacion de materiales arqueologicos submergidos del siglo XVI en Pinar del Rio, Cuba. Paper presented at the Fifteenth International Congress for Caribbean Archaeology, San Juan, Puerto Rico.

Reed, M. 1983. *The Georgian triumph, 1700–1830.* London: Paladin Books.

Rees, C. 1944. C. Rees to Herbert McKinney, May 12, 1944. Estate of Herbert A. McKinney, courtesy of Andrew McKinney, Nassau, Bahamas.

Reeves, M. 1996. "To Vex a Teif": An African-Jamaican ritual feature. Poster presented at the annual meeting of the Society for American Archaeology, New Orleans.

Reeves, R. 1989. San Felipe del Morro guardhouse restroom conversion. *SHA Newsletter* 22(1):32.

Registrar General's Department [RGD]. 1789. Land grant to Wade Stubbs. Bahamas Records Alphabet Series, B-1, 12, 1789. Nassau, Bahamas.

Registrar General's Department [RGD]. 1791. Land grant to Joseph Hunter. Bahamas Records Alphabet Series Book F-1, 90, 1791. Nassau, Bahamas.

Registrar General's Department [RGD]. 1792. Indenture between George Gray with Mary his wife and James Menzies. Bahamas Records Alphabet series U, 24, 1792. Nassau, Bahamas.

Registrar General's Department [RGD]. 1797. Inventory of assessment of William Moss. Bahamas Records Alphabet Series E-2, 34–47, 1797. Nassau, Bahamas.

Registrar General's Department [RGD]. 1798. Apraisement [sic] of the Plantation Negroes, Stock, etc. belonging to the late Archibald Campbell. Bahamas Records Alphabet Series E-2, 107–111, 1798. Nassau, Bahamas.

Registrar General's Department [RGD]. 1799a. Inventory and appraisement of the estate of John Moultrie. Bahamas Records Alphabet Series E-2, 152–163, 1799. Nassau, Bahamas.

Registrar General's Department [RGD]. 1799b. Inventory and appraisement of the estate of the late George Gray. Bahamas Records Alphabet Series E-2, 194–202, 1799. Nassau, Bahamas.

Registrar General's Department [RGD]. 1799c. Indenture between Lewis Johnston and William Wylly. Bahamas Records Alphabet Series H-2, 275–278, 1799. Nassau, Bahamas.

Registrar General's Department [RGD]. 1801. Inventory of assessment of Doctor John Bell. Bahamas Records Alphabet Series E-2, 290–295, 1801. Nassau, Bahamas.

Registrar General's Department [RGD]. 1805. Manumission of Sarah. Bahamas Records Alphabet Series W-2, 215–217, 1805. Nassau, Bahamas.

Registrar General's Department [RGD]. 1809. Indenture between John Forbes and William Wylly. Bahamas Records Alphabet Series X-2, 341–344, 1809. Nassau, Bahamas.

Registrar General's Department [RGD]. 1817. Indenture between the executors for James Menzies and Alexander Smith. Bahamas Records Alphabet Series K-3, 71, 1817. Nassau, Bahamas.

Registrar General's Department [RGD]. 1818. Indenture between John McCartney with Jane his wife and Henry Moss. Bahamas Records Alphabet Series G-3, 504, 1818. Nassau, Bahamas.

Registrar General's Department [RGD]. n.d. Index to land grants and transactions. Nassau, Bahamas.

Reitz, E. 1982. Report on fauna from excavations at Area 19, Puerto Real, Haiti. Ms. on file, Florida State Museum, University of Florida, Gainesville.

Reitz, E. 1986. Vertebrate fauna from Locus 39, Puerto Real, Haiti. *Journal of Field Archaeology* 13:317–328.

Reitz, E. 1990. Early Spanish subsistence at Puerto Real, Hispaniola. In *Proceedings of the Eleventh International Congress for Caribbean Archaeology,* edited by A. G. Pantel, I. Vargas Arenas, and M. Sanoja Obediente, pp. 442–447. San Juan: Fundación Arqueológica, Antropológica, e Histórica de Puerto Rico.

Reitz, E. 1992. The Spanish colonial experience and domestic animals. *Historical Archaeology* 26(1):84–91.

Reitz, E. J., and C. M. Scarry. 1985. *Reconstructing historic subsistence with an example from sixteenth-century Spanish Florida.* Special Publication Series No. 3. Society for Historical Archaeology.

Renkema, W. 1981. *Het Curaçaose plantagebedrijf in de negentiende eeuw.* Zutphen, The Netherlands: De Walburg Pers.

Richardson, R. 1992. A plea for professional guidance in the protection of our historical patrimony. Paper presented at the Twenty-fifth Annual Meeting of the Society for Historical Archaeology, Kingston, Jamaica.

Richmond, I. 1969. The plans of Roman villas in Britain. In *The Roman villa in Britain,* edited by A. L. F. Rivet, pp. 49–70. London: Routledge & Kegan Paul.

Rigsarkivet. 1728–1739. St. John landlister. Copenhagen, Denmark.

Rigsarkivet. 1755–1915. St. John matriklen. Copenhagen, Denmark.

Rigsarkivet. 1831. St. John landfoged skiftedokumenter, 1778–1859. Copenhagen, Denmark.

Rigsarkivet. 1841–1911. Folketaellingslisterne [Census] for St. Jan: 1841, 1846, 1850, 1856, 1860, 1870, 1880, 1901, 1911. Copenhagen, Denmark.

Riley, S. 1983. *Homeward bound: A history of the Bahama Islands to 1850.* Miami: Island Research.

Rivera, V., and C. Solis-Magana. 1993. La cerámica Criolla. Paper presented at the Fifteenth International Congress for Caribbean Archaeology, San Juan, Puerto Rico.

Rivero de la Calle, M. 1973. La mutilación dentaria en la población negroide de Cuba. *Ciencias Biológicas,* series 6, 38:1–21.

Roe, P. G. 1994. Ethnology and archaeology: Symbolic and systemic disjunction or continuity? In *History of Latin American archaeology,* edited by A. Oyuela-Caycedo, pp. 183–208. Aldershot, Hampshire: Avebury.

Römer, R. 1990. A call for attention for the historic monuments of the Netherlands Antilles. In *Building up the future from the past,* edited by H. Coomans, M. Newton, and M. Eustatia, pp. 9–16. Zutphen, The Netherlands: De Walburg Pers.

Römer, R. 1991. *De sociale geschiedenis van Curaçao.* UNA Publication No. 35. Curaçao: University of the Netherlands Antilles.

Romero, L. 1981a. *La Haban arqueología.* Revolución y Cultura 107. Havana, Cuba.

Romero, L. 1981b. Sobre las evidencias arqueológicas de contacto y tranculturación en el ambito cubano. *Santiago* 44:71–108.

Rosalia, R. 1996. *Represhon di kultura: E lucha di Tamboe.* Ph.D. dissertation, Leiden University. Curaçao: Instituto Stripan Pers.

Rousseau, X. 1996. Le fort Delgrès à Basse-Terre. In *Monumental* 12 (March): *Spécial départements français d'Outre-Mer,* pp. 43–46. Paris: Ministère de la Culture.

Rousseau X., M. Pichon, and Y. Vragar. 1997. *Le cimetière du Morne Dauphine, Saint Claude (Guadeloupe).* Rapport de sondage inédit, Service régional de l'archéologie. Basse-Terre, Guadeloupe: Direction Régionale des Affaires Culturelles (DRAC).

Royal Commission on the Historical Monuments of England and West Yorkshire Metropolitan County Council. 1986. *Rural houses of West Yorkshire, 1400–1830.* London: Her Majesty's Stationery Office.

Royal Gazette and Bahama Advertiser [*RGBA*]. 1804. Sale of Negroes. Vol. 1, no. 32 (October 26).

Royal Gazette and Bahama Advertiser [*RGBA*]. 1805. Public sales. Vol. 2, no. 115 (August 13).

Royal Gazette and Bahama Advertiser [*RGBA*]. 1806. To be sold. Vol. 3, no. 230 (September 19).

Royal Gazette and Bahama Advertiser [*RGBA*]. 1820. On Monday last. Vol. 7, no. 724 (October 25).

Royal Gazette and Bahama Advertiser [*RGBA*]. 1822. Died. Vol. 7, no. 854 (March 23).

St. Jan Probate Records. 1831. St. Jan probate records for 1831.

St. Thomas and St. John Recorder of Deeds. 1800–1960. Hansen Point: Newfound Bay I, Newfound Bay II files.

St. Thomas and St. John Recorder of Deeds. 1894. Contract between the Sewer and George families, August. Book U, pp. 183–189.

St. Thomas and St. John Recorder of Deeds. 1913. Declaration of July 3.

Salas, R. S. 1989. The sinking of the *San José:* A chapter in Colombian underwater archaeology. In *Modern technology for the search and salvage of underwater treasure.* Stockholm: Royal Swedish Academy of Engineering Sciences.

Sale, K. 1990. *The conquest of paradise.* New York: Plume Books.

Saltus, A. 1973. Spanish ceramics from the shipwreck *San José*. Ms. on file, Coastal Environments, Inc., Baton Rouge, Louisiana.

Sanders, S. 1988a. Architectural style on St. Eustatius, Netherlands Antilles. Master's thesis, Department of Anthropology, College of William and Mary, Williamsburg, Virginia.

Sanders, S. 1988b. Architectural survey of the town of Oranjestad, St. Eustatius, Netherlands Antilles: An interim report on the initial survey. Manuscript on file, Department of Anthropology, College of William and Mary, Williamsburg, Virginia.

Santiago, P. J. 1980. *Estudios sobre comercio maritimo, naufragios y rescate submarinos en la Republic Dominicana.* Santo Domingo: Museo Casas Reales.

Satchell, V. 1989. Pattern of abandonment of sugar estates in Jamaica during the late nineteenth century. *Caribbean Geographer* 2:251–267.

Sauer, C. 1966. *The early Spanish Main.* Berkeley: University of California Press.

Saunders, G. 1983. *Bahamian Loyalists and their slaves.* London: Macmillan Caribbean.

Saunders, G. 1985. *Slavery in the Bahamas, 1648–1838.* Nassau: Nassau Guardian.

Saunders, G., and D. Cartwright. 1979. *Historic Nassau.* London: Macmillan Caribbean.

Saunders, H. C. 1991. *The other Bahamas.* Nassau: Bodab.

Schaw, J. 1971. *Journal of a lady of quality.* Edited by Evangeline and Charles Andrews. New Haven: Yale University Press.

Sears, W. H., and S. O. Sullivan. 1978. Bahamas prehistory. *American Antiquity* 43(1): 3–25.

Shanks, M., and C. Tilley. 1987. *Re-constructing archaeology.* Cambridge: Cambridge University Press.

Shapiro, G. 1983. A soil resistivity survey at sixteenth century Puerto Real, Haiti. *Journal of Field Archaeology* 11:101–110.

Sheridan, R. 1960. Samuel Martin, innovating sugar planter of Antigua, 1750–1776. *Agricultural History* 34 (3):126–139.

Sheridan, R. 1973. *Sugar and slavery.* Baltimore: Johns Hopkins University Press.

Siebert, W. H. 1972a. *Loyalists in East Florida, 1774 to 1785: The most important documents pertaining thereto, edited with an accompanying narrative.* Vol. 1, *The narrative.* Reprint of 1929 edition. Boston: Gregg Press.

Siebert, W. H. 1972b. *Loyalists in East Florida, 1774 to 1785: The most important documents pertaining thereto, edited with an accompanying narrative.* Vol. 2, *Records of their claims for losses of property in the province.* Reprint of 1929 edition. Boston: Gregg Press.

Siebert, W. H. 1975. Loyalist exodus to the West Indies: Legacy of revolution. In *The American Revolution and the West Indies,* edited by C. W. Toth, pp. 210–225. Port Washington, N.Y.: Kennikat Press.

Skowronek, R. 1987. Ceramics and commerce: The 1554 Flota revisited. *Historical Archaeology* 21(2):101–111.

Skowronek, R. 1992. Empire and ceramics: The changing role of illicit trade in Spanish America. *Historical Archaeology* 26(1):109–118.

Sloane, H. 1707. *A voyage to the islands of Madeira, Barbados, Nieves, S. Christopher, and Jamaica with the natural history of the herbs and trees, four-footed beasts, fishes, birds, insects, reptiles etc. on the last of these islands.* London.

Smith, G. 1986. A study of colono ware and non-European ceramics from sixteenth-century Puerto Real, Haiti. Master's thesis, Department of Anthropology, University of Florida, Gainesville.

Smith, H. 1962. *El Morro.* Notes in Anthropology 6. Tallahassee: Florida State University.

Smith, K. B., and F. C. Smith. 1987. *To shoot hard labor: The life and times of Samuel Smith, an Antiguan workingman, 1877–1982.* Scarborough, Ontario: Edan's.

Smith, K. B., and F. C. Smith. 1989. *To shoot hard labour: The life and times of Samuel Smith, an Antiguan workingman, 1877–1982.* London: Karia Press.

Smith, M. E. 1982. The process of sociocultural continuity. *Current Anthropology* 23(2):127–142.

Smith, M. S., T. C. Loftfield, and F. Paulssen. 1994. Preliminary investigation of orange micaceous earthenware from the early colonial period Charles Towne Colony, Cape Fear River, North Carolina: Implications for local manufacture. Paper presented at the Materials Research Society Meeting, Materials Issues in Art and Archaeology IV, Cancún, Mexico.

Smith, R. C. 1978. New World shipwrecks, 1500–1800: A compendium of sites salvaged or excavated. Ms. on file, Institute of Nautical Archaeology, Texas A&M University, College Station, Texas.

Smith, R. C. 1985. The search for the caravels of Columbus. *Oceanus* 28(1):73–77.

Smith, R. C. 1987. The search for the lost caravels. *American Archaeology* 6:109–114.

Smith, R. C. 1991. Florida Bureau of Archaeological Research: Pensacola shipwreck survey. *SHA Newsletter* 24(2):37.

Smith, R. C., D. H. Keith, and D. C. Lakey. 1985. The Highborn Cay wreck: Further exploration of sixteenth century Bahamian shipwreck. *International Journal of Nautical Archaeology and Underwater Exploration* 14:63–72.

Smith, R. C., D. Lakey, T. Oerthing, B. Thompson, and R. Woodward. 1982. Sevilla la Nueva: A site survey and historical assessment of Jamaica's first European town. Ms. on file, Institute of Nautical Archaeology, Texas A&M University, College Station, Texas.

Smith, R. C., M. Myers, D. Lakey, D. Keith, B. Thompson, K. C. Smith. 1985. Symposium: The potential contributions of nautical archaeology to understanding voyages of exploration and discovery in the New World. In *Proceedings of the Sixteenth Conference on Underwater Archaeology,* edited by P. F. Johnston, pp. 109–119. Special Publication Series No. 4. Society for Historical Archaeology.

Smith, V. T. C. 1992. *Fire and brimstone: The story of the Brimstone Hill fortress, St. Kitts, West Indies, 1690–1853.* Basseterre: Brimstone Hill Fortress National Park Society.

Solis, C. 1984. Archaeological testing of Casa Rosa scarp wall project area, San Juan Historic District, San Juan, Puerto Rico. Ms. on file, U.S. Army Corps of Engineers, Jacksonville, Florida.

Solis, C., and V. Calderon. 1993. Generos mas comunes: Comercio colonial de siglos XVIII y XIX, San Juan Bautista, Puerto Rico. Paper presented at the Fifteenth International Congress for Caribbean Archaeology, San Juan, Puerto Rico.

South, S. 1977. *Method and theory in historical archaeology.* New York: Academic Press.

South, S. 1990. From thermodynamics to a status artifact model: Spanish Santa Elena. In *Columbian consequences,* vol. 2, edited by D. H. Thomas, pp. 329–342. Washington, D.C.: Smithsonian Institution Press.

Stahl, A. 1992. The coinage of La Isabela, 1493–1498. *Numismatist* 105(10):1399–1402.

Steane, J. M. 1985. *The archaeology of medieval England and Wales.* London: Croom Helm.

Steen, C. R. 1990. *The inter-colonial trade of domestic earthenwares and the development of an American social identity.* Volumes in Historical Archaeology 9. Columbia: South Carolina Institute of Archaeology and Anthropology, University of South Carolina.

Stein, H. 1980. Culture and ethnicity as group fantasies: A psychohistoric paradigm of group identity. *Journal of Psychohistory* 8:21–51.

Stienstra, P. 1988. The economic history of gold mining on Aruba, Netherlands West Indies, 1824–1920. In *Studies in honour of Dr. Pieter Wagenaar Hummelinck,* edited by L. J. van der Steen, pp. 227–254. Natuuretenschappelijk Studiekring voor Suriname and de Nederlandse Antillen No. 123. Utrecht: Koninklijke van de Gaarde.

Stine, L. F., M. A. Caback, and M. D. Groover. 1996. Blue beads as African-American cultural symbols. *Historical Archaeology* 30(3):49–75.

Stoffers, A. L. 1956. *The vegetation of the Netherlands Antilles.* Utrecht: Drukkerij en Uitgeversmaatschappij V/H Kemink en Zoon.

Sued-Badillo, J. 1978. *Los Caribes: Realidad o fábula?* Río Piedras, Puerto Rico: Editorial Antillana.

Sued-Badillo, J. 1992. Facing up to Caribbean history. *American Antiquity* 57(4):599–607.

Sypkens-Smit, M. 1982. Archeologisch materiaal van Sint Maarten/Saint Martin. Report submitted to the Department of Culture, Sint Maarten.

Tattersall, J. 1993. Catalina and the missing caravel: A new inquiry into the mystery of *Navidad.* Paper presented at the Fifteenth International Congress for Caribbean Archaeology, San Juan, Puerto Rico.

Taylor, R. 1974. Town houses in Taunton, 1500–1700. *Post-Medieval Archaeology* 8:63–79.

Teenstra, M. 1836. *De Nederlandsche West-Indische Eilanden in der zelver tegenwoordiger toestand.* Amsterdam: Sulpke Pers.

Temminck-Groll, C. 1982. Fort Amsterdam, Sint Maarten. *Sticusa Journal* 12(86):6–7.

Temminck-Groll, C. 1989. Government Guesthouse St. Eustatius: Geschiedenis en restauratie. Report for Plan-D2, Willemstad, Curaçao.

Ten Kate, H. 1917. Oudheden: De West Indische Eilanden. In *Encyclopedia van Nederlandse West-Indie, 1914–1917,* pp. 543–546. Amsterdam: Elsevier.

Terrell, M. 1994a. The Jews of Nevis and their synagogue. *Nevis Historical and Conservation Society Newsletter* 34:4–7.

Terrell, M. 1994b. The Jewish synagogue: 1994 dig. *Nevis Historical and Conservation Society Newsletter* 36:13–14.

Thomas, D. H., ed. 1990. *Columbian consequences.* vol. 2. Washington, D.C.: Smithsonian Institution Press.

Thomas, S. A. 1990. The development of plans and policies toward preservation of the historic urban core of St. John's, Antigua. Master's thesis, Department of Environmental Design, University of Calgary, Calgary, Canada.

Thompson, R. F. 1981. *Four moments of the sun.* Washington, D.C.: National Art Gallery.

Thompson, R. F. 1983. *Flash of the spirit.* New York: Vintage Books.

Trigger, B. 1967. Settlement archaeology: Its goals and promise. *American Antiquity* 32(2): 149–161.

Trigger, B. 1968. The determinants of settlement patterns. In *Settlement archaeology,* edited by K. C. Chang, pp. 53–78. Palo Alto, Calif.: National Press Books.

Trigger, B. 1984. Alternative archaeologies: Nationalist, colonialist, imperialist. *Man* 19:355–370.

Triplett, D. 1995. Town planning and architecture on eighteenth century St. Eustatius. Master's thesis, Department of Anthropology, College of William and Mary, Williamsburg, Virginia.

Turnbaugh, S. P., ed. 1985. *Domestic pottery of the northeastern United States, 1625–1850.* Orlando, Fla.: Academic Press.

Turner, G. 1992. An archaeological record of plantation life in the Bahamas. *Journal of the Bahamas Historical Society* 14(1):30–40.

Turner, G. 1993. An archaeological record of plantation life in the Bahamas. In

Amerindians, Africans, Americans: Three papers in Caribbean history, by G. Lafleur, S. Branson, and G. Turner, pp. 107–125. Department of History, University of the West Indies, Mona, Jamaica.

Tyson, G. F., Jr. 1984. A land use history of St. John, 1718–1940 (preliminary report). Report on file, Virgin Islands National Park, St. Thomas–St. John.

Tyson, G. F., Jr. 1987. Historic land use in the Reef Bay, Fish Bay, and Hawksnest Bay watersheds, St. John. Biosphere Reserve Research Report No. 19. Virgin Islands Resource Management Cooperative, St. Thomas, U.S. Virgin Islands.

Tyson, G. F., and A. R. Highfield, eds. 1994. *The Kamina folk: Slavery and slave life in the Danish West Indies.* Virgin Islands Humanities Council, St. Thomas, U.S. Virgin Islands.

Ubelaker, D. H., and J. L. Angel. 1976. Analysis of the Hull Bay skeletons, St. Thomas. *Journal of the Virgin Islands Archaeological Society* 3:7–14.

U.S. Bureau of the Census. 1917. St. John census returns. Washington, D.C.

van Alphen, W. 1990. Goldmines on Aruba: A concatenation of failures. In *Building up the future from the past,* edited by H. Coomans, M. Newton, and M. Eustatia, pp. 64–73. Zutphen, The Netherlands: De Walburg Pers.

van Buren, M. 1999. Tarapaya: An elite Spanish residence near colonial Potosí in comparative perspective. *Historical Archaeology* 33(2):101–115.

van den Bor, W. 1981. *Island adrift: The social organization of a small Caribbean community: The case of St. Eustatius.* Leiden: Department of Caribbean Studies, Royal Institute of Linguistics and Anthropology.

van der Hoeven, F. 1992. Saving historical monuments in an uncontrolled environment: Disaster management as a way of life in Sint Maarten. Paper presented at the Twenty-fifth Annual Meeting of the Society for Historical Archaeology, Kingston, Jamaica.

van der Valk, B. 1992. The physical environment of Golden Rock. In *The archaeology of St. Eustatius: The Golden Rock site,* edited by A. Versteeg and K. Schinkel, pp. 14–30. Special Publication No. 2. St. Eustatius: St. Eustatius Historical Foundation.

van Koolwijk, A. 1879. Letter registered no. 77. Leiden: Rijksmuseum voor Volkenkunde.

van Nooyen, R. 1985. *Historia di pueblo di Boneiru.* Kralendijk: Bonaire Offset.

van Nooyen, R. 1995. *De slavenparochie van Curaçao rond het jaar 1750: Een demographie van het Katholieke volksdeel.* Report No. 11. Curaçao: Archaeological-Anthropological Institute of the Netherlands Antilles.

Varlack, P., and N. Harrigan. 1992. *American paradise: A profile of the Virgin Islands of the United States.* St. Thomas: Research and Consulting Limited.

Vaz, E., and J. Cruxent. 1975. Determination of the provenience of the majolica pottery in the Caribbean area using its gamma ray induced thermoluminescence. *American Antiquity* 40(1):71–81.

Vega, B. 1979. Arqueología de los Cimarrónes del Maniel del Bahoruco. *Boletín del Museo del Hombre Dominicano* 12:11–48.

Veloz Maggiolo, M. 1974. Remanentes culturales indígenas y africanos en Santo Domingo. *Revista Dominicana de Antropologia e Historia* 7–8:19–26.

Veloz Maggiolo, M., and A. C. Fuentes, eds. 1996. *Ponencias del Primer Seminario de Arqueología del Caribe.* Altos de Chavón: Museo Arqueológico Regional.

Veloz Maggiolo, M., and J. Guerrero. 1986. Las Antillas del descubrimiento: Arqueología y etnología. *Hoy: Isla Abierta* 6(269):6–8.

Veloz Maggiolo, M., and E. Ortega. 1992. *Fundación de la Villa de Santo Domingo: Un estudio arqueo-historico.* Colección Quinto Centario, Serie Historia de la Ciudad. Santo Domingo, Dominican Republic: Comision Dominicana para la Celebracion del V Centenario.

Versteeg, A. H., and K. Schinkel. 1992. Conclusions. In *The archaeology of St. Eustatius: The Golden Rock site,* edited by A. Versteeg and K. Schinkel, pp. 228–229. Special Publication No. 2. St. Eustatius: St. Eustatius Historical Foundation.

Vescelius, G. S. 1977. A bibliography of Virgin Islands Archaeology. *Journal of the Virgin Islands Archaeological Society* 4:1–16.

Viola, H. J., and C. Margolis. 1991. *Seeds of change.* Washington, D.C.: Smithsonian Institution Press.

Vlach, J. M. 1986a. *Back of the big house: The architecture of plantation slavery.* Chapel Hill: University of North Carolina Press.

Vlach, J. M. 1986b. The shotgun house: An African architectural legacy. In *Common places: Readings in American vernacular architecture,* edited by D. Upton and J. M. Vlach, pp. 58–78. Athens: University of Georgia Press.

VROM. 1994. *Protected historical sites and buildings on Sint Maarten: First group.* St. Maarten: Department of Public Housing, Physical Planning and Environment, Island Government of St. Maarten.

Walker, J. 1982. Report on salvage excavations and analysis of La Perla, San Juan. Ms. on file, Instituto Nacional de Cultura Puertoriqueña, San Juan, Puerto Rico.

Wallerstein, I. 1974. *The modern world-system: Capitalistic agriculture and the origins of the European world-economy in the sixteenth century.* New York: Academic Press.

Walter, E. V. 1988. *Placeways: A theory of human environment.* Chapel Hill: University of North Carolina Press.

Warmington, R. 1976. Rebuilding of "Le Belle" Inn, Andover, 1534. *Post-Medieval Archaeology* 10:131–141.

Watters, D. R. 1980a. Observations on the historic sites and archaeology of Barbuda. *Journal of Archaeology and Anthropology of the Walter Roth Museum of Anthropology* 3:125–154.

Watters, D. R. 1980b. *Transect survey and prehistoric site locations on Barbuda and Montserrat.* Ph.D. dissertation, University of Pittsburgh, Pittsburgh. Ann Arbor: University Microfilms.

Watters, D. R. 1987. Excavations at the Harney site slave cemetery, Montserrat, West Indies. *Annals of Carnegie Museum* 56 (18):289–318.

Watters, D. R. 1994. Mortuary patterns at the Harney site slave cemetery, Montserrat, in Caribbean perspective. *Historical Archaeology* 28(3):56–73.

Watters, D. R. 1997. Historical documentation and archaeological investigation of Codrington Castle, Barbuda, West Indies. *Annals of Carnegie Museum* 66:229–288.

Watters, D. R., and R. B. Miller. 2000. Wood identification in historic sites: Inferences for colonial trade and modification of vegetation on Barbuda. *Caribbean Journal of Science* 36(1–2):19–30.

Watters, D. R., and D. V. Nicholson. 1982. Highland House, Barbuda: An eighteenth century retreat. *Florida Anthropologist* 35:223–242.

Watts, D. 1987. *The West Indies: Patterns of development, culture, and environmental change since 1492.* Cambridge: Cambridge University Press.

Webster, M. 1993. *Merriam Webster's collegiate dictionary.* 10th ed. Springfield, Mass.: Merriam Webster.

West, T. 1971. *The timber-frame house in England.* New York: Architectural Book.

Westergaard, W. 1917. *The Danish West Indies under company rule.* New York: Macmillan.

Westermann, J. H., and H. Kiel. 1961. *The geology of Saba and St. Eustatius.* Utrecht: Natuurwetenschappelijke Studiekring voor Suriname en de Nederlandse Antillen.

Wheeler, M. 1964. *Roman art and architecture.* London: Thames & Hudson.

Wheeler, M. M. 1988. *Montserrat, West Indies: Chronological history.* Plymouth: Montserrat National Trust.

Whitehead, N. L., ed. 1995. *Wolves from the sea: Readings in the anthropology of the native Caribbean.* Leiden: Koninklijk Instituut voor Taal-, Land-, en Volkenkunde.

Wignall, S. 1982. *In search of Spanish treasure: A diver's story.* North Pomfret, Vt.: David & Charles.

Wilkie, L. A. 1993. Continuities in African naming practices among the slaves of Wade's Green plantation, North Caicos. *Journal of the Bahamas Historical Society* 15(1):32–37.

Wilkie, L. A. 1994a. *"Never leave me alone": An archaeological study of African-American ethnicity, race relations, and community at Oakley plantation.* Ph.D. dissertation, Archaeology Program, University of California, Los Angeles. Ann Arbor: University Microfilms.

Wilkie, L. A. 1994b. Archaeological evidence of an African-American aesthetic. *African-American Archaeology* 10:1,4.

Wilkie, L. A. 1996a. House gardens and female identity on Crooked Island. *Journal of the Bahamas Historical Society* 18:33–39.

Wilkie, L. A. 1996b. Medicinal teas and patent medicines: African-American women's consumer choices and ethnomedical traditions at a Louisiana plantation. *Southeastern Archaeology* 15(2):119–131.

Wilkie, L. A. 1996c. Transforming African-American ethnomedical practices: A case study from West Feliciana. *Louisiana History* 37(4):457–471.

Wilkie, L. A. 1997. Secret and sacred: Contextualizing the artifacts of African-American magic and religion. *Historical Archaeology* 31(4):81–106.

Wilkie, L. A. 1999. Evidence of African continuities in the material culture of Clifton plantation, Bahamas. In *African sites archaeology in the Caribbean,* edited by J. B. Haviser, pp. 264–275. Princeton: Markus Wiener; Kingston: Ian Randle.

Wilkie, L. A. 2000a. *Creating freedom: Material culture and African-American identity at Oakley plantation, Louisiana, 1845–1950.* Baton Rouge: Louisiana State University Press.

Wilkie, L. A. 2000b. Culture bought: Evidence of creolization in the consumer goods of an enslaved Bahamian family. *Historical Archaeology* 34(3):10–26.

Wilkie, L. A., and P. Farnsworth. 1995. Archaeological excavations on Crooked Island. *Journal of the Bahamas Historical Society* 17:34–36.

Wilkie, L. A., and P. Farnsworth. 1996. Preliminary results of the 1996 archaeological excavations at Clifton plantation. *Journal of the Bahamas Historical Society* 18:50.

Wilkie, L. A., and P. Farnsworth. 1997. Daily life on a Loyalist plantation: Results of the 1996 excavations at Clifton plantation. *Journal of the Bahamas Historical Society* 19:2–18.

Wilkie, L. A., and P. Farnsworth. 1999a. Trade and the construction of Bahamian identity: A multiscalar exploration. *International Journal of Historical Archaeology* 3(4):283–320.

Wilkie, L. A., and P. Farnsworth. 1999b. 1999 archaeological investigations at Clifton plantation: A preliminary report. *Journal of the Bahamas Historical Society* 21:41–46.

Wilkie, L. A., and P. Farnsworth. 1999c. Archaeological reconnaissance and test excavations within the boundaries of the proposed Clifton Cay development project, 1999. Ms. on file, Department of Anthropology, University of California, Berkeley.

Wilkie, L. A., and P. Farnsworth. 2000. Archaeological reconnaissance and test excavations at Clifton plantation, New Providence, Bahamas, April–May, 1999. Ms. on file, Department of Anthropology, University of California, Berkeley.

Willey, G. 1953. *Prehistoric settlement patterns in the Viru Valley, Peru.* Bureau of American Ethnology Bulletin 155. Washington, D.C.: Smithsonian Institution.

Williams, A. R. 1997. Montserrat: Under the volcano. *National Geographic* 192(1):58–75.

Williams, J. 1993. Review of Ewen: From Spaniard to Creole. *Historical Archaeology* 27(3):118–119.

Williams, M. 1986. Sub-surface patterning at Puerto Real: A sixteenth-century Spanish town on Haiti's north coast. *Journal of Field Archaeology* 13:283–296.

Willis, R. 1976. The archaeology of sixteenth-century Nueva Cadiz. Master's thesis, Department of Anthropology, University of Florida, Gainesville.

Willis, R. 1982. Nueva Cadiz. In *Spanish colonial frontier research,* edited by H. Dobyns, pp. 27–40. Albuquerque: Center for Anthropological Studies.

Willis, R. 1984. Empire and architecture at sixteenth-century Puerto Real, Hispaniola: An archaeological perspective. Ph.D. dissertation, Department of Anthropology, University of Florida, Gainesville.

Wilson, S. M. 1989. The prehistoric settlement pattern of Nevis, West Indies. *Journal of Field Archaeology* 16(4):427–450.

Wilson, S. M. 1990. *Hispaniola: Caribbean chiefdoms in the age of Columbus.* Tuscaloosa: University of Alabama Press.

Wilson, S. M. 1993a. Caribbean diaspora. *Natural History* 102(3):54–59.

Wilson, S. M. 1993b. Structure and history: Combining archaeology and ethnohistory in the contact period Caribbean. In *Ethnohistory and archaeology: Approaches to postcontact change in the Americas,* edited by J. D. Rogers and S. M. Wilson, pp. 19–30. New York: Plenum Press.

Wilson, S. M., ed. 1997. *The indigenous people of the Caribbean.* Gainesville: University Press of Florida.

Wilson, S. M., and J. D. Rogers. 1993. Historical dynamics in the contact era. In *Ethnohistory and archaeology: Approaches to postcontact change in the Americas,* edited by J. D. Rogers and S. M. Wilson, pp. 3–18. New York: Plenum Press.

Wing, E. 1961. Animal remains excavated at the Spanish site of Nueva Cádiz on Cubagua Island, Venezuela. *Nieuwe West-Indische Gids* 2:162–165.

Wing, E. 1989. Evidences for the impact of traditional Spanish animal uses in parts of the New World. In *The walking larder,* edited by J. Clutton-Brock, pp. 72–79. London: Unwin Hyman.

Wolf, E. R. 1982. *Europe and the people without history.* Berkeley: University of California Press.

Woodward, R. 1981. The surface collection from Sevilla la Nueva. Ms. on file, Institute of Nautical Archaeology, Texas A&M University, College Station, Texas.

Wright, I. 1934. *Nederlandse zeevaarders op de eilanden in de Caraibische Zee en aan de kust van Columbia en Zuid Amerika gedurende de jaren 1621–1648.* Utrecht: Kemink en Zoon.

Wynter, S. 1984. New Seville: Major dates, 1509–1536; major facts; major questions. Ms. on file, National Historic Trust, Kingston, Jamaica.

Yacou, A. 1992. *Christophe Colomb et la découverte de la Guadeloupe.* Paris: Editions caribéennes.

Yacou, A., and J. Adelaide-Merlande, eds. 1993. *La découverte et la conquête de la Guadeloupe.* Pointe-à-Pitre, Guadeloupe: CERC, and Paris: Karthala.

Yentsch, A. 1994. *A Chesapeake family and their slaves: A study of historical archaeology.* New York: Cambridge University Press.

Zachs, S. 1985. An eighteenth century plantation support structure on the Caribbean island of Montserrat. Master's thesis, Department of Anthropology, Brown University, Providence, Rhode Island.

Zucchi, A. 1995a. Arqueologia historica en la barra de Maracaibo (Venezuela): Fortificaciones y asentamientos. In *Proceedings of the Fifteenth International Congress for Caribbean Archaeology,* pp. 83–94. Centro de Estudios Avanzados de Puerto Rico y el Caribe, San Juan, Puerto Rico.

Zucchi, A. 1995b. Spanish burial practices of the seventeenth and eighteenth centuries (Venezuela). Paper presented at the Sixteenth International Congress for Caribbean Archaeology, Guadeloupe.

CONTRIBUTORS

Douglas Armstrong, Department of Anthropology, 209 Maxwell Hall, Syracuse University, Syracuse, NY 13244

Norman F. Barka, Department of Anthropology, College of William and Mary, Williamsburg, VA 23187

André Delpuech, Equipe Archéologie des Amériques, Maison René Ginouvès de l'Archéologie et de l'Ethnologie, 21 allée de l'Université, 92023 NAN-TERRE Cedex, France

Charles R. Ewen, Department of Anthropology, East Carolina University, Greenville, NC 27858

Paul Farnsworth, Department of Geography & Anthropology, Louisiana State University, Baton Rouge, LA 70803

Conrad "Mac" Goodwin, Department of Anthropology, 250 South Stadium Hall, The University of Tennessee, Knoxville, TN 37996

Jay B. Haviser, Director, The Jacob Gelt Dekker Institute for Advanced Cultural Studies, Klipstraat 9, Willemstad, Curaçao, Netherlands Antilles

Thomas C. Loftfield, Laboratory of Coastal Archaeology, Department of Anthropology, University of North Carolina at Wilmington, 601 South College Road, Wilmington, NC 28403

Lydia M. Pulsipher, Department of Geography, 408 G and G Building, The University of Tennessee, Knoxville, TN 37996

David R. Watters, Division of Anthropology, Edward O'Neil Research Center, Carnegie Museum of Natural History, 5800 Baum Boulevard, Pittsburgh, PA 15206

Laurie A. Wilkie, Department of Anthropology, 232 Kroeber Hall, University of California, Berkeley, CA 94720

INDEX

271, 273, 275, 277–280, 283–299, 300;
body art, 278; as consumers, 280–281,
284, 298, 299, 300; "liberated," 236,
277–278; names of, 278. *See also* Akan;
Amina; Angolas; Ashanti; Bakongo;
Canga; Congoes; Contabutta; Ebo;
Free Blacks; Fulani; Ga'anda; "Guinea
born"; Ibo; Konkomba; Kwakwa;
Mandingo; Negroes; Quaqua; West
Africans; Windward Coast Negroes;
Yoruba
Agorsah, Kofi, 84
agrarian economy, 136–137
agricultural produce: bananas, 276; beans,
146, 201, 276; cassava, 146, 179, 193,
201; cocoa, 138, 179, 193, 201; coconut,
179; coffee, 44, 50, 119, 138; fruit trees,
146, 148, 151, 192; ginger, 122, 179, 193;
indigo, 44, 47–49, 94, 119, 122, 138,
167; lime juice, 168; maize, 146, 201,
276; melons, 276; okra, 276; peanuts,
131, 201, 276; peas, 276; peppers,
146; pineapple, 201; plantains, 276;
potatoes, 276; pumpkins, 276; sesame,
276; sisal, 63, 132, 134; sorghum, 276;
squash, 146, 201, 276; sweet potatoes,
131, 132, 134, 146, 150, 193, 201, 276;
tannia, 201; taro, 276; tobacco, 44,
94, 119, 120, 122, 136, 138, 167, 292;
vanilla, 201. *See also* charcoal; cotton;
dyewood; gold; muscovado; rum; salt;
sugar
agricultural reform movement, 267–270
agriculture, 66, 75, 108, 112, 119, 120,
122–126, 131, 134, 136–140, 145–152,
169–176; mixed farming, 236, 237
Akan, 147, 279
amateur archaeologists. *See* avocational
archaeologists
American: mainland colonies, xix; rebels,
108, 140
American Revolution, 9, 64, 77, 97, 103,
108, 129, 140, 236, 261, 266

American South, xvii, 279, 280, 281, 285,
291, 292, 295, 298
Amerindian: contributions, xxiii; culture,
207; population, xxiii.
Amerindians, 10, 23, 24, 25, 26, 29, 30, 32,
40, 63, 73, 74, 84, 91, 92, 119, 145, 167,
207, 208, 219–220. *See also* Arawaks;
Caquetio Arawaks; Caribs; indigenous
people; Kalinagos
Amerindian sites, xxiii, 97; En Bas
Saline, 18; Morne Cybèle, 31. *See also*
Pre-Columbian sites
Amina, 147
Amsterdam, 122
anchorages, 71, 74, 105, 129, 136, 139, 212
Andros, 237; Long Bay Cays, 237
Anglo-American culture, 195
Angola, 263
Angolas, 263
Anguilla, xx, 61, 85, 86, 89, 90
animal pens, 112, 114, 192, 245, 281
animals, 150; butchering, 179; cattle, 131,
132, 134, 176, 182, 292; chickens, 195,
276; goats, 169, 176, 195; hides, 122,
138; hogs, 132, 193, 195, 208, 276, 292;
horses, 131, 137; livestock, 66; meat,
179; mules, 131; sheep, 131
Annual Meeting of the Society for
American Archaeology, 4
anthropologists, 92, 279
anthropology, 83, 84
Antigua, 84–91, 96–99, 174, 179;
Blockhouse Hill, 96; English Harbour,
84, 85, 96
Appea, 278
Aragon, 5
Arawaks, 6, 8, 18, 23, 63
archaeological: collections, 98; sampling,
153; societies, 85, 86, 88, 97, 99
archaeological excavations of: Anse
de la Petite Chapelle, 41–44; Anse
Sainte-Marguerite, 54–57; Anse
du Vieux-Fort, 53; Baillif, 40–41;

147; marine shell, 283; metal, 18, 26,
46–47, 55, 57, 109, 197, 246, 279, 280,
283; musket balls, 36; *Nkisi* charms,
291–292, 298; Obeah bottles, 280;
personal adornment, xxii, 297–299;
tiles, 185, 187, 221, 224, 225, 267;
wooden, 36, 226, 229. *See also* pipes;
ceramics
Aruba, 60–68, 74–75, 78, 79, 80, 81, 132,
134; geography of, 61; geology of, 61
Ashanti, 294
Ashton, Catherine Ann, 157
Asia, 175, 201
Asians, 74, 94
Auger, Governor, 34
Aulinagan, 25. *See also* Marie-Galante
avocational archaeologists, xxi, 13, 72, 83,
85, 88, 99
Ayscue, George, Sr., 214
Ayubi, E. N., 75

Baart, J., 70
bagasse, 185, 200, 225
Bahama Islands, xxii, xxiii, 6, 17, 83, 88,
89, 97, 234–271, 272–300; architectural
heritage, xxii; historical overview,
236–237; House of Assembly, 272,
273, 275; plantations, 234–300; slave
registers, 277, 278; society, 236;
traditions, 234–271. *See also* Andros;
Caicos Islands; Cat Island; Crooked
Island; Egg Island; Exuma; Grand
Turk; Long Cay; Long Island; Middle
Caicos; Nassau; New Providence;
North Caicos; Rum Cay; Samana Cay;
San Salvador; West Caicos
Bahamas. *See* Bahama Islands
Bahamians, 235, 236, 267
bakehouses, 254
baking ovens, 108, 110, 111–112, 126, 134,
161, 179, 190
Bakongo, 263, 277, 278, 289, 290, 291,
292, 296, 297, 300; cosmograms,
291–293, 296–298; graves, 289; pottery,

289, 290, 291, 294. *See also* Congoes;
Kongo People
banks, 135
Barbados, xxii, 82–84, 87, 88, 90, 92, 97,
207–233, 238, 266, 269; Alleyndale, 238;
Carlisle Bay, 212; ceramic manufacture,
219–233; Cromwellian invasion, 212;
defenses, 208–219, 232; geographic
position of, 208; Holetown, 211, 214;
House of Assembly, 219; population
size, 218; St. James Parish, 231; St. John
Parish, 214; Scotland District, 226;
settlement and early development,
211–212
Barbotin, Maurice, 33, 52
Barbuda, 84, 86, 89, 90, 96
Barka, Norman F., xxi, xxii, 68, 69, 70
barns, 187, 191, 241, 276, 281
bars, 135
basements, 110, 126, 188
Basse-Terre, 21, 29, 31–35, 38–39, 40,
45, 50, 52, 53, 58; archaeology in, 39;
layout, 39
bees, meaning of, 294–297
Bégot, Danièle, 45
Belgrove, William, 200
belief systems: Creole, 166, 202
Belize, 83
Bell, John, Dr., 242; estate inventory, 242
Benjamin, Guy, 163
Bequette, K., 70
Bermuda, 110, 140
Bisschop Grevelink, A. H., 129
Black Caribs, 92
Black Harry, 128
"black sugar." *See* muscovado
Blacks, 155, 167, 237, 272, 276. *See also*
African Americans; Africans
Blanken, W. Lieutenant, 129
Blondel, François, 34, 38
boatbuilding, 146, 157, 159, 164, 179
boats, 276
Bodu, Pierre, 31

body art: "country marks," 278, 288, 297; hair braiding, 288, 297; piercings, 288, 297; scarification, 278, 288, 297, 298; tattooing, 288, 297

Bonaire, 60, 61, 63–67, 74, 75, 78, 238; geography of, 61; geology of, 61

Bonaparte, Napoleon, 24

Bonnissent, Dominique, 36

Booi, F., 74

Bosch, G., 74

Boston Public Library, 179

Bourbons, 9

Braudel, Fernand, 5

braziers. *See* coal pots

Brazil, 279

Brenneker, P., 72, 74

Breton, Père R., 24, 27–30

Bridgetown, 214

Brimstone Hill Fortress National Park, 84

Britain. *See* Great Britain

British Caribbean. *See* British West Indies

British Colonial Office, 273; correspondence, 275

British colonies, 272; crown, 86; North American, 97–98, 140, 236

British Commonwealth, 82

British Guiana. *See* Guyana; Demerara

British Honduras. *See* Belize

British islands. *See* British West Indies

British Loyalists, 236, 237, 240, 246, 254, 261, 262, 264, 265, 268, 270

British Navy, 217–218

British Virgin Islands, 83, 148, 150, 154, 157, 159. *See also* Tortola; Virgin Gorda

British West India Regiments, 97, 277

British West Indies, xx, xxi, 82–90, 93, 94, 98, 108, 123, 140, 159. *See also* Anguilla; Antigua; Bahama Islands; Barbados; Barbuda; British Virgin Islands; Cayman Islands; Dominica; Grenada; Guyana; Jamaica; Monserrat; Nevis; St. Christopher; St. Lucia; St. Vincent;

Tobago; Trinidad; Turks and Caicos Islands

Brito, N., 68, 72, 73, 76

Brugman, F., 71

buccaneers. *See* pirates

Buisseret, David, 238

burials, 53–57, 70, 73, 74, 196–199, 279, 280

bussels, 147. *See also* Africans

Caicos Islands, 237, 238, 254. *See also* Middle Caicos; North Caicos; West Caicos

calabash gourds, 179

Campbell, Archibald: estate inventory, 241, 242

Campbell, P. F., 214, 217

Canada, 97, 99, 236

Canga, 263

cannibals, 27

capital investment, 6, 152, 174, 211

Caquetio Arawaks, 63

Carib problem, 92

Caribbean: architecture, xxi; culture, xix, xxiii, xvii, 166, 177–178, 180, 207; geographer, 93; heritage, xvii; immigrants, 74; identities, xxi, xxii; island colonies, xix, xx; landscapes, xxi; researchers, 4, 9, 17, 75–77, 83, 88, 90, 94, 98, 99

Caribbean peoples, xvii, xix, xx, xxi, xxii, xxiii, 84, 99; Antiguans, 84; Barbadians, 221; British Virgin Islanders, 157; Dominicans, 84; Kittians, 84; Netherlands Antillean, 60, 75; Vincentians, 84. *See also* East Enders

Caribs, xxi, 23, 25–32, 33, 58, 92

Carlson, Shawn Bonath, 219

Carolinas, 236, 265

Caron, A. P., 147

Caroucaera, 25. *See also* Guadeloupe

carpenters, 140

Cartwright, David, 237, 242

Carty, John "Montserrat," 165
Castile, 5, 25
catchments, 174, 182, 190, 191, 192
Cat Island, 17, 237
cattle feed, 185, 200
"Cavaliers." *See* Royalists
Cayman Islands, xx, 83, 86
cemeteries, 43, 44, 52–58, 70, 73, 108,
  114, 116, 123–124, 128, 131, 132, 135,
  140; Anse du Vieux-Fort, 53; Anse
  Sainte-Marguerite, 54–57; Benners
  Family Graveyard, 123; Berkel Family
  Cemetery, 135; Bishop Hill Cemetery,
  70; Bransby Site, 199; Catholic
  Cemetery, 135; Duinkerk Cemetery,
  135; Government Cemetery, 135;
  Groebe Family Graveyard, 123; Jewish,
  123; leper, 131; Morne Dauphine, 53–54;
  plantation, 123, 132; Raisins Clairs
  Beach, 52; slave, 52–58, 175, 178, 190,
  196–199, 279; Kongo Cemetery, 135;
  Salem Cemetery, 135; Schotsenhoek
  Cemetery, 128
census data, 171, 173
Central Africa, 278, 294
Central America, 6, 8, 21, 92
ceramic decoration: annular, 194, 196, 286,
  288, 289; banded, 195, 196, 285, 287;
  bird motifs, 291, 297; Chinese motifs,
  blue printed, 124; cut-sponge, 194, 196;
  floral motifs, 291; geometric motifs,
  289, 290, 291, 294; hand-painted, 194,
  196, 285–289, 291; minimally, 285, 286;
  mocha, 196, 285–289; shell-edged,
  194, 285–288; sponged, 194, 196, 285;
  transfer-printed, 194–196, 285, 286,
  287, 296; undecorated plain white,
  194, 285, 286
ceramics, xxii, 36, 47, 50, 90, 94, 98,
  104, 108, 114, 124, 137, 146, 175, 190,
  192, 193, 197, 201, 214–233, 280, 283,
  284–292, 296; African, 289; African
  potters, 227–232; Afro-Caribbean,
90, 94, 193, 197, 201–202, 228–233,
279–280, 288; Afro-Jamaican, 229,
230; Amerindian, 231; analysis of
color, 286–288; analysis of decoration,
194–195, 286; analysis of design motif,
288–292; analysis of vessel form, 195,
219; architectural, 221, 224–225; as
display items, 192, 195; Barbadian
made, 219–233; basalt wares, 286;
"Buckley-type" pan, 197; Colono
wares, 228–230; Colono wares in
Northeast U.S., 228, 230; Colono
wares in Southeast U.S., 228–230, 233,
280, 291, 292; conaree, 226–227, 232;
cottage ceramic industry, Barbados,
226; creamware, 124; English potters,
226, 227, 230, 232; European, 225–229;
for sugar industry, 220, 221–224, 230,
233; gurglets, 226; local industry, xxii;
manufacture, 219–233; mean ceramic
date formula, 90; mean ceramic dating,
283; molasses drip jars, 221–224, 226;
molded white-bodied ceramics, 194,
286; pearlware, 124; pitchers, 226;
porcelain, 285; pottery manufactory,
220–221; price indexing, 285; redwares,
locally made, xxii; spouted water jugs,
226, 227; stonewares, 285; symbolic
value, 193–194; waster piles, 220–221;
whitewares, 194–195; yabbas, 229, 279;
Yoruba pottery, 289, 290, 291, 294. *See
also* unglazed red earthenware
ceramic studies: Afro-Caribbean, 90, 94,
228–233; Afro-Jamaican, 229, 230;
British, 90, 193–195, 219–233, 284–292;
of Clifton plantation, 284–292;
Spanish, 14–15
Chanca, Diego Alvarez, 25
Chapman, W., 266, 267
charcoal, 146, 152, 164
Charles I of England, 211, 212
Charles I of Spain, 5
Charles II, 6

Charles V. *See* Charles I of Spain

Chesapeake region, 291, 292

Chicago, 18

Chinese, 65

Christian V, 145

cisterns, 34, 108, 110, 114, 134, 174, 182, 185, 187, 188, 191, 200

Clarke, H. 264

clothing, 150, 197, 199, 278, 297, 298

coal pots, 226, 227; iron 163

Codrington College, 219–233; history of, 220

Codrington family, 220; Codrington, Christopher III, 220

Codrington Trust, 220

coffins, 53, 54, 55, 197–198; decoration, 44, 55, 197

Cold War, 15, 20

College of William and Mary, xxi, 68–70, 78, 177

colleges. *See* Codrington College

Collins, Dr., 267, 268, 269

Colon, Fernando, 26

Colonial domination. *See* colonialism

colonialism, xix, xx, 24, 95, 144

colonization: Dutch, 67, 83, 119; English (British), 83, 167, 208, 211–212; European, 92, 104, 107, 166; French, 24, 27, 29, 32–34, 41, 44, 53, 83

Columbian Consequences, 11

Columbian Quadracentennial, 17

Columbian Quincentennial, xvii, xx, 3, 9–11, 19

Columbus, Christopher, 5, 6, 10, 11, 16, 17, 20, 22, 24–27, 32, 63, 92, 107; first voyage, 5, 6, 11, 17, 92; first landfall, 17; fourth voyage, 16; second voyage, 6, 25, 63, 92; house at Isabella, 18

commercial activities, 83; economy, 136–137; sites, xxi, 69, 74, 75, 90, 91, 94, 108, 112, 119, 123, 127–128, 132, 135

Compagnie des Iles d'Amerique, 32

Congo. *See* Bakongo

Congoes, 263, 277. *See also* Bakongo; Kongo people

Congo Jim, 278

Congo region (W. Africa), 135

Conquest of Paradise, 10

consumer culture, 275

Contabutta, 277. *See also* Congoes

Contact period, xxi, 9–12, 15, 17–19, 88, 91–92, 97; research, xxiii

contact period sites: Kelbeys Ridge Site, 71

contract archaeology. *See* cultural resource management

cooking practices, 163

cooking shed, 161, 190

cooks, 277, 283

coppers, 173

corrals. *See* animal pens

cotton, 119, 122, 132, 134, 138, 145, 146, 148, 152, 167, 168, 176, 236, 237, 268; houses, 247; plantations, 145, 146, 149, 154, 161, 236, 268; storage buildings, 176

Courtaud, Patrice, 54–57

Courteen, Sir Peter, 211; Sir William, 211

courthouse, 112

craftsmen, 103, 274

Craton, Michael, 238–240, 263, 268

Creole: communities, 142, 144, 155; culture, 166, 202; house forms, 268; language, 166, 202; musical traditions, 166, 202

Creoles, 142, 144, 147, 236, 270, 273, 277, 278; Anglo-Bahamian, 236

Creutzer, Johan Jacob, 146–147

Croitzer, Johan Jacob. *See* Creutzer, Johan Jacob

Crooked Island, 237, 241, 242, 243, 250–254, 256–257, 260, 274

Cruxent, Jose M., 14, 18, 72

Cuba, 6, 8, 11, 15, 20, 91, 277, 291

Cudjoe, 278

River, 25; Matouba, 54; Port-Louis, 45;
See also Basse-Terre; Grande-Terre; La
Désirade; Les Saintes; Marie-Galante
Guinea, 147
"Guinea born," 263
Guinea Coast, 265
Guischard family, 54
Gulf Coast, 6
Guyana, 83, 85, 91. *See also* Demerara

Haiti, xx, 6, 27, 291
Hall, Douglas, 181, 193
Hall, N. A. T., 91
Hamilton, Alexander, 85–86
Handler, Jerome S., 219, 221, 225, 226,
227, 279, 280
Hannum, James, 168
Hansen, Governor Jens, 147, 148, 150
Hapsburgs, 5, 6
Hardin, K., 68
Haviser, Jay B., xx, xxi, 68, 69, 70, 71, 73,
74, 78
Hay, James, Earl of Carlisle, 211
Henry, John J., 161
Henry, Salome Rebecca, 161
Herskovits, Melville, 280
Heyliger, Commander Johannes, 110, 129
Highfield, A. R., 147
Higman, Barry, 263, 278
Hints to Gentlemen of Landed Property, 267
Hispaniola, 6, 8, 9, 16, 26, 38, 91, 149; Cap
Hatien, 17
historians, 92, 238, 279
historical archaeologists, xvii, xix, xxi,
xxiii
historical archaeology, cultural impact of,
xvii, xix, xx, xxii, xxiii, 75
Historical Architecture of the Caribbean,
238
historical societies, 85, 86, 88, 99
historic districts, 90, 94; on Nevis, 87
historic preservation, 70, 79, 84–87, 95,
99

history: discipline of, 84, 85; Spanish
colonial, 5–9, 25–29, 32
hoes, 179
Hofman, Corinne, L., 31, 71
Holdren, Cody A., 97
Holland. *See* Netherlands, Kingdom of
Hollander, Paul, 168
Holy Roman Empire, 5, 6
Honychurch, Lenox, 86
Hoogland, Menno, 31, 71
horticultural plots, 176, 179, 201
hospitals, 135
hotel keepers, 140
hotels, 135, 139
Houël, Governor Charles, 31, 33, 34, 36, 38
house: building, 179; floors, 237, 239, 247,
254, 255, 257, 259, 262; sites, 144, 153,
157, 161, 163, 175, 192–196, 281, 292
houses, 108, 110, 111, 112, 114, 128, 137, 139,
144; African style, 235, 261–266; brick,
108, 122, 126, 131, 264; drivers, 281,
282, 283, 292, 294, 296, 297, 298, 300;
lath and plaster, 262, 265; managers,
50; modern stone, 108, 109, 133–134;
modern wood, 108–109, 133–134; mud
walls, 261, 265; planters, 44, 50, 91, 94,
112, 144, 161, 173, 176, 178, 182, 187–192,
195, 196, 201, 220, 241, 243–247, 249,
253, 254, 255, 256, 259, 260, 281, 285,
286, 287, 292, 298; overseers', 112, 245,
255; slave, xxi, 45, 52, 71, 73, 110, 112,
122, 161, 174, 182, 192, 193, 194, 220,
229, 234–271, 280–283, 285, 286, 292;
tabby plastered, 262; traditional stone,
108–110, 119, 122, 124, 130, 137, 174,
187–190, 235, 237, 238, 239, 241, 243,
245, 246, 247, 249, 250–257, 259, 260,
264, 266–271, 281; traditional wood,
108, 109, 110, 122, 124, 130, 133, 137,
174, 179, 192–193, 237, 238, 239–243,
259, 260, 262; wattle and daub, 238,
242, 261–266, 269, 270, 271; wattle
and plaster, 237, 242, 243, 254, 255,

256, 257, 259, 260, 261, 262, 265, 266, 270, 271; Welgelegen estate, 110; West African, 73, 263, 270; workers, 50, 71

Houses of Parliament, 174

houseyards, 179, 181, 259, 280

Howes, Kingsley, 168

Howson, James, 165

Howson, Jean, 179, 192–196

Hughes, Christian, 161

human bones, 27, 41, 42, 44, 52, 53, 196–199; skeletal remains, 33, 44, 52–57, 196, 199, 202, 279; teeth, 280

human ecology, 178

humanistic research approaches, 179–182

Hunter, Joseph, 257

hurricanes, 38, 39, 40, 41, 44, 50, 53, 128, 132, 147, 149, 154, 168–169, 176, 188; Hugo, 176; Luis, 41; Marilyn, 40, 53

hydraulic water systems, 50, 182, 190–191, 200

Iberian Peninsula, 5

Ibo, 278

identities, development of, xxii; ethnic, 236

indentured servants, 91, 97, 166, 167, 171, 202, 220; descendants of, 176

independent nations, xix, 83

indigenous peoples, 8, 10, 84, 92, 145; archaeology of, 9, 11, 15; of Lesser Antilles, 8; Spanish impact on, 4–5, 8, 10, 17. See also Amerindians

indigo works, 47–49; Le Gouffre, 48–49

industrial archaeology, 75; sites, 74, 94, 112

Inquisition, 5

interdisciplinary studies, 88, 180, 201

international agencies, 84, 87–88

International Association for Caribbean Archaeology, 88

Ireland, 166

Irish heritage, 166, 202–203

Italy, 140

Jack, 277, 282, 297

jails. See prisons

Jamaica, 6, 8, 9, 15, 16, 83, 84, 86, 90, 91, 94, 99, 144, 149, 179, 181, 193, 229, 230, 232, 233, 236, 266–269, 279, 280; Kingston, 267; St. Anne's Bay, 16

Jamaica Journal, 93

"Jamaica Train," 200. See also sugar, boilers

James, S., 14

James I of England, 211

Jamestown, xvii

John Carter Brown Library, 179

Johnston, Lewis, 247, 262

Jones, S. L., 265, 266

Joris, Charles, 148

Joris, William, 148

Journal of Archaeology and Anthropology of the Walter Roth Museum of Anthropology, 93

Journal of the Barbados Museum and Historical Society, 92

Journal of the Virgin Islands Archaeological Society, 93

Juliana, E., 72

Junkanoo, 278

Kalinagos, 27

Keegan, William F., 17

Kembeck, Antoni, 149

Kent, Nathaniel, 267

Khudabux, M. R., 73

kilns, 18, 221, 225, 229, 231

Kirby, Earle, 85

kitchens, 72, 110, 116, 190, 229, 241, 254, 255, 281, 283, 286, 287, 292, 298

Klein Bonaire, 61

Klein Curaçao, 61, 66

Kongo people, 135. See also Bakongo; Congoes

Konkomba, 265

Kozy, Charlene, J., 238

Kwakwa. See Quaqua

130, 135; Aruba Archaeological Museum, 74; Barbados Museum and Historical Society, 85; Bonaire Museum, 74; Curaçao Museum, 72; Florida Museum of Natural History, Bullen Research Library, 3; Grenada National Museum, 86; Hamilton House Museum of Nevis History, 85; Institute of Jamaica museums, 86; Leiden Ethnological Museum, 68, 72; Museum of Antigua and Barbuda, 86, 88–89; National Archaeological Anthropological Museum, 72; Nelson's Dockyard Museum, 85; Saint Vincent Archaeological Museum, 86; Schoelcher Museum, 52; Smithsonian Institution, 10; Smithsonian Museum of Natural History, 180, 181; Walter Roth Museum of Anthropology, 85

Myers, J. E., 15

Nagelkerken, W., 69, 70, 73
Nassau, 237, 238, 246, 257, 267, 273, 274, 276, 277, 292, 299; Baintown, 277; "Over the Hill," 277
national: consciousness, xxi; heritage, 83–84, 87; identities, xix, 80, 81, 83–84, 86, 94; nationalism, 4, 77–78, 80, 83–84; patrimony, xxi, 84, 86, 87, 94, 99
National Historic Landmark, 16
national trusts, 86, 97, 99; Bahamas National Trust, 250, 257; Monserrat National Trust, 86, 176, 177
Native American sites. *See* Amerindian sites
Native Americans. *See* Amerindians
native inhabitants. *See* indigenous people
naval facilities, 95, 96, 97
Navigation Acts, 225
navigation skills/seamanship, 66
Neaga House. See slave, villages
Neave, James, 174, 192, 200
Neave and Willet, 173, 174

Netherlands, Kingdom of, 60, 121, 136, 212, 218
Netherlands Antilles, 60–81; government, 75
Nevis, 85–88, 90, 91, 190; Charlestown, 87
New England, 230
New Providence, 237, 238, 243, 246, 260, 273, 277, 278, 285, 300. *See also* Nassau
New Spain, 27
newspaper advertisements, 243, 247, 254, 255, 263, 278
New World, 3, 5, 6, 8, 9, 14, 17, 27, 196, 207, 228, 280
Nicholson, Desmond, V., 84, 85, 86
Nigeria, 277
Nissen, 157
Non-governmental organizations, xxi, 85–88, 98; Anguilla Archaeological and Historical Society, 85; Antigua Archaeological Society, 86; Antigua Historical and Archaeological Society, 86; Caribbean Conservation Association, 87, 88; Dominica Institute, 86; Friends of English Harbour, 84; Island Resources Foundation, 87, 88; Museums Association of the Caribbean, 87, 88, 98; Nevis Field Research Center, 87; Nevis Historical and Conservation Society, 86–87; St. Eustatius Historical Foundation, 78, 130; St. Lucia Archaeological and Historical Society, 86; St. Lucia National Trust, 86, 89; Society for the Restoration of Brimstone Hill, 84
North America, 9, 19, 77, 90, 97, 103, 104, 140, 174, 228, 267; British West Indian connections to, 97–98
North Americans, xvii, 76, 77, 80, 83, 87, 134, 137
North Caicos, 243, 254
North Carolina, 97, 98, 221, 226; Brunswick County, 221; Cape Fear